Spirit Flowing Like Water

CHURCH OF SWEDEN
Research Series

§

The Church of Sweden Research Series promotes research investigating the intersections of church, academy, and society. Its focus is on theology that is in lively conversation with the pressing issues of the world today, both from an academic and from an ecclesial perspective. What is the role of the churches in ever changing ecological, political, cultural, social and religious contexts? How is Christian teaching and practice affected by these changing currents? And how is the Lutheran tradition evolving amid such challenges? Through monographs and anthologies, the series makes available Swedish and Scandinavian scholarship in the English-speaking world, but also mirrors the worldwide connections of the Church of Sweden as part of its own identity.

General editor of CSRS (since 2020): Michael Nausner

VOLUMES PUBLISHED

1. Göran Gunner, editor, *Vulnerability, Churches and HIV* (2009)
2. Kajsa Ahlstrand and Göran Gunner, editors, *Non-Muslims in Muslim Majority Societies with Focus on the Middle East and Pakistan* (2009)
3. Jonas Ideström, editor, *For the Sake of the World. Swedish Ecclesiology in Dialogue with William T. Cavanaugh* (2010)
4. Göran Gunner and Kjell-Åke Nordquist, *An Unlikely Dilemma. Constructing a Dialogue Between Human Rights and Peace-Building* (2011)
5. Anne-Louise Eriksson, Göran Gunner, and Niclas Blåder, editors, *Exploring a Heritage. Evangelical Lutheran Churches in the North* (2012)
6. Kjell-Åke Nordquist, editor, *Gods and Arms. On Religion and Armed Conflict* (2012)
7. Harald Hegstad, *The Real Church. An Ecclesiology of the Visible* (2013)
8. Carl-Henric Grenholm and Göran Gunner, editors, *Justification in a Post-Christian Society* (2014)
9. Carl-Henric Grenholm and Göran Gunner, editors, *Lutheran Identity and Political Theology* (2014)
10. Sune Fahlgren and Jonas Ideström, editors, *Ecclesiology in the Trenches. Theory and Method Under Construction* (2015)
11. Niclas Blåder, *Lutheran Tradition as Heritage and Tool* (2015)
12. Ulla Schmidt and Harald Askeland, editors, *Church Reform and Leadership of Change* (2016)
13. Kjell-Åke Nordquist, *Reconciliation as Politics. A Concept and its Practice* (2016)

14. Niclas Blåder and Kristina Helgesson Kjellin, editors, *Mending the World? Possibilities and Obstacles for Religion, Church, and Theology* (2017)
15. Tone Stangeland Kaufman, *A New Old Spirituality? A Qualitative Study of Clergy Spirituality in the Nordic Context* (2017)
16. Carl Reinhold Bråkenhielm, *The Study of Science and Religion. Sociological, Theological, and Philosophical Perspectives* (2017)
17. Jonas Ideström and Tone Stangeland Kaufman, editors, *What Really Matters. Scandinavian Perspectives on Ecclesiology and Ethnography* (2018)
18. Dion Forster, Elisabeth Gerle, and Göran Gunner, editors, *Freedom of Religion at Stake. Competing Claims Among Faith Traditions, States, and Persons* (2019)
19. Marianne Gaarden, *The Third Room of Preaching. A New Empirical Approach* (2021)
20. André S. Musskopf, Edith González Bernal and Maurício Rincón Andrade, editors, *Theology and Sexuality, Reproductive Health, and Rights. Latin American Experiences in Participatory Action Research* (2022)
21. Karin Johannesson, *Thérèse and Martin. Carmel and the Reformation in a New Light* (2023)
22. Harald Hegstad with Steinunn Arnþrúður Björnsdóttir, Magnus Evertsson, Jonas Adelin Jørgensen, and Jyri Komulainen, editors, *Baptism in Times of Change. Exploring New Patterns of Baptismal Theologies and Practices in Nordic Lutheran Churches* (2025)
23. Ryszard Bobrowicz, Anna Hjälm, Ulrich Schmiedel, editors, *Living in A World of Neighbours. Activists and Academics in Conversation about Multi-Faith Refugee Relief* (2025)
24. Nausikaa Haupt, Olle Kristenson, Michael Nausner, Gregory A. Ryan, editors, *Spirit Flowing Like Water. New Conversations on Receptive Ecumenism* (2025)

Spirit Flowing Like Water

New Conversations on Receptive Ecumenism

Edited by
NAUSIKAA HAUPT,
OLLE KRISTENSON,
MICHAEL NAUSNER, and
GREGORY A. RYAN

Foreword by
SOFIA CAMNERIN

PICKWICK *Publications* • Eugene, Oregon

Sankt Ignatios Press, Stockholm, Sweden

SPIRIT FLOWING LIKE WATER
New Conversations on Receptive Ecumenism

Church of Sweden Research Series 24

Copyright © 2025 Wipf and Stock Publishers. All rights reserved. Except for brief quotations in critical publications or reviews, no part of this book may be reproduced in any manner without prior written permission from the publisher. Write: Permissions, Wipf and Stock Publishers, 199 W. 8th Ave., Suite 3, Eugene, OR 97401.

Pickwick Publications
An Imprint of Wipf and Stock Publishers
199 W. 8th Ave., Suite 3
Eugene, OR 97401

www.wipfandstock.com

PAPERBACK ISBN: 979-8-3852-2809-6
HARDCOVER ISBN: 979-8-3852-2810-2
EBOOK ISBN: 979-8-3852-2811-9

Cataloging-in-Publication data:

Names: Haupt, Nausikaa, editor. | Kristenson, Olle, editor. | Nausner, Michael, editor. | Ryan, Gregory A., editor. | Camnerin, Sofia, foreword.

Title: Spirit flowing like water : new conversations on receptive ecumenism / edited by Nausikaa Haupt, Olle Kristenson, Michael Nausner, and Gregory A. Ryan ; foreword by Sofia Camnerin.

Description: Eugene, OR: Pickwick Publications, 2025. | Church of Sweden Research Series 24. | Includes bibliographical references and index.

Identifiers: ISBN 979-8-3852-2809-6 (paperback). | ISBN 979-8-3852-2810-2 (hardcover). | ISBN 979-8-3852-2811-9 (ebook).

Subjects: LCSH: Ecumenical movement. | Ecclesiology. | Lutheran Church. | Anglican Communion. | Roman Catholic Church.

Classification: BX8.3 S76 2025 (print). | BX8.3 (ebook).

VERSION NUMBER 06/16/25

Unless otherwise noted, Scripture quotations are from New Revised Standard Version Bible, copyright © 1989 National Council of the Churches of Christ in the United States of America. Used by permission. All rights reserved worldwide.

Verses from "Guds källa har vatten tillfyllest" by Bo Setterlind (1978) used with permission.

Contents

Foreword: Listen to What the Spirit is Saying to the Churches | xi
—*Sofia Camnerin*

Introduction | xix
—*The Editors*

List of Contributors | xxv

Part I: *Transforming Ecumenism*

Prologue to Part One: Homily | 3
—*Anders Arborelius, OCD, and Karin Johannesson*

1. Receptive Ecumenism as an Instrument for Ecclesial Transformation | 7
—*Paul D. Murray*

2. On Being Ecumenically Unfashionable: A "Faith and Order" Reflection on Receptive Ecumenism | 22
—*Susan Durber*

3. Why Unity for its Own Sake is not Enough: Principles of Receptive Ecumenism and the Vision of Sobornicity Revisited | 33
—*Ivana Noble*

4. A Methodist Reception of the Petrine Ministry? | 47
—*Dominic Robinson, SJ and David Carter*

5   Framing Receptive Ecumenism as Pilgrimage in the Context of
    the *Joint Declaration on the Doctrine of Justification* | 55
    —Tony Franklin-Ross

6   From Suspicion to Gratitude: Pentecostal Perspectives on
    Receptive Ecumenism | 69
    —Cheryl Bridges Johns

7   Lutherans and Pentecostals in Dialogue: A Happy Marriage? | 88
    —Johannes Habib Zeiler

8   Ecumenism—Receptive and Cruciform | 101
    —Elizabeth Woodard

9   Discerning the Impasse: A Spirituality of Receptive Ecumenism | 111
    —Paul Lakeland

Part II: *Encounters in Context*

Prologue to Part Two: Listening Churches | 121
—Sven-Erik Fjellström

10 Friendship, Spirituality, and Imagination: Historical Approaches to
    Current Challenges in Receptive Ecumenism | 125
    —Sara Gehlin

11 Receptive Ecumenism and Mission: Transformed Ecumenism
    for Transformed Societies | 138
    —Callan Slipper

12 "Mutual Flourishing" in the Church of England: An Opportunity for
    Internal Receptive Ecumenism? | 147
    —Diane Ryan

13 Transforming Ecumenism Through an Ecumenism of
    the People | 158
    —Joan Patricia Back

14 Searching for a Deeper Unity: Towards Relational Receptive
    Ecumenism Through the Lens of Interchurch Families | 170
    —Doral Hayes

15 When the Legwork Fails: A Local Experience of Forgetting
    Receptive Ecumenism | 183
    —Erik Ringheim

16 Towards a Model of Transformative Ecumenical Asceticism in
    Sophrony Sakharov and Basil Pennington | 193
    —Emil M. Mărginean

17 Receptive Ecumenism and Ecumenical Mission: Two Sides of the Same Coin | 203
    —Risto Jukko

18 Listening, Discipleship, and Church in Mission: An Evangelical Perspective | 221
    —Bertil Ekström

Part III: *Expanding the Horizon*

Prologue to Part Three: River Ecumenism | 229
—Sven-Erik Fjellström

19 A Living Conversation: Mutual Learning within the Lutheran Community | 232
    — Chediel Sendoro and Karin Johannesson

20 Touchstone and Transformation: Christian Relationships with Judaism as Challenge and Tool for Receptive Ecumenism | 245
    —Clare Amos

21 Wider Ecumenism: A Pilgrimage towards Cosmic Christ Consciousness | 259
    —Mathew Chandrankunnel, CMI

22 Receiving and Beyond: Receptive Ecumenism and Wider Ecumenism | 279
    —Peniel Rajkumar

23 Recognition of Others and Receptive Ecumenism | 288
    —Risto Saarinen

24 Recognizing Our Gifts: Re-reading Receptive Ecumenism with Risto Saarinen | 299
    —Gregory A. Ryan

25 Becoming Through Participation: Flourishing Together at Multiple Boundaries | 312
    —Michael Nausner

Index of Names | 325

Foreword

"Listen to What the Spirit Is Saying to the Churches" (Rev 2:7)

SOFIA CAMNERIN

WHAT IS THE SPIRIT saying to the churches? I hope readers of this volume, like the participants in the Sigtuna conference, will take the opportunity to widen our hearts, sharpen our ears, and listen to what the Spirit is saying to the churches. And when we listen carefully, it is also important that we try to hear the silenced voices, the cracked voices—and also to listen to what is silenced in ourselves. What is the Spirit whispering? What is our heart, in which the Spirit intercedes, telling us? I have many rich experiences of transforming impact from my years in the worldwide ecumenical community, and I share some here in the hope that they will shed light on some perspectives I find crucial.

I have been actively involved in the ecumenical movement for nineteen years now. In 2006 I was elected to the Central Committee of the World Council of Churches (WCC). It was truly life-changing to participate in the purple walk on one of the first days of the 9th Assembly of the WCC in Porto Alegre in 2006. This was a manifestation to mark the end of the decade to overcome violence against women. Thousands of people marched in purple. Purple: the color of regret and lent, of shared pain, but also of strength, since power is born in suffering. "Three times I appealed to the Lord about this, that it would leave me," says Paul, "but he said to me, 'My grace is sufficient for you, for my power is made perfect in weakness'" (2 Cor 12:8–9).

It was life-changing to realize how interconnected faith and action are to most Christians around the world. During the first years of my participation in the Central Committee meetings, I made use of breaks and other in-between-spaces to ask the other members what the greatest challenges for their churches were. I got answers like "how we can rebuild the school in our village since the old one is threatened by rising water levels," or "how we can manage to help all the children who have been orphaned because their parents died of HIV/Aids." I have often asked myself what I would have answered if someone had asked me the same question. Sometimes they did and probably I said something about secularization and how our church in Sweden can improve evangelism among people who (very often) have everything. They are already on the top of Maslow's pyramid of needs.

Certainly, I was challenged by the obvious integration of belief and action among the others I met. I have also been deeply moved by speeches, like the one the late Archbishop Desmond Tutu gave, also in Porto Alegre, when he said that "it is important to remember we overcame apartheid through the crucial help of the united world church."[1] Such impact—overcoming apartheid—is born from within and from below and is, I would say, at its core: peace, love, silent listening to the Spirit.

Nathan Söderblom, the pioneering Archbishop of the Church of Sweden and one of the founders of the Sigtuna Foundation, said in his Nobel prize speech:

> It is my belief that "leaving ourselves in peace" with our self-conceit and evil passions does not lead to real peace. Peace can be reached only through fighting against the ancient Adam in ourselves and in others.[2]

When Söderblom planned for the Stockholm meeting in 1925 he hoped for a spiritual revival in a world wounded by war, greed, and nationalism. He saw the ecumenical movement as a revival movement carried by praise and prayer, and his vision of the ecumenical revival applied to nothing less than the saving of the whole world, and that saving of the whole world presupposed the visible unity among all Christians.

---

1. Tutu, "Transform Your World," 350.
2. Söderblom, Nobel Lecture.

Do we still believe that visible unity is that crucial, that the salvation of the whole world depends on it? And if so, why is there not more urgency? Why do we not do everything we can to embrace each other, hold each other accountable, honor each other, be totally honest to each other, demonstrate our wounds to each other, welcome and love each other, search for one another? Can meeting together for receptive ecumenical listening and learning be a step in a revival movement for the salvation of the whole world?

When Söderblom, as newly elected archbishop, met students for the ministry he encouraged them to love humans, not humanity, and, as Jesus's servants, to be aware of the ally they have in every human being. He told them not to be lords or masters but shepherds of God's flock that is under God's care, not lording it over those entrusted to them, but being examples to the flock. Söderblom thought that it is impossible to preserve peace of the heart without giving one's life in the service of peace and love. Change begins from within and below and is preserved in living it out.

In the Sermon on the Mount, given during the Roman occupation of Palestine, Jesus proclaims: "Blessed are the peacemakers, for they will be called children of God" (Matt 5:9). The words he spoke must have appeared impossible and provoking. He expressed them when Palestine was occupied, and yet the words seemed possible, since Jesus said them. He spoke with authority, as we know from other contexts in the New Testament. We read in Colossians: "As you therefore have received Christ Jesus the Lord, continue to live your lives in him, rooted and built up in him and established in the faith, just as you were taught, abounding in thanksgiving" (Col 2:6–7). In these verses the preposition "in" is crucial: living "in" him; rooted "in" him; "in" faith. The connection between receiving and living is evident in the opening: "As you therefore . . . " (other possible translations are "Just as you . . .," or "Since you . . ."). Here is a link between receiving, incorporation into Christ through baptism, the life in Christ, and the lived life in Christ.

Since Jesus Christ is our peace, the one who we have been clothed in through faith and baptism, we also live *in* this peace and peace is as much prayer as action. Therefore, let us be observant of the preposition "in," the simultaneity that is covered by it, the prayer and breathing in the Spirit, as well as the action. Let us seek stillness, remain rooted, and yet not be naïve. We know that dominating, destructive forces are strong and must be resisted. It is always necessary to protest against egoistic, protectionist, violent, nationalistic forces. As peacemakers we cannot avoid wounds. We cannot ignore perpetrators, nor invaders. To become a peacemaker is not equal to distributing cheap grace or quick forgiveness. We must equip ourselves with time and patience, and remember the wave, the movement back and forth to our inner wells and the lived faith, build our strength in union with the Lord and walk closely with our neighbors. Peacemakers keep their eyes and ears open, and their hearts warm, and they acknowledge their own vulnerability. It is necessary for a peacemaker to take injuries seriously and always respect victims, to combine justice with peace and seek restoration. Integrity is important in conflict situations, both for the peacemakers themselves and for the various parties in the conflict. Different parties must be respected, and their integrity secured. Peace-making takes time and must take time. Both victims and perpetrators need time to heal and repent, to take responsibility for suffering they may have caused others or may have been affected by.

In the Swedish pre-meeting before the 11th General Assembly of the WCC in Karlsruhe, Germany (2022), we had a conversation on the theme: "Christ's love moves the world to reconciliation and unity" and discussed whether "love" is too weak a term to use, when we have a brutal, unacceptable war taking place here in Europe, near the venue of the Assembly. We stated that the theme was intended as a deepening of what had already been the fact, namely that we, as churches, are supposed to walk together, to stay together. And we will now answer Jesus's command—to love one another. Someone said that love is not too weak in times of war. When there is obviously no peace, we can still love one another. However, that doesn't sound easy, to love one another, to love the perpetrator. Even the invader?

Söderblom was installed as archbishop in 1914, the same year as World War I broke out. He insisted that the church's sympathy must be with the most vulnerable. The church must be independent from political parties. Christendom had been powerless in preventing the war. He warned against nationalism when it is distorted into self-righteousness. 16 years later in 1930 he held his Nobel-prize-lecture and said: "Our generation has lived through not only a world catastrophe, but also through a violent inner revolution. People with unshakable faith in progress, believing that the world was on the road to Paradise, suddenly found themselves in the darkest hell of hatred and duplicity." He continued with strong self-critical words about how the church, which had been called the Prince of Peace, had not fulfilled its duty.

"We sang every Sunday 'Glory be to God on high, and on earth peace,'" he said, and "every Christmas Day we proclaimed 'Eternal peace must be secured and sustained by law and justice.'"[3] He emphasized that some people realized that more could have been done for peace by a Christendom united at least in its most essential principle: to live according to the commandment of love. He stressed that religion and morality should be based on the following two major premises: 1) the commandment of love transcends all frontiers; 2) the Christian concept of justice is generated by a continuous process of divine creation. For Söderblom, the values of Christendom transcend those of individual nations, that nationalism must be replaced by Christian brotherhood/sisterhood and that the church should take the lead in showing the world the unity of Christ's followers in their obedience to Him.

He also spoke about public opinion and that Christians should realize that they are partly responsible for public opinion and should serve love and truth in public, national, and international life, as well as in their personal relations. They should try to understand others, their thoughts, languages, and behavior. Therefore, the church must fight against all glorification of violence, and against any force contrary to the rule of law, and she must preach that nations and communities, like individuals, must act according to the principles of truth, justice, and love. If peace is to become a reality on our earth, it must be founded in the hearts of the people. Here, Söderblom highlighted the importance of conversion. It is a struggle to win peace: it requires struggle against schism, against fear, against Mammon, against hatred and injustice. And the struggle must also be directed toward the primitive man [sic.] within us, he said. World peace will be realized only if God conquers the hearts of the people.

The Central Committee of the WCC in June 2022, prior to the General Assembly, was my last meeting on that board. However, I have stepped down now and serve in other ways. Nevertheless, I will still be active in the ecumenical movement and walk very closely to the WCC. On the agenda on this my last meeting was, of course, the war in Ukraine and the role of churches both there and here. As members in the Central Committee, the Russian Orthodox delegation was also in the room. I was a bit nervous before that meeting and said to people who were going to go to the Assembly in Karlsruhe, that this meeting would be a kind of test. What happened in the Central Committee at that time could also be expected

---

3. Söderblom, Nobel Lecture.

to take place in Karlsruhe. I had many questions, such as if every delegate should stay in the room or leave in anger? How should the committee act if some churches wanted to expel the Russian Orthodox Church? And if so, who expels who? Are we not one? Who is the subject and who is the object in a community where we are all members?

A statement on the war in Ukraine was prepared and we started our discussion there. Some delegates stated that their church's board expected the suspension or exclusion of the Russian Orthodox Church. Some delegates stressed that we must stay together, but clearly emphasize that war is against the will of God and that legitimation of war must be condemned. Some delegates replied that no one is innocent and asked why the West is expanding their military line of defense. One delegate from Armenia almost shouted out in tears and asked where the rest of us were, when they needed us. The Russian delegates got the floor in the end. They opened with words like: "It is not easy to stand here in front of you, when you all blame us. We did not start the war; we are against war. We also suffer. Our people are also in Ukraine." A young Russian Orthodox delegate pleaded: "Please do not destroy the future for us, we want to be part of the ecumenical movement now and in the future."

Not everything was being said, we would have needed more time and conversations in smaller settings. Nevertheless, we agreed on a strong statement, I think, that was later published.[4] And we all stayed in the same room. We listened to each other. We shared space and perhaps took a small step towards Jesus's call to us to become peacemakers. Still, I had wanted more closeness and more vulnerability, more honesty- and perhaps more languages than words.

Septemmy E. Lakawa underlines the importance of poetry when it comes to experiences of suffering and trauma. According to her, the testimony of the cross in the New Testament is presented as a poetic testimony. The cross is the place of ongoing and unspeakable suffering. Processing of trauma needs more languages than the written. The "language of silence," the "language of the wounded," is a language that has been rejected by missionaries and evangelists who favored the written word. Such wordless language is needed for bodies that remember the trauma, violence, and terror of war. Art becomes important then and the space that arises between death and resurrection, the place of the

---

4. World Council of Churches, Statement on the War in Ukraine by the WCC Central Committee meeting, 15-18 June 2022, https://www.oikoumene.org/resources/documents/wcc-central-committee-statement-on-the-war-in-ukraine accessed 2025-04-16.

testimony of the Spirit, the poetic testimony. Vulnerability needs to be in focus. Jesus takes on the suffering and remains with the suffering, even if the suffering does not pass, as for traumatized victims.[5]

The theme of the Sigtuna conference underpins the present volume: *"listen to what the Spirit is saying to the churches"* (Rev 2:7). In times of war—between the nations, against nature, in the market, in society—let us listen to what the Spirit is saying and listen closely. Let us also try to hear the silenced voices, the wounded and cracked, and the voices whispering or perhaps singing, dancing, or creating, in vulnerability. Let us listen to the Spirit within us, among us, and let us seek and live out her peace embraced by love.

BIBLIOGRAPHY

Biel, Michael, et al., eds. *Witnessing Christ. Contextual and Interconfessional Perspectives on Christology*. Stuttgart: Kolhammer 2020.

Söderblom, Nathan. Nobel Lecture: https://www.nobelprize.org/prizes/peace/1930/soderblom/lecture/. [2025-04-16]

Tutu, Desmond. "Transform Your World: The Search for Unity." In *God, in Your Grace: Official Report of the Ninth Assembly of the World Council of Churches*, edited by Luis N. Rivera-Pagan, 349–53. Geneva: WCC Publications, 2007.

World Council of Churches. Statement on the War in Ukraine by the WCC Central Committee meeting, 15-18 June 2022, https://www.oikoumene.org/resources/documents/wcc-central-committee-statement-on-the-war-in-ukraine.

---

5. Biel et al., eds.) *Witnessing*, 165–75.

Introduction

The Editors

At the heart of Receptive Ecumenism is a simple principle, that "further ecumenical progress is indeed possible, but only if each of the traditions . . . makes a clear programmatic shift from prioritizing the question 'What do our various others first need to learn from us?' to asking instead 'What do we need to learn and what can we learn—or receive—with integrity from our others?'"[1] From this wellspring, opened by the Catholic theologian Paul Murray at the inaugural international symposium on Receptive Ecumenism, Durham, England, in January 2006, this ethic has flowed worldwide and watered ecumenism in many different contexts and traditions. To mention just three examples, Receptive Ecumenism was chosen as a theological method for the most recent round of Catholic–Anglican international dialogues (ARCIC III). It also underpinned the ecumenical prayer gathering preceding the 2023 Catholic Synod in Rome (itself the largest listening exercise the Catholic Church has ever done), through a conversation between a monk of the ecumenical Taizé community with the former secretary of the Global Christian Forum, Rev Dr Larry Miller, who had encountered Receptive Ecumenism at the Third International Conference, held in Fairfield, USA, in 2014. On more familiar ecumenical territory, at the 70th Anniversary of the WCC

1. Murray, "The Reception of ARCIC I and II in Europe and Discerning the Strategy and Agenda for ARCIC III," 212.

in 2018, the Archbishop of Canterbury, Justin Welby, called it "One of the most important of recent ecumenical developments . . . It turns negotiated frontiers into open borders."[2]

Alongside such ecclesial adoption there has been a steady stream of scholarly articles, monographs and edited volumes engaging the subject with constructive creativity and critique. Indeed, a recent entry in this Church of Sweden Series, *Thérèse and Martin: Carmel and the Reformation in a New Light* by Karin Johannesson is described by the author as a work of Receptive Ecumenism.[3]

The entries in the present volume are drawn from the fifth Receptive Ecumenism International Conference, held at Sigtuna, Sweden, in 2022, following a two-year delay due to Covid-19. The Conference was organized by the Swedish Christian Council, University College Stockholm, and the Sigtuna Foundation, which itself has an important history in ecumenism and peacebuilding.[4] We chose as a conference theme, "Transforming Ecumenism," aware that in English "transforming can be understood as a verb—"to transform ecumenism"—but also as an adjective—"an ecumenism which transforms." Both this notion, and the subtitle "Listen to what the Spirit is saying to the churches" were eagerly taken up by contributors and are reflected in many of the entries in this volume.

One of the interesting things about the Sigtuna conference, and in turn part of the rationale for this publication, was the sense that the study and practice of Receptive Ecumenism had achieved a certain maturity. This could be seen in the confident and courageous decision to organize a conference by the Swedish team, aware that important work in Receptive Ecumenism was being done not just in England and Australia, but in Scandinavia, including Sara Gehlin's groundbreaking work in conversation with peacebuilding and with feminist critique. The conference therefore set out to include more presentations and participants for whom English was not a primary language, and who were rooted in traditions other than Catholicism and Anglicanism. The strong Lutheran presence was particularly significant in this regard, as were the Pentecostal and Orthodox contributions. The "new maturity" could also be seen when alongside experienced ecumenists and professors (including Paul

2. https://www.archbishopofcanterbury.org/news/ecumenical-spring-archbishop-justins-speech-world-council-churches-70th-anniversary (16 February 2018).

3. Johannesson, *Thérèse and Martin*, 3.

4. See https://sigtunastiftelsen.se/en/.

Murray, the initiator of Receptive Ecumenism), the conference heard from ministers, emerging scholars, and doctoral students who have discovered Receptive Ecumenism for themselves through practice or research. To those who had attended earlier conferences, it was evident that the subject had now truly taken on a life of its own, a desire expressed by Murray at the Third International Conference in 2014.

However, *Spirit Flowing Like Water* is not primarily intended as a record of the Sigtuna conference. We make no attempt to follow the structure or order of that event, and the papers have been revised, some entirely rewritten, for publication. Rather this volume is a contribution to the academic conversation on this topic, reaching into new conceptual and contextual areas, as well as consolidating some fundamental principles. At the same time, it is offered as inspiration and aid for those working in ecumenical situations at any level. It does not contain a single blueprint, but it does share stories, offering resources and hopefully wisdom—as well as numerous cautions and critiques.

The book is divided into three parts, each preceded by a short meditative "prologue" which both echoes the important prayer time woven into the Sigtuna conference and acknowledges the deep relationship of Receptive Ecumenism to Spiritual Ecumenism. We are grateful to Sofia Camnerin, who contributed so much to the conference, for providing a Preface to the overall volume drawn from her opening address.

Paul Murray opens *Part One—Transforming Ecumenism,* setting the scene for these conversations, acknowledging that "new chapters" do not come from nowhere, and that Receptive Ecumenism has roots deep in Christian thoughts and practice. At the same time, he highlights certain innovations and distinctive attributes, including how Receptive Ecumenism differs from some "kenotic" ecumenism, and expands on the role of the Spirit. Both themes are taken up by authors throughout the volume. In their chapters, Susan Durber and Ivana Noble offer that rare thing in academic conversation—genuinely constructive criticism—in very different ways, reflecting respectively on Receptive Ecumenism through a Faith and Order lens, and in dialogue with selected Orthodox and philosophical resources. The relationship of Receptive Ecumenism to established dialogues is taken up by Dominic Robinson, SJ, with David Carter, and by Tony Franklin-Ross, with a focus on Catholic, Methodist, and Lutheran initiatives, including the 1999 Joint Declaration on the Doctrine of Justification, a milestone which also inspires Elizabeth Woodard's chapter on "Cruciform Ecumenism." Cheryl Bridges John presents a very important contribution from a Pentecostal perspective, eloquently demonstrating that Pentecostal churches have more to contribute than "a sort of worship vibe." Johannes Zeiler's response is surely only the beginning of a vital conversation between established denominations and Pentecostal churches, using Receptive Ecumenism. Finally, Paul Lakeland introduces a theme which will be echoed throughout the volume, the *spirituality* of Receptive Ecumenism.

In *Part Two—Encounters in Context*, Sara Gehlin imaginatively plays with the double meaning of "strand" as shoreline and thread. She models her multi-stranded ecumenical proposal by weaving together friendship, spirituality, imagination and history in a critical and constructive manner. The Church of England provides ground for two chapters drawing on the experience of Anglican priests, with Callan Slipper critically and creatively exploring the nature of a "mission-shaped church," and Diane Ryan using the notion of "internal Receptive Ecumenism" to examine an ongoing lack of reconciliation around women's ministry. Practical and spiritual dimensions of Receptive Ecumenism are explored in different ways by Joan Patricia Back's reading of Chaira Lubich and the Focolare community; by Doral Hayes, who combines her experience of interchurch families with the evolutionary theology of Thomas Oord; and in Erik Ringhem's unflinchingly honest account of pain and learning when ecumenism goes wrong. A rather different perspective on spirituality is offered by Emil Marginean's thoughtful parallel reading of two spiritual masters from East and West. Finally in this part, we return to the theme of mission, with a comprehensive presentation (Risto Jukko) and response (Bertil Ekström) showing Receptive Ecumenism and ecumenical mission as two sides of the same coin. A missional dimension had not been strongly evident in previous discussions of Receptive Ecumenism, so this represented an important development, preceded by the publication of *Sharing and Learning: Bible, Mission, and Receptive Ecumenism* in 2021.[5]

Part Three—Expanding the Horizons, begins with another kind of "internal" Receptive Ecumenism, this time not *within* a single church but *between* churches of the Lutheran tradition, refusing to allow painful differences in doctrinal and ethical understanding to prevent them from joining together and learning together. Here Karin Johannesson (Church of Sweden) is joined by Bishop Chediel Sendoro (Evangelical Lutheran Church of Tanzania). Tragically, as the final manuscript was

---

5. Jakobson, Jukko, and Kristenson, eds., *Sharing and Learning*.

being prepared for publication, we learned of Bishop Sendoro's death in a road traffic accident. Our prayers are with his community and his family; may he rest in peace and rise in glory.

Expanding the horizons, at the boundary of how "ecumenism" might be defined, Clare Amos sensitively explores Jewish–Christian relations in light of Receptive Ecumenism, with Barth and Kasper as key conversation partners. Mathew Chandrankunnel and Peniel Rajkumar each argue for a "wider ecumenism" encompassing interfaith dialogue and uncover a concern for ecumenism outside of the global North that can "unthink the West." A different kind of horizon is opened in the chapters by Risto Saarinen and Gregory Ryan, who engage in a reading of Receptive Ecumenism alongside theoretical studies and concrete sites of theological recognition of difference. The volume ends with Michael Nausner's chapter reaching for the planetary horizon of eco-ecumenism, yet rooted in a deeply personal disposition of vulnerability and awareness of the *multiple* boundaries at which each of us is situated.

A collaborative volume such as this incurs many debts of gratitude in addition to the generous efforts of the contributors, and the editors would like to acknowledge a few of those here. The conference out of which the present anthology emerged would not have been possible without the generous support and hospitality of the Sigtuna Foundation, and its director, Alf Linderman, and the Christian Council of Sweden, particularly Karin Wiborn and Sofia Camnerin. The conference was initiated and organized to no small extent by the leaders and administrators of Stockholm University College, and thanks are due to both the former dean Owe Kennerberg and the intermediate dean Pekka Mellergård, and not least to Sophia Tonneman who ably juggled the many administrative challenges which always are a part of international conferences. We are grateful for the support of Veljko Birač at Sankt Ignatios Press who has walked with us from the very start of the development of this volume, and for Hugh Doyle's careful proof-reading and copy-editing. The editors express heartfelt thanks to the family of the late Bo Setterlind, who kindly allowed us to publish a verse from his wonderful 1978 hymn, *Guds källa har vatten tillfyllest*.

As we sang in Sigtuna, so with this volume:

> *Guds källa har vatten tillfyllest,*
> *en gåva av strömmande liv,*
> *den äger vad alla behöver,*
> *det räcker för dig och för mig.*

God's wellspring is brimming with water,
a generous flow giving life.
What everyone needs, it possesses;
sufficient for you and for me.[6]

BIBLIOGRAPHY

Jakobson, Petter, Risto Jukko, and Olle Kristenson, eds. *Sharing and Learning. Bible, Mission, and Receptive Ecumenism.* Geneva: WCC Publications, 2021.

Johannesson, Karin. *Thérèse and Martin: Carmel and the Reformation in a New Light.* Eugene, OR: Pickwick Publications, 2023.

Murray, Paul D. "The Reception of ARCIC I and II in Europe and Discerning the Strategy and Agenda for ARCIC III." *Ecclesiology* 11/2 (2015) 199–218.

Setterlind, Bo. (1978). "Guds källa har vatten tillfyllest." In *Den Svenska Psalmboken*, no. 236. (1986).

Sigtuna Stiftelsen. https://sigtuna stiftelsen.se/en.

World Council of Churches. https://www.archbishopofcanterbury.org/news/ecumenical-spring-archbishop-justins-speech-world-council-churches-70th-anniversary (16 February 2018).

---

6. No. 236 in *Den Svenska Psalmboken* (1986). Swedish text, Bo Setterlind, 1978. Our translation.

Contributors

Clare Amos worked in the field of interreligious dialogue for the Anglican Communion (2001–2011) and for the World Council of Churches (2011-2018). She continues to teach and write in the fields of biblical studies, interreligious dialogue and spirituality, and has published a well-received commentary on Genesis, *Birthpangs and Blessings* (2022). In May 2024 she presented the David Goodbourn lecture for Churches Together in Britain and Ireland focusing on religion and violence. Clare was awarded a Lambeth Doctorate in Divinity in 2012 to mark her contribution to theological education and interreligious engagement in the Anglican Communion.

Anders Arborelius, OCD, is bishop of the Roman Catholic Diocese of Stockholm, Sweden. He has a Master of Arts in modern languages—English, Spanish, and German—from Lund University and has studied Theology and Philosophy in Bruges and Rome. In Rome, he obtained a Licentiate in Spirituality from the Carmelite Pontifical Theological Faculty. In 2017 he was appointed Cardinal by Pope Francis—the first Swedish cardinal in history. Cardinal Arborelius is a member of the Dicastery for the Clergy, the Dicastery for Bishops, the Dicastery for the Eastern Churches, and the Dicastery for Promoting Christian Unity. Since 2020 he is also a member of the Vatican's Council for the Economy.

Joan Patricia Back, originally from England, is a member of the Focolare community in Ireland. She worked at Centro "Uno" Focolare's international ecumenical secretariat in Rome from 1975–2014 where she was co-director from 2008–2014. She is a teacher of ecumenical studies at the Focolare's formation schools, a member of Focolare's interdisciplinary study center at Rocca di Papa (Rome). In Ireland she is a member of the Irish Inter Church Committee and Focolare's ecumenical coordinator. Her PhD in Theology is from the Pontifical Lateran University in Rome.

Sofia Camnerin (PhD in Systematic Theology, University of Uppsala) is Secretary General of the Christian Council of Sweden and was Academic Dean and Vice President at University College Stockholm 2018–2021. Before that she served in the first leadership team of the Uniting Church of Sweden 2012–2020. She is pastor in the Uniting Church in Sweden. She has also been a member of the Central Committee of the World Council of Churches (2006–2022). She is the author of several books and her research-field covers reconciliation, disability, pastoral care, and ecumenism.

David Carter is a Methodist local preacher in Bristol. He is involved in ecumenical research and is active in local ecumenism. Formerly, he was secretary to the Theology and Unity Group of Churches Together in England and a member of the British Methodist Roman-Catholic dialogue.

Mathew Chandrankunnel, CMI, is a Catholic priest belonging to the Carmelites of Mary Immaculate. He studied physics, philosophy and theology and did his doctorate at the University of Leuven, Belgium on Foundational Problems in Quantum Mechanics. He was appointed at Dharmaram Vidya Kshetram and Christ University, Bangalore as Professor of Philosophy of Science and has been visiting professor at many universities. He is the author of numerous books including *Ascent to Truth: The Physics, Philosophy and Religion of Galileo Galilei* and *The Philosophy of Quantum Mechanics*. From 2016–2021 he was the first Catholic Director of the Ecumenical Christian Centre, Bangalore, and works with NGOs and State Governments to transform underdeveloped societies through science and technology.

Susan Durber is a retired minister of the United Reformed Church and a former Moderator of the Faith and Order Commission of the World Council of Churches. She has served pastorates in Manchester, Salford,

Oxford, and Taunton. She is a former Principal of Westminster College in Cambridge and has worked as Christian Aid's Theology Advisor. She is the World Council of Churches President from Europe.

Bertil Ekström is an ordained Baptist pastor, born in Sweden and raised in Brazil by missionary parents. He has worked for more than forty years as a missionary sent by Örebromissionen/Interact (Sweden) to Latin America. Engaged in the World Evangelical Alliance since 1992, he was the Executive Director of the Mission Commission of WEA between 2006 and 2019. Currently, he is the Mission Director of the Convention of the Independent Baptists of Brazil (CIBI).

Sven-Erik Fjellström has served as a minister in the Church of Sweden on parish and diocesan levels, as well as some years in the Lutheran Church in Zimbabwe. Before retirement he worked for seven years as Ecumenical Officer at the Church of Sweden national office. During that time he was engaged as pedagogical resource in the Pilgrimage on Mission Theology initiated by the Christian Council of Sweden 2016-2019. This task also included participation in the Fourth Receptive Ecumenism International Conference in Canberra, 2017.

Tony Franklin-Ross is an ordained presbyter-theologian in the Methodist Church of New Zealand and is active in a range of domestic and international ecumenical projects. Tony is the Chairperson of the Ecumenical Relationships Committee of the World Methodist Council, and a member of the multilateral working group of communions associated with the *Joint Declaration on the Doctrine of Justification*.

Sara Gehlin is a senior lecturer at University College Stockholm, Sweden. Her recent works include the book *Pathways for Theology in Peacebuilding: Ecumenical Approaches to Just Peace*. She carried out her doctoral studies at Lund University, Sweden. Sara has also worked at the Church of Sweden Research Department in Uppsala and has been a post-doctoral researcher at the Faculty of Theology, University of Helsinki, Finland. She has worked with Receptive Ecumenism in Sweden since 2014 as a work group member of the Christian Council of Sweden, and she is a commissioner for the World Council of Churches' Commission on Education and Ecumenical Formation.

Doral Hayes is Principal Officer for Ecumenical Development and Relations at Churches Together in England, and a licensed lay minister in the Diocese of Oxford, Church of England. Doral holds an MA in Contemporary Christian Theology and is undertaking doctoral research into the experience of interchurch families. Publications include "The Scandal and Celebration of Ecumenical Worship: What can we learn from worshipping alongside those from other Christian traditions?" in *Preaching the Uncontrolling Love of God*, edited by Jeff Wells, Vikki Randall, Nichole Torbitzky and Thomas Jay Oord (2024).

Nausikaa Haupt is an Ecumenical Officer at the Catholic diocese of Stockholm, and Catholic coordinator at the Christian Council of Sweden, and was one of the organizers of the Fifth Receptive Ecumenism International Conference in Sigtuna 2022. She is a member of numerous Christian Council groups, including ecumenical theology (former Faith and Order) and missionary theology. Nausikaa obtained a Master of Divinity from Uppsala university, and has a LLM Canon Law from Cardiff university and a Iuris Canonica Licentiate, (Master of Canon Law) from KU Leuven.

Karin Johannesson is bishop in the Church of Sweden, Uppsala Diocese since March 2019. She is Associate Professor of Philosophy of Religion at the Faculty of Theology, Uppsala University. Her publications in English include *God pro Nobis: On Non-Metaphysical Realism and the Philosophy of Religion* (2007) and *Thérèse and Martin: Carmel and the Reformation in New Light* (2023).

Cheryl Bridges Johns is Director of the Global Pentecostal House of Studies at the United Theological Seminary, Dayton, Ohio, USA and is ordained in the International Pentecostal Holiness Church. She researches and teaches in various fields like Practical Theology, Spiritual formation and Ecumenism. Among other honorary assignments she has served as President of the Society for Pentecostal Studies. She authored the books *Pentecostal Formation* and *Seven Transforming Gifts of Menopause* as well as numerous articles for academic journals.

Risto Jukko (PhD, ThD) is currently serving as the Director of the Office for Global Mission of the Evangelical Lutheran Church of Finland. Between 2018 and 2022 he held the position of Director of the Commission of World Mission and Evangelism of the World Council of Churches in

Geneva, Switzerland. He is also Adjunct Professor of Ecumenics at both the University of Helsinki and the University of Eastern Finland.

Olle Kristenson is a retired priest in the Church of Sweden. He holds a PhD in Mission studies from Uppsala University. Before retirement he was theological advisor at the Christian Council of Sweden and was in that position project coordinator for the Fifth International Conference on Receptive Ecumenism in Sigtuna 2022.

Paul Lakeland is the Aloysius P. Kelley SJ Professor of Catholic Studies and Director of the Center for Catholic Studies at Fairfield University in Connecticut. He is the author of ten books that address the issues of ecclesiology, cultural theory and religion and literature.

Emil M. Mărginean completed his doctoral studies in Theology in 2018 at Babeș-Bolyai University in Cluj-Napoca, Romania. He is currently a research member of the Orthodox Research Institute of St. John Chrysostom. His research focuses on the confluence of Eastern Orthodox spirituality, contemporary asceticism, digital media and artificial intelligence.

Paul D. Murray is Professor of Systematic Theology within the Department of Theology and Religion at Durham University where, from 2007 to 2023, he was also the founding Director of the Centre for Catholic Studies. He is the initiator of Receptive Ecumenism. From 2011 to 2018 he was a member of, and now Consultor to, the Anglican–Roman Catholic International Commission. His current monograph projects are: *Healing the Wounds of the Church: The Theology and Practice of Receptive Ecumenism*; and *Catholicism Transfigured: Conceiving Change in the Church*. In January 2024 he was installed as a non-residentiary Ecumenical Canon of Durham Cathedral.

Michael Nausner is a systematic theologian and Senior Researcher at the Unit for Research and Analysis of the Church of Sweden. He received his PhD from Drew University in 2005 and taught Systematic Theology at Reutlingen School of Theology between 2005 and 2017. His research interest has revolved around issues of intercultural and postcolonial theology, theology of migration and the exploration of participation as a theological concept. Lately he has focused on the intersection of theology, ecology, and climate. His publications include *Eine Theologie der Teilhabe* (2020) and *Eco-Justice as Mutual Participation* (2022).

Ivana Noble is Professor of Ecumenical Theology at the Protestant Theological Faculty of Charles University in Prague, where she is currently Director of the Ecumenical Institute. She is a priest in the Czechoslovak Hussite Church and a former president of Societas Oecumenica. For five years, she led a research project investigating Orthodox Theology in the West, and currently she leads Charles University Centre of Excellence on Theological Anthropology in Ecumenical Perspective. Among her many publications are *Essays in Ecumenical Theology Vol.1* (2019) & *Vol.2* (2022), and *Theological Interpretation of Culture in Post-Communist Context* (2010).

Peniel Jesudason Rufus Rajkumar is "Global Theologian" with USPG (United Society Partners in the Gospel). He teaches at Ripon College Cuddesdon and has served the WCC as program executive for Interreligious dialogue and cooperation and as professor at the Ecumenical Institute in Bossey. His research and teaching interests include ecumenism, Christian social ethics, mission and World Christianities, interreligious dialogue, and liberation theologies. He is the author of many books and articles and recently edited *Faith(s) Seeking Justice: Dialogue and Liberation* (2021) which explores interreligious theologies of liberation from Christian, Muslim, Hindu and Buddhist perspectives.

Erik Ringheim is a Lutheran pastor in the Church of Sweden. He holds a Bachelor of Theology in New Testament Exegesis and a Masters degree in Systematic Theology with a paper on territorial Ecclesiology in Church of Sweden. Erik has represented Church of Sweden in various ecumenical gatherings such as Lutheran World Federation and Christian Council of Sweden. Erik serves as pastor and vice vicar in the parish of Sollentuna in the diocese of Stockholm.

Dominic Robinson SJ is parish priest of Farm Street, the Jesuit church in Central London. He is Vice-Chair of the Society for Ecumenical Studies, a member of the Department for Dialogue and Unity of the Catholic Bishops' Conference of England and Wales and a lecturer in Dogmatic Theology at St Mary's University, Twickenham.

Diane Ryan is a parish priest in the Church of England, serving parishes in the Diocese of Durham. She has published on the place of Receptive Ecumenism in interchurch families and their church communities, and on the Victorian social reformer, Octavia Hill.

Gregory A. Ryan (PhD, Durham) is Assistant Professor in Catholic Theology at the Centre for Catholic Studies, Durham University. He serves as Academic Director of the Northern Diaconal Formation Partnership, training permanent deacons for eight Catholic dioceses in Northern England and Wales. His publications include *Hermeneutics of Doctrine in a Learning Church* (2020) and *Receptive Ecumenism as Transformative Ecclesial Learning: Walking the Way to a Church Re-formed* (2022).

Risto Saarinen is Professor of Ecumenics at the University of Helsinki. From 2014 to 2019 he directed the Center of Excellence "Reason and Religious Recognition" funded by the Academy of Finland. Saarinen is the author of *Recognition and Religion* (2016) and *Luther and the Gift* (2017).

Chediel Sendoro Rt. Rev. Chediel Sendoro (1970–2024) was bishop of Mwanga Diocese of the Evangelical Lutheran Church in Tanzania from 2016. He worked with ecumenical bodies including the United Evangelical Mission (UEM) and Christian Council of Tanzania and was involved in inter-religious forums in Tanzania.

Callan Slipper (PhD, Lancaster University) is a theologian and writer. He is Chair of Churches Together in England and of the Society for Ecumenical Studies and is also a member of the Focolare Movement's international study center, the Abba School. An ordained priest in the Church of England, he lives in London in a community of the Focolare Movement. Until 2022 he was National Ecumenical Officer for the Church of England's Council for Christian Unity. He is author of *Five Steps to Living Christian Unity* and *Enriched by the Other: A Spiritual Guide to Receptive Ecumenism*.

Elizabeth Woodard is a Catholic theologian and lay ecclesial minister. She holds a PhD in systematic theology from the Catholic University of America in addition to a Master of Divinity and a Master of Sacred Music from Boston University. Her work as a retreat leader, public speaker, and spiritual director can be seen on unityhopeful.com. She serves as a pastoral associate at a parish in the archdiocese of Boston and teaches in the graduate and permanent deaconate programs at St. Meinrad Archabbey and Seminary. She is a composer and practitioner of choral music.

Johannes Zeiler is an ordained priest in the Church of Sweden and holds a PhD in World Christianity and Interreligious Studies from Uppsala University, Sweden. He currently serves as Canon Chancellor at Linköping Cathedral, Sweden. He earlier served as Ecumenical Officer at the Church of Sweden Central Office particularly in relation to the Lutheran World Federation and the Christian Council of Sweden. His research interests include global Christianity, ecumenical theology, and mission. He is the co-chair of the International Lutheran-Pentecostal Dialogue Commission.

Part I

Transforming Ecumenism

Prologue to Part One
I–Thou–We

BISHOP KARIN JOHANNESSON *and*
CARDINAL ANDERS ARBORELIUS, OCD

OPENING HOMILY FOR THE FIFTH
INTERNATIONAL RECEPTIVE ECUMENISM
CONFERENCE, SIGTUNA, JUNE 2022

KJ: God speaks in every moment. If God had not spoken, there would not have been a single nanosecond. Time began when God created heaven and earth by saying: "Let there be." Without words, our cosmos would not exist. When the time was right, God spoke again, in a new way, through Jesus Christ. In him, the Word became flesh. When he was teaching, people were amazed because his words had authority. They were healing and revealing. They still are today.

Currently—at every moment—the Church throughout the world declares the wonders of God in many different tongues. Faith comes from hearing the word about Christ. We in the churches are often very keen on finding the right words for talking about Christ. How can we be just as careful about listening to him when he speaks to us today?

AA: To listen is really a grace. We have to learn to become responsive to the silent whisper of the Holy Spirit deep inside us. There are usually so many loud voices with all kinds of messages in our contemporary world. In order to listen we have to be silent and to be empty. Then we can receive the fullness of God's love. In my Carmelite tradition we try to learn from Mary to be silent, to listen and to be responsive. Together with her we can receive the Eternal Word of God who became flesh in Jesus Christ in our heart.

Every word from Jesus is a grace for each one of us. When we really can listen to him and be responsive to his love something will change. We will change. The word of Jesus can re-create us and make us new. We need his loving word in order to realize that he loves us in a unique and personal way. That is also the reason why everyone will find a personal accent and understanding of the words of Jesus. He can love each one with a preferential love. At the same time, we become more and more united to each other when we listen together to the word of Jesus. It is the wonderful task of the Holy Spirit to make all of us aware of this love that unites us in the church.

KJ: During our conference here in Sigtuna, we get the opportunity to rejoice in the Spirit in a very special way. Our gathering is a way of celebrating that the Spirit gives us the grace to listen to God and to one another. We may listen to God every day but sometimes it is extra important that we do it together, as a community, as churches. Recently, the bishops of the Church of Sweden visited Norway. In the cathedral in Trondheim, we had the opportunity to listen to a sermon given by the Lutheran theologian and bishop Olav Fykse Tveit. Currently, he is Preses of the Bishops' Conference of the Church of Norway. Before he was elected to that position, he was the general secretary of the World Council of Churches for ten years. His doctoral dissertation is entitled *Mutual Accountability as Ecumenical Attitude,* so it fits in well with our conference.

In Nidaros Cathedral, Olav Fykse Tveit quoted from a famous Norwegian poem that begins with the words "It is no longer relevant to say 'I'; instead, we have to say 'we.'" This stanza sounds much more poetic in the Norwegian original text, but I think that you can understand the main point even if my English translation has its shortcomings. This poem was written during the Second World War. Inspired by the poem, Olav Fykse Tveit emphasized that in times of war, anxiety, great challenges for humanity and creation, it is not time for exaggerated individualism or unnecessary conflicts. Instead, in such times we need to listen together to the Spirit with great attention. We have to say "we"—even if we do not agree on everything—because we must handle big challenges that we can only solve together. How do we participate in God's mission in our world today? To know what to do, say and pray we have to listen to what the Spirit is saying to the churches.

AA: The Holy Spirit can help us to leave our own "I" behind and enter into the "we" of the human family and of the Church. Then we also get a glimpse of the mystery of the Holy Trinity, the divine "We." Gradually, we can grow into a more trinitarian atmosphere, where everything reminds us of God's own reality and mystery. Our human reality should reflect this interior mystery of God, where "I" live in a constant communion with "Thou." Then it will be quite natural to live together as "we."

I can only become a real "I" in my loving dialogue and relation with a "Thou." My prayer is not only my own business, it is a constant grace and gift from "Thou." When I learn to live like that, in a loving communion with the divine "Thou," it becomes quite natural to live like that in communion with every human "Thou." Then it will be evident that we can live together as a human community, a human "we" reflecting the divine "We."

This is not merely a childish way of playing with words. Still, as the adopted children of the Father, we need not always to be like the serious grown-ups. We are allowed to be a bit childish and play in the presence of God. The scheme "I–Thou–We" can be very helpful in order to see how the Holy Trinity can be reflected in so many ways. It is not only important in dogmatical theology. It helps us to get a better understanding of Christian spirituality, social doctrine—and even Receptive Ecumenism.

KJ: This conference gives us the opportunity to make new friends and to deepen the bonds of friendship that we have already established in the past. We meet here in Sigtuna as a "we." In plenary sessions and short paper sessions, we will engage in dialogues about our common challenges and opportunities. During the conference, we also meet each other as an "I" and as a "you." At dinner tables and during coffee breaks we will get to know each other through conversations that will sometimes broaden our views in an unexpected way.

As we get to know each other we can at the same time get to know God better. Bible studies and common prayers will help us to discern what the Spirit is saying to the churches. In addition, every meeting that we are involved in during the conference is such an opportunity. Every human being has something to teach us about God. Receptive Ecumenism is about seeing and receiving such gifts with gratitude.

AA: Hopefully this conference can help us all to become more receptive to the special gifts and charisms of other Christian traditions and denominations. It is thrilling indeed to discover some new and unknown treasures that can help us to become more receptive to God's providence and grace.

Every single human being has a message of God for me when I look upon him and her as a "Thou," a "you." It is the same really when we look upon another church or denomination. There is always a hidden secret, a hidden treasure to discover, if we really use the gifts of the Holy Spirit and let ourselves be guided by his light. Historical wounds and misunderstandings can be overcome when we try to look upon other denominations in that way. We have seen that the crucial issue of grace and good deeds that was so painful and divided us at the time of the Reformation has been overcome.

When we become more receptive to God's message in other churches, we can also become more receptive to the needs of humanity. As believers and followers of Jesus we are sent to the world, to the poor, to those who suffer and are persecuted. We have to look upon them as a "Thou" identified with Jesus himself. The church may never forget that she is sent out to serve all those in need and bring them the love and care of Jesus. If we want to be the disciples of Jesus we have to be receptive to the voices of those who have no voices. Jesus will send us out after this conference in order to show the world that he is the Risen Lord who has come to save those in need.

1

Reforming Ecumenism

Receptive Ecumenism as an Instrument for Ecclesial Transformation

PAUL D. MURRAY

INTRODUCTION

THE TITLE OF THE Fifth International Receptive Ecumenism Conference, "Transforming Ecumenism—'Listen to what the Spirit is Saying to the Churches' (Rev 2:7)," and the title of this chapter, each express some key convictions and fundamental commitments that have been at work in Receptive Ecumenism from the outset and to which we need to keep returning.[1] This chapter accordingly starts by reflecting on some of these key convictions and fundamental commitments, beginning with that refrain that runs through the book of Revelation, "Listen to what the Spirit is saying to the churches," and with the understanding and experience it here references of Receptive Ecumenism as a movement of the Spirit. The focus then turns to Receptive Ecumenism as at once a transforming of contemporary ecumenism, a further encouraging of the

---

1. Building on the pioneering work that Dr Sara Gehlin had previously done in introducing Receptive Ecumenism in various Scandinavian contexts, I remain immensely grateful for the creative, sensitive, and patient work that Rev. Dr Olle Kristenson and colleagues on the Organizing Committee and Program Committee did in organizing and hosting the Fifth Receptive Ecumenism International in June 2022.

intrinsically transformative potential and effects of ecumenism, and as an event and instrument of ecclesial transformation. Following that are some reflections on differing ways of understanding ecclesial conversion, the continuing place of traditioned identities and difference, and the kind of full communion in redeemed diversity that is envisaged. Finally, having pointed to some examples of Receptive Ecumenism in practice, the chapter closes by noting the strong resonance between current Catholic explorations of more synodal ways of being and the orientation, practice, and potential of Receptive Ecumenism. Is this the moment when receptive ecumenical learning can help serve the transformation of the Catholic Church and so help serve the ecumenical journey?

LISTEN TO WHAT THE SPIRIT IS SAYING TO THE CHURCHES

Recurring throughout the literature is the conviction that before Receptive Ecumenism is offered as a thought-through distinctive strategy for contemporary ecumenism—which it *is*—and before it is promoted and adopted as a total ethic for Christian living—which it properly can be—Receptive Ecumenism first needs to be understood and engaged as a movement of the initiating–transforming Spirit of Christ.[2] Its manner of first coming to somewhat inchoate semi-consciousness and initial experimental practice in my own teaching experience, followed by its subsequent reflected and more informed articulation, all had the feel of a stirring and moving of the Spirit about it; a moving of the Spirit that was opening an unexpected new chapter for me personally and, possibly, also opening a fresh new chapter for the wider ecumenical movement.[3] In turn, the way in which time and time again it found ready, sometimes surprising, resonance in the hearts and minds of others—not universally but frequently and recurrently—similarly had a feel of the movement and synchronicity of the Spirit about it. It was as though the Spirit had also been preparing the way for the reception of Receptive Ecumenism in the felt needs and desires of others.

Further, given that with the Spirit there is always freedom, creativity, and particularity of action as well as recognizable form in

2. E.g., see Murray, "Afterword. Receiving of Christ in the Spirit"; "Foreword. Receptive Ecumenism as a Leaning-in to the Spirit of Loving Transformation"; "Discerning the Call of the Spirit to Theological-Ecclesial Renewal"; and "Foreword: Serving the Spirit of Receptive Ecumenism."

3. See Murray and Murray, "The Roots, Range, and Reach of Receptive Ecumenism."

non-identical repetition, it has always been recognized that Receptive Ecumenism cannot be a one-size-fits-all franchise that is the same in all contexts. It needs always to be worked out in relation to the particular questions, difficulties, needs, and possibilities that are "live" in any given context. So also, it has been emphasized that Receptive Ecumenism is not a one-stop shop nor a technique for delivering fixed end-results but a dynamic process in which each of us repeatedly listens—and listens again, and again, and again—to what the Spirit is saying to each of us as church in our specific ecclesial contexts in the here and now. Receptive Ecumenism as a way of ecclesial "life in the Spirit" is a matter of hearing and responding to the particular ways in which the Spirit is now calling and drawing us in the particularities of our circumstances, to become more fully, more freely the Church of Christ; more authentic witnesses to, heralds, and sacraments of the Kingdom in our ecclesial lives, structures, and being together.

As has just been referenced under the actions of listening, hearing, and responding, the Receptive Ecumenism literature variously speaks of there being three broad, recurrent, and intertwined movements in the dynamics of ecclesial existence under the new law of the Spirit. At an earlier point, in a metaphorical register more visual than aural, Joseph Cardijn famously referred to them as see, judge, and act. Encompassing both of these sensory registers, the formative thinking that has shaped Receptive Ecumenism frequently refers to these three movements of life under the Spirit as: attending to what is; discerning what might be; and enacting the future in love.[4]

"Attending to what is," or "attending to the reality of things," represents a deliberate step away from ecclesial idealism. It is a step away from prioritizing conceptual abstraction and doctrinal definition as the first way of understanding our ecclesial existence, and a step towards taking our respective lived realities seriously: both the true, the good, and the beautiful; *and* all the messy imperfections, contradictions, and incoherences that attending to the reality of things inevitably discloses. To put this another way, attending to our respective ecclesial realities represents a step away from ecclesial defensiveness and any false sense of completeness in ourselves, and a step towards recognizing both that each tradition falls short of the glory of God and that precisely here in our respective fallen states we are each—each ecclesial tradition, each

---

4. See Murray, *Reason, Truth, and Theology in Pragmatist Perspective*.

ecclesial community—uniquely called to healing and greater flourishing in the loving communion of God in Christ and the Spirit.

To be clear, this is not about those who are truly secure and strong condescending to adopt a pretense of vulnerability. It is about us being brought to recognize that we already *are*, in reality, both vulnerable and considerably less than we might be and should be. Each of our traditions has had to live through its own version of this disillusioning process. For many of us this has been tied up with things like the clerical sexual abuse crisis, or coming to recognize our shameful historic complicity in the slave trade, or the exclusion of women from full voice and participation, or the fact of our becoming increasingly marginal to the wider cultural and societal contexts in which we are situated, or the anticipation of our projected numeric decline to earthly "completion." Despite the very many things that we each rightly treasure and gratefully regard as God-given in our respective ecclesial traditions, the process of attending to our lived ecclesial realities evokes in us both a sense of need concerning what is limited and wounded, and a sense of desire for health, healing, *salus*, and salvation. This is where Receptive Ecumenism finds its true locus, in the lived lives of our holy yet fallen, wonderful yet wounded ecclesial traditions; and it is perhaps fitting to recognize how well this dual regard for the respective realities of our ecclesial existences as holy yet fallen, wonderful yet wounded coheres with the Lutheran sensibility concerning the church collectively and each member thereof as *simul iustus et peccatore* and, hence, as in a state of *semper reformanda*.

"TRANSFORMING ECUMENISM" AND "RECEPTIVE ECUMENISM AS AN INSTRUMENT FOR ECCLESIAL TRANSFORMATION"

In reflecting on the pneumatological context and character of Receptive Ecumenism as referenced by the refrain from the book of Revelation, we have already begun to say a fair bit about Receptive Ecumenism as "transforming ecumenism," and this in two senses: firstly, relating to the proximate aims of Receptive Ecumenism; and, secondly, concerning the place of Receptive Ecumenism relative to the broader family of ecumenical approaches and strategies. In the first case, we are dealing with the notion of Receptive Ecumenism as having transformative potential *within* ecclesial traditions: the potential for being "an instrument of ecclesial transformation"; or as the title for the second edited volume from Oxford University Press puts it, *Receptive Ecumenism as Transformative Ecclesial Learning: Walking the Way to a Church Reformed*.[5] In the second case, we are dealing with Receptive Ecumenism as representing something of a transformation in our wider ecumenical ways of working. It is entirely understandable, perhaps even inevitable, that we have already begun to touch on these matters whilst reflecting in pneumatological frame. As earlier alluded to, in Christian tradition the Spirit *is* the initiating–transforming power of God, the Love-in-act of God, in which all things are brought into being, held in being, and drawn to their consummation in the loving communion of God. In as much, then, as Receptive Ecumenism really is a pneumatological reality, change-agency will be written into its DNA.

Taking first the notion that Receptive Ecumenism represents a transformation of ecumenism itself—of our ecumenical ways of proceeding—this can be both overplayed and underplayed. Let us remind ourselves that a key part of the context for Receptive Ecumenism is the dual recognition that in the more mature dialogues and well-developed engagements across traditions, it is the case *both* that much mutual corrective learning about each other has now been achieved—churches have been able to resolve many false points of division by achieving far more helpful, less prejudicial understandings of each other than we used to have—*and* that real, long-term, substantive differences have come into clearer focus that do not lend themselves to relatively easy resolution through processes of clarification, interpretation, and harmonization. Accordingly, with this dual recognition in view, at the heart of Receptive Ecumenism is the conviction that, for now, the most appropriate and effective way forward is to switch things away from continuing to ask what our others might fruitfully learn about and from us, to asking instead what our own tradition might most fruitfully learn from our others in ways that speak into our own felt difficulties and needs. The closely related further conviction is that pursuing this path will lead both to various changes *within* the respective traditions and, thereby, over time to significant changes in the relationships *between* the traditions.

In some key respects this proposed receptive ecumenical way of proceeding is in creative continuity with what has gone before in the ecumenical movement. In other respects, there is real freshness here. I earlier alluded to Receptive Ecumenism as possibly opening a new chapter for

5. See Murray, Ryan, and Lakeland, *Receptive Ecumenism as Transformative Ecclesial Learning*; and Murray. *Receptive Ecumenism and the Call to Catholic Learning*.

the modern ecumenical movement. Well, the point is that as is generally the case in books so also in Christian life, "new chapters" do not just appear out of nowhere. Even when they take things in fresh directions not previously explicitly foreseen, they generally pick up and build on things that have gone before such that in retrospect the freshness of the new can be read as being in creative continuity with what has gone before.

Similarly, many, if not most, of the key attitudes and commitments at work in Receptive Ecumenism can be identified as having already been at work throughout the modern ecumenical movement. Take Receptive Ecumenism's commitment to relationality, and its openness to being changed by our encounters with our ecumenical others, as also the conviction that the quality of the lived lives of the churches in communion is ultimately more important than doctrinal resolution alone. All of this can already be found in the ecumenical movement, particularly so in its Life and Work manifestations. Similarly, take the receptive ecumenical conviction that, vital though they are, living, praying, and working together can never in themselves be a full and adequate resolution of the ecumenical problem for as long as communion-dividing differences of theology, structure, and procedure remain unresolved. That is a conviction strongly shared with prior strategies in Faith and Order ecumenism, as too is the conviction that critical-constructive theological labor has an essential role to play in this process of healing. Indeed, in these regards Receptive Ecumenism is most properly understood not as a move away from Faith and Order ecumenism but as a development within it, in a way that also draws strongly on core Life and Work instincts.

Further, as well as the various ways in which Receptive Ecumenism can be seen to continue with key respective aspects of Life and Work ecumenism and Faith and Order ecumenism, it is also possible to identify notable anticipations of Receptive Ecumenism and key influences on its explicit articulation in earlier bodies of ecumenical writing. For example, from amongst many other significant reference points, of particular importance for me in relation to my own ecclesially-situated, Catholic-specific articulation of Receptive Ecumenism, have been the work of Yves Congar, the Vatican II documents, and Pope John Paul II's 1995 encyclical, *Ut Unum Sint*. It would be interesting if theologians and ecumenists of other ecclesial traditions were, in a similar way, to mine the resources of their own traditions in order to identify the relevant reference points and anticipations that would enable Lutheran-situated, Orthodox-situated,

Pentecostal-situated—and so on—accounts of Receptive Ecumenism to be articulated with dynamic integrity.

So, Receptive Ecumenism belongs within the modern ecumenical movement and has grown from it, with all manner of precedents and anticipations in place. As a way of expressing this, I have sometimes co-opted the sub-title of William James's lectures on *Pragmatism* and referred to Receptive Ecumenism as a *New Name for some Old Ways of Thinking*. But while there is some truth in that, is it not quite right either; and certainly not if it is taken to imply that Receptive Ecumenism is really just the same old, same old, but now with a new, fancy-sounding title.

What distinguishes Receptive Ecumenism is that whilst it continues, in long frame, to hold to the core Faith and Order concern to serve the structural and sacramental communion of the one divided Church of Christ, it does not make this the immediate objective. In a somewhat lateral, counter-intuitive manner, rather than applying itself, in the main, to seeking immediately to overcome remaining communion-dividing differences *between* traditions, Receptive Ecumenism turns the proximate focus away from this concern—believing that it is generally not directly achievable at this point—and focuses instead on felt difficulties *within* traditions and on how these might be helped by transformative learning *across* traditions. The dual conviction is: a) that as relevant changes occur *within* traditions through receptive ecumenical learning from *across* traditions, this will serve to alter the relationships *between* the traditions; such that b) over time, as consequence of this, yet more things will become possible which are currently unforeseeable and apparently impossible. This transformative process is envisaged as continuing as, on the one hand, each tradition comes to greater flourishing in its own right through receptive learning from its others and, on the other hand, the traditions collectively thereby also come to closer communion with each other in Christ and the Spirit.

So yes, Receptive Ecumenism fits within the wider ecumenical movement that has incubated it and variously anticipated it, but it is also distinctive relative to what went before on account of this primary strategic emphasis on serving the needs for ecclesial transformation *within* traditions through receptive ecumenical learning from *across* traditions. This does two things simultaneously. It addresses immediate needs *within* traditions by drawing upon fresh logic, fresh ways of thinking, and fresh ways of being and doing from other traditions; and, at one and the same time, it also serves the longer-term aim of healing the differences *between* the traditions so that they can become reconfigured and resituated as valued distinctions in communion rather than as contested divergences that continue to separate.

This last point needs emphasizing. In seeking to further the long-term ecumenical goal of full ecclesial communion *between* the currently separated traditions by pursuing ecclesial transformation *within* the traditions, Receptive Ecumenism seeks not the reduction of the traditions but their respective greater flourishing and fulfilment. Similarly, it seeks not the reduction of ecclesial diversity to a bland uniformity but a genuinely reconciled diversity in full communion and with full mutual recognition. Something of this distinctiveness can be usefully, if briefly, indicated by contrasting the theology and practice of conversion towards greater flourishing and fulfilment that is at work in Receptive Ecumenism with the theology and practice of kenotic conversion espoused by the Groupe des Dombes.

TRUE AND FALSE ECCLESIAL CONVERSION AND TRANSFORMATION: FROM SELF-EMPTYING TO ENRICHED IDENTITY

My final chapter in the 2022 volume, *Receptive Ecumenism as Transformative Ecclesial Learning*, is entitled, "Growing into the Fullness of Christ: Receptive Ecumenism as a Way of Ecclesial Conversion." In that chapter, having first spent some time showing that understanding Receptive Ecumenism as a way of ecclesial conversion is an integral, pervasive, and distinctive dimension of the theology and practice of Receptive Ecumenism, the second part clarifies the particular understanding and practice of ecclesial conversion that is at work in Receptive Ecumenism. It does this by conducting an appreciative comparative reflection on the Groupe des Dombes's theology of ecclesial conversion as expressed in their ground-breaking 1991 text, *Pour la conversion des Eglises*, which is shaped by a Philippians 2-influenced theology of self-emptying. By contrast, influenced by the theology of Christian existence as continual conversion to the gospel of life that is to be found in the *Spiritual Exercises* of Ignatius of Loyola, Receptive Ecumenism is presented as being marked by an understanding and practice of ecclesial conversion as oriented in the particularities of one's existence towards growth into ever greater fullness.

To be more precise, the chapter recognizes that there are many points of positive connection and real resonance between what the Groupe des Dombes is seeking to do in *Pour la conversion des Eglises* and the positive and always particularized theology of continual ecclesial conversion, transformation, and reform that is at work in Receptive Ecumenism. Nevertheless, the chapter marks critical distance from the Groupe's core adoption of the now widely used but, I think—together with others—overworked and frequently problematic notion of kenosis as self-emptying and self-abasement, from Philippians 2. Most particularly, critical distance is marked from the Groupe's drawing from this an emphasis on the essential role of an openness to the emptying, relinquishing, and diminishing of our various particular ecclesial identities if the goal of full structural and sacramental ecclesial communion is to be achieved. As precedent for this emphasis, the Groupe endorses the words of the Reformed theologian, Johannes Hoekendijk, when, speaking at the 1960 Lausanne youth conference, he said: "There will be no unity until we are ready to die as a Reformed, Lutheran, Orthodox in the expectant hope of a resurrection in the presence of Christ, and his one church."[6]

By contrast, whilst Receptive Ecumenism certainly looks for the freeing of the traditions from all that needlessly limits and distorts them—for their freeing and redeeming, we might say, from all that is of the corrupting effects of sin rather than the flowering of grace in each of them—Receptive Ecumenism also steadfastly maintains the lasting significance of each one of these diverse particular expressions of Christian ecclesial existence. For Receptive Ecumenism a diversity of traditioned-expressions is necessary for true catholicity, with each contributing to the full flourishing and full showing of the manifold one Church of Christ. Far from thinking of the various ecclesial traditions as each being on a journey towards the absorption of the many into a great undifferentiated unity, Receptive Ecumenism charts a path towards the particularity of each coming to full shining in all its particular glory in a reconfigured and redeemed whole. As such, the appropriate primary registers in Receptive Ecumenism's understanding and practice of ecclesial conversion are not those of loss, emptying, or substantive diminishment, as for the Groupe, but of freeing, transforming, reconfiguring, and fulfilling in service of enriched and expanded communion.

---

6. Groupe des Dombes, *For the Conversion of the Churches*, 24.

Underpinning and inspiring this approach is the conviction that the authentic divine-dynamic of the Spirit and the communion of the Trinity, as disclosed in Jesus, and into which we are drawn, is one of life-giving, self-giving Love, from life unto life, not one of self-emptying. In orthodox, evangelical, catholic understanding, the life-giving, self-giving Love of God in creation, incarnation, and sanctification represents not the emptying or diminishing of God's being-in-act in any way but the authentic expression of its overflowing fullness.

It is in accordance with this understanding of the core divine dynamic that Receptive Ecumenism views ecumenical ecclesial conversion not, primarily, as a relinquishing and diminishing of respective ecclesial identities but as a freeing of them to become more fully what they most truly are through expansion rather than diminishment. The vision is that that which is thwarted in the ecclesial existence of one can be tended to and enhanced by that which is fluent of grace in another. As I have frequently said, when viewed from the Catholic perspective this is about us becoming more, not less, Catholic precisely by becoming, for example: appropriately more Anglican, by becoming more synodal; appropriately more Methodist, by becoming more connexionally Catholic; appropriately more Pentecostal, by becoming more charismatically Catholic; appropriately more Lutheran by having a much stronger and more effective sense of our ecclesial falling short and our moment-by-moment dependence on the forgiving, healing, and renewing grace of God; and so on.[7] Far from this representing conversion from traditioned distinctiveness to a basic commonality, this is a journey towards a dynamic community of redeemed diversity in which the distinctiveness of each is enriched by learning from transposed aspects of the other traditions to the point of achieving mutual recognition across differences that need no longer divide. None ceases to be who they are. The promise and hope is that all will be freed to become more fully and more fluently who we most deeply already are and are called to be.

But what does this imply for the ways in which we might anticipate a fully redeemed, one Church of Christ, healed of its current communion-dividing differences? Some key images that have been used in the Receptive Ecumenism literature are that of a polyphonous choir singing in harmony, wherein each distinct voice is required to play its part in the performance of the whole; or that of a fully-decked, fully illuminated

---

7. E.g., Murray, "Receptive Ecumenism and Catholic Learning: Establishing the Agenda."

family Christmas tree. Not one with the uniformity of color and style that one finds in shopping arcades but one with the kind of non-uniform, organic assemblage of diverse particular items, gathered ad hoc on trips, collected, and passed on through generations, each treasured in its uniqueness, and then brought into concert with each other in the dressing of the tree. Here, each unique ornament gathered over years, each with its own story, is needed for the whole showing. I love to look at our decked tree from various different angles and perspectives, letting my eyes go slightly out of focus in order to enjoy its shimmering unity, before then bringing them back into focus and appreciating each ornament in its particularity of relation with the others.

Of course, whilst such images might provide some helpful orientation, they inevitably also prompt the need for greater practical definition, delineation, and example, together with relevant theological scrutiny and legitimation. So let me close by pointing to some places where the beginnings of such can be found.

PRACTICAL EXAMPLES

Perhaps the first place to point to is the first Oxford University Press edited volume, published in 2008 under the title, *Receptive Ecumenism and the Call to Catholic Learning: Exploring a Way for Contemporary Ecumenism*. That volume contains a number of studies of various ways in which the structures and processes of Catholic exercise of governance and authority might be appropriately reimagined and reformed with dynamic integrity through real receptive learning from a number of other traditions. Following that first project and as complement to it was a multi-year, more practically and more locally-focused collaborative study in partnership with the major church groupings in the North-East of England.[8]

Perhaps of even more immediate significance and applicability for those of you working at the level of local church are the many practical initiatives that have been developed and the associated resources these have produced. As recounted by Geraldine Hawkes in her chapter in *Receptive Ecumenism as Transformative Ecclesial Learning*, this has been a particularly well-developed feature of local ecumenical life in Australia.[9]

---

8. See Pound, "Receptive Ecumenism and the Local Church." There is a full report available on the website for the Centre for Catholic Studies at Durham University, see: https://www.durham.ac.uk/research/institutes-and-centres/catholic-studies/research/constructive-catholic-theology-/receptive-ecumenism-/project-3/.

9. See Hawkes, "Australian Practices of Receptive Ecumenism."

Similarly, as Sara Gehlin recounts in her chapter in a volume put together by Vicky Balabanski and Geraldine Hawkes following the Fourth Receptive Ecumenism International in Canberra, 2017, it has also been a significant feature in Sweden due, not least, to her own energetic leadership over many years now, and as strongly supported by the Christian Council of Sweden under the then leadership of Olle Kristenson.[10]

A further interesting local project in Receptive Ecumenism, initiated and supported by the National Board of Catholic Women in England and Wales, and conducted by Rev. Dr Gabrielle Thomas, was focused on lay and ordained women's experiences in the UK churches, both good and bad, and at what the various participants and the churches to which they belonged might learn from each in these regards.[11] Similarly, also included within *Receptive Ecumenism as Transformative Ecclesial Learning* are a number of studies treating the potential for transformative receptive ecumenical learning relative to issues of race, gender, and sexuality.

But still the question might be asked as what realistic chance there is that any of the divided ecclesial traditions might really take upon itself the challenge of formally recognizing its difficulties and publicly committing to a serious process of sustained receptive ecumenical learning with real transformative potential at every level of the church's life? In response, I first offer the historical reminder as resource for the nurturing of hope that in the middle years of the last century many were asking themselves an analogously dispiriting question about whether the Catholic Church could ever reform itself before, seemingly from nowhere but in fact emerging from well-prepared ground, Pope John XXIII opened the Second Vatican Council with ecclesial reform and ecumenical engagement as central to the agenda. Second, in our own ecclesial moment, I point to Pope Francis's recent opening of space for the Catholic Church to progress its Vatican II-rooted journey towards more synodal ways of being and working at every level of Catholic structure, process, habit, and norm.

This represents not only the most significant development to-date in the reception of Vatican II but also a reforming initiative of even greater potential ramifications than the council itself. Whereas the council was

---

10. See Gehlin, "Receptive Ecumenism: A Pedagogical Process."

11. Thomas, *For the Good of the Church*. The project report is available from the Centre for Catholic Studies Website, at: .https://www.durham.ac.uk/research/institutes-and-centres/catholic-studies/research/constructive-catholic-theology-/receptive-ecumenism-/project-5/.

an event and conversation of the bishops and their near exclusively male theological advisors, the synodal process is an event of and for the whole church, and an opening to a conversation in which all rightly need to be involved. Now the point is that this is not a learning process that the Catholic Church can manage from its own familiar resources and occluded memory. Outside of the religious orders, the Eastern rite churches, and experiments in ecclesial base communities and the like, we in the Catholic Church cannot remember how to do this. As such, it is a process that will only succeed if the Catholic Church at parochial, diocesan, national, regional, and international levels attends closely to what can be variously learned from the long and varied relevant experiences, both good and bad, in the other Christian traditions.[12]

In his own significant contribution to *Receptive Ecumenism as Transformative Ecclesial Learning*, the Irish theologian, David Ford, likens Receptive Ecumenism to being in an analogous state to Catholic *ressourcement* theology in the late 1950s.[13] The key thinking had been done and all the potential was there for major impact and ecclesial reform but the right circumstances had not yet arisen to release this to full effect . . . until, that is, Pope John XXIII's announcement of Vatican II. Pope Francis's opening of space for the Catholic synodal pathway could feasibly end-up being of similar significance relative to Receptive Ecumenism. Perhaps now is the moment when the Catholic Church's need and desire will meet with what has already been grown in the other traditions and is now ready to be put to work. Let us, then, fear not in the ecumenical movement: we *can* trust in where the Spirit is drawing us because the Spirit is always going before us. It is into our future in God that we are being drawn, and in that we *can* trust.

CONCLUSION

The essential argument of this chapter and the central argument and sustained demonstration in the 2022 second Oxford University Press volume, is that Receptive Ecumenism as an instrument of transformative ecclesial learning is *both* a powerful way to intra-ecclesial reform and

---

12. Of relevance here is the "Learning on the Way" research project, exploring the relevance of Receptive Ecumenism to the Catholic synodal pathway, that is being conducted by the Centre for Catholic Studies, see: https://www.durham.ac.uk/research/institutes-and-centres/catholic-studies/research/constructive-catholic-theology-/receptive-ecumenism-/project-7/#d.en.1322117.

13. Ford, "Mature Ecumenism's Daring Future."

renewal *and*, thereby, the most appropriate and effective way open to us in our current context to moving towards the inter-ecclesial ecumenical goal of fullness of communion and embraced diversity in Christ and the Spirit. As I close that volume by praying, so also I now pray for each of us and those who will engage the work subsequently:

> May we each continue to walk this way
>
> In dynamic faith, sure hope, and active love;
>
> And may we thereby tend together to the healing
>
> Of the wounded one church of Christ
>
> In the life-giving, self-giving Love of God, the Spirit,
>
> Amen

BIBLIOGRAPHY

Ford, David F. "Mature Ecumenism's Daring Future: Learning from the Gospel of John for the Twenty-First Century." In *Receptive Ecumenism as Transformative Ecclesial Learning: Walking the Way to a Church Re-formed*, edited by Paul D. Murray, Gregory A. Ryan, and Paul Lakeland, 414–28. Oxford: Oxford University Press, 2022.

Gehlin, Sara. "Receptive Ecumenism: A Pedagogical Process." In *Receptive Ecumenism: Listening, Learning, and Loving in the Way of Christ*, edited by Vicky Balabanski and Geraldine Hawkes, 111–22. Adelaide: ATF, 2018.

Groupe des Dombes. *Pour la conversion des Eglises*. Paris: Editions du Centurion, 1991. English translation: *For the Conversion of the Churches*. Translated by James Greig. Geneva: WCC Publications, 1993.

Hawkes, Geraldine. "Australian Practices of Receptive Ecumenism." In *Receptive Ecumenism as Transformative Ecclesial Learning: Walking the Way to a Church Re-formed*, edited by Paul D. Murray, Gregory A. Ryan, and Paul Lakeland, 275–86. Oxford: Oxford University Press, 2022.

Murray, Paul D. "Afterword. Receiving of Christ in the Spirit: The Pneumatic-Christic Depths of Receptive Ecumenism." In *Receptive Ecumenism: Listening, Learning, and Loving in the Way of Christ*, edited by Vicky Balabanski and Geraldine Hawkes, 157–70. Adelaide: ATF, 2018.

———. "Discerning the Call of the Spirit to Theological-Ecclesial Renewal: Notes on Being Reasonable and Responsible in Receptive Ecumenical Learning." In *Leaning into the Spirit: Ecumenical Perspectives on Discernment and Decision-Making in the Church*, edited by Virginia Miller, David Moxon, and Stephen Pickard, 217–34. Cham, Switzerland: Palgrave Macmillan, 2019.

———. "Foreword. Receptive Ecumenism as a Leaning-in to the Spirit of Loving Transformation." In *Receptive Ecumenism: Listening, Learning, and Loving in the Way of Christ*, edited by Vicky Balabanski and Geraldine Hawkes, xv–xxiii. Adelaide: ATF, 2018.

———. "Foreword: Serving the Spirit of Receptive Ecumenism." In Antonia Pizzey. *Receptive Ecumenism and the Renewal of the Ecumenical Movement: The Path of*

Ecclesial Conversion, xi–xii. Brill's Studies in Catholic Theology 7. Leiden: Brill, 2019.

———. "Growing into the Fullness of Christ: Receptive Ecumenism as a Way of Ecclesial Conversion." In *Receptive Ecumenism as Transformative Ecclesial Learning: Walking the Way to a Church Re-formed*, edited by Paul D. Murray, Gregory A. Ryan, and Paul Lakeland, 463–79. Oxford: Oxford University Press, 2022.

———. *Reason, Truth, and Theology in Pragmatist Perspective*. Leuven: Peeters, 2004.

———. "Receptive Ecumenism and Catholic Learning: Establishing the Agenda." In *Receptive Ecumenism and the Call to Catholic Learning: Exploring a Way for Contemporary Ecumenism*, edited by Paul D. Murray, 5–25. Oxford: Oxford University Press, 2008.

Murray, Paul D. ed. *Receptive Ecumenism and the Call to Catholic Learning: Exploring a Way for Contemporary Ecumenism*. Oxford: Oxford University Press, 2008.

Murray, Paul D. and Andrea L. Murray. "The Roots, Range, and Reach of Receptive Ecumenism." In *Unity in Process: Reflections on Ecumenism*, edited by Clive Barrett, 79–94. London: DLT, 2012.

Murray, Paul D., Gregory A. Ryan, and Paul Lakeland, eds. *Receptive Ecumenism as Transformative Ecclesial Learning: Walking the Way to a Church Re-formed*. Oxford: Oxford University Press, 2022.

Pound, Marcus. "Receptive Ecumenism and the Local Church." In *Receptive Ecumenism as Transformative Ecclesial Learning: Walking the Way to a Church Re-formed*, edited by Paul D. Murray, Gregory A. Ryan, and Paul Lakeland, 211–24. Oxford: Oxford University Press, 2022.

Thomas, Gabrielle. *For the Good of the Church: Unity, Theology and Women*. London: SCM, 2021.

2

On Being Ecumenically Unfashionable
A *"Faith and Order" Reflection on Receptive Ecumenism*

SUSAN DURBER

INTRODUCTION

I HAVE A FRIEND, now in later life, who feels that she is destined to be old-fashioned. When she was in her twenties it was quite the thing to look mature and sophisticated, to wear a little black dress and a string of pearls, like Audrey Hepburn. But when she reached her forties and actually possessed a string of pearls, it was then fashionable to be youthful and informal, to wear jeans, sandals and T-shirts.

I feel something of the same about what some people would call, and rarely flatteringly, classic Faith and Order ecumenism. When I was young and a theological student at Oxford, ecumenism, and particularly its Faith and Order expression, was full of excitement, drama and hope. I thought of the drafters of *Baptism, Eucharist and Ministry*[1] as heroes and never dreamt that I might follow in their footsteps. However, now that I have been among those who draft Faith and Order texts, who debate into the night, work at the relationships and face the rigors of jet lag or "Zoom lag" to do it, it is no longer quite the thing. Even within the ecumenical

---

1. World Council of Churches, *Baptism, Eucharist and Ministry*, 1982.

movement itself, Faith and Order can sometimes seem like a Cinderella figure (or even an ugly sister), dull as ashes, while the party is elsewhere. I have noticed references within some of Paul Murray's writings (and he would not be alone in this), to Faith and Order work that seeks convergence and consensus as belonging to an *earlier* phase of ecumenism (along with Life and Work ecumenism).[2] Faith and Order is often seen as institutional and formal, as failing to make progress in recent times, and as now needing renewal. I have seen the responses of the churches to Faith and Order's second convergence text, *The Church: Towards a Common Vision*,[3] and I have read the letters that say that another text, from the Commission on World Mission and Evangelism, *Together Towards Life*,[4] was better, more grounded in real experience, more resonant. I find myself at the unglamorous end of the ecumenical movement, and there are days when I envy those in the T-shirt and jeans part.

I also have a story to tell about how the church I belong to, the United Reformed Church in the United Kingdom (the URC), once seemed to be in the vanguard of the ecumenical movement and in tune with the age, but now seems tired, out of favor and declining. The URC, a united church, was formed in 1972 when Presbyterians and Congregationalists joined together, fully expecting more unions to come very swiftly, at least with the Methodists and the Church of England. We spent little time even choosing our name, because it was forecast to be temporary, gone within a few years. But the greater unions we looked for did not happen and we are left as orphans now. The separate movements that came together at that moment in 1972 had their own roots in the Reformation period and in the events of 1662, a time when the more Puritan ministers were ejected from the Church of England. The word "puritan" itself has also morphed in popular culture from proud boast to unfashionable slur. I remain proud of the church and the traditions from which I come, but I cannot deny that part of our story is a story of loss, about being on the losing side of history, about finding yourself disregarded and ignored, not the eager subject of enquiry or interested attention of people from other traditions any more. At World Council of Churches meetings today, people are sometimes called to meet in confessional groups and I find myself, along with people from the Churches of North and South India, or the United Church of Canada, feeling that we are somehow being

2. Murray, *Introducing Receptive Ecumenism*, 1–2.
3. World Council of Churches, *The Church: Towards a Common Vision*, 2013.
4. World Council of Churches, *Together Towards Life*, 2013.

marginalized for being united, for answering the very call to the churches for which the ecumenical movement stands! Institutional, or structural, unity does not seem to be expected now, and the churches that have gone down this route are left feeling marooned.

IS RECEPTIVE ECUMENISM MORE ATTRACTIVE TODAY THAN FAITH AND ORDER?

You might detect, in my story, a kind of resentment of the way in which Receptive Ecumenism now attracts more attention, more delight, than Faith and Order. It seems that I find myself metaphorically wearing a black dress and pearls when now everyone thinks we should be wearing jeans. Of course, something that can describe itself as "a fresh new strategy in Christian ecumenism"[5] is going to sound more exciting than a movement that can look back to formal black and white photographs of its first conference in 1927. But I am delighted, *truly and unreservedly*, to be part of anything that arouses anyone to excitement again about ecumenism and that invites us to meet each other and to grow towards God's future, with honesty and openness. I have come to a significant moment in my own life, when I am ready to let go of much that I would once have clung to, and even if the gifts amongst what I have lost are not always appreciated or their source not recognized, I see now that there are ways in which it doesn't matter. What matters is that *together* we find ways to bear witness to Christ in the world. I am ready to let go of the labels for the sake of the fruits. If Receptive Ecumenism is about transformative learning from our ecclesial others, if it is about growth in relationship with God and each other, if it is a Spirit-filled sharing in the fullness of Christ, then this is exactly what I long for, and indeed have worked for within Faith and Order.

FAITH AND ORDER AS IT REALLY IS

An ecumenical journey often begins with the breaking down of caricatures and stereotypes. It cannot end there, but it must often begin there. I want to break down the stereotypes of Faith and Order, some of which, admittedly, we sometimes even peddle ourselves. And I want to show that in this part of the ecumenical movement there is already a good deal of transformative learning going on.

---

5. Murray, *Introducing Receptive Ecumenism*, 1.

Faith and Order has always been about enabling the churches to call one another to visible unity in common faith, in sacramental life and in ministry and mission. It has always been said, within the World Council of Churches and within the Faith and Order movement that became part of it, that unity should not be imagined as some kind of Platonic abstract, but that it has to be visible and tangible, for this is how the incarnate God works. But it has never been suggested that the visibility of this unity should take any particular form, and it is certainly not imagined to be "structural" in the sense of corresponding to any particular church's structural form. It is not about going "back" to Rome or Constantinople or even Geneva, Jerusalem or Corinth. The recent Roman Catholic response to the Faith and Order text *The Church: Towards a Common Vision* speaks of all the churches being "on the road" (in via) towards that full visible unity for which Christ prayed.[6] This is not an ecumenism of return, but a conversion to a new future, together. It is also about looking for ways in which the unity that *God* gives is made somehow visible, tangible, experiential, among us. This is a little different from suggesting that we envisage or are pushing for a kind of absorption into one great undifferentiated unity of structure. The Toronto statement of 1950[7] made this clear. And no-one in Faith and Order now, is under any illusion that any kind of structural unity is just around the corner.

The formal ecumenical movement (in so far as it is really formal) has also often been criticized for separating out doctrine from action, justice and peace from life and work, mission from unity. This is a perceptive criticism and sometimes these kinds of separations and silos have damaged the movement and have prevented some vital conversations. But there have always been ways in which these separations have simply not held and ways in which they have been constantly and faithfully subverted. If ever one of these "sets" tries to do ecumenism without the others, then we are in trouble. This is why, for example, Faith and Order has, more recently, worked not only on the traditional doctrinal divisions, but has asked questions like, "What can we say together theologically, with one voice, about the climate emergency?" And, hearing from the churches that it is moral questions that most often cause division between or among churches, the Faith and Order Commission has worked on moral discernment, not seeking to provide ecumenical

6. World Council of Churches, *Churches Respond*, Vol. 2, 161–221.
7. World Council of Churches, Toronto Statement.

answers to the difficult questions (for that would please no-one), but trying to help all of us appreciate and understand the reasons why we differ and how we each approach ethical questions, digging down to the deep foundational discourses that undergird our moral statements and affirmations. And this is not only about revealing the surface, soft wood differences, but also about getting more honestly and openly at the hardwood differences that cause painful division.

Faith and Order is also sometimes seen as being "best china" ecumenism, the polite negotiation of high-level doctrinal issues around conference room tables, where we present the most "official" of our traditions, or where a kind of pure Calvinism that never actually walked in Geneva engages with a form of Orthodoxy that can only be found in the pages of the Fathers. I can understand why this is so, and perhaps it happens in some places, but Faith and Order work as it is now is not like this. Those who participate are all too vulnerable, too human, too near the surface to bring to discussions that take place over years anything other than the real deal, the wounds we bear, sometimes the defensiveness that reveals our underbelly, and the need we all have to be heard. Ecumenism under the Faith and Order banner is as much rooted in human realities, in geopolitics, in human fears and hopes, in the personal and the spiritual, as other forms of human interaction. How else can you proceed when every meeting begins with the sharing of the realities of our contexts, including hunger, war, violence, the longing for a post-colonial or decolonized future, and experiences of pandemic and climate change? The challenge is to hear one another as fully as human beings can, to resist the caricatures of one another that we might be tempted to hide behind, and to build good, trusting relationships over years.

WE ARE ALL LOOKING FOR A RENEWAL OF THE ECUMENICAL MOVEMENT

The WCC 11th Assembly's theme, *Christ's love moves the world to reconciliation and unity* was the first to include the word "love." This has led people to reflect on the significance that such a word might have for an ecumenical movement that stands in need of renewal. Many have felt the energy drain from our movement, known the disappointment at slow "progress," and the loss of hope and excitement. Perhaps it can only be the love nurtured between us, the quality of our relationships, that can remake the bedrock of what we do. And this love must come from and be inspired by the love of the Triune God that we see embodied most perfectly in Jesus Christ. Paul Murray has referred to "the holy erotics of Receptive Ecumenism,"[8] but this sense of the need for the restoration of passion, excitement and desire reaches more widely too, into Faith and Order, and indeed the whole of the work of the World Council of Churches.

In a text reflecting on the theme of the Assembly we read that,

> As human beings, we know so well that unity and love belong together. The very word "communion" (*koinonia*), a word that we often choose above the term "unity," implies the kind of unity that happens when people love one another. In our most intimate lives we may experience, if we are truly blessed and if it is our vocation, the wonder of the kind of love that brings human beings together in such a way that they are made one—not just physically but, we might say, spiritually.[9]

This is as close as the World Council of Churches could come to an expression of something like a "holy erotic," or what has been termed an "ecumenism of the heart." It is only from love that we shall find the impetus to engage in the kind of relationship building and attentive being together that might make our unity, and our fruitfulness in the Spirit, possible. We can imagine an ecumenism that brings together the whole of our human being; head and thought, feet and action, hands and service, heart and love, so that we are not only thoughtful scholars or bold activists, not only those who pray faithfully or who engage in sacrificial good works, but all of these, held together in love, moving together along what St Paul calls, in 1 Corinthians 12:31, "a still more excellent way."

Present-day Faith and Order work and Receptive Ecumenism are not so very far apart. While Receptive Ecumenism speaks of "a holy erotics," Faith and Order has the virtues of something more like a long and faithful marriage. Relationships need the charge of desire, but they also need the patient discipline that is unglamorous, determined, loyal in times of weakness, enduring in days of poverty and famine. The repetitions of Faith and Order conversations, the spiral that means that as the generations turn we need to keep going back to where we started and do it again, these things need doing so that small steps can be made, so that sometimes we look back and can see just how far we have come.

---

8. Murray, "Foreword. Receptive Ecumenism as a Leaning-in to the Spirit," xxii.
9. World Council of Churches, *Christ's Love Moves the World*, 19.

We might conclude that the churches' responses to *The Church: Towards a Common Vision* reveal no major break-throughs, but they do show that we now agree on more than we disagree, that it is unremarkable to speak about "the whole people of God," and that we all recognize that the church is both sign and servant of the mission of God to the world.[10] We have, actually, come a long way, but it's a long game.

REFLECTING ON RECEIVING AND ON GIVING, ON VULNERABILITY AND POWER

I return to my reflection about my own small united church. As I read of Paul Murray's conviction regarding Receptive Ecumenism that the ecumenical journey need not be about loss, but about growth, I feel a twinge of pain. For some of us at the moment there is real loss, as our ecclesial communities, perhaps with the gifts they carry, are being seriously wounded or even apparently lost, and with them, our power to speak. We might say that if all ecumenical partners came into discussions with the same power, the same respect and dignity, then it would be different. But the landscape is not flat, there are wide divergences of power and sometimes we all need protection.

I have long admired, and tried to follow the advice of Receptive Ecumenism, that we need to move from defending our traditions and guarding their treasures against attack or misunderstanding and rather ask what gifts we need to *receive* from other traditions so that we may grow into the fullness of the stature of Christ. On a recent visit to Armenia I was suddenly asked to say a little about my own church in the UK, and I realized how unusual it was for the conversation to be that way round. I didn't get out "the best china" or stick to the usual narrative, but I spoke about my church's wounds and vulnerabilities and, even though I could not boast of great successes or triumphs, it was a profoundly empowering conversation. It occurred to me afterwards that one reason it may have been possible to have the conversation in that way is that the churches in Armenia are *themselves* so very vulnerable, and indeed that the whole nation is vulnerable. Mutual vulnerability makes for real and deep conversation, but in those circumstances when the power balance in a discussion is so unequal (either in perception or reality) it is much harder to share woundedness in ways that make for mutual flourishing. I am less likely to reveal the wounds of my church

---

10. See: World Council of Churches, *What are the Churches Saying.*

to an ecclesial other that I know, for example, is ready to take over our buildings for a cheap price once we are done.

If Receptive Ecumenism is indeed about the receiving of gifts then it will be helpful to reflect a bit more on what it might mean to exchange gifts, about the power relations that might be implied in the act of giving. I am reminded of an extraordinary piece of writing by Jacques Derrida about the idea of "gift."[11] His insight is that we all suffer from an irresistible temptation to turn gift into *exchange*. A gift should be something that comes without a price, asking nothing in return. The essence of a gift is precisely that it is *not* an object of exchange. But we find it hard to stop turning every gift into a kind of transaction or deal. At Christmas we worry when we receive a present from someone we hadn't sent one to, or we are hurt because we gave someone a gift and they didn't give us one! Derrida suggests that sometimes even gratitude for a gift can function as a kind of payment in return or in exchange, and then the gift is strictly no longer a gift. Being Derrida, he takes the logic of this as far as it will go and argues that there is a sense in which *a real gift could only be one we don't even notice we have received.*

I have had a few experiences of the gifts of my tradition being received by others without them even noticing. I was once introduced to a well-known author at a dinner party. On hearing that I am a minister of the United Reformed Church, he looked puzzled and then asked, "Do you have hymns?" I thought about those from my tradition who transformed music for worship, of Isaac Watts who wrote what is probably the greatest hymn in the English language, *When I survey the wondrous cross*. Do we have hymns?! You could say that we gave them to you, I thought. But I pause now to ask myself, in light of Derrida's insight, whether it really matters whether anyone knows what they have been given, and who am I to take offence when it is unrecognized? Is it only really a true gift when it has been received unknowingly? Is it then most truly a gift?

There was another occasion when I realized that at least one person from another tradition had noticed a gift that my tradition had given, though his insight is exceptional. In 2012 there was a service in Westminster Abbey to mark the 350th anniversary of the events of 1662, when there was a major disruption in English ecclesial life and many ministers were expelled from or left the Church of England. From then on there was both "church" and "chapel" in England, two cultures, as the Presbyterians

---

11. See, Derrida, *Given Time: 1 Counterfeit Money*—Carpenter Lectures 2017

and the Independents settled outside the established church, later to be joined by others. The preacher at the service to mark the anniversary of this disruption and to heal some of its memories was the then Archbishop of Canterbury, Rowan Williams.[12] He preached on a text dear to Receptive Ecumenism, Ephesians 4:13.

> ... until all of us come to the unity of the faith and of the knowledge of the Son of God, to maturity, to the measure of the full stature of Christ.

Before a congregation of Church of England bishops, clergy and laity, and of ministers and members of the United Reformed Church, Rowan argued that our Christian faith is something constantly growing, moving towards greater maturity, and that we need the kind of challenges that push us away from an infantile faith. He said that it was those who followed the path of dissent in 1662 who pushed the *Church of England* towards a mature faith and a mature presence in society. This high Anglican Archbishop spoke in appreciative terms of the gifts given to the life of church and nation by the Reformed tradition. He told us about a gift that we had given without recognizing that we had, and I doubt that many of the Anglicans present had ever thought they had received it from us either. Perhaps that is the true nature of gift.

I suspect that so much of this exchange of gifts happens without us noticing or naming it. Many of the gifts we share come without labels or announcement. They are simply given and we are better for receiving them, even if we do not know what has been given. There are gifts that I, in my church, have received from others, some of which I recognize and others that I surely don't. And indeed, it is in the nature of gift to be just that, gift, grace, unearned or unexpected, not grasped or chosen, but simply "given." It is somehow this quality of receiving, this openness to accept what is given, that is the key and distinctive note of Receptive Ecumenism. This makes it different from what is sometimes, admittedly, known in Faith and Order, the sort of contest and struggle, the defensiveness and even something like violence that sometimes breaks the best china and that leaves fragments lying on the ground. When ecumenism is too much like either diplomacy or war it is self-defeating. When it is the gracious receiving of gifts then it can be breathtakingly beautiful.

---

12. See his sermon delivered that evening.

LETTING GO OF DEFENSIVENESS, OWNERSHIP, AND LABELS FOR THE SAKE OF GOD'S NEW FUTURE

Within the drama of ecumenism, I see now that I have to let go of that for which I have sometimes longed, the dignity of recognition. I have wanted a "return" on the gifts that I believe my tradition is giving or giving up. I look for the "thank you" note, the acknowledgement. What I have to accept is simply the joy of seeing the gifts I have treasured find a new home in a renewed church, even if the gift tag is misplaced and even if no-one pauses to say thank you. In the same way, I have to accept in my turn that I have inherited a great wealth of riches in the faith whose sources I certainly do not always understand or know. And perhaps we are at a moment, certainly in the European context, where we must be sure that the gifts of the Christian faith, the faith that truly transformed some of the barbarism of classical culture, continue to be received into our secular world, even if their source is unrecognized and unacknowledged. What matters is that we share in God's mission of love to the world God is creating.

Receptive Ecumenism is, undoubtedly, enabling more people to share in the vision of a church growing into the fullness of the maturity of Christ, and in the deepest mysteries of our common faith. I share its sense of longing, not for a future uniformity, but for a true communion between diverse people. My own particular church does not seem to be journeying towards greater flourishing, *as itself alone*, but I hope that as those of us within it are invited into the wider space of a renewed church, we shall find ourselves restored. I have to let go of the indignity of being unfashionable, of being Cinderella in the ashes, of doing the equivalent of peeling ecumenical vegetables in the basement kitchen while the dancing happens elsewhere. I have to remember that they will have no food at the party unless someone does *this* work, and that this is my task. The work of Faith and Order, patient, slow and unfashionable as it is, is not an older or earlier phase to be ended in favor of the newer one of Receptive Ecumenism. Rather, these are both necessary strands within the one ecumenical movement which can, in their different ways, bring grace and hope. I am content to do my part, and to wait and see whether I too shall be transformed and join the dance, put on those pearls and strut my stuff.

BIBLIOGRAPHY

Derrida, Jacques. *Given Time: 1 Counterfeit Money*. Carpenter Lectures. Translated by Peggy Kamuf. Chicago: University of Chicago Press, 2017.

Murray, Paul D. "Foreword. Receptive Ecumenism as a Leaning-in to the Spirit of Loving Transformation." In *Receptive Ecumenism: Listening, Learning, and Loving in the Way of Christ*, edited by Vicky Balabanski and Geraldine Hawkes, xv–xxiii. Adelaide: ATF, 2018.

———. "Introducing Receptive Ecumenism." *The Ecumenist* 51/2 (2014) 1–8.

Williams, Rowan. A Sermon for the Service of Reconciliation, Healing of Memories, and Mutual Commitment for the Church of England and the United Reformed Church, Westminster Abbey, February 7th, 2012. http://rowanwilliams.archbishopofcanterbury.org/articles.php/2346/joint-church-of-england-and-united-reformed-church-service-of-reconciliation-and-commitment.html.

World Council of Churches. *Baptism, Eucharist and Ministry*. Faith and Order Paper No.111. Geneva: WCC Publications, 1982.

World Council of Churches. *Christ's Love Moves the World to Reconciliation and Unity. A reflection on the theme of the 11th Assembly of the World Council of Churches in Karlsruhe 2022*. Geneva: WCC Publications, 2021.

World Council of Churches. *Churches Respond to The Church: Towards a Common Vision, Volumes 1 and 2*, Faith and Order Papers Nos. 231 and 232. Geneva: WCC Publications, 2021.

World Council of Churches. *The Church: Towards a Common Vision*. Faith and Order Paper No. 214, Geneva: WCC Publications, 2013.

World Council of Churches. *Together Towards Life. Mission and Evangelism in Changing Landscapes*. Geneva: WCC Publications, 2013.

World Council of Churches. *Toronto Statement*. Geneva: WCC Publications, 1950. https://www.oikoumene.org/resources/documents/toronto-statement.

World Council of Churches. *What are the Churches Saying about the Church? Key Findings and Proposals from the Responses to The Church: Towards a Common Vision*. Faith and Order Paper No. 236. Geneva: WCC Publications, 2021.

3

Why Unity for Its Own Sake Is not Enough

Principles of Receptive Ecumenism and the Vision of Sobornicity Revisited

IVANA NOBLE

INTRODUCTION

IN ONE OF THE conversations during the last Consultation of the Societas Oecumenica, a colleague asked: What is the new and specific contribution of Receptive Ecumenism to the understanding of Christian unity? After I had listed some of its values and principles, she remained unconvinced about its novelty, claiming that she had experienced something very similar with her colleagues whom she had got to know quite closely during years of working on bilateral dialogues. This conversation made me think about the nature of the contribution of Receptive Ecumenism and its understanding of Christian unity and inspired an idea to think about it in terms of a theological manifesto.[1]

Manifestos are proclamatory. They do not necessarily need to bring new ideas; rather, they endeavor to push already existing and helpful ideas into action. As Galia Yanoshevsky says, manifestos are "akin to programmatic and prescriptive discourse"; the knowledge they operate

---

1. This text is part of the research funded by Charles University Centre of Excellency: Theological Anthropology in Intercultural Perspective (UNCE/24/SSH/019).

with "aspires to change reality," it is the type of knowledge that is discovered, it "is asserted rather than developed," and when successful it has an "epiphanic" quality.[2] In this sense, we are drawn to the linguistic roots of the word manifesto, from the Latin *manifēstō* (I exhibit, make public), in its adjectival form, *manifēstus* (apparent, palpable, plain, clear, visible, manifest).

Manifestos as a genre have been present in the religious, political, artistic, literary, and philosophical realms. In a way, we could say that Christian creeds and confessions preceded modern manifestos. These latter have usually been published as pamphlets, brochures or journal articles and have represented particular sets of convictions, principles and values that demonstrated why the political, social or cultural status quo was non-acceptable, and thus called for action that would bring a welcome change, sometimes, but not necessarily always sketching out a possible program.[3] Thus we have manifestos of Communism (Karl Marx and Friedrich Engels, 1848); Symbolism (Jean Moréas, 1886); Futurism (Filippo Tommaso Marinetti, 1909); Dadaism (Hugo Ball, 1916; Tristan Tzara, 1919); Surrealism (André Breton, 1924) or Personalism (Emmanuel Mounier, 1938), just to mention some of the most famous examples. They have in common that they bear witness to alternative outlooks in times of crisis.[4] This, indeed, was another feature that I found important for considering the actual and the possible contribution of Receptive Ecumenism in our times.

Before our societies managed to recover from the Covid-19 crisis, the Russian invasion of Ukraine took away hopes for a more tranquil future and brought to the center of our attention the new and the prevailing problems of this still young century. The war started in 2014 in Donbass, and it had already taken away the dream of peaceful coexistence in post-totalitarian Europe. Confrontations with a growing number of terrorist attacks coming from radical Islamist groups, and massive numbers of refugees coming from Syria, Afghanistan and Iraq confronted Europe with its limits when it came to solidarity with those who came from other races, cultures and religions, with these limits often being dressed up in a populist rhetoric of "Christian values." The nationalism of Central

---

2. Yanoshevsky, "Three Decades," 264–65. She draws here on Hélène Millot, "Arts poétiques," 212–13.

3. See Yanoshevsky, "Three Decades," 262, with reference to Claude Abastado, "Introduction à l'analyse des manifestes," 3.

4. See Dumasy and Massol, eds. *Pamphlet*, 12.

European governments as well as Brexit uncovered how the priority of short-term economic interests, social acceptability of lies in the realm of high politics, and the usage of "fake news" can do long-term harm. All these different crises have an impact on the search for a joint action to help Ukraine and prevent World War III. Moreover, Christians must deal with a massive abuse of religion for political aims, and seek for those convictions, principles and values that neither denominationally (e.g., within Orthodoxy), nor ecumenically (e.g., within the WCC) question what kind of unity is holy and unbreakable, and where unity for its own sake needs to be left behind. In this light, the principles of Receptive Ecumenism may be a helpful guide, and in this contribution, I will argue that its kind of a manifesto can be fruitfully expanded for a critical reception of the vision of an open sobornicity.

THE NATURE OF THE PRINCIPAL CHANGE ENVISAGED BY RECEPTIVE ECUMENISM

> Receptive Ecumenism is both a way of thinking and a process that enables unity to be built by receiving gifts from others. It challenges us to not think of what others might benefit from receiving from us, but instead invites us to recognize our needs and to put ourselves in the place of being a recipient.[5]

These words are used as an introduction to a course "Embracing the Other: A resource for groups to explore Receptive Ecumenism together—asking what our church tradition can learn from others," available on the web page of Churches Together in England. The concept of the new approach has been developed by Paul Murray and his team at Durham University since 2005,[6] and various projects and conferences that followed have contributed together to what I call the Receptive Ecumenism Manifesto.

Paul Murray has characterized it as follows:

> Receptive Ecumenism starts with humble recognition of the wounds, tears, and difficulties in one's own tradition and asks how the particular and different gifts, experiences, and ways of

---

5. See https://cte.org.uk/about/ecumenism-explained/receptive-ecumenism/course-embracing-the-other/.

6. For the development of the idea, its roots and forms, see especially Murray, "Receptive Ecumenism and Catholic Learning"; Murray, "Receptive Ecumenism and Ecclesial Learning;" Paul Murray and Andrea L. Murray, "The Roots, Range, and Reach," 79–94.

proceeding in the other traditions can speak to and help to heal these wounds that elude the capacity of one's own tradition to heal itself.[7]

In his lecture for the International Theological Institute at the Catholic School of Theology, Paul Murray speaks of yet another crisis, affecting the very concept of ecumenism, and in particular, hope for any real progress on the way of full and visible ecclesial unity.[8] According to Murray such progress is possible, but it needs to involve an inversion of perspective, something that he calls a fundamental "counter-instinctual move," in which the different Christian traditions will recognize their weaknesses and shortcomings and will start receiving help from each other. In this way he transposes "the evangelical call to growth and conversion" from the personal to "the institutional, structural, and formal ecclesial dimensions of Christian existence."[9]

Gregory Ryan later called this key principle of Receptive Ecumenism an "expansive catholicity,"[10] explaining that it is possible to retain one's integrity even when a tradition shows its shortcomings and wounds. And it is precisely in doing so that it can borrow with gratitude from others what it itself does not have. As each tradition is missing different things, this type of exchange of gifts can lead to a greater flourishing of a Christian ecclesial life.[11] Murray speaks about this principle of "greater flourishing," saying that

---

7. Murray, "Introducing," 7.

8. Murray says: "Many have grown impatient and downsized the ecumenical goal to seeking simply to get along and do as many good things together as possible: if you like, Life and Works ecumenism instead of Faith and Order ecumenism . . . But whilst such things as shared prayer and witness are as crucial to ecumenism as oxygen to life, no matter how much getting along with each other and doing good things together we have, they alone are never going to solve the ecumenical problem, which in Catholic understanding is to do with the broken sign-value we give of our communion in diversity in the Trinitarian life of God. For this, the aspiration of formal institutional ecumenism remains basic. But it is this very aspiration which is now so difficult to pursue in any meaningful way—at least as we have thus far done . . . Receptive ecumenism does not foreclose the traditional Faith and Order concern to work for the structural and sacramental unity of the churches and settle for something less." Murray, "Receptive Ecumenism as a Catholic Calling," 6, 8.

9. See Murray, "Receptive Ecumenism as a Catholic Calling," 8.

10. See Ryan, *Hermeneutics*, 198–203.

11. "The basic principle of RE [Receptive Ecumenism] is that of attending to one's own ecclesial shortcomings by receiving with integrity from the ecumenical other. This involves a commitment to critical—but constructively-oriented—discernment in one's own community or tradition, combined with a constructive—yet

for all the many particular gifts and strengths to be found in each tradition, each also variously falls short of the glory of God; each has specific characteristic difficulties and limitations, open wounds in need of healing, that can be highly resistant to resolution from within the tradition's existing resources.[12]

The paths away from this resistance towards a greater flourishing that he recommends involve accepting one's vulnerability, something that, in his view, all of the traditions need to do.[13] And here he offers what I believe to be a pragmatic motivation: Christians and churches can assume that such a process towards greater and fuller life "will take each tradition to new places—in the first instance for their own health and flourishing but in such fashion as will also open up fresh possibilities, currently unforeseeable, for their relating to each other."[14]

I think that the emphasis on such a dynamic way of relations, where, indeed, unity does not arise merely as some abstract concept deprived of real life, has a very strong transformative potential. My question, however, is whether the inverted perspective that Murray emphasizes does not need to be still more radical. I wonder whether Murray's prioritizing the health and flourishing of one's own tradition, in fact, does not create an obstacle for ecumenical relations, as it lacks a deeper level of mutuality. At times, his understanding of the importance of one's own becoming as a kind of obtaining "what we already are,"[15] seem to need the other just as a help to achieve that.

In the next section I will first look at what Receptive Ecumenism can borrow from Emmanuel Levinas's change of the priority towards the other, and from his argument that without such change Christians will keep missing their Evangelical calling. The following section, then, will explore how a longer Orthodox tradition of sobornicity can enrich the "manifesto" of Receptive Ecumenism.

---

appropriately critical—reception of other churches and traditions for fruitful growth, reparative healing, and greater Christian and human flourishing. In these critical-constructive interactions, the faithful hope embodied in RE is that new ways of growing together might become possible, even where apparently insurmountable obstacles presently exist." Ryan, "Reception," 8.

12. Murray, "Receptive Ecumenism as a Catholic Calling," 8.

13. Murray speaks about "being prepared to show our wounds to each other." Murray, "Receptive Ecumenism as a Catholic Calling," 9.

14. Murray, "Receptive Ecumenism as a Catholic Calling," 8.

15. Murray, "Receptive Ecumenism and Catholic Learning," 282.

THE OTHER AS THE "FIRST INSTANCE"— BORROWING FROM EMMANUEL LEVINAS

Murray's notion of Receptive Ecumenism calls for a deeper conversation with the challenge presented by Emmanuel Levinas, namely reversing the priority perspective towards the other. I am aware that Murray is aware of that challenge,[16] but as I have pointed above, he does not integrate it sufficiently into his project. Here I will show that Emanuel Levinas's inversion of perspective, where the other plays the central role, is both helpful and problematic. From his earliest writings Emmanuel Levinas addressed the danger of the prioritizing of the subject, the "I" or the "we."[17] He inverted the perspective as he gave total priority to the other, the one who does not belong, but is coming as a stranger.[18] In encountering the face of the other, I am confronted with his/her demand: "Thou shalt not commit murder."[19] He interprets this command both physically, as no to killing, and metaphorically, as no to killing of the otherness of the other. In the case of the current ecumenical theology, this emphasis of Levinas is helpful not only regarding confessional traditions but also different lived situations of people and communities that may include more irregularity than classical ecumenism, drawing on confessional perspectives, allows for. According to Levinas, this encounter places the other before the "I" or "we." The face of the other demands response—and thus responsibility. Human identity, in Levinas, does not come from the self, but the self finds resources in responding to the other.[20]

16. See Murray, "Receptive Ecumenism and Catholic Learning," 290.

17. It has its roots in the experience of the Second World War and the Shoah (Holocaust), where the persecuted were not treated as a priority but as an added extra, who did not have the chance to be spared. See e.g. Levinas, *Totality and Infinity*, 21, 24–28; see also the dedication to *Otherwise than Being*, where Levinas writes: "To the memory of all those who were closest among the six million assassinated by the National Socialists, and of the millions on millions of all the confessions and all nations, victims of the same hatred of the other man, the same anti-Semitism." See also his critique of substituting the other for the self, Levinas, *Otherwise than Being*, 13. A good analysis of why Levinas's direct references to war and Holocaust are rare is in Plant, "Levinas and the Holocaust."

18. See Levinas, "The Proximity of the Other," in, *Alterity and Transcendence*, 97. In *Totality and Infinity* Levinas speaks about the particularity of the other, saying: "The other that dominates me in his transcendence is thus the stranger, the widow, and the orphan, to whom I am obliged." Emmanuel Levinas, *Totality and Infinity*, 215; he says further: "Man as other comes to us from the outside, a separated—or holy—face. His exteriority, that is, his appeal to me, is his truth." (291).

19. See Levinas, *Totality and Infinity*, 199.

20. Levinas says: The subject "consists in being able to respond to this essential

> It is only in approaching the Other that I attend to myself . . . The face I welcome makes me pass from phenomenon to being in another sense: in discourse I expose myself to the questioning of the Other, and this urgency of response . . . engenders me for responsibility; as responsible I am brought to my final reality . . . To be attentive is to recognize the mastery of the Other, to receive his command, or, more exactly, to receive from him the power to command.[21]

Levinas insists that the relationship is asymmetrical: "I am responsible for the Other without waiting for reciprocity, . . . Reciprocity is *his* affair."[22] Levinas goes as far as placing the self into the position of a hostage of the other.[23] This position, however, is relativized by the fact that we do not live only in dual relationships (the other—I), but that there are also other players. These in Levinas's terms come under the concept of the Third. The relation between the other and the Third, e.g., when the other does injustice to the third, also has a claim on me and relativizes the totality of the claim of the other and provides some space to breathe. Yet, the inverted position of the I/we—and the other/others remains.[24] The main problems for which Levinas was criticized could be summarized as follows: the lack of reciprocity that does not need to be seen only as a kind of business exchange, reducing human freedom to the demand of response, the lack of the right to discern when it comes to the demand of the other, and in effect, opening the door to both a deep self-alienation and abuse of the other, when the third is not directly involved.[25] With that

---

destitution of the Other, finding resources for myself." Levinas, *Totality and Infinity*, 215. Tim Noble points out that in *Totality and Infinity* "this response is still related to the needs of the I, inasmuch as it is seen as a way in which the I can break out of the imprisonment of totality, and through the encounter with the other escape from the fatal insatiability of the demands of the I (for food, shelter, love, and so on). Because the other is what I can never be, this other allows me to leave behind these desires and thus sets me free. In *Otherwise than Being* Levinas turns his attention even more to this other, who opens the way up to transcendence and who commands me in a way that I cannot refuse." Ivana Noble and Tim Noble, "Hospitality," 49.

21. Levinas, *Totality and infinity*, 178.
22. Levinas, *Ethics and Infinity*, 98.
23. For the description of the subject as hostage, see Levinas, *Otherwise than Being*, 112.
24. Levinas explains that "social reality . . . inevitably entails the existence of the third party." Levinas, *Entre Nous*, 18; see also Emmanuel Levinas, *De Dieu*, 134.
25. One of the strongest criticisms came from another Jewish scholar, Gillian Rose. She criticised his "new ethics," arguing that in general the commands of substitution and sacrifice of the self only deepen the trauma that they want to heal. This risks further

in mind, Levinas's critique of giving the first place to oneself or one's own is nevertheless valid.

When it comes to Receptive Ecumenism, Levinas's ideas can be transposed in two ways that I believe are helpful, in order to subvert the "first instance" of the health and flourishing of one's own tradition. First, his critique of the dominance of the "I" is relevant, as it shows that in a crisis, such dominance is willing to sacrifice the well-being of the other in order to save the self. Second, allowing Christians of other traditions to be and remain other, includes also that the projections of what the other players in the other traditions have to give to us is slightly more problematic. It is necessary to take on board that in different contexts the traditional confessional communities have undergone different developments and also inner crises and fragmentation. So, besides and sometimes instead of a helpful borrowing from a tradition, what takes place in settings where such mutual exchange of gifts works is more complex and less easily reduced to a common denominator. Besides working with a plurality of traditions, practices and religious subcultures within confessions, it needs to take on board also the fluidity and multiplicity of the religious belonging of a number of our contemporaries. The picture of what can be grasped when facing the other is already quite complex, and we need to pay equal attention to the fact that others in their being and becoming will always also become an ungraspable mystery that we must not kill.

A critical reception of Levinas may help Receptive Ecumenism to recognize that in life there are some situations that require sacrifices and other situations where sacrificial mechanisms do harm. The critique concerns discernment between situations when priority treatment of the I or "the we" need to be "fractured" so that new life can enter in,[26] and when the lack of self-respect, and self-love is only destructive. There are also other themes that Levinas does not treat sufficiently, such as the beauty of the other, or the desire for the life that one sees in others. Here Levinas may need to be complemented by mimetic theory,[27] or the approaches

---

deprivation by creating what Rose calls "an unhappy consciousness" caused by denying full subjectivity both to the self and to the other. See Rose, *Judaism and Modernity*, 8–9.

26. A Catholic Orientalist Louis Massignon speaks about the example of Abraham, in whom we can see how hospitality can "fracture" one's identity to the degree of losing one's old name and receiving a new one. See Massignon, "Visitation de l'étranger: Réponse à une enquête sur Dieu," in *Parole donnée*, 281–82.

27. See Girard, *Violence and the Sacred*, 146; *Things Hidden*, 301. For a good summary of the "scapegoat mechanism," Kirwan, *Discovering Girard*, 14–37.

emphasizing non-possession.²⁸ In the following part dedicated to a possible contribution of the idea of open sobornicity, I will return to these aspects of the relating to the other as well.

OPEN SOBORNICITY

Another way to address the problem of priorities is with the help of the notion of open sobornicity. The concept has its roots in the Slavophile movement in nineteenth-century Russia. Influenced by the movement of Romanticism and by the desire to construct a specifically Slavic contribution, Alexei Khomyakov came up with the notion of "sobornicity" as the basic union of truth and mutual love in the Church. He saw such an ideal in the way he imagined the pre-Petrine Russian village, a place of the ongoing presence of peasant solidarity.²⁹

When Nikolai Berdyaev, already in emigration after the Bolshevik Revolution, rephrases Khomyakov's notion, it is interesting that instead of truth he places freedom into the process of open dialectics. He says: "The Church is the order of love and freedom, and represents their union."³⁰ And instead of drawing on the romanticized Russian village utopia, he grounds this vision of unity in Christ, whom he sees as the embodiment of both freedom and love, and who is, according to Berdyaev, "our eternal contemporary."³¹ It is worth noting that Berdyaev saw the effects of the lack of freedom or love not only in the society that forced him to leave, but often also in the church, and often among people who would place themselves in the position of defenders of the "Orthodox truth." Berdyaev's critique is still very relevant. He says:

> People of a conservatively "orthodox" mindset, esteeming themselves as bearers of Orthodox truth, have defended the right to serfdom, to a despotic state, army and military, the death sentence and flogging, nationalism, total enmity towards other peoples and anti-Semitism, they have defended the injustice of man, have denied freedom of conscience and thought,

---

28. See e.g. "The Poor in Spirit." In Skobtsova, *Essential Writings*, 104–6.

29. Khomyakov, *The Church Is One*. The original was written in Russian in 1846 and published posthumously in 1864. For the critical analysis, see Parushev, "The Slavophiles and Integral Knowledge," in Noble et al, *Wrestling*, 121–55, here 141–42.

30. Nicolas Berdyaev, *Freedom and Spirit*, 330.

31. Berdyaev, "Ещё о христианском," 69–72, cited in Lowrie, *Christian Existentialism*, 265.

have expelled from the Church all human creativity, have been cruel and pitiless towards man on the basis that he is a sinner.[32]

Fr Dumitru Stăniloae, who experienced the harshness of the Romanian Communist prisons, when writing years after on the church in its broadest sense, came back to the notion of sobornicity too, and his adaptation may be most useful for Receptive Ecumenism.[33] He says:

> [Sobornicity] has to be the gathering (*sobor*) of the whole world, where all Christians bring together their understanding of the whole revealed divine reality and of the whole human reality seen in the light of integral revelation. By so doing, they share their understanding with all and each can participate in the understanding of all.[34]

Like Khomyakov and Berdyaev, Stăniloae focusses here more on the human relationships and the inner life of the church rather than on its visible administrative structures.[35] And here comes the main point that I think can help Receptive Ecumenism to expand and be transformed. Stăniloae emphasizes that people as personal reality are not only capable of exercising freedom, but also of being and becoming "witnesses" of divine glory and goodness; they are capable of the reciprocity of love, and thus of growing into communion with God, with each other and with nature.[36] This is, according to Stăniloae, valid also in the church, where people are called to respond to God's gifts by returning the gifts with their "own valuable stamp . . . [making] of them human gifts as well."[37] And as the church lives in the world, it includes all that the church is, also from the human perspective.

---

32. Berdyaev, "Concerning Authority."

33. For more detail, see my earlier studies: Noble, "Doctrine of Creation" and "Symbolic Mediation." See Stăniloae, *The Experience of God*, 20.

34. Stăniloae, "Sobornicitate" 172. The translation is taken from Turcescu, "Eucharistic Ecclesiology, 101–102.

35. See Stăniloae, "The Holy Spirit," 56.

36. See Stăniloae, *The World*, 20.

37. Stăniloae *The World*, 25. For Stăniloae "God is in relation with the entire movement of the world" (*The World*, 12), and that involves all the stages of the world after it has been weakened by the fall, and God sends always new creative energies to the world to counteract new tricks of the evil, to liberate, strengthen and protect the good, to preserve the world and move it towards communion with God (see *The World*, 203, 206–7).

In ecclesiology Stăniloae wrestled, however, with the following tension.[38] In his *Dogmatic Theology* we find passages adhering to an ecclesiology of concentric circles, according to which the Orthodox Church is the only church in the full sense and other Christian confessions are so only incompletely.[39] He softens this position by recognizing that no particular church family gives a privileged union with Christ, nor does celebrating liturgy and sacraments according to the "right" rites give, without qualification, privileged access to the gifts of the Spirit.[40] But there is a second category, namely that of open sobornicity, in other words with a communion that is open both to the Spirit and to various others.

Stăniloae argues here that the Holy Spirit bestows communion among the different people without taking away their distinct ways of living their Christian life. He speaks about people living in different traditions rather than about traditions in abstract. People are turned to each other, making bonds between each other and teaching each other that "the gift of each exists for the sake of the others."[41] Open sobornicity is a gathering that can encompass the whole world and where all Christians bring together all of their experiences and understanding of the revealed divine reality and while participating in it, exchange their gifts.[42]

As we have seen, Stăniloae was not free of convictions about the privileged place of the Orthodox Church in the divine plan with humankind. However, the more he got to know people from other confessions whom he could understand and respect, the more he appreciated that the love of the Holy Trinity, which is the source, the ongoing stream of life and the aim of human personal as well as communal life reaches far beyond the Orthodox or any other church.[43] Stăniloae grew in appreciating ideas of Western theologians, reciprocated their friendship, and

---

38. See Stăniloae, "The Holy Spirit," 56.

39. A similar position is displayed when Stăniloae speaks about liturgically and sacramentally expressed church unity in official ecumenical work. See Stăniloae, *Theologia Dogmatică*, 266–68; see also Roberson, "Dumitru Stăniloae on Christian Unity," 104–25.

40. Lucian Turcescu points out that here Stăniloae's position departs from Christocentric eucharistic ecclesiology, see Turcescu, "Eucharistic Ecclesiology," 98.

41. Stăniloae, "The Holy Spirit," 54. There are links here with his theology of the world. See Stăniloae, *The Experience of God*, 3, 18, 37, 87, 89.

42. See Stăniloae, "Sobornicitate deschisă," 172.

43. Divine generosity speaks through "all the modes of revelation and expression of God into the world or in life." Bordeianu, *Dumitru Stăniloae*, 29, citing Stăniloae, "Sobornicitate deschisă."

participated in official ecumenical activities on behalf of the Romanian Orthodox Church. Thus, he can be more appreciated for developing a very helpful model of open sobornicity rather than for its consistent implementation in practice.[44] We can, then, take from his interpretation of sobornicity as open the emphasis on relations being mutual, without the need to define a privileged first place where the healing of tradition happens. For Stăniloae belonging to a tradition is not a possession but a gift, and the openness to other people and traditions needs to go hand in hand with an openness to the transformative and sometimes unpredictable ways of the Spirit.

CONCLUSION

In this chapter I have tried to show how Receptive Ecumenism locates the call to unity within the complex dynamics of shared and broken Christian life. Taking seriously both the redemptive possibilities of healing and the hope in the Spirit preceding, accompanying and surprising human effort, Receptive Ecumenism announces that one should not give up on a genuine progress in recognition of the value of others, or even in sacramental hospitality. I have approached Receptive Ecumenism as a kind of manifesto, and thus pointed out that the clarity of what people who gather under that manifesto are willing/planning to do plays a prime role. I have argued that for the genuine progress in ecumenical efforts to which Receptive Ecumenism is dedicated, a stronger critique of the mentality that gives priority to the healing of one's own tradition is needed. The alternative ways of looking at the problem involved first Levinas's inversion of the perspective. With him we can say that healing of one's own tradition is possible only when the other is given a selfless priority. As we have seen, giving the central place to the other (and to the third), however, still works with a hierarchy of priorities that may be sometimes helpful to balance the centrality of the self, but at other times a hindrance to a genuine mutuality.

Other alternatives included subversion of the hierarchy between the I/we and others. *Sobornicity,* as the union of love and truth (Khomyakov), love and freedom (Berdyaev), or open sobornicity as a non-possessive

---

44. Clark states that even Bordeianu, one of the biggest advocates of the ecumenical potential of open sobornicity, concludes that others, like the local Orthodox churches in America, managed to put it into practice in dialogue and lived relations with other Christians and churches much more than Stăniloae. See Clark, "Nationalist and Trinitarian Visions," 223, referring to Bordeianu, *Dumitru Stăniloae,* 209–14.

exchange of gifts (Stăniloae), complements the lack of mutuality in the Levinasian concept, without regressing back to the domination of the personal or the collective self.

To conclude, the vision of "expansive catholicity"[45] envisaged by Receptive Ecumenism, which would lead to a "greater flourishing"[46] of all, as all will participate in the mutually supportive journey towards the greater glory of God, needs to include this ascetic element of subverting the dominance of the interests of one's own tradition. That would make it harder, but in a way, more grounded.

BIBLIOGRAPHY

Claude Abastado. "Introduction à l'analyse des manifestes." *Littéature* 39 (1980) 3–11.
Berdyaev, Nicolas. "Concerning Authority, Freedom and Humanness." http://www.berdyaev.com/berdiaev/berd_lib/1936_409.html.
———. "Ещё о христианском пессимизме и оптимизме: Ответ протоиерею С. Четверикову." *Put* 48 (1935).
———. *Freedom and Spirit*. London: Centenary, 1948.
Clark, Roland. "Nationalist and Trinitarian Visions of the Church in the Theology of Dumitru Stăniloae." *Studii Teologice* 2 (2013) 207–25.
Dumasy, Lise and Chantal Massol, eds. *Pamphlet, utopie, manifeste XIXe–XXe siècles*. Paris: L'Harmattan, 2001.
Girard, René. *Things Hidden Since the Foundation of the World*. Stanford: Stanford University Press, 1987.
———. *Violence and the Sacred*. Baltimore: Johns Hopkins University Press, 1977.
Khomyakov, Alexei. *The Church Is One*. London: Fellowship of St. Alban and St. Sergius, 1968.
Kirwan, Michael. *Discovering Girard*. London: DLT, 2004.
Levinas, Emmanuel. *Alterity and Transcendence*. New York: Colombia University Press, 1999.
———. *De Dieu qui vient à l'idée*. Paris: Vrin, 1982.
———. *Entre Nous: Thinking of the Other*. London: Continuum, 2006.
———. *Ethics and Infinity: Conversations with Philippe Nemo*. Pittsburgh: Duquesne University Press, 1985.
———. *Otherwise than Being, or Beyond Essence*. Pittsburgh: Duquesne University Press, 1998.
———. *Totality and Infinity*. Pittsburgh: Duquesne University Press, 1987.
Lowrie, Donald. *Christian Existentialism: A Berdyaev Anthology*. London: Allen & Unwin, 1965.
Massignon, Louis. *Parole donnée*. Paris: Seuil, 1983.
Millot, Hélène. "Arts poétiques, préfaces et manifestes: La légitimation de l'écriture par le savoir au XIXe siècle." In *Ecriture/savoir: Littérature et connaissance à l'époque moderne*, edited by Alain Vaillant, 205–27. Saint-Etienne: Printer, 1996.

---

45. See Ryan, *Hermeneutics*, 198–203.
46. See Murray, "Receptive Ecumenism as a Catholic Calling," 8.

Murray, Paul D. "Introducing Receptive Ecumenism." *Ecumenist* 51.2 (2014) 1–8.
———. "Receptive Ecumenism and Catholic Learning: Establishing the Agenda." In *Receptive Ecumenism and the Call to Catholic Learning: Exploring a Way for Contemporary Ecumenism*, edited by Paul D. Murray, 5–25. Oxford: Oxford University Press, 2008.
———. "Receptive Ecumenism and Ecclesial Learning: Receiving Gifts for Our Needs." *Louvain Studies* 33 (2008) 30–45.
———. "Receptive Ecumenism as a Catholic Calling: Teaching on Ecumenism from Blessed Pope John Paul II to His Holiness Pope Francis." Vienna, 19th November 2014, at https://iti.ac.at/fileadmin/user_upload/user_upload/News-Events/pdfs/Dr-Paul-Murray-Vienna-Receptive-Ecumenism-Lecture.pdf, 1–11.
Murray, Paul D., and Andrea L. Murray. "The Roots, Range, and Reach of Receptive Ecumenism." In *Unity in Process: Reflections on Receptive Ecumenism*, edited by Clive Barrett, 79–94. London: DLT, 2012.
Noble, Ivana. "Doctrine of Creation within the Theological Project of Dumitru Stăniloae." *Communio Viatorum* 49 (2007) 185–209.
———. "Symbolic Mediation of Wholeness in Western Orthodoxy: Introduction to the Theme," *Logos: A Journal of Eastern Christian Studies* 56.1–2 (2015) 265–75.
Noble, Ivana and Noble, Tim. "Hospitality as a key to the relationship with the other in Levinas and Derrida." *Acta Universitatis Carolinae Theologica* 6.2 (2016) 47–65.
Ivana, Noble, Katerine Bauerov, Tim Noble, Parush Parushev, eds. *Wrestling with the Mind of the Fathers*. Crestwood, NY: St. Vladimir's Seminary, 2015.
Plant, Bob. "Levinas and the Holocaust: A Reconstruction." *Journal of Jewish Thought and Philosophy* 22 (2014) 44–79.
Roberson, Ronald G. "Dumitru Stăniloae on Christian Unity." In *Dumitru Stăniloae: Tradition and Modernity in Theology*, edited by Lucian Turcescu, 104–25. Iași: Center for Romanian Studies, 2002.
Rose, Gillian. *Judaism and Modernity: Philosophical Essays*. Oxford: Blackwell, 1983.
Ryan, Gregory A. *Hermeneutics of Doctrine in a Learning Church: The Dynamics of Receptive Integrity*. Studies in Systematic Theology 23. Leiden: Brill, 2020.
———. "The Reception of Receptive Ecumenism." *Ecclesiology* 17.2 (2021) 7–28.
Skobtsova, Mother Maria. *Essential Writings*. Maryknoll, NY: Orbis, 2003.
Stăniloae, Dumitru. *The Experience of God: The Orthodox Dogmatic Theology II: The World: Creation and Deification*. Translated and edited by Ioan Ioniță and Robert Barringer. Brookline, MA: Holy Cross Orthodox Press, 2005.
———. "The Holy Spirit and the Sobornicity of the Church." In *Theology and the Church*. Crestwood, NY: St Vladimir's Seminary, 1980.
———. *Theologia Dogmatică" ortodoxă" II*. Editura Institutului Biblic. Bucharest, 1978.
———. "Sobornicitate deschisă" [Open Sobornicity] *Ortodoxia* 23 (1971) 165–80.
Turcescu, Lucian. "Eucharistic Ecclesiology or Open Sobornicity?" In *Dumitru Stăniloae: Tradition and Modernity in Theology*, edited by Lucian Turcescu, 83–103. Iași: Center for Romanian Studies, 2002.
Yanoshevsky, Galia. "Three Decades of Writing on Manifesto: The Making of a Genre." *Poetics Today* 30.2 (2009) 257–86.

4

A Methodist Reception of the Petrine Ministry?

Dominic Robinson SJ *and* David Carter

INTRODUCTION

BEFORE VATICAN II NO one would have envisaged the possibility of a Methodist reception of the Petrine ministry. However, by the fourth quinquennium of the international Methodist–Roman Catholic dialogue, Methodists hinted at it as an ultimate possibility. In "Towards a Statement on the Church," they said, "Methodists accept that whatever is properly required for the unity of the whole church must by that very fact be part of God's will for his Church. A universal primacy might well serve as a focus for the unity of the whole Church."[1]

Today, we sometimes feel that the Ecumenical Movement has not succeeded because it has not yet led to reunion between the major churches. However, it has led to a widespread change in attitudes by members of the ecumenically engaged Christian traditions towards each other and above all in relations between Catholics and the western churches. Most recently there has been the fillip of Receptive Ecumenism, making us all ask not just what it is that we may commend from our respective traditions to others, but also what it is that we need to learn from each other. It provides

---

1. Joint Commission, "Statement on the Church," §58.

a specific context for Methodists to consider how far a central global ministry of personal leadership might enhance our connectional structures in the service of God's mission throughout the world.

Three common characteristics have increasingly deepened the Catholic–Methodist relationship. Both are missionary churches, seeking to fulfil the Lord's instruction to go into all the world and preach to every nation—this has particularly been the case for Catholics since the sixteenth century and for Methodists since the late eighteenth century. Both believe in the essential interdependence and interconnectedness of the universal church at every level.[2] In the Wesleyan tradition, the ministers in Conference meet to watch over the church and each other in faith and love. Here the Catholic Church, it should be stated, has a differing view of the principles of synodality. The Catholic Church stresses collegiality amongst the bishops across the globe with the Bishop of Rome as of ultimate importance and authority in decision making for the whole church. Pope Francis exercises the role of bridge builder in discerning a universal way on questions of faith and order. This has been evinced most recently in the decision not to accept the majority view of the Amazon Synod to ordain *viri probati* (married men of proven virtue) to priesthood and to persist with a discernment in the ordination of women to the diaconate, despite the first delegated commission declaring this as inconclusive. Nevertheless, the Synod on Synodality is showing a greater concern to represent inter-connectedness, as the continental phase clearly shows differing local positions.

Finally, and significantly, both share a rich tradition of teaching and action on social justice, particularly recognized since the beginning of the present pontificate, which has roots both in the teaching and practice of the early Methodists and in the practice of Rome in the first centuries and, later, under a whole series of pontiffs since Leo XIII. Both traditions receive fresh inspiration from Pope Francis, in act and teaching alike.

SEARCHING TOGETHER

The key early turning point in the relationship of the two communions was, of course, the Second Vatican Council, in particular the open and frank invitations to the communions of what were then called "separated brethren" to send observers to the Council, observers who were most

---

2. For unity in faith, mission and sacramental life as ultimate goal, see MRCIC §20. See also Robbins and Carter "Connexion and *Koinonia*," 320–36.

specifically welcomed to give their reactions to the unfolding debates and to the decrees that resulted from them. The most significant of the Methodist observers was the American Albert Outler, initially skeptical, but who ended his term of service by paying deep tribute to the decree *Lumen Gentium*.[3] Outler, himself, had for some time, been seeking to recall American Methodism to both its Wesleyan and earlier patristic roots—he wanted a Methodist *ressourcement* to match the Roman Catholic one.

The decree on ecumenism, *Unitatis Redintegratio*, proposed the method of dialogue as a way of developing rapprochement and mutual learning; it even talked of "searching together with the separated brethren into the divine mysteries," which held the promise, for Methodists and others, to be a way of developing relationships very differently from the pre-Vatican II era. The first three communions to respond to the invitation were the Lutheran World Federation, the Anglican Communion, and the World Methodist Council. By 1967, these three dialogues were launched. The MRCIC (Methodist Roman Catholic International Commission) dialogue, in particular, was characterized both by a degree of realism about the distance previously existing between the two communions and yet also by a real desire to learn from and with each other. From 1981 onwards, there was commitment by both churches to seek unity in faith, mission and sacramental life.

It was in the next dialogue report in 1986 that the Methodists made a key statement, effectively acknowledging that whatever is necessary for the unity of the Church must, by that fact, be necessary for the Church. "A universal primacy might well serve as focus of and ministry for unity of the whole Church."[4]

UT UNUM SINT

Most significant in our context was John Paul II's encyclical *Ut Unum Sint* of 1995. A very large part of this was devoted to the necessity for dialogue, integral to every human community. Both the very real advances in dialogue and those still needing to be made were clearly spelled out, as specified in the five key points for further consideration with the separated western churches .[5] On all of these, further progress has since been made

3. Outler, *Methodist Observer*, explores his reactions to Vatican II.
4. Joint Commission, "Statement on the Church," §58.
5. *Ut Unum Sint*, §79. The points are the relationship between Scripture and Tradition, the Eucharist, ordination as a sacrament, the magisterium of the Pope and bishops, the Virgin Mary as Mother of God and intercessor.

in the MRCIC dialogue, the last of these dealing with Marian devotion, discussed primarily through the British national Catholic–Methodist dialogue and expressed in its publication *Mary, Mother of the Lord: Sign of Grace, Faith and Holiness*.[6] The ninth dialogue, on the two gospel sacraments, made great progress on baptism and eucharist, largely through a joint reading of Charles Wesley's "Hymns on the Lord's Supper," an act of Catholic reception and Methodist re-reception.

A particularly important statement in *Ut Unum Sint*, was that "the Spirit has allowed conflicts to serve in some circumstances to make explicit certain aspects of Christian vocation. In spite of fragmentation, which is an evil from which we need to be healed, there has resulted a rich bestowal of grace which is meant to embellish the *koinonia*" (§85).

It builds on the Vatican II statement that "whatever is wrought by the Holy Spirit in the hearts of our separated brethren can contribute to our own edification." (§4). It also anticipates the development, in the next decade, of Receptive Ecumenism and created the right context for John Paul II's most remarkable proposal, that he wanted to consider ways in which his uniquely preserved ministry as Bishop of Rome could be adjusted to provide for a shared and mutually agreed primacy within the universal church, which would, "while in no way renouncing what is essential to its mission, nevertheless be open to a new situation" (§95). Moreover, he wanted to involve the leaders and theologians of the other communions in a "patient and fraternal dialogue on this subject . . . keeping before us only the will of Christ for His Church and allowing ourselves to be deeply moved by his plea 'that they all may be one'" (§§95–96).

This proposal naturally attracted enormous interest. As far as Methodism was concerned, Geoffrey Wainwright, then the leading Methodist ecumenist and co-chair of MRCIC, advocated a meeting of church leaders, presided over by the Pope, to consider what were the most urgent issues in world mission and evangelism on which the churches might be able to address the world together.[7] With the succession of Pope Francis, much was to change, including the giving of renewed attention to *Ut Unum Sint* as the Pontifical Council for Christian Unity currently seeks to raise its proposals for reconsideration in the

---

6. Largely the work of the late bishop Michael Evans, a member then of both the national and international Roman Catholic–Methodist Commissions.

7. First proposed at a conference in 1998. Wainwright also made further similar comments in the early years of Benedict's pontificate. See Wainwright, "Petrine Ministry Universal Church," 284–309.

light of the very extensive work that has been done on Petrine primacy and related issues since 1996.

The report of the latest MRCIC dialogue quinquennium was completed in 2021 and made public in 2022. Its title, "God in Christ Reconciling," certainly indicates that it hopes to move the two communions closer to each other. It is insistent that in both communions there can be no doubt that Pope Francis has every possible chance of being regarded as the Pope with whom Methodists can most easily identify.

We say this on the basis of his overall winsomeness of character, the relevance and soundness of his practical teaching on the difficult issues confronting all humankind and his proposals for a thoroughly synodical church, a church whose leaders, the bishops, have a duty to listen to the *sensus fidelium* of the *whole* church. We add the latter, in light of the 2015 report of the International Theological Commission, which accepted that the *sensus fidelium* is at work in *all* Christian communities and is not limited to those in present communion with the Bishop of Rome.[8]

AN ECUMENICAL *KAIROS*?

Francis's three major works, *The Joy of the Gospel*, *Laudato Si*, and *Fratelli Tutti*, all resonate with traditional and contemporary Methodist emphases. For Methodists, Francis encapsulates all the key concerns in our pilgrimage of faith and discipleship. It should be noted, from the Catholic perspective, that these common trends towards listening and discerning in common for the good of the universal Church, are to be placed in the context of Francis's understanding of communal discernment rooted in the creative tension between firm magisterial teaching and the primacy of conscience. This is grounded in the very difficult contemporary pastoral context of discernment on significant moral questions in the document *Amoris Laetitia*. This document, alongside the others of the pontificate and now of the ongoing synodal process, expresses a creative tension which Catholicism embraces. Methodism too will be aware of these creative tensions in discernment for the good of the universal church.

Synodality, "the way that God wants for the Church in the third millennium,"[9] (Francis's words), will, perhaps, particularly appeal to

---

8. *Sensus Fidei*, §§56, 86. David Carter discusses this and the other issues in "Petrine Ministry," 60–82.

9. Pope Francis was speaking at a ceremony at the Vatican commemorating the

Methodists as they see the emergence of a providential way ahead for the Catholic Church, as parallel, in some ways, to their own early experience of the development of ministerial and lay partnership. Both churches will be acknowledging the prophetic role of the laity and the many charisms for service in the Church with which they are endowed.

In the light of all this, one may ask whether there could be a *kairos* moment for the wider Christian community comparable to the one recorded in 451 at the Council of Chalcedon when all the fathers acclaimed the definition of the two natures of Christ given by Pope Leo I and said, "Peter has spoken through Leo." It could even, in the light of the recent decision of the five communions which are signatories to the Joint Declaration on Justification, be an occasion for them to begin to consider *together* how the Petrine ministry might be jointly received, possibly in a differentiated form which would involve more immediate jurisdiction on a wider level in the Catholic Church as such, whilst also acting as a more general leadership in prophetic discernment for the other communions.[10] A purely Methodist–Catholic search for a joint reception needs to be complemented by the insights of the other three signatories of the "Joint Declaration on Justification" (JDDC), with whom both Methodism and the Catholic Church enjoy long-standing ecumenical relationships.[11] Are five better together than two? There is a lot of work to be done and prayer to be offered.

On a more immediate level, what can we learn about the nature of the dialogues in process. How significant might the synodical process prove?

It was in this context that David Carter, wrote his article "A Wider Role for the Petrine Ministry," in which he suggested five functions that the Petrine minister could exercise on behalf of all the ecumenically engaged churches and, in particular, on behalf of the five communions now pledged to work further forward from that basis.[12] The first function could be that of acting as a universal spokesman for the Christian church

---

50th Anniversary of the Institution of the Synod of Bishops on October 17, 2015.

10. We owe this idea to the thought of Harding Meyer, who in an article, once proposed the possibility of a differentiated reception of episcopal ministry by Protestant churches. *Ecumenical Trends* (October 2005), 1–8.

11. The other three signatories are the Lutheran World Federation (1999) and the Anglican Communion and the World Alliance of Reformed Churches (2018). As we understand it, they are pledged to do further work towards consensus on other key theological issues.

12. Carter, "Petrine Ministry," 60–82.

in dialogue with other religions and even people of good will with no religious allegiance as such. The second would be encouraging mutual respect and learning between all the communions, Receptive Ecumenism as something to be taken for granted. Thirdly, a universal Petrine minister could act as arbitrator in disputes affecting any of the ecumenical partners, particularly over jurisdiction. Fourthly, the Petrine minister could remind churches of their need for a balanced approach to both teaching and practice within and across the *oikoumene*. Finally, he would continue the great tradition of his Catholic predecessors in their regular teaching through encyclicals on key issues of concern and relevant mission and diaconal ministry for both church and world.

We believe that the five points mentioned in the penultimate paragraph summarize the case for such a ministry, particularly in a world as fully globalized as that of the early twenty-first century. We recognize, however, that there are remaining problems for all the ecumenical partners of the Catholic Church over the Vatican I definition of papal infallibility and that elements of historic distrust of the Catholic Church inherited from the past within Methodism need addressing in some quarters. Nevertheless, we believe that the progress of the MRCIC to date gives us confidence that the question can be sensitively, and, hopefully, increasingly fruitfully addressed.

BIBLIOGRAPHY

British Methodist/Roman Catholic Committee. *Mary, Mother of the Lord: Sign of Grace, Faith and Holiness: Towards a Shared Understanding*. London: Catholic Truth Society, 1995.

Carter, David. "A Wider Role for the Petrine Ministry?" *One in Christ* 54/1 (2020) 60–82.

Francis, Pope. "Address of His Holiness Pope Francis for the Commemoration of the 50th Anniversary of the Institution of the Synod of Bishops." Vatican, October 17, 2015.

———. *Amoris Laetitia*. Vatican City: Libreria Editrice Vaticana, 2016.

———. *Evangelii Gaudium*. Vatican City: Libreria Editrice Vaticana, 2013.

———. *Fratelli Tutti*. Vatican City: Libreria Editrice Vaticana, 2020.

———. *Laudato Si'*. Vatican City: Libreria Editrice Vaticana, 2015.

International Theological Commission. *Sensus Fidei: In the Life of the Church*. London: Catholic Truth Society, 2014.

John Paul II, Pope. *Ut Unum Sint*. Vatican City: Libreria Editrice Vaticana, 1995.

Joint Commission of the Roman Catholic Church and the World Methodist Council. "Towards a Statement on the Church," Nairobi, 1986.

Methodist–Roman Catholic International Commission. "God in Christ Reconciling: On the Way to Full Communion in Faith, Sacraments, and Mission." Report of the Joint International Commission for Dialogue Between the World Methodist Council and the Roman Catholic Church, 2022.

Meyer, Harding. *Ecumenical Trends*, October 2005, 1–8.

Robbins, D., and D. Carter. "Connexion and *Koinonia*, a Wesleyan Contribution to Ecclesiology." *One in Christ* 34 (1998) 320–36.

Outler, Albert C. *Methodist Observer at Vatican II*. Westminster, MD: Newman, 1967.

Vatican Council II. *Lumen Gentium*. Vatican City: Libreria Editrice Vaticana, 1964.

———. *Unitatis Redintegratio: Decree on Ecumenism*. Vatican City: Vatican Publishing House, 1964.

———. *Gaudium et Spes*. Vatican City: Libreria Editrice Vaticana, 1965.

Wainwright, Geoffrey. "How Can the Petrine Ministry Be of Service to the Unity of the Universal Church?" In *A Primatial Ministry of Unity in a Conciliar and Synodal Context*, edited by James F. Puglisi, 284–309. Grand Rapids: Eerdmans, 2010.

5

Framing Receptive Ecumenism as Pilgrimage in the Context of the *Joint Declaration on the Doctrine of Justification*

Tony Franklin-Ross

"Always be ready to make your defense to anyone who demands from you an accounting for the hope that is in you" (1 Peter 3:15)

ECUMENICAL PILGRIMAGE

THE HOPES AND EXPERIENCES of a pilgrimage will be different for each pilgrim, whether it be the intent, the spiritual discovery or insights gained, the route, or destination. The act of devotion that is encompassed by the pilgrim often evokes a deep spirituality beyond the physical journey. The hope may not always be clear from the beginning of the pilgrimage, but be discovered along the way, or even change and arise in ways unforeseen from the outset.

In various forms, the act of religious pilgrimage dates from ancient times through to contemporary expressions. Nevertheless, the "touchstones" of the spiritual experience of the journey are an openness to both fleeting and lasting encounters along the way, with others of different walks of life, with God or the Divine, and with oneself. These encounters expose the pilgrim to learning or self-discoveries, predicated by an openness to be changed through the pilgrimage (most likely in a way that was not pre-determined). The spirituality of a pilgrimage also arises through encountering milestones along the way. These milestones might be physical or spiritual, including moments of reconciliation or release from the past, moments of peace for the present, or a reframed sense of the future; whether within oneself, one's relationship(s) with others and with the Divine. The goal, the location of the conclusion of the pilgrimage, whilst nevertheless important from the outset of the journey, is only a part of the overall experience when the pilgrimage is viewed with hindsight.

A contemporary resonance to pilgrimage is expressed in the ecumenical project of the last century. Much of what I have just described can be affirmed in ecumenism: encounters with a variety of fellow pilgrims whether fleeting or long term, intentional and unintentional insights, moments of spiritual discovery. These spiritual milestones might arise through moments of rapprochement, *metanoia*, learning and change towards expressions of visible unity. Whilst the goal of ecumenism is the full unity of the church, as a destination it is still some way off—but nevertheless invokes a devotion to continue the journey.

In the context of the *Joint Declaration on the Doctrine of Justification* (JDDJ), I explore ecumenical pilgrimage as a particular lens when relating to Receptive Ecumenism. The evolving experience from the two communions that comprised the original bilateral agreement of JDDJ, to the subsequent association of other communions into a multilateral, evokes an ecumenical pilgrimage. From this, I will commend three aspects of ecumenical spirituality as part of the continuing ecumenical pilgrimage for JDDJ.

RECEPTIVE ECUMENISM AS PILGRIMAGE

With the premise that the theology of Receptive Ecumenism is a spirituality as much as a methodology, I suggest that the image of a pilgrimage is an expression of this spirituality.

Essentially, Receptive Ecumenism encourages making a safe space for learning, for receiving the giftedness of the other, for conversion and for growing more fully into who God made us to be, of becoming more authentically what God has called us to be (whether as individuals, communities of faith, or communions). Though such an approach might be engaged within one's own tradition, mutual acceptance is not insisted upon those encountered from other traditions, although it might be hoped for. This is an ecumenical spirituality that moves from doctrinal and ecclesiological convergence constructs, to one of taking a lived reality of revealing and affirming one's own wounded hands, welcoming the grace of gift of the other to minister healing to the Church as the wounded body of Christ.[1]

Such spirituality indicates something that is dynamic and is an orientation towards the other; possibly invoking a Spirit-given moment of metanoia, conversion, or even healing. This involves grappling with how to remain true to one's own traditions, even whilst cultivating an openness to the receptions of others' views that do not reflect one's own.[2]

Receptive Ecumenism is both freshly dynamic and intentionally relational, involving listening and accompaniment that occurs over and over. This ecumenical spirituality of Receptive Ecumenism invokes a pilgrimage through meeting and honoring the other encountered on the way as fellow pilgrims; to be touched by something of the other person that changes or moves oneself in the moments of encounter on the pilgrimage journey. Ecumenical pilgrimage evokes vulnerability to a movement from differences-that-divide to differences-that-unite. But this does not mean that one should deny or diminish our own giftedness and ways of working out our distinctive gifts. We are each called also to embody deeply our own tradition, so that others might also learn from us, as their needs suggest. As a spiritual fulfilment of ecumenical unity, when communions are living together well, they are living with God in their mutual presence.

The Joint Declaration on the Doctrine of Justification as Pilgrimage

The JDDJ presents an example of Receptive Ecumenism that gives expression to an ongoing pilgrimage. Whilst JDDJ is most known as a significant bilateral document for the Lutheran and Roman Catholic churches, JDDJ now has a life beyond that origin through wider applications and associations.

Walter Kasper, influential in the formation of the JDDJ, anticipated:

---

1. Murray, "Introducing Receptive Ecumenism," 4–5. See also Murray, "Receptive Ecumenism and Catholic Learning," 12.

2. Rusch, *Ecumenical Reception*, 76.

> It is my firm conviction that one day too we will rub our eyes in amazement that God's Spirit has broken through the seemingly insurmountable walls that divide us and given us new ways through to each other and a new communion. Hopefully we shall not have to wait another four hundred years.[3]

One such moment of "rubbing our eyes" is the unfolding of the bilateral JDDJ into a multilateral agreement as other communions voluntarily respond to affirm a desire of association with JDDJ through their own lens of theology.

Paul Murray characterizes Receptive Ecumenism as church communions seeing each other in a new light, enabling mutual recognition of the other's Christian faith where once ignorance or hostility towards each other prevailed.[4] Correspondingly, JDDJ presents an expression of a journey with fellow pilgrims, leaning into the Spirit of diverse unity through differentiated consensus through the voices of the other churches, listening to what the Spirit is saying to the churches, and being willing to be transformed: thus, effecting Receptive Ecumenism as an ecumenical pilgrimage.

Indeed, aside from providing a space for other communions to make mutual association with JDDJ, it also seeks to lay the groundwork for extending the implications of justification into matters of baptism, eucharist and ministry, and further through to Christian witness and justice. These are the open possibilities of discovery, of milestones as yet undetermined, that witness to the ongoing journey of this ecumenical pilgrimage.

Milestones Rather Than the Finish Line

The Protestant Reformation, as grounded in 1517 and Martin Luther, engaged the theology of justification as a central issue; not just for Luther but also for other Reformation movements such as that of John Calvin. The interpretation of justification given by Luther and Calvin raised fundamental problems for Roman Catholicism, which gave rise to intense controversies, and mutual condemnation.

Approaching the 500th anniversary of the Reformation, JDDJ arose from the Lutheran and Roman Catholic churches' intentional engagement in a process of examining divisive questions and historic condemnations.

---

3. Kasper, "The Joint Declaration," 21.
4. Murray, *Receptive Ecumenism and the Call to Catholic Learning*, 33–34.

More than thirty years of national and international dialogues and wider scholarship fed into the creation of the JDDJ document. Significantly, JDDJ declares that the Lutheran and Roman Catholic churches are no longer in a church-dividing dispute about the doctrine of justification; and that the condemnations of the 16th century do not apply to current church teaching. Essentially resolving the 500-year-old division, the two communions affirm that they are able to articulate a common understanding of justification by God's grace through faith in Christ.

Speaking about the Lutheran–Catholic dialogue, Pope Francis said, "We have the opportunity to mend a critical moment of our history by moving beyond the controversies and disagreements that have often prevented us from understanding one another."[5] The breakthrough was not through a perfect agreement, but rather a "differentiated consensus." The approach of Receptive Ecumenism is reflected in the methodology of section four of the JDDJ, where subsections are placed in the following order: first a statement of Lutheran–Roman Catholic consensus, then a Lutheran perspective, and finally a Catholic perspective. JDDJ does not require the dialogue partners to accept each other's perspectives, but to view them as tolerable and as the basis for further ecumenical pilgrimage. Therefore, JDDJ should not be seen as concluding a particular bilateral ecumenical project on the doctrine of justification for the two communions. It is a milestone, but one that in the wider ecumenical spirituality and prayer of other churches, becomes an opportunity for furthering Receptive Ecumenism.

A continuing ecumenical pilgrimage is envisaged in three ways, with opportunities for further milestones. First, JDDJ provides a basis for broadening reflection on other questions requiring further mutual discernment, including mission, ministry and eucharist. Second, justification grounds a call to evaluate church and Christian life in today's world, and especially their impact on matters of justice and peace, and how justification relates to transformation in personal and community life in recognition of human dignity and human rights. Third, JDDJ is being received beyond the first bilateral participants to encounter additional pilgrims.

The potential for further pilgrims is significant to the image of an ecumenical pilgrimage. As noted by William Rusch, one of the questions raised early in this progress towards the JDDJ itself was whether

---

5. Underwood, "Pope Francis's Lutheran Reconciliation."

the basic bilateral consensus on justification could be extended to other communions. He suggested, "The discussion on the Joint Declaration and its larger impact on Churches in the ecumenical movement should and will continue."[6]

Methodist theologian Geoffrey Wainwright, influential in the World Methodist Council's process of engaging with the JDDJ discussions, noted that Methodists could have simply offered polite congratulations to the Lutherans and Roman Catholics.[7] Rather, in 2006 after studying JDDJ, the World Methodist Council (WMC) declared its assent to make a *Statement of Association* with the JDDJ. It did so on the basis that Methodist theological understandings can also affirm the Declaration, as indirect inheritors of the Reformation, though with a particular emphasis on John Wesley's perspective on sanctification. It was discerned that the WMC would not sign the JDDJ itself, since they did not participate in the condemnations of the Reformation era; rather it was by way of a *Statement of Association* that WMC affirmed and added their own differentiated consensus to that expressed within the JDDJ.

This opened a pathway for others: in 2016 the Anglican Communion, and in 2017 the World Communion of Reformed Churches, extending the JDDJ family to its now five communions in multilateral fellowship.[8] Each communion has approached the possibility of association through a process of discernment, whereby each has sought to both describe, from its own self-understanding and particular theological perspective, its agreement with the doctrinal implications of the JDDJ, while also adding its voice to the differentiating consensus on the Doctrine of Justification. Each additional association is marked with a formal liturgical celebration of association, with representatives of all the communions.

"Notre Dame"—Furthering the JDDJ Pilgrimage

In 2019, a consultation of these five communions, held at Notre Dame University (USA), generated a fresh mutual statement in response to JDDJ, termed the *Notre Dame Statement* (NDS). This is not a further doctrinal treatise, but rather a statement that expresses an intention of

---

6. Rusch, *Justification and the Future*, xi.

7. Wainwright, "The Lutheran–Roman Catholic Agreement," 20.

8. In 2023 the Old Catholic Church of the Union of Utrecht advised that it is considering an association with JDDJ.

living into the pastoral, practical, and spiritual experience of multilateral association with JDDJ based on the affirmation:

> . . . we wish to make more visible our common witness, in worship and service, on our journey together towards visible unity, walking together, praying together and working together. In this new reality in our common life, we shall review the application of the Lund Principle of 1952: "that churches should act together in all matters except those in which deep differences of conviction compel them to act separately" which we have all affirmed.[9]

From this basis, hope is expressed for fresh ways in which the five communions can work in realizing a deeper communion towards the full visible unity, along with an imperative of proclaiming the good news of salvation, through compassion and working for justice in facing similar challenges of the contemporary world. The significance of NDS is that it identifies that JDDJ was: "the beginning of something and not the end." That is to say, it created a vision and a sense of purpose, and it gave language to growing in unity.[10] NDS affirms the essence of the journey of JDDJ which I interpret as resonating with Receptive Ecumenism, and pilgrimage.

The JDDJ Steering Committee (formed by communion general secretaries and ecumenical officers, or equivalent) in October 2019 reflected living into the NDS.[11] All five communions mutually seek to further the pilgrimage together, and to engage together in acts of joint witness. It was acknowledged that though church unity is the final goal that is driving JDDJ, the potential of the JDDJ is not yet fully utilized in the ecumenical activities of the five communions, in that a commitment to multilateral ecumenism has not yet transformed the system of bilateral dialogues in the spirit of the JDDJ process. It was therefore suggested that we create new language and new imagination to express together who we already are and, indeed, that JDDJ should shape the framework of ecumenical relations among the five communions.

---

9. "Notre Dame Consultation Statement."
10. "Notre Dame Consultation Statement."
11. Taken from Notes at the JDDJ Steering Committee Meeting on Oct 8th, 2019; held in Christiansfeld, Denmark.

SPIRITUALITY FOR RECEPTIVE ECUMENICAL PILGRIMAGE

I suggest three touchstones as a spiritual theology of Receptive Ecumenism, shaped through a lens of pilgrimage, as already exhibited in the JDDJ journey, as potential language for the continuing pilgrimage.

Ecumenical Catholicity

Miroslav Volf describes "catholic personality" as an openness for learning to value our own and others' identities and to relate across the differences which presents the embodying of embrace rather than exclusion.[12] To adopt a catholic personality is, for Volf, part of becoming a Christian: we become in Christ a new creation in which there is space, through the Spirit, to receive "the other." Indeed, a catholic personality is one which is enriched by otherness and is only catholic by virtue of the multiple "others" that become reflected in it. The Spirit breaks through the barriers and self-enclosed worlds that we inhabit and calls us to come to God, and re-creates us and sets us on a path of continued sanctification—furthering a catholic personality.

Volf suggests an ecclesiological implication of this: a catholic person requires a "catholic community." As a "church among churches," Volf accommodates multiple churches as reflecting that the church universal has taken root in many cultures, yet all are part of the one. Therefore, reflecting a catholic personality on a communal level catholic spirit of embrace, every church must be open to all other churches, and each church needs the others in order to properly be itself.

To affirm being part of the *one holy catholic and apostolic church*, Volf draws together "ecumenical personality" and "catholic community" to advocate the term "ecumenical catholicity." Thus, the minimum requirement of catholicity should be in exhibiting an openness to other churches, whereas churches that close themselves off from other churches effectively deny their own claim to catholicity. Accordingly, the optimal expression of catholicity is to maintain and deepen ties to other churches, past and present, with a view to an eschatological future catholicity.

Embodying a "catholic personality" takes diversity seriously as being part of the very nature of the church. The concepts of "catholic personality" and "ecumenical catholicity" are visible through the JDDJ pilgrimage. As observed of JDDJ:

12. Volf, *"A Vision of Embrace."*

> Yes, patience is necessary, just as it is when we nourish the soil in the garden. However, in this process Christians together begin to see themselves in the larger context . . . we are reminded that we may not have the whole picture; that we have gifts that we may share with each other.[13]

It is therefore valid to have differences, whereby each church may have something to hear from others in appreciation, teach the others in modesty; which leads to a willingness to understand each other better and critique one's own tradition, to continue further in the conversation and dialogue, and seek further expression of communion.

Empathetic Ecumenism

David Carter offers "empathetic ecumenism" to express a discipline of standing in the shoes of one's ecumenical partner; seeking to understand their living within the broad totality of Christian discipleship, through understanding the things that concern them, particularly when coming to issues with different perspectives.[14] As an expression of Receptive Ecumenism, this enables shared insights that enable greater trust and honoring of each other. As noted by Kasper, "We held out our hands to each other as churches and we do not wish to let go ever again."[15]

The empathy towards each other's communion is affirmed in the Roman Catholic–Lutheran document *From Conflict to Communion*:

> We should always begin from the perspective of unity and not from the point of view of division, in order to strengthen what is held in common, even though the differences are more easily seen and experienced. We must let ourselves continuously be transformed by the encounter with the other and by the mutual witness of faith.[16]

When JDDJ arose as a fruit of the Lutheran–Roman Catholic bilateral dialogue, observer communions who had empathy for the conversation took notice. Later the five communions reflected that "It was evident also that the hands joined together in Augsburg needed to reach out to a wider circle of participants.[17]

13. Kessler, *Receive One Another*, 64, 68–69.
14. Carter, "Progress towards Anglican–Methodist Unity," 211.
15. Kasper, *That They All May Be One*, 127.
16. *From Conflict to Communion*.
17. Lutheran World Federation, *Biblical Foundations*, ix.

The Methodist Association Statement gave a lead for the methodology that paved the way for others to explore their response to the JDDJ. A grounding was made from the perspective of Methodist traditions. This included a particular resonance with John Wesley's sermon *On the Catholic Spirit*, in which he reflects in the following posture towards a person with a different theological position: "Is your heart right as my heart is with your heart, then give me your hand, and do not worry about the differences that do not matter to the core of faith, and witnesses of the heart of the Gospel of Christ."[18]

Empathetic reflection occurred in relation to Methodism's discernment on the doctrine of justification: in relation to Lutherans, by referencing an indebtedness to the biblical teaching on justification by Luther and other reformers as engaged by John and Charles Wesley; and in relation to Roman Catholic tradition by acknowledging its embrace of elements which belong to the Catholic tradition of the early church, both East and West. Further, a Methodist perspective was added as its own contribution to the discussion, through the Wesleys' emphasis on prevenient grace and sanctification.[19]

JDDJ held wider appeal to other communions with an empathy for the significance of the JDDJ. This empathy also allows for a space where the direction of the pilgrimage is not yet determined but further milestones may well arise. NDS furthers the hope to continue mutual journeying towards visible unity.

Differentiated Consensus

William Rusch identified as critical to ecumenical methodology that one's own confessional identity is not to be given up, whilst at the same time developing a fellowship of varying confessional identities living, practicing and showing further visible unity. Rusch suggests two levels of consensus outlined by this method: an articulated identified agreement while also articulating remaining differences, which are nevertheless considered as admissible and not called into question by the agreement or challenge what is agreed.[20]

---

18. Wesley, *Sermons*, 450.

19. *Synthesis: Together to Holiness*. World Methodist Council, Lake Junaluska; 2010. §27–34.

20. Rusch, *Ecumenical Reception*, 120–21. See JDDJ §40.

Rusch suggests that JDDJ, along with the *Leuenberg Agreement* (1973), are key processes that moved differentiated consensus "out of the realm of theory and into the area of practice and acceptance."[21] In the JDDJ, neither the Lutherans nor the Roman Catholics give up the doctrinal statements of the sixteenth century, nor do they disown their respective traditions, but are enabled to understand them afresh and in a deeper way. New scholarship and dialogue over some time enabled a place to recognize and re-receive respective traditions.[22]

Rather than JDDJ becoming a "new confessional statement" or a "compromise document," it enables communions to continue to hold to different understandings or positions as not being contrary to each other, nor exclusive of the other. Thereby, diversity of expression is offered in a way that enriches the faith understanding of each contributor to the dialogue.[23] The JDDJ association statements did not conclude the differentiated consensus process, such as a published differentiated consensus on biblical perspectives of justification.[24]

Kasper notes the JDDJ process of differentiated consensus: "The differences that remain are not contradictory statements but rather are seen to complement and to 'complete each other.'"[25] Kasper observes that JDDJ did not seek to demand a full consensus, whereas differentiated consensus understands that *the one, holy, catholic and apostolic church* is an organic whole of complementary opposites. With the Church modelled as the image of the triune God who is oneness in diversity, JDDJ points the way forward and opens a wider perspective.[26]

It is affirmed in NDS:

> We have found that the method of the differentiating consensus has proved to be a fruitful means of overcoming controversies by identifying common substance and distinguishing from its different confessional expressions. Thus, this type of consensus encompasses both agreements and differences.[27]

---

21. Rusch, *Ecumenical Reception*, 125.
22. Kasper "The Joint Declaration," 16.
23. Edward Cassidy in Rusch, 87.
24. See *The Biblical Foundations*.
25. Kasper "The Joint Declaration," 18.
26. Kasper. *That They May Be One*, 129–30.
27. "Notre Dame Consultation Statement," 56.

This has exhibited Receptive Ecumenism in the self-reflection gained through engagement with other traditions and perspectives.

CONCLUSION

Geoffrey Wainwright published a keynote paper in 2000 asking the question: *Is the Reformation over?*[28] JDDJ offers a significant turning point, not just for the communions closest to the 16th century crisis of divisions; yet holds latent potential.

As an evolving pilgrimage of Receptive Ecumenism, JDDJ has seeded a spiritual process where the communions journey together as pilgrims, with a means of discovery and learning about each other, not relying on bilateral dialogues alone (nor negating their continuing role) but relate multilaterally with other communions in their pilgrimage of observing and discernment. NDS extends the milestone of JDDJ into an intentional continuing pilgrimage, seeking to express ecumenical catholicity through encounters with fellow present and future pilgrims to this journey.

The differentiated consensus affirmed in the original bilateral agreement of JDDJ has not been appropriated by other communions, rather empathy has evoked a changed relationship by and with other communions who have each developed their own associations in response to JDDJ as mediated by their own tradition. This reception through self-reflection, occasioned (but not exclusively) through rapprochement or *metanoia*, invokes an integrity between fellow pilgrim communions that hopes to transform the whole Body of Christ through being a catholic community—knowing that "the whole" is itself but a temporary grouping of pilgrims that is open to being a changing group as the pilgrimage continues and encounters others. This process has invoked Receptive Ecumenism towards a self-informing change in each communion and as a multilateral group together.

The JDDJ pilgrimage has gone beyond the bilateral theological positions, through extending the family of communions associated with the core JDDJ document, and now together living into the hopes of NDS. It offers a renewal of relationships through empathetic ecumenism, between communions in a multilateral plurality that is not static but invites further exploration, so that the JDDJ should not settle into a status quo nor dare to sense completeness to this journey. The sense of a catholic

---

28. Wainwright. *Is the Reformation Over?*

personality of the communions, to bring a recognition of the ecumenical catholicity through a space of engagement of multiple communions, without any posturing of "seniority." This has presented the sense of being more fully catholic travelling towards further milestones of unity.

The relationships have expressed becoming mutually informing and transformational through the encounter of fellow pilgrims and of God. And it is my contention that this presents an expression of Receptive Ecumenism, and with hope for further new and unforeseen potential for discoveries of pilgrimage for fellow pilgrims along the way—indeed exploring and discovering future milestones as yet unmapped, towards the goal of visible unity.

BIBLIOGRAPHY

Avis, Paul. *Reshaping Ecumenical Theology: the Church Made Whole?* London: T. & T. Clark, 2010.

Carter, David. "Methodist and the Ecumenical Task." In *The Unity We Have & the Unity We Seek: Ecumenical Prospects for the Third Millennium*, edited by Jeremy Morris and Nicholas Sagovsky, 53–76. London: T. & T. Clark, 2003.

———. "Progress towards Anglican–Methodist Unity." *One in Christ* 48 (2014) 194–214.

Chapman, David M. "Consensus and Difference: The Elusive Nature of Ecumenical Agreement." *Ecclesiology* 8 (2002) 54–70.

Cracknell, Kenneth, and Susan J. White. *An Introduction to World Methodism*. Cambridge: Cambridge University Press, 2005.

From Conflict to Communion: Lutheran–Catholic Common Commemoration of the Reformation in 2017. Grand Rapids: Eerdmans, 2016.

Joint Declaration on the Doctrine of Justification—20th Anniversary Edition. Geneva: Lutheran World Federation, 2019.

Junge, Martin. "Our Journey Ahead: Reflections on the Joint Declaration on the Doctrine of Justification." *Ecumenical Review* (2019) 252–66.

Kasper, Walter. *That They All May Be One: The Call to Unity*. New York: Continuum, 2004.

———. "The Joint Declaration on the Doctrine of Justification: A Roman Catholic Perspective." In. *Justification and the Future of the Ecumenical Movement: The Joint Declaration on the Doctrine of Justification*, edited by William G. Rusch, 12–22. Collegeville, MN: Liturgical, 2003.

Kessler, Diane C., ed. *Receive One Another: Hospitality in Ecumenical Perspective*. Geneva: WCC Publications, 2005.

Lutheran World Federation, *The Biblical Foundations of the Doctrine of Justification: An Ecumenical Follow-Up to the Joint Declaration on the Doctrine of Justification*. New York: Paulist, 2012.

Murray, Paul D. "Introducing Receptive Ecumenism." *Ecumenist* 51/2 (2014) 1–8.

———, ed. *Receptive Ecumenism and the Call to Catholic Learning: Exploring a Way for Contemporary Ecumenism*, Oxford: Oxford University Press 2008.

"Notre Dame Consultation Statement" in *Joint Declaration on the Doctrine of Justification—20th Anniversary Edition*, 55–58. Geneva: Lutheran World Federation, 2019.

Rusch, William G. *Ecumenical Reception: Its Challenge and Opportunity*. Grand Rapids: Eerdmans, 2007.

———. *Justification and the Future of the Ecumenical Movement: The Joint Declaration on the Doctrine of Justification*. Collegeville, MN: Liturgical 2003.

Ryan, Gregory A. "The Reception of Receptive Ecumenism." *Ecclesiology* 17 (2021) 7–28.

Synthesis: Together to Holiness. Lake Junalaska, NC: World Methodist Council, 2010.

Underwood, Kieren. "Pope Francis's Lutheran Reconciliation on Reformation Anniversary." *The Trumpet*, Nov 5, 2016. Available at https://www.thetrumpet.com/article/14296.19.0.0/religion/christianity/pope-franciss-lutheran-reconciliation-on-reformation-anniversary (accessed 2 September 2024).

Volf, Miroslav. "Living with the 'Other.'" *Journal of Ecumenical Studies* 39/1–2 (2002). 8–25.

———. "A Vision of Embrace: Theological Perspectives on Cultural Identity and Conflict." *Ecumenical Review* 47/7 (1995) 195–205.

Wainwright, Geoffrey. *Is the Reformation Over? Catholics and Protestants at the Turn of the Millennia*. Milwaukee, WI: Marquette University Press, 2000.

———. "The Lutheran–Roman Catholic Agreement on Justification: Its Ecumenical Significance and Scope from a Methodist Point of View." *Journal of Ecumenical Studies* 38 (2001) 20–42.

———. "World Methodist Council and the Joint Declaration on the Doctrine of Justification." *Pro Ecclesia*. 16/1 (2007) 7–13.

Wesley, John. *Sermons on Several Occasions*. London: Epworth, 1948.

Wicks, Jared, SJ. "Lutheran–Roman Catholic World Level Dialogue: Selected Remarks." In. *Celebrating a Century of Ecumenism*, edited by John A Radano, 55–76. Geneva: WCC Publications, 2012.

6

From Suspicion to Gratitude

Pentecostal Perspectives on Receptive Ecumenism

CHERYL BRIDGES JOHNS

INTRODUCTION

RECEPTIVE ECUMENISM REPRESENTS A shift from traditional ecumenical dialogue in that it focuses on a more radical openness to the other in order to learn from the other. In Receptive Ecumenism there is openness to acknowledging the Holy Spirit as the key agent in uniting the body of Christ as well as the power of the Holy Spirit to transform the church. In light of Receptive Ecumenism's openness to the Spirit, this chapter addresses the question, "Is there a place for Pentecostals within this ecumenical space?" If so, what might that space look like?

ECUMENISM IN TRANSITION

At the close of the twentieth century people were using phrases such as "the ecumenical winter" to describe loss of optimism and energy that once characterized the quest for the visible unity of the church. At that time, Konrad Raiser best summed up the mood: "The contemporary movement is marked by uncertainty, stagnation, and a loss of direction and vision.

There is even little shared understanding of what is meant by the word *ecumenical*.[1] Raiser saw the proper label for that time as "transition."

For Pentecostals such as myself, this period of transition was one in which we developed a hermeneutic of suspicion regarding the capacity of traditional ecumenical structures to authentically engage our movement. In my plenary address at the first international meeting of the Global Christian Forum in 2007 (Limuru, Kenya), I used the words of Matthew Arnold to define what I understood to be the state of the ecumenical movement: "We are living in a past that is dead and a future unable to be born." I also noted that "[a]s never before, we are in need of a rebirth for the sake of the visible unity of the church."[2] At that time, it was my desire to see a greater unity between the global North and the global South. I suggested that each part of world-wide Christianity had gifts to offer to the other, and that the churches of the North and the South should be seen as "equal partners in shaping the ecumenical future." To accomplish this vision, I offered the tasks of re-conception, re-visioning, and conversion. Re-conception involves taking stock of the resources found within the North as well as the South. The task of re-visioning requires the ecumenical movement to discern the paradigm shifts necessary in following the Spirit's leading of the churches. The task of conversion requires what Andrew Walls describes as "not substituting a new element for the old—or adding a new element to the old, but changing the direction of what is already there."[3]

I understood this definition of conversion as being in line with the call at the WCC Assembly in New Delhi (1968) for death and re-birth, but I underestimated the investment that had been given to traditional ecumenical structures. My call for death and re-birth was not received well. As a matter of fact, people were pretty upset. Many of those present at this meeting saw me as someone seeking to burn down the ecumenical house.

In 2007 there were hints about the ending of the ecumenical winter and the arrival of a new season, but those signs were hard for some to grasp. The old wineskins had been dependable. Many people thought they just needed adjusting to adapt to the changing face of global Christianity. The structures of the old ecumenical wineskins were built at a time when Christianity was centered in the Global North. For most of the twentieth

---

1. Raiser, *Ecumenism in Transition*, 33.
2. See Bridges Johns, "When East Meets West and North Meets South," 473.
3. Walls, "Eusebius Tries Again," 21.

century, churches of the Reformation dominated ecumenical discussions. Beginning in the early part of the twentieth century, the Orthodox joined in various ecumenical initiatives. Their participation may be characterized by both common agreement and a great deal of dissent.[4]

At Edinburgh 1910, Pentecostalism was only a tiny blip on the screen. But, by the end of the twentieth century the landscape had drastically changed. The formal ecumenical movement represented only twenty per cent of worldwide Christianity. Through the latter part of the twentieth century, in awareness of these changes, leaders of the ecumenical movement invited those "others" such as Roman Catholics, Evangelicals, and Pentecostals to the ecumenical table. As one of those who entered the movement in the early 1990s, it became clear that Pentecostals were being invited to a table as guests. It was not our table, and the grammar of those who sat around it was foreign language we needed to learn.

The belief that Pentecostalism represented more of a sociological than a theological movement has been one of the main hindrances in engaging Pentecostals as full participants in formal ecumenical discussions. To many, Pentecostals represented a "haven of the masses," or "religion among the oppressed." Another blinder was the idea that Pentecostalism represented a spirituality devoid of deep theological underpinnings—a sort of worship vibe. Sarah Wilson, for instance, in her study of bilateral dialogues writes about Pentecostalism that "it's not terribly helpful to think about the differences between the Lutherans and Pentecostals as primarily doctrinal . . . since Pentecostalism so often assumes a basic Reformation Protestant outlook as the foundation for their own particular contributions."[5]

In spite of these blinders, during the latter part of the twentieth century, effort was made to include Pentecostals in ecumenical structures such as Faith and Order and various other divisions of the World Council of Churches. Pentecostals were often part of bilateral and multilateral dialogues. But, at other times, the idea that Pentecostalism represented a spirituality rather than a theological development contributed to the idea that the best thing Pentecostals could add to the ecumenical movement was some sort of "devotional flavor." For instance, in many ecumenical

---

4. For a good overview of the Orthodox participation in the WCC see Held, "Orthodox Participation in the WCC."

5. Wilson, "Six Ways Ecumenical Progress is Possible." David Sang-Ehil Han offers an insightful analysis of Wilson's "ecumenical blinders." See Han, "Changing Paradigms in Global Ecumenism," 127.

gatherings it became a common practice to invite local Pentecostals to "showcase" their worship, as if they were a novelty to be experienced and not authentic theological dialogue partners. No wonder some of us developed a hermeneutic of suspicion.

A good example of this remarkable oversight can be seen as late as 2006 at the World Council of Churches General Assembly in Porto Alegre, Brazil: When I received a copy of the program, I noticed that the plenary sessions were devoted to themes such as economic justice, Christian identity in a pluralistic world, church unity and the future of ecumenism, youth and overcoming violence. All of these topics represent crucial issues in the world and in the life of the churches, but what a missed opportunity to explore the new forms of Christianity emerging in the Global South! This is not to say that Pentecostals were not present in the work of this Assembly. They were there and contributed to the discussions.

The organizers of Edinburgh 2010 went to great lengths to include what they saw as the five main streams of Christianity: Catholic, Orthodox, Protestant, Evangelical, and Pentecostal. Furthermore, there was effort to include representatives from Asia, Europe, Latin America, North America, and Africa. During the conference Pentecostals got together and drafted a statement, part of which read:

> We appreciate that Pentecostals are recognized in a positive way. At the same time, we leave with the challenge to find fuller expressions of global Pentecostalism in an ecumenical context. We also noticed a disparity of the language used and concerns expressed between the Global North and Global South. We must be careful that the academic voices of the North do not wash away the narrative claims of the South. As Pentecostals we are acquainted with both linguistic traditions, we realize that we can play an important role as bridge builders.[6]

Through the years, there have been those who made concerted efforts to understand the unique gifts and challenges that Pentecostals bring to global Christianity. Richard Shaull, who in his address at the 1966 World Council of Churches Conference on Church and Society, called for a "conversion to the poor,"[7] was one of the first to see the

6. Quoted in: Ma, Kärkkäinen, Asamoah-Gyadu, eds., *Pentecostal Mission and Global Christianity*, 7.

7. Richard Shaull, "Order, Power, and Politics," World Conference on Church and Society (Geneva, Switzerland), July 13–14, 1966. Shaull spent the latter years of his life

major theological distinctions of Pentecostalism, especially as the movement is configured in the Global South. In the late 1980s, Shaull returned to Brazil where decades earlier he had helped construct the Base Communities movement. Upon returning, he found a vastly different landscape than the one he left.

Shaull identified four major challenges that Pentecostals present to historic churches of the Reformation:

- To accomplish the movement of the Spirit in a church of the poor.
- To discern new dimensions of the nature of God's redemptive action in the world.
- To explore the meaning of salvation as a new *experience* of liberation for the poor.
- To recapture the power of the Spirit for the reconstruction of life here and now.[8]

Shaull concluded that the soteriology of Pentecostalism in the Global South was drastically different than that of the North. Coming out of the Reformation, Protestantism emphasizes salvation as redemption from the guilt of original sin. Among Brazilian Pentecostals, the focus on the human problem is how humanity is often "poor, impotent, and condemned to insignificance." In this regard, salvation is less about a forensic identity and more about "the presence and power of the resurrected Christ and of the Holy Spirit as the source of life and hope, the power to make it through each new day, and the guarantee of victory over demonic forces."[9] Shaull summarized this vision of salvation as the "reconstruction of life in the face of death."

Wes Granberg-Michaelson is another ecumenist who has made efforts to explore Pentecostalism as well as the ever-widening gap between Christianity in the Global North and that of the East and South. In his book, *From Times Square to Timbuktu*, Granberg-Michaelson observes that the churches of the formal ecumenical movement and those that are part of Pentecostal, independent, evangelical, and indigenous

---

investigating Pentecostalism, in particular, Pentecostalism in Brazil. It was at that time that he had a "third conversion," namely to the religion of the poor. See Shaull and Cesar, *Pentecostalism and the Future*. See also Barreto, "Understanding Richard Shaull's Third Conversion."

8. Shaull and Cesar, *Pentecostalism and the Future*, 123.
9. Shaull and Cesar, *Pentecostalism and the Future*, 145.

churches have functioned in two separate spheres. This divide, which is both doctrinal and stylistic, is "the most pressing challenge to the unity of the church in the twenty-first century."[10]

As it became clearer that the existing ecumenical structures were unable to support the changing landscape of global Christianity, in 1998 Konrad Raiser asked that Hubert Van Beek launch an investigative committee to explore the contours of a separate space. Van Beek relentlessly pursued this task, making great effort to dialogue with Evangelicals and Pentecostals as to the nature and methodology of a new ecumenical space. At that time, I was impressed with Van Beek's genuine humility and willingness to hear the concerns of non-WCC Christians. In 2000 Van Beek convened a meeting of sixty leaders from various traditions for a meeting in Pasadena, California. This meeting helped launch what was to become the Global Christian Forum.

The methodology of the Global Christian Forum differs from traditional ecumenism in that the Forum calls for the grammar of narrative, the telling of stories in order that the Spirit of Christ be recognized in the other. Pentecostals and other Christians from the global South have found a place within this framework. In his account of being at the first international Global Christian Forum meeting in Limuru, Daniel Okoh, International Chairman of the Organization of African Instituted Churches (OAIC) wrote, "leaders of AICs identified with the practice of telling stories of our faith journeys because in Africa story telling is a major means of communication in all spheres of life. It gave members of all the Christian Traditions opportunity to interact with one another in an atmosphere of fraternal love."[11]

About the same time as the emergence of the Global Christian Forum, Paul Murray envisioned a new way for churches to come together in the quest for unity: Receptive Ecumenism. As with the Global Christian Forum, Receptive Ecumenism, with its emphasis upon authentic dialogue and sensitivity to the Holy Spirit, offers a possible space for Pentecostals to engage other Christians.

---

10. Granberg-Michaelson, *From Times Square to Timbuktu*, 19.
11. Okoh, "I was in Limuru."

FROM A HERMENEUTIC OF SUSPICION TO A HERMENEUTIC OF GRATITUDE

The rise of the Global Christian Forum as well as the emergence of Receptive Ecumenism are signs of what may be called "the ecumenical spring."[12] The jury is still out regarding how Pentecostals will impact these two movements, but I do have hope that we can make some significant contributions. This hope is a move from a hermeneutic of suspicion to one of gratitude.

During the latter part of the twentieth century, when Pentecostals were included in ecumenical gatherings and structures, we were often given the task of relating our "otherness" to their "sameness." We were asked to give a "Pentecostal perspective" on things. "In other words, most of our energy was placed in defining who we were and how we fit into the ecumenical journey. We were the 'hobbits' on the ecumenical quest, invited but considered strange and irrelevant."[13] A significant change occurred at the first international gathering of the Global Christian Forum in that two plenary speakers were Pentecostal, Wansuck Ma and myself. It's significant to note that we were not asked to give a "Pentecostal Perspective on the Global Christian Forum." We were asked to speak as if we were an integral and founding part of the Forum who were capable of giving direction to this gathering. *For many of us, acknowledging this hermeneutical difference is critical for the future of ecumenism.*

The methodology of Receptive Ecumenism, namely the dual tasks of asking what we need to learn from other traditions and seeking to discern what gifts we offer to others, is a concrete expression of what I called for in Limuru. In anticipation that Receptive Ecumenism offers a way ahead for the ecumenical movement, in this chapter I attempt to step back into the larger conversation with gratitude. Following a brief assessment of the epistemology of Receptive Ecumenism, I will attempt to model its methodology from the stance of my own tradition. Murray describes Receptive Ecumenism as offering the possibilities of "real growth and real change within each of the churches, and not just warmer and better relationships between the churches." It offers what he insightfully describes as an "ecumenism of wounded hands." Notes Murray, "We show our wounded hands to the other in the hope that

---

12. Banks. "Hopes for an Ecumenical Spring."
13. Bridges Johns, "Re-modeling our Ecumenical House," 150.

the other can minister to each other from their strengths."[14] It is my understanding that Pentecostals offer many gifts to the global church. It is also my understanding that Pentecostals have wounded and sometimes, even dirty hands.

A BRIEF ASSESSMENT OF THE EPISTEMOLOGY OF RECEPTIVE ECUMENISM

Receptive Ecumenism is not meant to replace the methodology of more formal engagements. Rather, in the words of Murray, Receptive Ecumenism seeks to put the ecumenical movement's "formal theological aspect back clearly in its proper place as the critical-constructive faculty of diagnosing, re-imagining, and testing in the way of Christian life."[15] In this sense, Receptive Ecumenism not only offers an alternative methodology, but it also offers a needed corrective to the epistemology of traditional ecumenism. For the most part, the work of Faith and Order as well as bilateral dialogues, have been grounded in what may be called a theory-to practice way of knowing. Dialogues are held and papers are written teasing out the nuances of doctrine and ecclesial polity. Following these dialogues, the work is distributed to the churches for reception. Sometimes documents such as "Baptism, Eucharist, and Ministry" (1982) garner years of receptive engagement, while others seem to slip through the radar of church leaders, and especially the laity.

During the mid-to late twentieth century, the *praxis* epistemology of liberation theologies offered its own challenge to the ecumenical movement. In response to Shaull and other voices, such as Paulo Freire, the WCC began to see that the quest for Christian unity could not be separated from the work of constructing more humane forms of human community, and that it is exactly in the pain of injustice and oppression that reflection needs to begin. Praxis epistemology differs from theory to practice in that it asks for reflection and action to be integrated into a whole. During my doctoral program I studied with Paulo Freire and wrote my dissertation as a response to his work.[16] Freire was critical of traditional Roman Catholicism as well as Pentecostals. He saw these expressions of Christianity as "opiates," and as he pointedly told me, they are "death loving." Over the years Freire suffered major

---

14. Murray, "Receptive Ecumenism's Distinctive Contribution."
15. Murray, "Receptive Ecumenism as a Leaning-in," xxiii.
16. See Bridges Johns, *Pentecostal Formation*.

disappointments when the educational programs he helped set up in emerging democracies were overtaken by new authoritarian regimes. As Karl Marx warned, revolutionary praxis has a way of hardening into ideology. The new "transforming" ideology can easily become oppressive, and yes, even "death loving."

The Achilles heel of praxis is its inability to acknowledge that human reflection and action is often tainted by self-interests. In our quest to transform the world we are often blinded by our own desires for power, and we frequently fail to see the whole picture. While praxis is an important and necessary epistemological element for the ecumenical movement, I believe it needs to find a deeper epistemology, a way of knowing that is more faithful to the biblical witness. This way of knowing may be summed up using the phrase of philosopher Martha Nussbaum: "love's knowledge."[17]

The Hebrew word for knowing, *yada*, conveys a knowing characterized by relationship. Instead of the Greek form of *theoria*, which conveys a "standing back from" in order to know, *yada* conveys embrace. *Yada* is a form of love's knowledge that is centered in the affections. Thus, we see how the Apostle John kept reiterating that one does not know God unless they love God. Likewise, one does not know another person unless they love that other person. *Yada* involves emotions, but it is more than that. The affections are at the core of being human. They unify mind, heart, and action.

When a pneumatic dynamic is added to *yada*, our knowing of the world takes on another dimension. As seen in the Paraclete Sayings of John 14–15, the Holy Spirit is sent to the disciples as the "second Jesus." The Spirit would lead them into all truth and reveal the world. The epistemology of Pentecost is one in which knowledge is taken out of the hands of the philosopher-kings and distributed to "all flesh." It's a radical epistemology, one that is able to be more critical than the critical reflection offered in praxis. In this sense, it is not helpful to place the Holy Spirit in the ghetto of the emotions. The logic of the Spirit is that which holds the possibility of leading to great scientific discoveries as much as compelling us to love the world. Furthermore, the criticism of the Spirit supersedes the knowing subject's ability to know and read the world. This way of knowing is not antirational; it is trans-rational, inviting all the faculties of critical reasoning, while at the same time,

---

17. See Nussbaum, *Love's Knowledge*.

open to the dimension of eternity. As James K.A. Smith writes: "This incipient epistemology is not *antirational,* but antirationalist; it is not a critique or rejection of reason as such but rather a commentary on a particularly reductionistic model of reason and rationality, a limited, stunted version of what counts as 'knowledge.'"[18]

Smith sees in Pentecostal spirituality "a sort of inchoate epistemic grammar, perhaps best described as a hermeneutic—a tacit understanding of what constitutes 'knowledge' and the means by which we know." It is a spirituality that offers a critique of "idolatrous constructions of reason—rational*isms* of various stripes."[19] Smith's analysis of the epistemology found in Pentecostalism closely relates to Walter Hollenwegers's assessment that Pentecostal religion, especially that found among the poor, "tears down the cathedrals of the intellect."[20]

I see signs that Receptive Ecumenism offers possibilities for the way of love's knowledge. Elizabeth Welch observes: "Receptive Ecumenism is about identifying the Spirit's presence at work in each other and, through that identification, being led by the Spirit towards the communion which is God's gift."[21] Welch goes on to point out that the renewed emphasis on the Trinity has opened possibilities of seeing how the relationality found within God and flowing outward toward creation, serves as the ground for our knowing. She makes the observation that in order to have the depths of communion we must acknowledge the transformative power of the Holy Spirit. When seen in this light, knowledge is a gift. It is the form of knowing that refuses to objectify the world, and in that refusal, opens the possibility of communion.

I love Murray's description of Receptive Ecumenism as a "leaning-in to the Spirit of Loving Transformation."[22] In this phrase he captures the essence of the human response to God's invitation to participate in his economy toward the healing of all creation. Murray draws attention to the center of this response residing in what St. Bonaventure would refer to as *affectus*. This way of knowing "is a spiritual practice and mode of understanding which needs to be explicitly theologically inflected, reflected, shaped, and scrutinized throughout by the power of intellect (*intellectus*) and reason (*ratio*). Working in inextricable association with

18. Smith, *Thinking in Tongues*, 53.
19. Smith, *Thinking in Tongues*, 53.
20. Hollenweger, "The Social and Ecumenical Significance of Pentecostal Liturgy."
21. Welch, "The Holy Spirit and Communion."
22. Murray, "Receptive Ecumenism as Leaning-in," *xv–xxiii*.

the receptive spiritual soul of Receptive Ecumenism is a beating theological heart and intentional mind-set."[23]

Receptive Ecumenism calls for love's knowledge that invites critical, constructive analysis. It does not, as Murray points out, substitute the hard work of analyzing, probing, and criticizing. It is important, however, that such thoughtful engagement is framed within the bounds of epistemic humility—an acute awareness of one's inability to truly know the world apart from the Spirit's transforming presence. *It is my understanding that epistemic humility is the key to Receptive Ecumenism.* When we are open to see ourselves in the eyes of the other, and to receive their reading of us as a gift rather than as a threat, we can move toward authentic unity. Thus, Receptive Ecumenism calls for both self-knowledge as well as knowledge of the other, a looking within as well as a looking outward.

WE BRING THESE GIFTS IN WOUNDED HANDS

Murray points out that Receptive Ecumenism is a "matter of starting with honest, repentant recognition of one's own tradition's significant difficulty in some specific regard and, with this clearly in view, then turning with a sense of urgent need to examine what might be potentially helpful in another tradition in some equally specific regard."[24] In this last section of my paper, I would like to offer, briefly, a Pentecostal expression of Receptive Ecumenism. I do so, knowing I cannot adequately represent a complex and highly diverse worldwide movement. I can, however, faithfully speak as someone situated in the movement for many decades and as a student of its theologies. First, I will discuss what I consider to be three important gifts of Pentecostalism. Second, I will testify of the wounded hands that hold these gifts, in hope that together, we can find healing.

We Bring These Gifts

Pentecostals bring gifts to the ecumenical table. For the purposes of this paper, I will identify three gifts of Pentecostalism: the possibility of re-enchantment of Christianity, a Spirit-Christology, and the possibility of serving as interlockers between the global North and South.

---

23. Murray, "Receptive Ecumenism as Leaning-in," *xvi*.
24. Murray, "Receptive Ecumenism as Leaning-in," *xx*.

The Possibility of Re-enchantment

Charles Taylor describes the modern world as "disenchanted." Disenchantment has been a long process of de-centering from the sacred canopy of the cosmos, as well as a process of centering humanity as *the subject* over the world. Prior to the Enlightenment, people "lived in an enchanted world, one that was filled with divine presence. This presence could, at any time, impinge upon their daily lives."[25]

We have discovered that in order to join the march of progress, disenchantment is a heavy, but seemingly necessary burden to bear. Speaking to science students at Munich University in 1917, Max Weber admonished: "the fate of our times is characterized by rationalization, and above all, by the 'disenchantment of the world.'"[26] Weber went on to say that if the students could not bear this burden, they could "return to the arms of the old churches."

As Weber would point out, Protestant Christianity was an active partner in the dis-enchantment project. During the late nineteenth century and up to the mid-twentieth century Christians, especially Protestant Christians, were eager to join in the scientific revolution. What is often missed is how much fundamentalist Protestantism, especially that which later became known as "the Princeton School," was an attempt to fit Christianity into the scientific paradigm. During the same year as Weber's lectures, American theologian, B.B. Warfield addressed a group of Presbyterian seminary students. He attempted to rid them of any sense of the supernatural world, believing these miracles and divine intervention left the earth with the apostles. Warfield warned the students to avoid "heathen modes of thought." By this he meant Roman Catholicism and the newly emerging Pentecostal movement. During the twentieth century both liberal Protestantism and fundamentalist Protestantism sought to become accepted as part of the rational and scientific project. As a result, at the beginning of the twenty-first century, Protestants are poor stewards of the great mystery of the Gospel.

We are at a point in human history in which there's a growing longing for re-enchantment. Smith describes this longing as "haunting." He uses the words of novelist Julian Barnes, the poster child of British secularization, to describe this feeling: "I don't believe in God, but I miss

---

25. Taylor, *The Secular Age*, 25.
26. Weber, "Science as Vocation," from Max Weber. *Essays in Sociology*, 155.

him."[27] Haunting can be seen in the popularity of grand myths such as *Lord of the Rings* and *Harry Potter*. It's also found in people returning to pre-Christian religions as well as the number of Protestants returning into the arms of "the old churches."

Pentecostalism arose at the height of the modern project, but in many respects, it represents a protest to its iron cage. Harvey Cox describes this Pentecostal protest as "revenge upon the secular city."[28] It is my understanding that Pentecostals can help re-enchant Christianity by bringing back mystery and by offering a worldview that affirms "the dynamic, active presence of the Spirit not only in the church, but also in creation."[29]

The Pentecostal vision of the inter-relational dynamics of the natural and the supernatural worlds have implications for a vision not only of Christian unity, but also that of cosmic unity. This cosmic unity is the quest of the feast of Pentecost, namely re-uniting that which has been separated: heaven and earth, men and women, and different ethnicities. Pentecost also unites the natural elements—wind, fire, and human bodies into cosmic harmony. Most Pentecostals fail to see the cosmic implications of their movement. However, I believe that Pentecostalism has the potential to help nurture the harmony of creation, one envisioned by Hildegard of Bingen: "Fire has flames and sings in praise of God. Wind whistles a hymn to God as it fans the flames. And the human voice consists of words to sing paeans of praise. All creation is a single hymn in praise to God."[30]

Re-enchantment is but one gift of Pentecostals to the body of Christ and to the world at large. I consider this gift to be one of our most precious ones. There are signs that Pentecostals are grasping the enchanting power of their movement. Theologians such as Amos Yong, James K.A. Smith, Wolfgang Vondey, and Daniela Augustine are teasing out the dynamic pneumatic epistemological, ontological, and socio-political implications of Pentecostal theology.[31]

---

27. Smith, "From Ex-carnation to Re-enchantment."

28. Cox, *Fire from Heaven*.

29. Smith, *Thinking in Tongues*, 39. See also Bridges Johns, *Re-enchanting the Text*.

30. Hildegard of Bingen, *Analecta Sacra*, 352. Quoted in: Schipperges, *Hildegard of Bingen*, 27.

31. See Smith, *Thinking in Tongues*; Stephens, ed. *An Amos Yong Reader*; Augustine, *The Spirit and the Common Good*. Bridges Johns, *Re-enchanting the Text* is my offering to this emerging conversation.

Renewal of Spirit Christology

The flourishing of Trinitarian theology has made way for the re-emergence of Spirit Christology. Telford Work points out that the reduction and separation of the Spirit from the ministry of Christ can be traced to an over-reaction to Christological adoptionism, a belief that the "Son's sonship was mistakenly perceived to have begun at some point in his earthly life through the coming of the Holy Spirit."[32] He notes that this over-reaction led to a stress on the Son's sonship and the Spirit's role as proceeding from the Father and the Son. This stress created a minimalizing of the Spirit's role in the Trinitarian life and in the ministry of Christ.

A Spirit Christology offers the understanding that Jesus did nothing apart from the Holy Spirit. It helps to recover the understanding of the Spirit as the One who "conceives, anoints, and empowers Jesus's work in the created order, not just the One who points to it and carries it on in Jesus's absence."[33] A common misunderstanding about Pentecostals is that we over-emphasize the Holy Spirit, but if you were to look carefully at our written material, especially that from our early days, it is easy to see that it is Jesus who is the focus of our affections. The basic Pentecostal paradigm of the "Five-Fold Gospel": Jesus as Savior, Sanctifier, Baptizer in the Spirit, Healer, and Coming King, leaves little room to imagine that we neglect Christology in favor of Pneumatology. What we do offer is the intimate connection between the Holy Spirit and the ministry of both the Incarnate Jesus and the Jesus sent to us by the Spirit. We have a vision of the real presence of Jesus, one who by the power of the Spirit, continues to walk among us, saving, healing, and delivering. Shaull's research in Brazilian Pentecostalism led him to conclude that the movement offered "the Spirit as present in history of the resurrected Jesus." Writes Shaull: "*In Pentecostalism, poor and broken people discover that what they read in the Gospels is happening NOW in their midst. This same Jesus is present with them, doing what he did in Galilee two thousand years ago . . . He is present in the world, doing in their lives and communities what he did then—through the Holy Spirit.*"[34]

In terms of the work of ecumenism, a Spirit Christology helps to bridge the gap between the more *Logos* centered discussions and the search for the depths of *koinonia*. We could say that just as Jesus did nothing

---

32. Work, *Living and Active*, 111.
33. Work, *Living and Active*, 113.
34. Shaull, *Pentecostalism and the Future*, 185.

apart from the Spirit, we too cannot become one without the Spirit, and that the work of the Spirit among us can be seen in both the critical engagement of dialogues as well as in times of shared testimonies, fellowship, and shared mission. In addition, as participants in the quest for Christian unity, Pentecostals do not want to remain in the ecumenical movement's "Spirit-ghettos" of heart-felt worship or zeal for mission.

Pentecostals as Interlockers

In the Pentecostal statement at Edinburgh 2010, we offered ourselves as bridge builders between the academic voices of the North and the narrative voices of the South. Out of necessity, Pentecostals who are involved in the ecumenical movement have learned to be bilingual. When I arrived at the 1993 World Conference on Faith and Order in Santiago de Compostela, I was introduced to an elder in the Faith and Order Movement. He greeted me warmly and then said: "I would encourage you to work hard to learn the language of Faith and Order. After a while, you will fit right in." What he did not think to add was: "What language do you bring to the table, and how might we learn from you how to speak that language?"

Thirty years have gone by since that conversation, but I often think of it. In many ways the ecumenical movement has made great strides in learning the languages of those churches that have not historically been represented within its ranks. On the other hand, there is a long way ahead, one characterized by epistemic humility and the willingness to speak in other tongues. To this end, Pentecostals can offer help in bridging the gap in ecumenical discourse. We can help build a future in which the primary discourse is not dominated by the vocabulary of the global North, as well as one in which those from the global South acquire a new vocabulary.

With Wounded Hands

Writes Murray: "The process of attending in the Spirit to the difficulties in our own tradition can break up the ground and awaken a sharpened sense of need in us which can prepare us for the recognition of attractive graced gift in the other."[35] In light of this comment, I would like to close this paper by attending to some reflection of two difficulties I see present within the Pentecostal tradition: failure to live out the gift

---

35. Murray, "Receptive Ecumenism as Leaning-in," *xxi*.

of radical inclusion, and alignment with fundamentalist theology and forms of Christian Nationalism.

In spite of its many gifts, all is not well within the Pentecostal movement. We have grown numerically faster than we have matured. As a result, we are often like adolescents on a quest for identity—going after every new fad, rapidly exchanging theological partners, and looking for affirmation in all the wrong places.

The Loss of the Gift of Radical Inclusion

At its inception, the movement was graced with, using terms from David Tracy, "the sheer excess of gift." In 1907, the Azusa Street meeting, known as the primal heart of the movement, stood in stark contrast to the dominant U.S. society. In an age of Jim Crow, with its violence against blacks, the gathering was led by William Seymour, a black man. Many other ethnicities were part of this mission. Before women could vote in national elections, at Azusa Street women as well as men served as leaders. The meeting was also characterized by the mixing of people from various socio-economic backgrounds.

As the years passed, in the United States, the sheer excess of Azusa Street was difficult to maintain. There were no holding containers for such radical expressions of the Christian faith, and eventually the movement adapted to normative societal patterns. I once heard an African American bishop lament that "[h]ad Pentecostals held on to the gift of racial unity, there might not have been need for the March on Washington."[36]

In other areas of the world, the radical inclusiveness of Pentecostalism can be seen in varying degrees. For instance, in Latin America, the "liberation of the laity" and the empowerment of women have been a driving force in the movement's growth. However, if we look closely, we can see how Pentecostal churches, in their alignment with populist and sometimes authoritarian leaders, have looked the other way regarding the loss of human rights.

---

36. This comment was made in the address of bishop George D. McKinney at the "Pilgrims on the Sawdust Trail" gathering at Beeson Divinity School, October 3, 2001.

Identifying with Fundamentalism and Nationalism

Across the globe, in reaction to perceived threats of liberal democracies, religious fundamentalism is on the rise. Pentecostals have not been immune to seeking safety within the confines of the binary thinking represented in rigid doctrinal ideology. Writing in 1998, Cox noted that Pentecostalism, with its emphasis on experience, was in many ways antithetical to fundamentalism's rigid orthodoxy. He rightly pointed out the antagonism early Pentecostals experienced at the hands of fundamentalists, and how it was a mistake to lump Pentecostalism together with the category of "fundamentalism." He also noted that feeling they had to make a choice between liberalism and fundamentalism, some Pentecostals, especially those in the U.S., worked to find affinity with fundamentalist theologies. For Cox, it remained to be seen if Pentecostals would continue to offer an experiential "third way" between fundamentalism and liberalism.[37]

Today, due to fear and insecurity, many Pentecostals are letting go of their "third way" and aligning themselves with fundamentalist theologies, especially those related to Christian Nationalism. In countries such as the U.S and Brazil, Pentecostals have adopted the talking points of what is known as the "Religious Right." The Religious Right represents a merger between fundamentalist theology and right-wing political ideology. In some cases, it is hard to tease out the political from the theological, for they have become one and the same. A growing number of Pentecostals are longing for a "strongman" to protect them, and this longing is woven together with a combative theology, leaving little room for nuance and dialogue.

In this terrible marriage, the relational, dynamic, and inclusive faith of Pentecostalism is being lost in favor of the perceived safety of hardened ideology. In the U.S. some Pentecostals have anointed Donald Trump as their savior and are willing to employ violence to help him return to power. Unfortunately, Pentecostals are some of the most ardent supporters of the right to own tactical, military style weapons, such as the AR15. In this sense, Pentecostals have not only wounded hands, our hands are stained with the blood of many innocent children. Speaking as a U.S. Pentecostal, I am aware of how we are in need of both healing and cleansing, and I come to this gathering with a broken heart and grief. Yet, I also come in hopeful awareness that the Holy Spirit is

---

37. Cox, *Fire from Heaven*.

even now at work sanctifying and uniting the church. I am filled with gratitude for the diversity of gifts found in the worldwide body of Christ as well as this new ecumenical day.

In summary, I see many possible intersections between Receptive Ecumenism and Pentecostalism. Openness to the Spirit, authentic dialogue, and the stated purpose of "leaning-in to the Spirit of Loving Transformation," offer points of serious engagement. On the other hand, I am left with questions. "How much of Receptive Ecumenism continues to operate out of the ethos of disenchanted modernity? Will those who lead and participate in this form of ecumenical dialogue be willing to let go of what Charles Taylor describes as the "buffered self," an understanding of the human as tightly bounded, "giving its own autonomous order to its life,"[38] and be open to the trans-rational and the mysterious? Christians are stewards of the mysteries of God (1 Cor 1:4). It is my hope that Receptive Ecumenism will continue to be a steward of the mystery of Christian unity.

BIBLIOGRAPHY

Augustine, Daniela. *The Spirit and the Common Good: Shared Flourishing in the Image of God.* Grand Rapids: Eerdmans, 2019.

Banks, Adelle M. "Hopes for an Ecumenical Spring." *Christian Century* (March 15, 2012).

Raimundo C. Barreto. "Understanding Richard Shaull's Third Conversion: Encountering Pentecostalism Among the Poor." *Koinonia* 16 (2004) 161–75.

Bridges Johns, Cheryl. *Pentecostal Formation: A Pedagogy Among the Oppressed.* 1998. Reprint, Eugene, OR: Wipf & Stock, 2010.

———. *Re-enchanting the Text: Discovering the Bible as Sacred, Dangerous, and Mysterious.* Grand Rapids: Baker Academic, 2023.

———. "When East Meets West and North Meets South: The Reconciling Mission of Global Christianity." In *The Ecumenical Movement: An Anthology of Key Texts and Voices,* edited by Michael Kinnamon, 472–75. Geneva: WCC Publications, 2016.

Cox, Harvey. *Fire from Heaven: The Rise of Pentecostal Spirituality and the Re-shaping of Religion in the Twenty-First Century.* Cambridge, MA: Da Capo, 1995.

Granberg-Michaelson, Wes. *From Times Square to Timbuktu: The Post-Christian West Meets the Non-Western Church.* Grand Rapids: Eerdmans, 2013.

Han, David Sang-Ehil. "Changing Paradigms in Global Ecumenism: A Pentecostal Reading." In *Pentecostal Theology and Ecumenical Theology,* edited by Peter Hocken, Tony Richie, and Christopher Stephenson, 111–30. Leiden: Brill, 2019.

Held, Heinz Joachim. "Orthodox Participation in the WCC: A Brief History." *Ecumenical Review* 55 (2009) 295–312.

Hollenweger, Walter. "The Social and Ecumenical Significance of Pentecostal Liturgy." *Studia Liturgica* 8/4 (1971–1972) 207–15.

---

38. Taylor, *The Secular Age,* 38–39.

Ma Wonsuk, Veli-Matti Kärkkäinen, and Kwabena Asamoah-Gyadu, eds. *Pentecostal Mission and Global Christianity*. Regnum Edinburgh Centenary Series 20. Oxford: Regnum, 2014.

Murray, Paul D. "Receptive Ecumenism as a Leaning-in to the Spirit of Loving Transformation." In Vicky Balabanksi and Geraldine Hawkes, eds. *Receptive Ecumenism: Listening, Learning, and Loving in the Way of Christ*, xv–xxiii. Adelaide: ATF, 2018.

———. "Receptive Ecumenism's Distinctive Contribution," Presentation at "'Heeding the Spirit: New Horizons in Receptive Ecumenism,'" online conference, 17 June 2021. Available at https://www.durham.ac.uk/research/institutes-and-centres/catholic-studies/research/constructive-catholic-theology-/receptive-ecumenism-/resources-and-publications-/.

Nussbaum, Martha. *Love's Knowledge: Essays on Philosophy and Literature*. Rev. ed. Oxford: Oxford University Press, 1992.

Okoh, Daniel. "I Was in Limuru: Global Christian Gathering in Limuru—My Story." In *Global Christian Forum*. https://globalchristianforum.org/i-was-in-limuru/ (accessed 2 September 2024).

Raiser, Konrad. *Ecumenism in Transition: A Paradigm Shift in the Ecumenical Movement?* Translated by Tony Coates. Geneva: WCC Publications, 1991.

Schipperges, Heinrich, ed. *Hildegard of Bingen: Healing and the Nature of the Cosmos*. Princeton: Wiener, 1997.

Shaull, Richard and Waldo Cesar. *Pentecostalism and the Future of the Christian Churches*. Grand Rapids: Eerdmans, 2000.

Smith, James K.A. "From Ex-carnation to Re-enchantment: Why Imagination is Crucial to Mission." Public Lecture, Dallas Theological Seminary, November 8, 2018.

———. *Thinking in Tongues: Pentecostal Contributions to Christian Philosophy*. Grand Rapids: Eerdmans, 2010.

Taylor, Charles. *The Secular Age*. Cambridge: Harvard University Press, 2007.

Walls, Andrew. "Eusebius Tries Again." In *Enlarging the Story: Perspectives on Writing World Christian History* edited by Wilbert R. Shenk, 1–21. 2002. Reprint, Eugene, OR: Wipf & Stock, 2011.

Weber, Max. *Essays in Sociology*. Oxford: Oxford University Press, 1946.

Welch, Elizabeth. "The Holy Spirit and Communion, Shaping Receptive Ecumenism." In *Receptive Ecumenism: Listening, Learning, and Loving in the Way of Christ*, edited by Vicky Balabanksi and Geraldine Hawkes, 49–60. Adelaide: ATF, 2018.

Wilson, Sarah Hinlicky. "Six Ways Ecumenical Progress is Possible." *Concordia Journal* 39/4 (2013) 1–23.

Work, Telford. *Living and Active: Scripture in the Economy of Salvation*. Grand Rapids: Eerdmans, 2001.

Yong, Amos. *An Amos Yong Reader: The Pentecostal Spirit*. Edited by Christopher A. Stephenson. Eugene, OR: Cascade Books, 2020.

7

Lutherans and Pentecostals in Dialogue
A Happy Marriage?

Johannes Habib Zeiler

SETTING THE SCENE

Cheryl Bridges Johns's excellent chapter on Pentecostalism in this volume points to the fact that the ecumenical landscape has undergone significant changes over the last twenty years. Pentecostals participate in and contribute to the ecumenical movement in general and to the vibrant and growing research field on Receptive Ecumenism in specific. Bridges Johns provides us with crucial snapshots that, put together, provide essential hermeneutical keys for those of us who encounter and dialogue with Pentecostals, as we try to understand the inner dynamics of the movement and articulate what could be learnt and held as common concerns across and beyond denominational borders.

My response will be divided into two separate parts. While the first part deals with three clusters of questions emanating from Bridges Johns's chapter, the second part identifies contemporary challenges among Lutherans across the globe. I argue that Lutherans and Pentecostals in this regard share similar, if not identical, challenges and therefore may find it fruitful to explore, address, and encounter many of these issues together.

I have had the privilege to participate in Lutheran–Pentecostal conversations, both on a global level and nationally in Sweden over the last decade.[1] Additionally, my academic background in Mission studies and World Christianity studies has widened my horizon concerning what is at stake. Pentecostals are found in many places, impacting, shaping, inspiring, and provoking every single church tradition all around the globe. Bridges Johns situates and problematizes the distinctiveness of Pentecostalism in a rapidly changing society and its diverse relationships with other Christian churches and traditions.

In her chapter, Bridges Johns does what Pentecostals often do, namely she gives a powerful testimony that is based on personal *experience* of an encounter with the living God, a testimony that is *relational* in character and that invites us to "walk and talk" together, a testimony that is opening a window to a *new reality* that is yet to be discovered, in this case an ecumenical engagement for the days and years to come. The institutional and individual dimensions are tightly knit together, clearly showing that the church never exists in general but always in particular.

PENTECOSTALISM IN WORLD CHRISTIANITY

My first point deals with Pentecostalism in world Christianity. Bridges Johns's way of mapping the diverse Pentecostal encounters with the ecumenical movement worldwide can be related to the African Pentecostal theologian Ogbu Kalu's ground-breaking study on African Pentecostalism in which he claims that the Pentecostal story "must be woven into the broader tapestry of Christian presence" and regional or local responses, not least when it comes to those voices that are not heard, marginalized, even silenced.[2] Bridges Johns sketches the contours of contemporary Pentecostalism in a global setting. She points to the fact that Pentecostalism is diverse and changes over time, is attentive to local contexts, guided by the Scriptures, driven by experience, cultivates distinct pastoral practices and theologies, and appears in different shapes depending on where and when it is studied. There is no doubt that many Pentecostal churches across the globe are strong civil society actors, heavily engaged in education and health services and thereby impacting the world. As Bridges Johns indicates, Pentecostalism should not be homogenized but always taken seriously and be acknowledged

---

1. Grenholm et al., "Lutherans and Pentecostals."
2. Kalu, *African Pentecostalism*, vii.

as a significant part of world Christianity. The field of Pentecostal studies has grown immensely over the last decades, and research is often carried out within different academic disciplines and from different perspectives, combining various methods in order to analyze a broad range of empirical data in the form of oral and textual sources.

But what about the future tracks and directions of Pentecostalism? Given that Christianity worldwide is diverse and poly-centric, that God's mission is multi-directional, what will Pentecostalism be like in, say, thirty years? Bridges Johns elaborates on three Pentecostal gifts to world Christianity: the possibility of re-enchantment; a Spirit Christology; and the possibility of serving as interlocutors between the so-called global South and North. What learning could be drawn *within* Pentecostalism from these three challenging gifts?

PENTECOSTAL IDENTITIES

My second point deals with the many underlying assumptions on the identity and self-understanding of Pentecostalism. Bridges Johns raises crucial questions on what it means to be respected and recognized as church, both in relation to other churches across the globe and within the Pentecostal tradition at large. Whether Pentecostals talk about themselves as movement or church or a mix of these terms is a hotly debated question and Bridges Johns touches on several of these underlying, ongoing theological discussions which are vital when trying to carve out why, how and by what means Christian unity should or could be embodied.

The North American Pentecostal church historian, Cecil M. Robeck, deeply engaged in ecumenical dialogues in the context of the World Council of Churches and beyond, has for decades been advocating for Pentecostals to dialogue and cultivate trustful relationships with other churches. More recently, when addressing a Roman Catholic audience, Robeck has argued that Pentecostals have an indisputable and unique contribution to make when exploring ways toward Christian unity in today's world. Arguing on the basis of the current demographic changes in World Christianity, with the continuing rise of Pentecostal and charismatic Christians across the globe, Robeck tentatively explores the future role and function of Pentecostal/charismatic Christians from a global ecumenical perspective. He states: "I find it most helpful to think of Pentecostals/charismatics not in terms of 'Church' but as a uniquely powerful form of spirituality *within* the one, holy, catholic, and apostolic Church."[3] Robeck's argument, imagining these vibrant and rapidly growing churches as spiritual gifts and profound resources for the whole Church rather than as individual churches, is interesting and challenging both from an ecclesiological perspective and for its ecumenical implications. Robeck implicitly underlines the transformative aspects in all ecumenical endeavors, namely how and to what extent the churches involved are ready to be transformed by the Spirit and drawn out of their self-centeredness when encountering one another.

There is no doubt that the "charismatization" and "pentecostalization" of the so-called mainline churches, particularly in the global South, have paved the way for new ecumenical initiatives and learnings. The fact that a growing number of Lutherans, Anglicans, Baptists, Catholics, and Orthodox Christians understand themselves as charismatics has created a seedbed for a fruitful conversation on the role of the Spirit in the life of the church. Bridges Johns invites her readers to reflect further on Christian unity and Pentecostalism and the fact that all Christians claim the presence/activity of the Spirit. How may Christian unity be expressed in a fragmented and polarized world today and in the future?

JOINT WITNESS AND SERVICE

My third point deals with joint witness and service. In line with Bridges Johns's references to early twentieth-century Sweden and the strong Pentecostal engagement in democracy when advocating for full participation of men and women in church and society, it is worth mentioning the current links and relationships between Lutherans and Pentecostals, not least when it comes to the powerful advocacy work that is carried out in the context of the Christian Council of Sweden on migration, climate justice, and the public debate on religious rights and freedom of speech. Whether they understand themselves as primarily confessional or experiential, conservative or liberal in their theological understanding, the churches—in all their diversity—come together and speak with one voice for the sake of the common good in society.

The Lutheran theologian, Kenneth Appold, co-chair of the six-year Lutheran-Pentecostal Study Group which was initiated by the Institute for Ecumenical Research in Strasbourg, underlines in a report from 2010 that the teaching and practice of the many gifts of the Spirit must be at the center in Lutheran–Pentecostal conversations. He argues:

---

3. Robeck, "Can We Imagine," 66.

Lutherans can learn from Pentecostals that charisms are in fact bestowed upon all Christians and are not limited to particular offices. Those charisms, furthermore, are diverse. Lutherans need to do a better job not only of acknowledging them but also of integrating them into the life of the church."[4]

From there, Appold takes the field of *diakonia* as a crucial example of how such charisms are put into practice. He defines *diakonia* as Christ-inspired service, dependent upon charisms. In other words, diakonia depends on the full range of spiritual gifts and on those people who receive and exercise these gifts—contributing to the Christocentric approach to service, to encountering Christ in the neediest and least fortunate among us.

The process of discerning what the Spirit calls the churches to say and do in a certain situation or context requires therefore a robust curiosity and a radical openness for each other's "otherness." We all know this is hard work and a risky business to engage in. Someone's otherness is easily seen as an exotic element and, as Bridges Johns indicates, in relation to Pentecostal engagement in the ecumenical movement, thought to be something that needs to be tamed or normalized through adaptation or assimilation into an even greater "sameness."

Speaking powerfully on the move from a hermeneutic of suspicion to one of gratitude, Bridges Johns reminds me of what is expressed in the second ecumenical imperative in the Lutheran–Catholic document *From Conflict to Communion*, which could be applied in all ecumenical encounters and fits perfectly in the context of Receptive Ecumenism. It states: "Lutherans and Catholics must let themselves continuously be transformed by the encounter with the other and by the mutual witness of faith."[5]

Bridges Johns underlines the importance of taking spiritual and pastoral practices from local situations as a crucial departure point for joint theological reflection and mutual learning. I very much resonate with that. Interestingly, some of the most recent Lutheran initiatives on a global level have, as far as I understand, methodologically speaking, been based upon the principles of Receptive Ecumenism without even mentioning the term and its underlying theory and method. The global Lutheran Pentecostal Dialogue as well as the most recent study process on Lutheran identities carried out by the Lutheran World Federation,

---

4. Appold, "Lutheran Reactions," 84.
5. *From Conflict to Communion*, 88.

have both an empirical and praxis-oriented approach when analyzing the role of the Spirit in the life of the church in dialogue with other Christian traditions.[6]

What could the churches learn from their mistakes, when things go wrong—sometimes terribly so—particularly regarding issues linked to certain pastoral practices, such as exorcism and deliverance ministries, which often are embedded in biblical narratives and enforced through specific religious rituals? When the Lutheran–Pentecostal dialogue met for its fourth meeting in Antananarivo, Madagascar, in order to reflect on the practice and ministry of healing we were invited to a Lutheran prayer service. The characteristics of a "typical Lutheran" or a "typical Pentecostal" were no more. To put it mildly, we were all confused and some of us were upset, while others tried to adjust or adapt to the cultural, ritual and liturgical practices on site. Afterwards, we tried to understand what had taken place before our eyes. New questions were brought to the table: on the necessity of discerning the spirits, on the misuse and abuse of power, on biblical principles for sound ministries for healing when not having access to proper health care and hospitals. Animated discussions followed. And it was the Pentecostals who offered us guidance, who gave us a critical corrective, and guided us forward.

In other words, I believe that Lutherans have so much to learn from Pentecostals and indeed we need each other's experience, encouragement, and critique. However, having said that, Lutheran–Pentecostal relations are yet to be further explored. Over the last decade, the Lutheran World Federation has published several study documents that relate to issues that both Lutherans and Pentecostals would identify as key though these have not yet been sufficiently analyzed in the dialogue between the two traditions. The second part of this chapter, therefore, highlights four areas in which Lutherans could benefit and learn vastly from Pentecostalism through mutual reflection and common action.

MISSION AND MINISTRY AS PUBLIC EVENTS

The LWF study document *The Church in the Public Space* from 2016 situates the church and its missionary task in its wider societal context.[7]

---

6. For example: Lange et al. *International Lutheran–Pentecostal*; Rimmer and Peterson, *We Believe*.

7. As the document deals with the self-understanding of the church and its role in society it also shed light on issues related to a theology of mission which correspond well to many of the leading perspectives and thoughts outlined in the LWF mission

In line with contemporary Lutheran discourse, mission is understood as "holistic mission." Based on the teaching in the Bible and guided by the gifts of baptism and Holy Communion, Christians are called to serve in mission "in proclamation, prophetic diakonia and advocacy work, of which its voice in the public space is an integral part."[8] The document points out that there is no contradiction between mission and the engagement in the public space. The missionary task of the church goes beyond the walls of the church and is carried out in the public sphere. In other words, the proclamation of the gospel is a fundamentally public endeavor. For this to happen, however, it is essential for the church to continuously "listen to the Word of God."

Clearly, the document draws special attention to the fact that the Christian church has a public dimension. Guided by its vision of "the common good" the church speaks and acts outside as well as inside its walls. God's mission brings life in abundance to all people, not only to church members. The document states: "When churches isolate themselves from the broader concerns of their societies they lose the chance to be salt and light to the world (Matt 5:13–16)."[9] Five areas in which the church engages in the public sphere are mentioned: engagement for refugees, overcoming exclusion (overcoming racism, advocating just relationships etc.), gender justice, climate justice, and peaceful inter-religious relations.[10]

Through its presence and its various activities, the church may contribute to "creating public space that is inclusive, just and peaceable."[11] Moreover, the document examines the theological rationale for its public and contextual engagements. In this regard the baptismal vocation becomes the key through which Christians are sent to the world as participants of God's mission. The gifts of baptism and Holy Communion thus guide, direct, shape, and strengthen the church's witness.

AREAS OF CONTESTATION AND NEGOTIATION

The fact that the largest Lutheran churches in the world today are found in sub-Saharan Africa signals the dramatic demographic changes during

---

document *Mission in Context*.

8. *Bible Life Lutheran Communion*, 18.
9. *Church Public Space*, 16.
10. *Church Public Space*, 29–30.
11. *Church Public Space*, 11.

the last century: World Christianity has moved from the Northern hemisphere to the global South with clear implications for Lutheran perceptions on mission and ministry.[12] As already noted, mission is polycentric in nature and, through the missionary activities in churches worldwide, carried out in various geographical directions. The Indian theologian Sathianathan Clarke points out that "the missional turn of Christian identity and practice in contemporary world Christianity has come from the local, non-Northern, post-Western communities."[13]

When the LWF General Secretary Martin Junge in 2014 addressed an international audience of Lutherans under the heading "A Communion of Churches in Mission" he called the churches across the globe to participate on equal terms.[14] All churches and missionary agencies, he argued, regardless of their geographical location, would find themselves "both at the sending and the receiving end" at one and the same time.[15]

Mission as accompaniment, as a joint venture, has thus come increasingly to the fore. But with new metaphors come new demands in terms of developing adequate structures for mutual reflection, learning, and transnational cooperation, not least when dealing with asymmetrical power relations (related to financial or human resources, decision making and so on.) Therefore, many churches are actively seeking ways for mutual reflection and sharing as an expression of the interdependency upon one another as churches in mission. The idea of "reverse mission" (various mission initiatives from the South to the North), different exchange programs for youths, or global partner consultations in various forms have been implemented in several LWF member churches in order to underline the significance of the poly-centric character of mission.

Along similar lines, issues related to biblical hermeneutics have recently been identified as of crucial importance.[16] As indicated in the study document from 2016, *The Bible in the Life of the Lutheran Communion*, the fact that Lutherans hold the Bible in high esteem does not imply that there are no disputes about the Bible or how it could or should

---

12. The estimated number of church members presented on the LWF website; Ethiopian Evangelical Church Mekane Yesus (10.4 million members) and Evangelical Lutheran Church in Tanzania (7.9 million members). https://www.lutheranworld.org/content/member-churches (accessed March 8, 2023).
13. Clarke, "World Christianity," 197.
14. Jukko and Rusama, *Your Kingdom Come*.
15. Jukko and Rusama, *Your Kingdom Come*, 41.
16. *Bible Life Lutheran Communion*.

be interpreted in different contexts.[17] The document ends with five recommendations under the following headings: reaffirm the Lutheran emphasis that the heart of the Bible is its salvific message; commit ourselves to learning from one another globally about the ways in which the Bible can best be heard in our diverse contexts; commit ourselves to ongoing dialogue about points of biblical interpretation on which members of the LWF disagree; commit ourselves to supporting theological education that effectively prepares pastors, teachers and leaders to interpret the Scriptures, and; commit ourselves to encouraging the Church to recognize the Bible as a resource for social commitment.[18]

The message of *The Bible in the Life of the Lutheran Communion* has clear implications for how churches within the Lutheran communion relate to one another in their joint participation in God's mission. As noted in the document, Lutherans are called to proclaim the Gospel "to all nations" (Luke 24:46–47).[19] Issues related to the interpretation of the Bible, the fact that its message is culturally and contextually bound, have become important identity markers for many of the Lutheran churches across the globe. The issue of biblical hermeneutics thus could not be ignored when striving for bilateral/multilateral church relations. For instance, it was important for the Church of Sweden as well as for the Ethiopian Evangelical Church Mekane Yesus to outline their respective principles and views on the interpretation of the Bible and the practical consequences thereof after having re-negotiated their relationship due to the issue of same-sex marriages.[20]

---

17. The document argues that there are a number of controversies within the Lutheran communion today that are related to "the right interpretation of the Holy Scripture and its consequences for our respective contexts," for example, the ordination of women and questions of sexuality. See: *Bible Life Lutheran Communion*, 8–9.

18. *Bible Life Lutheran Communion*, 29–30.

19. *Bible Life Lutheran Communion*, 29.

20. The Ethiopian Evangelical Church Mekane Yesus (EECMY) still accepts financial support for its diaconal engagements from the Church of Sweden and from the Evangelical Lutheran Church in America. However, sending missionaries to the EECMY or contributing financially to projects such as theological education has, at least for the time being, come to an end. See the following link: https://www.lutheranworld.org/news/elca-global-mission-and-eecmy-dassc-sign-memorandum-understanding (accessed March 8, 2023)

RELIGION AND DEVELOPMENT

The academic field of "religion and development" has rapidly increased over the last decades. A growing body of research has drawn attention to the role of the churches across the globe when encountering the marketization of the field of education or the social and health services.[21] Issues related to how and why churches and Christian communities understand themselves as agents of societal change have been hotly debated. On what grounds do they motivate, legitimize, and operationalize their various engagements in society as health providers, as owners of schools, colleges and universities, or as actors within the field of agriculture and sustainable development?

Lutheran churches in the Global South motivate such engagements in terms of holistic mission for which they seek funding and support amongst their global partners. But the idea of keeping proclamation and service together, as an expression of God's holistic mission, is challenged by complex structures and policies from the donor community urging them to differentiate, even separate, these two aspects. Since the Lutheran churches in the Nordic countries, for instance, are heavily dependent on state funded money when administering many of the development projects in the Global South, they implicitly work with this differentiation in mind. Simply put, the state might be willing to financially support local development projects related to the refugee camps in South Sudan or to particular health institutions in Latin America whereas funding for projects dealing with bible schools, church planting, or ministerial formation have to be sought elsewhere. The present structure has clear implications—for all parties involved—for how terms such as "religion," "church," "mission" or "development" are thought of and articulated in official applications and documents. One might think that this practical aspect would be a minor technicality but it is of significant importance for the churches involved to further reflect on how holistic mission is actually talked about, theologically argued, and practically embodied in order for them to keep the different "dialects" comprehensively together in one single language.

ENCOUNTERING "THE OTHER"

Today many Lutheran churches across the globe find themselves challenged, even threatened and disturbed, by the presence of "a religious

---

21. Tomalin, "Introduction," 1–13; Deacon and Tomalin, "A History," 68–79.

other" be it Muslims or Pentecostal/Charismatic Christians. Issues on freedom of religion, religious extremism, and proselytism particularly have been mentioned in this regard as crucial issues for further reflection.

The Pentecostal theologian Veli-Matti Kärkkäinen indicates that it is of crucial importance for Pentecostals to further elaborate upon the issue of religious pluralism in relation to mission.[22] Their missionary zeal and openness to the Spirit, the fact that mission is highly experiential and relational in character, might serve as a significant departure point, he argues, to open up a new and wider perspective on mission when encountering people of other faiths. A similar perspective has been cultivated in the Roman Catholic context suggesting that the role of the Spirit in relation to the idea of mission could be seen as a clear invitation for further collaboration and reflection amongst "all people of good will."

What Kärkkäinen suggests for the Pentecostals could also apply to Lutherans, not least in the light of what the LWF 2004 mission document *Mission in Context* states about a Trinitarian approach to the concept of mission and its implications for interfaith dialogue: "a Trinitarian approach may provide the possibility of underlining the uniqueness of Christ, while at the same time confessing to the Holy Spirit's influence outside the church and God's work in creation and in other religions."[23] The document thus reaffirms the well-known position from the WCC Mission and Evangelism Conference in San Antonio (1996): "We cannot point to any other way to salvation than Jesus Christ; at the same time we cannot set limits to the saving power of God."[24]

Such Trinitarian "roominess," as Sathianathan Clarke wants to call it, opens up a new approach also within and between churches around the world when building vital links and establishing relationships with one another.[25] In his article on World Christianity and postcolonial mission, Clarke argues that the time has come for "ecumenicals" and "evangelicals" to search for a common witness and service in the world. He points out that both the Lausanne Movement and the Commission on World Mission and Evangelism (CWME) in their respective documents on mission take the Trinity as the departure point when elaborating a theology of mission.[26] Additionally, Clarke argues, these documents indicate that

22. Kärkkäinen, "Pentecostal Theology."
23. *Mission in Context*, 40.
24. *Mission in Context*, 40.
25. Clarke, "World Christianity," 204.
26. Clarke, "World Christianity," 199; *Cape Town Commitment*; *Together Towards Life*.

the marginalized in society play a significant role in the mission of the church as they are "agents of mission" and signal "the prophetic role" of the church.[27] The Roman Catholic theologian Stephen Bevans offers a similar perspective on mission in his analysis of the WCC mission document from 2013, *Together Towards Life*.[28] The Spirit is the principal agent of mission, he argues, calling and challenging the churches to "finding out where the Spirit is working, and joining in."[29] Clarke and Bevans eagerly invite churches of various denominational affiliations to further reflect upon how mission and evangelism may be creatively linked and intertwined in a dialectic relationship with one another.

CONCLUDING REMARKS

Cheryl Bridges Johns's profound contribution to the field of Receptive Ecumenism in this volume comes very timely given the significant influx from the Pentecostal and Charismatic churches to the wider ecumenical conversations worldwide over the last decades. It may provide Christians across the globe with inspiration, direction, and an important corrective as they discern what the Spirit is calling them to do, say and pray in today's world. Seen from that perspective, Lutheran–Pentecostal relations have the potential to grow, flourish, and journey together as one people of God into the future.

BIBLIOGRAPHY

Appold, Kenneth G. "Lutheran Reactions to Pentecostalism. A US Case Study." In *Lutherans and Pentecostals in Dialogue*, 58–84. Strasbourg: Institute for Ecumenical Research, 2010.
Bevans, Stephen. "Mission of the Spirit." *International Review of Mission* 103/1 (2014) 30–33.
The Bible in the Life of the Lutheran Communion. A Study Document on Lutheran Hermeneutics. Geneva: Lutheran World Federation, 2016.
The Cape Town Commitment. A Confession of Faith and a Call to Action (2011). https://www.lausanne.org/content/ctc/ctcommitment.
The Church in the Public Space. Geneva: Lutheran World Federation, 2016.
Clarke, Sathianathan. "World Christianity and Postcolonial Mission: A Path Forward for the Twenty-first Century." *Theology Today* 71 (2014) 192–206.

---

27. Clarke, "World Christianity," 203; Clarke refers to the following documents: *Cape Town Commitment* and *Together Towards Life*.

28. Bevans, "Mission of the Spirit," 30–33.

29. Bevans, "Mission of the Spirit," 30–33.

From Conflict to Communion. Lutheran–Catholic Common Commemoration of the Reformation in 2017. Leipzig/Paderborn: Evangelische Verlagsanstalt/Bonifatius, 2016.

Deacon, Gregory, and Emma Tomalin. "A History of Faith-based Aid and Development." In *The Routledge Handbook of Religions and Global Development*, edited by Emma Tomalin, 68–79. Routledge International Handbooks. London: Routledge, 2015.

Grenholm, Cristina, Johannes Habib Zeiler, and Ulrik Josefsson. "Lutherans and Pentecostals in Dialogue: From Local to Global." *Pneuma* 43 (2021) 250–72.

Jukko, Risto, and Jakko Rusama, eds. *Your Kingdom Come: The International Mission Partnership Consultation of the Evangelical Lutheran Church of Finland, Järvenpää, Finland, March 21–April 3, 2014.* Publication of the Evangelical Lutheran Church of Finland 12. Helsinki 2014.

Kalu, Ogbu. *African Pentecostalism: An Introduction.* Oxford: Oxford University Press, 2008.

Kärkkäinen, Veli-Matti. "Pentecostal Theology of Mission in the Making." *Journal of Beliefs and Values* 25/2 (2004) 167–76.

Lange, Dirk G., et al. *International Lutheran–Pentecostal 2016-2022 Dialogue Statement: "The Spirit of the Lord Is Upon Me."* Geneva: Lutheran World Federation, 2023.

Messenger, Jack, et al. *Mission in Context: Transformation, Reconciliation, Empowerment. An LWF Contribution to the Understanding and Practice of Mission.* Geneva: Lutheran World Federation, 2004.

Robeck, Cecil M. "Can We Imagine an Ecumenical Future Together? A Pentecostal Perspective." *Gregorianum* 100 (2019) 46–69.

Rimmer, Chad M., and Cheryl M. Peterson, eds. *We Believe in the Holy Spirit: Global Perspectives on Lutheran Identities.* Leipzig: Evangelische Verlagsanstalt, 2021.

Together Towards Life: Mission and Evangelism in Changing Landscapes (2012). In *Together Towards Life: Mission and Evangelism in Changing Landscapes—with a Practical Guide*, edited by Jooseop Keum, 1–40. Geneva: WCC Publications, 2013.

Tomalin, Emma. "Introduction." In *The Routledge Handbook of Religions and Global Development*, edited by Emma Tomalin, 1–13. Routledge International Handbooks. London: Routledge, 2015.

8

Ecumenism—Receptive and Cruciform

Elizabeth Woodard

INTRODUCTION

It is easy for ecumenists to consider our work finished. The era of anathematizing each other is, to a great extent, in the past. As I read the ecumenists of the past hundred years as a doctoral student at the Catholic University of America, however, I became convinced that it is as urgent a matter as ever. I decided to write my doctoral dissertation on this topic, which led me to a study of the Anglican–Lutheran dialogues of the 1990s. I defended my dissertation in 2017, the proclaimed 500th anniversary of the Reformation, and subsequently published it as *Cruciform Ecumenism*.[1] I called it this because I noticed that various ecumenists all had various adjectival claims to how ecumenism will reach its goal. I encountered missional ecumenism, that is, ecumenism based on acknowledging diverse Christians' common mission to preach the Gospel of Christ. John Armstrong is an important author in this respect. I encountered Receptive Ecumenism; ecumenism based on the principle of openness to the gifts of fellow Christians' ways of living the faith. Paul Murray first introduced me to this when I wrote to him to ask him to review my book. This is how I ended up writing this chapter. I felt, as one does when publishing a first book, that I needed to offer something new to the conversation,

---

1. Woodard, *Cruciform Ecumenism*.

something that would go past sharing, past receiving, past partnering, past anything already done, anything that allowed a potential reader to think we had "done enough," and rest in the easy and incomplete peace of our yet undivided faith. What power could be so great? I concluded: only the cross itself. This chapter aims to elaborate on this approach, and to place it into dialogue with the wider field of Receptive Ecumenism.

Only the power of the cross is capable of modeling true ecumenism for us. Consider, first, the identity of this crucified God. God is unified, while also being diverse. The Son was crucified, not the Father; they are not interchangeable. In God is a legitimate diversity. We know the Spirit is not the Father, and the Son is not the Spirit, yet they each are God. How is this unity-in-diversity held? Through perfect love. And how is it that you and I are invited into that perfect unity-in-diversity, that perfect love? Through the cross. Cruciformity is literally the shape of the divine love. It is the way you and I are sanctified and justified and brought from our brokenness into the wholeness, the very identity for which we were made.

And so, I decided, this is the only way to envision ecumenism as well. The way to unity with God cannot be other than the way to unity with each other. God opens his heart to us all; true, "In my Father's house there are many rooms," but there is only one house, and we must live peacefully within its walls. Cruciform ecumenism would go beyond tolerating one another's differences, and even beyond celebrating them. If it does not require sacrifice on my part, indeed, if it does not require a certain dying on my part, then it isn't the cross. Cruciform ecumenism, in short, invites us into unity with one another the same way the cross invites us into unity with God, and the same way that marriage invites spouses into unity with one another: through sacrifice.

In this chapter, I want to answer the question Paul Murray asked me: how much should we be willing to sacrifice? It is a good question; one we must take seriously. There are arguments that some might consider extreme, such as Ephraim Radner's *The End of the Church: A Pneumatology of Christian Division in the West*,[2] which takes the logic I just presented and uses it to justify an end to the institutional Church altogether. His beginning is not unlike my own: Christ sacrificed himself, and we make an idol of the Church when we refuse to do the same. This is, of course, not what I mean by cruciform ecumenism. True, Christ's cross took his life, but

---

2. Radner, *The End of the Church: A Pneumatology of Christian Division in the West*.

only insofar as it made way for eternal life. Simply deleting formal church structures isn't the solution. But I insist, clinging with rigidity to current structures at the expense of Christian unity, especially on the part of my own Catholic Church, without any sense of the Scriptural call to find your life only by losing it is to be obtusely bereft of the Spirit of God.

CRUCIFORMITY IN ANGLICAN-LUTHERAN DIALOGUE

At this point, I need a concrete illustration of what cruciform ecumenism looks like in practice. A wonderful example can be found in the aforementioned Anglican-Lutheran dialogues of the 1990s, which, in the US, Canada, and Northern Europe, resulted in *full visible* unity among the denominations. To be more specific about the dialogues about which I speak, I am referencing the following documents:

- Canada: 1998 *Called to Full Communion*[3] comes from the work done by the Joint Working Group of the Evangelical Lutheran Church in Canada and the Anglican Church of Canada in December of 1997.

- US: The Division of Theological Studies, Lutheran Council in the U.S.A., and the Standing Commission on Ecumenical Relations of the Episcopal Church conversed with each other from 1978–80 to produce the 1981 *Lutheran—Episcopal Dialogue*[4] (LED) and the 1991 *Toward Full Communion & "Concordat of Agreement."*[5] This last document was rejected by six votes, but the 1999 *Called to Common Mission: A Lutheran Proposal for a Revision of the Concordat of Agreement*[6] was accepted.

- Europe: The 1993[7] *Porvoo Common Statement*, representative of work between British and Irish Anglican Churches and Nordic and Baltic Lutheran Churches.

---

3. The Joint Working Group of the Evangelical Lutheran Church in Canada and the Anglican Church of Canada, *Called to Full Communion*.

4. Division of Theological Studies, Lutheran Council in the U.S.A. and the Standing Commission on Ecumenical Relations of the Episcopal Church. Cincinnati, *Lutheran—Episcopal Dialogue: Report and Recommendations*.

5. Norgren, Rusch, *"Toward Full Communion" and "Concordat of Agreement": Lutheran Episcopal Dialogue Series III*.

6. Evangelical Lutheran Church in America, *Called to Common Mission*.

7. *Together in Mission and Ministry*.

- International: *The 1987 Niagara Report* by the Anglican–Lutheran International Continuation Committee.

Each of these documents, in one way or another, summarizes their major roadblock to visible unity as being a question of authority. This is why my dissertation, and a giant part of the book, *Cruciform Ecumenism,* focuses on apostolic succession as a sort of case study. How did two denominations—Anglicanism and Lutheranism, who had such different views on authority—enter into full communion with one another?

Another way to put the question: When we survey the landscape of the world's denominations, what keeps us divided? Common answers might be: the relationships of Scripture and Tradition, women's ordination, gay marriage, the openness of the communion table. One central element stands at the center of all of these: authority. As an apostolic church, we claim that our authority comes from the apostles, that we have not created a church of our own, but that we aim to preserve the church the apostles handed on to us. Therefore, the fundamental question is: who is in charge *now* to define answers to these questions? In other words, who decides? Who are the ones guarding the apostolic faith?

The episcopate, that is, the exercise of leadership specifically in the office of bishop, is understood in Catholic and Anglican theology to be the locus of apostolicity. Successive generations of bishops who were ordained by bishops, who themselves were ordained by bishops and so on, back to the first bishops who were ordained by the apostles through the efficacious symbol of the laying on of hands, have handed on the apostolic faith and the gift of the Holy Spirit to one another. Authority rests there. This concept of historical episcopal succession is, for Catholics and Anglicans, the very locus of apostolic succession. The historic episcopate is, in short, constitutive of apostolic succession.

Other denominations (notably Lutheran), however, do not see the historic episcopate as the essential locus of apostolicity. Rather, they believe that the Holy Spirit has preserved the integrity of Christ's teachings, as handed on to the apostles, in the entirety of the faith, teachings, and practices of the Church. It does not reside exclusively in the episcopal office.

This is it. This is the whole disagreement. And hundreds and hundreds of pages of ink are spent arguing each side. Now, those pages are less of interest to us now than the pages that reveal how we might overcome these varying understandings, so I will jump right to that.

Anglicans posed a simple solution: that Lutherans be re-ordained by Anglican bishops, thereby legitimizing them. This, of course, was objectionable to Lutherans, who felt it asked them to sacrifice their definition of legitimacy. The Lutheran conversation partners had an instinct, therefore, to dig in their heels against the idea of historic succession being important *at all* in the church, let alone as the guarantor of apostolicity. They eventually moved enough to admit that historical episcopal succession could be a "sign, though not a guarantee" of apostolic succession. But ultimately, they maintained that historic succession doesn't guarantee that the integrity of the faith has been upheld. They use examples such as legitimately ordained Arian bishops to prove the point.

For decades, this is as far as it went. But in the 1990s, something happened. It happened in Canada. *Called to Full Communion* cites a piece written for the 1993 first joint Eucharist service.

A Tale of Two Sisters: A Reflection on Christian Unity:

> There once were two women, living in different countries, who discovered from old records that they were twin sisters. They had been separated when very young and sent to foster families when their own family broke up. Once they contacted each other, they began to write letters, but the letters didn't say very much. Neither of them quite trusted the other; each was afraid that the idea of a twin sister was at best a dream, and at worst some kind of scam.
>
> All that changed when they agreed to meet at their old family home, abandoned now and boarded up since the caretaker had died. They brought a picnic lunch, and as they sat in the garden and ate, their suspicions vanished. Each one, looking at the other under the apple tree, thought she saw herself— not like in a mirror, but in the flesh. They began to laugh together, to tell each other about their lives, their sorrows, their secret hopes. Then they finally summoned the courage to go into the house.
>
> It was dusty, many things were broken, and there were tangles of cobwebs and some scary dark corners. But under the debris they found things: the room they must have shared as infants, with a cot and toys still in it, and even some baby pictures of themselves. They . . . began dreaming of a way to bring children—their own sons and daughters, nieces and nephews—into the old house once again. When they parted, they promised not only to write but to meet again every year; and each swore to do

her best to find the other members of their scattered family, and to bring them as well to the next reunion.[8]

Here, I detect a shift in how the dialogues proceeded. The shift that enabled the Anglican–Lutheran dialogues to proceed differently *was not a theological one. It was an emotional one.* Suddenly, conversation partners paused their theological discussions long enough to recognize long-lost Christian brothers and sisters in the conversation partners, and somehow that was enough to shift the conversation from "here's what I'm not willing to let go of" to "here's what I can." *Nothing changed theologically.*

This led to some exciting forward movement in the dialogues. The Lutheran Conversation partners acknowledge: "Within the apostolicity of the whole Church is an apostolic succession of the ministry which serves and is a focus of the continuity of the Church in its life in Christ and its faithfulness to the words and acts of Jesus transmitted by the apostles. The ordained ministry has a particular responsibility for witnessing to this tradition and for proclaiming it afresh with authority in every generation."[9] Now, we did not spend much time on how much they argued against this, but I hope you see the significance there.

And the Anglican conversation partners, previously clinging to the sign of the historic episcopate, moved far enough to admit that apostolic succession may indeed have a broader definition than merely historic succession, and that it indeed involves the whole Church. By the mid-1990s, that side of the table "endorses the Lutheran affirmation that the historic catholic episcopate under the Word of God must always serve the gospel, and that the ultimate authority under which bishops preach and teach is the gospel itself."[10]

There is an almost imperceptible difference in theology. Neither denomination denies its aforementioned position. But they move from a position of stating that which they will not relinquish to a position of pondering what they could. The shift is more emotional, more spiritual, than theological. And yet it is intensely theological. It is a cruciform orientation to the conversation partner. And that is the crux of my point. Receptive Ecumenism rightly asks what a conversation partner has that we can receive. Cruciform ecumenism offers a next step. It asks what I,

---

8. Humboldt, *Called to Full Communion*, 38.
9. *The Porvoo Common Statement*, 40.
10. *Concordat of Agreement*, 100.

myself, can sacrifice. If sacrifice is not a part of our conversations, then how can we call them Christian?

This is what I mean by cruciform ecumenism. Not that Anglicans sacrificed the sign of episcopal succession. But that there had to be a dying to the self, of sorts, to the pride and to the comfort of what is familiar. This dying demanded new creativity. Can we do the difficult work of *wanting* to be united with each other enough to do the creative work involved?

This is how the creativity concluded in the Anglican–Lutheran dialogues. Both sides gave. They decided that, for future generations of bishops in both denominations, *both* Anglican and Lutheran bishops would lay their hands on those being ordained. This grafts all Lutheran bishops into the Anglican legitimacy within one generation while still honoring the presence of the Lutheran bishop. Look at what both sides had to sacrifice to make that work:

> Lutherans had to consent to the necessity of Anglican laying on of hands in this model.

They did not admit it was a "guarantee" of episcopal succession, but they did consent to its necessity henceforth. And Anglicans consented to acknowledge the *current* legitimacy of Lutheran clergy—that's right, the *current* generation of existing Lutheran bishops—without re-ordination.

The *Concordat* states that "the Episcopal Church hereby recognizes now the full authenticity of the ordained ministries presently existing within the Evangelical Lutheran Church of America."[11] This is a theological statement, but it was not made for theological reasons. It was made to acknowledge the legitimate path to the historic succession that these Lutherans took because *there is no other way* back to unity. The Episcopal Church declares that:

> hereby pledges, at the same time that this Concordat of Agreement is accepted . . . to begin the process for enacting a temporary suspension . . . of the 17th century restriction that 'no persons are allowed to exercise the offices of bishop, priest, or deacon in this Church unless they are so ordained, or have already received such ordination with the laying on of hands

---

11. *Concordat of Agreement*, 99.

by bishops who are themselves duly qualified to confer Holy Orders.[12]

Why temporary? Because after one generation, it would no longer be needed! The legitimacy would be restored. The Anglicans did not abandon permanently a sign that is essential to them. They simply made a way to graft the Lutherans back onto the tree of legitimacy in a way that didn't neglect their own theology.

THE CHALLENGE OF CRUCIFORM CATHOLICISM

Now my own Catholic Church would likely not be able to adopt this model, because it would immediately raise questions concerning the legitimacy of the sacraments. . Even though this single, passing generation of "illegitimate" successors to St. Peter is but the blink of an eye in God's timing, the question of legitimate sacraments is an issue in Catholicism in a way it never was in Anglicanism. And this is where I want to be sure to highlight again that cruciform ecumenism is not a sloppy casting off of essentials, but rather a disposition of sacrifice, with what *can* be sacrificed. And surely something can, no matter who the conversation partners are.

I spent extensive pages of my book examining if this model would work for Catholicism. It would be problematic for Catholics to offer the opportunity to confect the sacraments to someone not validly ordained, obviously. And yet, there are conceptual categories in which to talk about this. I spent some time looking at the difference between true invalidity and a mere "defect," for example. I did not reach a conclusive answer, but that is actually beside the point. The point is that cruciform ecumenism is not afraid to put in the work to get there, is not so busy digging in its heels about what is not permitted, that it misses the brotherhood of the people on the other side of the table. Cruciformity is, above all, an emotional and attitudinal shift before it is a theological one.

Cruciform ecumenism does not suggest we throw away matters of canon law and ecclesiastical polity in the name of unity. Such reconciliation would be shallow. Great care must be taken to retain precisely those gifts of each tradition that are given by God for the good of all his people. If Catholicism's gift is the possession of a holy law, we cannot abandon it in the name of reconciliation. Notice, too, that, in entering full communion, that is, in the sense that their clergy are

---

12. *Concordat of Agreement*, 100.

interchangeable, they do not lose their individual identities. They retained their denominational identities as Anglicans and Lutherans. Again, just as the Son is not the Spirit, the Lutheran need not become the Anglican for true unity to happen. As *Porvoo* states, "Visible unity . . . should not be confused with uniformity."[13]

We live in a broken world. And our age cries out for the saving power of the Gospel. But we mute the power of Christ and his Church when we fixate on lines that divide us. Non-Christians look at us and wonder, why should I believe a word you say about love? You clearly do not even love each other? This is the urgent problem that cruciform ecumenism seeks to rectify. We must be a model to the world of what sacrificial love looks like, the living embodiment of Christ crucified. The scandal of division threatens the efficacy of the Christian message, as Christians stand in hypocrisy when they tell the world how to love one another fully without maintaining unity among themselves. If God himself could offer himself unto death on a cross, are we exempt from seeing this as a model for our own ecumenical encounters? How can we refuse to live *kenosis*, as expressed in Philippians 2, in our ecumenical dialogues?

What right do we have to the carelessness or pride it takes to continue "murmuring and arguing" with one another?

God came into a broken world; he can therefore live in a broken church. Indeed, is not the Lord of Christians a Lord who works *primarily* through brokenness, death, and falling? What if, as Pope Francis stated, the Church is called to be "bruised, hurting, and dirty because it has been out on the streets, rather than a church which is unhealthy from being confined and from clinging to its own security?"[14] Unity with God will mean cruciformity and unity with each other. The Catholic Church needs to preserve essential Catholic orthodoxy, orthopraxy, and orthopathy, while allowing the constraints of legitimacy to stretch beyond their current limits. The power of Christ can accomplish in us what we are powerless to accomplish on our own. We need Christ and we need each other. The more we can grow in humility and love, the more we can grow in a spirit of curiosity and learning, the more we will be saved from our insular prisons. The crucifixion served as the locus for God's greatest redeeming act. May our current state of division serve for God's great power of resurrection as well. It must begin with cruciformity.

---

13. *The Porvoo Common Statement*, 23.
14. Pope Francis, *Evangelii Gaudium*, 49.

BIBLIOGRAPHY

Called to Common Mission: A Lutheran Proposal for a Revision of the Concordat of Agreement. *An agreement of Full Communion with the Episcopal Church as amended and Adopted by the Churchwide Assembly of the Evangelical Lutheran Church in America, August 19, 1999.* Chicago: Evangelical Lutheran Church in America, 1999.

Called to Full Communion: A Study Resource for Lutheran–Anglican Relations Including the Waterloo Declaration. The Joint Working Group of the Evangelical Lutheran Church in Canada and the Anglican Church of Canada, December 1997. Toronto: Anglican Book Centre, 1998.

Francis, Pope. *Evangelii Gaudium.* Vatican City: Libreria Editrice Vaticana, 2013.

Lutheran–Episcopal Dialogue: Report and Recommendations. The Division of Theological Studies, Lutheran Council in the U.S.A. and the Standing Commission on Ecumenical Relations of the Episcopal Church. Second Series 1976–1980. Cincinnati: Forward Movement Publications, 1981.

Norgren, William A., and William G. Rusch., eds. *"Toward Full Communion" and "Concordat of Agreement": Lutheran Episcopal Dialogue Series III.* Minneapolis: Augsburg, 1991.

Radner, Ephraim. *The End of the Church: A Pneumatology of Christian Division in the West.* Grand Rapids: Eerdmans, 1998.

Together in Mission and Ministry: The Porvoo Common Statement with Essays on Church and Ministry in Northern Europe. Conversations between the British and Irish Anglican Churches and the Nordic and Baltic Lutheran Churches. London: Church House Publishing, 1993.

Woodard, Elizabeth. *Cruciform Ecumenism: The Intersection of Ecclesiology, Episcopacy, and Apostolicity from a Catholic Perspective.* Lanham, MD: Lexington/Fortress Academic, 2018.

9

Discerning the Impasse
A Spirituality of Receptive Ecumenism

PAUL LAKELAND

"If a thought or a desire leads you on the road of humility, of self-abasement and of service to others, it is of Jesus; but if it leads you on the road of self-importance, of vanity and of pride, or on the road of abstract thought, it is not of Jesus." (Pope Francis)[1]

"We work in the present, not for the present." (Leon Blum)

"The Christian of the future will be a mystic, or will not exist at all." (Karl Rahner)

IN THIS CHAPTER I want to examine the parallels between Receptive Ecumenism's response to what I will call the impasse of Christian unity, and its connection to a personal spirituality adequate to respond to the social and political impasse of our world today. The virtues of the one bleed into the other, and vice-versa. It will be my contention that both, the ecclesial movement and the personal journey of faith, illustrate a way forward towards the resolution of the impasse. I will proceed by outlining Constance

---

1. Homily for Mass, Santa Marta, Vatican City, 7 January 2014.

Fitzgerald's understanding of impasse and relating it to the work of Receptive Ecumenism, suggesting how it might connect to the formation of a healthy contemporary spirituality, and finally utilizing Jesuit ideas of "the discernment of spirits" to take a small step beyond Fitzgerald's "prophetic hope" that is suggestive for the work of Receptive Ecumenism, and even, perhaps, for the fate of the earth.

But before all that, let me share with you two moments in the life of Yves Congar, OP, one of the undoubted giants of twentieth-century Catholic theology. The first was in 1937 when the young scholar, fired up with ecumenical zeal and fresh from the publication of his first book, *Divided Christendom*, was invited to participate in the Oxford Ecumenical Conference as a Roman Catholic observer. He requested permission to attend, which was denied by no less a person than Cardinal Pacelli, the future Pope Pius XII. From this point on Congar was under suspicion, suspended only during the four years he spent in a German prisoner of war camp, where presumably he could do no harm. Congar himself wrote of his relations with Rome during the decade from the end of the war until the mid-fifties as "an uninterrupted series of denunciations, warnings, restrictive or discriminatory measures and mistrustful interventions."[2] The second moment came in the mid-1950s when Congar, now a distinguished figure in the church, was silenced by papal order and sent into a kind of house arrest in Cambridge, England, under the suspicious eyes of his fellow Dominicans, who had been appointed his jailers. In 1956 he wrote to his mother on the occasion of her birthday, pouring out his unhappiness at Rome's treatment of him in a classic expression of the experience of impasse:

> Practically speaking, they have destroyed me as far as it was possible for them. Everything I believed and had worked on has been taken away: ecumenism, teaching, conferences, working with priests, writing for *Temoignage Chretien*, involvement in conventions, etc.
>
> They have not, of course, hurt my body; nor have they touched my soul or forced me to do anything. But a person is not limited to his skin and his soul. Above all when someone is a doctrinal apostle, he is his action, he is his friendships, he is his relationships, he is his social outreach; they have taken all that away from me. All that is now at a standstill, and in that way I have been profoundly wounded. They have reduced me to nothing

---

2. Congar, *Dialogue between Christians*, 34.

and so they have for all practical purposes destroyed me. When, at certain times, I look back on everything I had hoped to be and to do, on what I had begun to do, I am overtaken by an immense heartsickness.[3]

Congar's experiences were of impasse, something often defined softly as "being in a difficult position in which it is impossible to make any progress," but more trenchantly by Constance Fitzgerald:

> By impasse, I mean that there is no way out of, no way around, no rational escape from, what imprisons one, no possibilities in the situation . . . Every logical solution remains unsatisfying, at the very least . . . Any movement out, any next step, is canceled, and the most dangerous temptation is to give up, to quit, to surrender to cynicism and despair.[4]

The impasse presents itself in the moment, the past is of no value for overcoming it, and if hope in the future is the only way forward, there are no signs in the moment of impasse that the future will offer anything different from the present. Just so for Congar, who had no inkling that within two years the papacy would be transformed by Pope John XXIII, and that a year later the pope would ask him to become part of the preparatory commission for planning the Second Vatican Council. The way out of his impasse, it is important to note, was not of his own doing. It was the consequence of waiting patiently on the work of the Holy Spirit, and we will shortly have more to say about this idea of waiting.

I am sure that it is not hard for Christian ecumenists to see that the past five hundred years of the Christian Church have been marked by impasse. I picked Congar as an example because he seems to me to illustrate three important forms of impasse that can affect the Christian. The first is what we can call *existential* impasse, obviously something not restricted to Christians but, as Congar's experience illustrates, easily initiated for Christians by dysfunctions in their relationship to their church. The second impasse is *ecclesial*: the sorry history of fraught and sometimes violent negativity between and among various Christian communities of faith, or indeed within any particular faith community, as old as the Church of Corinth but particularly relevant since the time of the Reformation. And the third is the *ecumenical* impasse. For at least the last hundred years some believers in many Christian churches have

---

3. Congar, *Journal d'un théologien*, 427, my trans.
4. Cited in Cassidy and Copeland, *Desire, Darkness and Hope*, 79.

worked to overcome the ecclesial impasse, only to find that their best efforts towards reunion or at least rapprochement have been stymied, often enough by the very churches they are working to heal.

Christian ecumenists are well acquainted with institutional impasse. I offer just two obvious examples. As long ago as 1967, Anglican–Roman Catholic dialogue concluded that "since the time of the Reformation, the doctrine of Eucharistic sacrifice has been considered a major obstacle to the reconciliation of the Anglican Communion and the Roman Catholic Church," but that "it is the conviction of our commission that this is no longer true."[5] And, "whatever doctrinal disagreements may remain between our Churches, the understanding of the sacrificial nature of the Eucharist is not among them." In the same year, a less uncomplicated consideration of the Eucharist in Lutheran–Roman Catholic dialogue nevertheless concluded that "despite all remaining differences in the ways we speak and think of the eucharistic sacrifice and our Lord's presence in his supper, we are no longer able to regard ourselves as divided in the one holy catholic and apostolic faith . . ."[6] However, for all the good words of Christian ecumenists, fifty-five years on we are no closer to institutional acceptance of the work of these two commissions. If ecumenists were or are discouraged, they are experiencing the same threefold impasse evidenced in Congar's career.

Enter Receptive Ecumenism. And once again (and for the last time), Yves Congar. In retrospect, Congar wrote in *Chrétiens désunis* that ecumenism was "not a speciality" and that in fact "each individual's task lay in the first place at home among his own people." "Our business," he continued, "was to rotate the Catholic Church through a few degrees on its own axis in the direction of convergence towards others and a possible unanimity with them." His fundamental assumption was eschatological, seeing reunion—and not return of the separated brethren—as something asymptotically approached in the power of the spirit. With this vision, Congar anticipated much of Receptive Ecumenism's impulses and did much to incorporate his insights into the texts of Vatican II: listening and learning rather than teaching or critiquing, patience, and a conviction that there are many ways in which church is legitimately realized.

---

5. Anglican–Roman Catholic Consultation USA (ARC IV) Statement on the Eucharist (29 May, 1967), https://www.usccb.org/committees/ecumenical-interreligious-affairs/arc-iv-statement-eucharist.

6. https://www.usccb.org/committees/ecumenical-interreligious-affairs/eucharist.

Unlike Receptive Ecumenism, he paid a heavy price for his eirenicism. In the end, of course, like other suspected theologians of his generation, Henri de Lubac and Jean Daniélou in particular, he was "rewarded" with a cardinal's hat. (Those of you not familiar with Roman practices might like to know that the cardinalate was only awarded to them once they had passed the age of 80, after which they would be ineligible to vote in a papal conclave. Though not ineligible to be elected!)

Axiomatically, then, I take it that Receptive Ecumenism is the deliberate effort to break the ecclesial and ecumenical impasses of the last century. As is evident in any summary of the key principles of Receptive Ecumenism, the intellectual and affective posture of Receptive Ecumenism is marked by an intentionality of humble learning in an atmosphere of open listening. It is not driven by a set of strategic markers or a list of accomplishments to be achieved in a one-, five- or ten-year span. The disciplined attentiveness of Receptive Ecumenism means, I think, that there are no timelines, no clarity even about ends to be achieved. It is, I suggest, the Zen of Christian ecumenism. Of course, there is hope for the future, but the kind of hope that waits on the spirit, not the kind that is checking its watch on the hour to see how much progress is being made. To the degree that Receptive Ecumenism is changing the face of ecumenism, it is inspiring a new ecumenical culture. And I would suggest that what culture means to an institution or any collective, is analogous to what spirituality means to the individual participant in the collective.

Of course, "spirituality" itself may need a word or two of explanation outside the bounds of the Catholic tradition understood broadly, just, in fact, as the term needs rehabilitation within the Catholic tradition itself. Spirituality is not just piety. It is better described in part as life lived intentionally as an expression of fundamental convictions. In Christian dress, it is life shaped by the gospel message of the love of God. And, in the words of Pope Francis, it is missionary discipleship put into practice in the field hospital at the periphery, which is what and where the church should be. But all of this profoundly pastoral activity is an empty sham if it is not matched by a contrary movement of the heart. And this *sine qua non* is the life of prayer. Intentionality must be balanced by the cultivation of consciousness and receptivity. These two together are the markers of a spirituality of self-abandonment to the spirit, as they are also the vital dialectical processes of Receptive Ecumenism.

Which brings us to Constance Fitzgerald and her discussion of both personal and societal impasse. Impasse, she writes of the individual, "becomes the place for the reconstitution of the intuitive self."[7] Her insight, drawn from the Carmelite mystical tradition of John of the Cross, is that an impasse cannot be overcome through the usual processes of reason, logic and analysis. It is of the nature of impasse that it must be addressed through "second order change," in which the experience of powerlessness can lead to igniting the imagination to a new way forward. But as Americans, (for whom she is predominantly writing), who are educated to tackle problems through the exercise of reason, analysis, statistics and so on, she says "we stand helpless, confused and guilty before the insurmountable problems of our world."[8] Climate change, pandemic control and world hunger are just three obvious examples of societal impasse calling for second order change. Up against our failures to address such apocalyptic issues, just doing things the old ways evidently doesn't work. So, asks Fitzgerald, "is it possible we are going through a fundamental evolutionary change and transcendence, and crisis is the birthplace and learning process for a new consciousness and harmony?"[9] I wish I had her hopefulness, but I heartily concur that we need such fundamental change. Not new machinery or new insights, but a change of heart, a metanoia, a true conversion.

I would of course be the last person to suggest that ecumenical deadlock is a challenge on a par with global warming, but there are lessons in Receptive Ecumenism for the wider Christian community, lessons that suggest that Receptive Ecumenism might be a propaedeutic for healing the world, an urgent move in the direction of *Tikkun olam*, the Hebrew notion of "repairing the world." The role of Receptive Ecumenism relative to the longstanding methods of ecumenical dialogue clearly shows it to be an imaginative shift away from an ecclesial and ecumenical impasse. The genius of Receptive Ecumenism is that having recognized the impasse, it has not made the mistake of using some version of the old methods that have failed, but instead has taken an altogether more contemplative approach of humble listening to the spirit. This may be the way the ecumenical winter is finally ended. But while we remain in the listening and learning posture, perhaps forever, the practitioners of Receptive Ecumenism are embraced by a novel wisdom that has much wider application. It is, in other words, in the spirituality that Receptive

---

7. Cassidy and Copeland, *Desire, Darkness and Hope*, 80.
8. Cassidy and Copeland, *Desire, Darkness and Hope*, 92.
9. Cassidy and Copeland, *Desire, Darkness and Hope*, 92.

Ecumenism has taught its adherents, that its fundamental value may lie, not only for the church but also for the world.

If Receptive Ecumenism is truly to be seen as this kind of spirituality, the only danger would seem to be that it might be accounted too passive, and here, finally, is where Ignatian discernment plays its part. The *Spiritual Exercises* of St. Ignatius of Loyola are intended to lead the exercitant to "a decision about a state of life." The process of discernment of spirits helps to distinguish between the good and bad urges that play a role in all human decision-making. But haven't we so far stressed the way in which Receptive Ecumenism has promoted a spirituality of listening and been suspicious of ratiocination? The answer is yes. However, Ignatian discernment is less about reason and analysis than it is about being attuned to what is going on within oneself, to what the great Jesuit theologian Karl Rahner referred to as "the mysticism of everyday life." God is experienced, in Rahner's view, in words that Constance Fitzgerald would surely cherish, "most clearly and intensely, where the graspable contours of our everyday realities break and dissolve; where failures of such realities are experienced; when lights which illuminate the tiny islands of our everyday life go out."[10] Where, in other words, we confront impasse. In fact, Rahner thought that negative experiences were more fruitful than joyful ones, because "wherever space is really left by parting, by death, by renunciation, by apparent emptiness, provided the emptiness that cannot remain such is not filled by the world, or activity, or chatter, or the deadly grief of the world—there God is.[11] The mystic of everyday life, Rahner's unknown saint, is "one who with difficulty and without any clear evidence of success plods away at the task of awakening in just a few men and women a small spark of faith, of hope and of charity."[12]

In the moment of impasse, then, we encounter God more directly, and we do so in the fabric of ordinary daily life, not in some monastic cell. Here our consciousness is open to the promptings of the good and evil spirits, and discernment leads us to the grace-filled consciousness of what we are called to do, not what we necessarily want to do or relish doing. Ignatian discernment requires openness, generosity, courage, interior freedom, prayerful reflection on one's experience, having one's

---

10. Rahner, "Experiencing the Spirit," 81. Also see Imhof and Biallowons, *Karl Rahner in Dialogue*, 57, 83, 142, 183, 227, 245, and 293; Rahner, "Reflections on the Experience of Grace," 86–89; Rahner, "Experience of the Holy Spirit," 189–210.

11. Rahner, *Biblical Homilies*, 77.

12. Rahner, "Why Become or Remain a Jesuit?," *Madonna* (April 1987), 11.

priorities straight and not confusing ends with means.[13] May I suggest that just these virtues are those which Receptive Ecumenism requires for ecumenical success, and thus that it both needs them and inculcates them in the ecumenical practitioner. As we plod along as unknown saints, let's remember Rahner's most famous remark about the mystic: "the Christian of the future will be a mystic, or will not exist at all."[14]

BIBLIOGRAPHY

Cassidy, Laurie, and M. Shawn Copeland, eds. *Desire, Darkness, and Hope: Theology in a Time of Impasse. Engaging the Thought of Constance Fitzgerald OCD*. Collegeville, MN: Liturgical, 2021.

Congar, Yves. *Dialogue between Christians*. Westminster, MD: Newman, 1966.

———. *Journal d'un théologien: 1946–1956: Présenté et annoté par Etienne Fouilloux; avec la collaboration de Dominique Congar, André Duval et Bernard Montagnes*. Paris: Cerf, 2000.

Imhof, Paul, and Hubert Biallowons. *Karl Rahner in Dialogue*. New York: Crossroad, 1986.

Rahner, Karl. *Biblical Homilies*. Dublin: Herder & Herder, 1966.

———. "Experience of the Holy Spirit." In *Theological Investigations*, Vol. 18, 189–210. New York: Crossroad, 1983.

———. "Experiencing the Spirit." In *The Practice of Faith*. New York: Crossroad, 1983.

———. "Reflections on the Experience of Grace." In *Theological Investigations*, Vol. 3, 86–89. London: DLT, 1979.

———. "The Spirituality of the Church of the Future." In *Theological Investigations*, Vol. 20, 143–53. London: DLT, 1979.

---

13. See the advice of Warren Sazama SJ at: https://www.marquette.edu/faith/ignatian-principles-for-making-decisions.php

14. Rahner, "The Spirituality of the Church of the Future," 149.

Part II

Encounters in Context

Prologue to Part Two
Listening Churches

Sven-Erik Fjellström

I GUESS THAT MOST of us are quite familiar with the opening chapters of the Book of Revelation. Even if the intention was to bring comfort and encouragement to seven churches living in tough contexts in the first century, we must admit that the opening of the book is also quite harsh. Reading all the seven letters makes us feel as if we have stepped into a tense situation. A relationship that began in abundant love is revealed in these short letters to be now the kind of relationship that couples sometimes have when they have been married a long time and discussions become straight to the point and louder in tone. The energy of that first love has run out. In these verses hard words about compromising attitudes and corruption are uttered. We can probably understand why so many churches throughout history have preferred to take the name Philadelphia—the faithful and loving church!

A thought came into my mind. What if it would be possible to invite representatives from these seven churches to travel over time and space to be part of the conference in Sigtuna? Isn't this a place where we would like churches with such "broken china" and "wounded hands" to meet? In an anachronistic way, I allowed myself to wonder what might happen if these churches had the opportunity to meet with us, under the umbrella of Receptive Ecumenism. Wouldn't that have made things better for them? And, perhaps also for us?

Topics like friendship, spirituality, transformed societies and mutuality would certainly create bridges for common reflection. Wouldn't this also be a perfect place to dare to share some devastating ecumenical insights in a "broken china" spirit? In my imagination I saw us being transformed (to some extent at least) having heard and met each other. Honestly sharing our contexts would certainly also increase our curiosity about each other. And the mix in these seven churches of multicultural, multi religious and economic power struggles would certainly make some of us feel as if we have known each other for a very long time!

And what would they say to hearing two Bishops from two parts of the *same* Lutheran family (Sweden and Tanzania) sharing their experiences of humbly engaging with one another, despite their widely differing doctrinal interpretations?[1] May we all pray that we listen to the Spirit—while understanding that this includes and begins with listening to each other!

One of the churches in the book of Revelation, the lukewarm church of Laodicea, has probably had a great impact on many of us. At least we have heard many sermons about the risk of not being devoted enough.

> I know your works; you are neither cold nor hot. I wish that you were either cold or hot. So, because you are lukewarm, and neither cold nor hot, I am about to spit you out of my mouth. For you say, "I am rich, I have prospered, and I need nothing." You do not realize that you are wretched, pitiable, poor, blind, and naked. Therefore I counsel you to buy from me gold refined by fire so that you may be rich; and white robes to clothe you and to keep the shame of your nakedness from being seen; and salve to anoint your eyes so that you may see. I reprove and discipline those whom I love. Be earnest, therefore, and repent. Listen! I am standing at the door, knocking; if you hear my voice and open the door, I will come in to you and eat with you, and you with me. (Rev 3:15–20)

Over the years we might have seen many attempts to interpret what the initial intention of the message to the church in Laodicea could have been. Some archaeologists have been saying that the problem for Laodicea was probably that they had built their town too far away from two important water springs—one hot, the other fresh and cold. With long distance the water arrived through the aqueduct pipes being lukewarm. Surely many of us could agree that we know what it means in the twenty-first century to build a life pattern that is too distant from the sources of real life.

1. See chapter 19.

Other scholars suggest that the key verse to understanding the Laodicean situation is the *final* verse (Rev 3:20), where Jesus is *knocking* at the door. This interpretation suggests that Laodicea was situated in a region of frequent travelers, perhaps migrants fleeing to get a better life. Visitors should always be well treated—with warm wine in wintertime, with cold water in summertime, but also be invited for a meal together. Was the letter to Laodicea saying that their *hospitality* had become lukewarm?

I leave it up to you to decide where to put the emphasis, but I will say that perhaps the lukewarm hospitality perspective comes as a challenge also to our contexts today. At the back of our Bibles the Mediterranean maps were seen as maps of life, of the Gospel successfully reaching as far as Rome. Today most of us are in many ways affected by the news and statistics showing how the Mediterranean has become a sea of death. In Acts 27–28 we read about St Paul's survival from the deadly sea finding shelter on the island of Malta. What would he say about the statistics today?

Looking at these new "maps" in this way could make us ask how and where Laodicean context exists today. And a question for us the authors and readers of this volume might be to ask ourselves what contribution Receptive Ecumenism could give. Can the present migration situation *recharge* us with an attitude of working even more for open doors and curiosity about the "other"? Even for the unknown visitor knocking at our door?

In 1925, a major ecumenical conference took place in Stockholm. Today we understand that this influenced the activities of Life and Work, and the World Council of Churches. One of the initiators of the conference was the well-known Swedish Archbishop Nathan Söderblom. And one Swedish hymn in particular somehow united the participants in a special way. Their context then was also a context of war and peace, and of longing as churches to be part of a vision for our societies. Let us make their prayer our prayer also:

> *O jubilee day of the world's expectation*
>
> *when earth is God kingdom of blessed accord,*
>
> *when man's erring race finds the path of salvation*
>
> *and all shall acknowledge that Christ is the Lord,*
>
> *when sin has been banished and death slain forever*
>
> *and blessed redemption will part from us ever.*

It cometh, it cometh, the day of our longing
whose beams we behold in the clouds of the morn.
Though shades in the mists of the valleys are thronging,
the day on the summits already is born.
It cometh to quiet the tears of the grieving,
the hopes to fulfil of the faithful believing.[2]

---

2. Original Swedish Text, *Ack saliga dag* by N. Beskow. English translation, made for the 1925 Universal Christian Life Conference on Life and Works, by Charles Wharton Storck.

10

Friendship, Spirituality, and Imagination
Historical Approaches to Current Challenges in Receptive Ecumenism

Sara Gehlin

INTRODUCTION

As a new ecumenical current, Receptive Ecumenism evokes extensive engagement among ecumenists and scholars of theology today. For almost two decades, Receptive Ecumenism has progressed in contexts of inter-church encounter and theological study around the world. Developing as a branch of spiritual ecumenism, it appeals to the capacity of imagination and calls for genuine commitment to the deepening of ecumenical friendship. Hence, this article revolves around the three themes of friendship, spirituality, and imagination in order to explore Receptive Ecumenism as a new ecumenical current.

In the article, the novelty of Receptive Ecumenism stands out against the background of modern ecumenism as a century-old movement. Approaching Receptive Ecumenism with a view to ecumenical history, the present exploration involves discovering both the riches and challenges of this new ecumenical current. Specifically, the article addresses challenges that emerge when Receptive Ecumenism is being received in a context with a long ecumenical history, namely the Swedish context.[1]

FRIENDSHIP

The first step of the exploration implies facing a challenge that emerges with regard to ecumenical friendship. As a new current of ecumenism, Receptive Ecumenism has been discussed in terms of an advanced form of ecumenical engagement, which presumes existing bonds of friendship. According to theologian Antonia Pizzey, Receptive Ecumenism is a type of humble engagement with other churches which can only be undertaken on the basis of trust in the other. Therefore, it is dependent on already established ecumenical relations.[2] This calls for consideration of the role of Receptive Ecumenism in situations of ecumenical mistrust. If Receptive Ecumenism presumes existing bonds of ecumenical friendship, what role can it play in the absence of such friendship?

Given that Receptive Ecumenism presupposes the existence of friendship, the possible lack of friendship poses a clear challenge to Receptive Ecumenism. The exploration of this challenge has its point of departure in the geographical region of the Swedish capital Stockholm. Looking back in the history of ecumenism, Stockholm is the cradle of a current of ecumenism which has long historical roots: Life and Work ecumenism.[3] Even though the beginning of Life and Work ecumenism precedes the birth of Receptive Ecumenism by almost a century, its history provides significant guidance for the present exploration. Therefore, this article starts at the time of the dawn of Life and Work ecumenism and the historical event of the *Universal Christian Conference on Life and Work* in Stockholm in year 1925.

At Stockholm 1925, the conference participants found themselves in an historical situation of faltering friendship and deep mistrust between nations. It was the interwar period, and in the wake of the First

---

1. The Fifth International Conference on Receptive Ecumenism was carried out in Sigtuna, Sweden, in June 2022. The present article is based on the author's lecture in this conference.
2. Pizzey, *Receptive Ecumenism*, 20, 224.
3. Ehrenström, "Movements for International Friendship," 545–60. Important steps towards the organization of the 1925 Stockholm conference and the founding of the Life and Work movement were taken already in Geneva 1920, in a conference which gathered Protestant church leaders. See: Karlström, "Movements for International Friendship," 535–39.

World War ecumenical pioneers from the participating churches sensed the need to bring Christians together across national borders.[4] Many of them were inspired by internationalism, and their work for Christian unity went hand in hand with their engagement for peace among the nations. The young ecumenical movement created bridges of friendship between Christians across national borders in a time when nationalism was on the rise. The conference in Stockholm 1925 was a landmark in this long-standing work.[5]

Even though Stockholm 1925 was a sign of international ecumenical friendship, it is important to keep in mind that this conference did not attract the multifaceted representation of church traditions that ecumenical gatherings usually do today. The disappointment about this was caught in the well-known remark, noting that while Paul and John now were gathered, they were still waiting for Peter: a statement indicating that the Protestant and Orthodox participants in the conference wished that Catholic representatives would have joined them.[6]

If this suggests that the ecumenical circle of friends that developed in Stockholm 1925 felt incomplete because of the absence of Catholic members, this absence was partly the result of a not-so-friendly exchange of word that took place between representatives of the Catholic Church and the principal organizer of the Stockholm conference, the Swedish Lutheran Archbishop Nathan Söderblom. While Catholic representatives denounced Söderblom's theology as relativist, dogmatically groundless, and a modern heresy, Söderblom on his part referred to the Catholic Church as an institutional way, a method of absorption, and a sect. Not unexpectedly, the Catholic Church declined the invitation to the Stockholm conference.[7]

---

4. Söderblom, *Kristenhetens möte*, 445–53. Cf. Kinnamon, *Can a Renewal Movement*, 22.

5. Karlström, *Kristna samförståndssträvanden*, 3–11; Söderblom, *Kristenhetens möte*, 493–503, 533–35, 599–600, 840–43.

6. Söderblom, *Kristenhetens möte*, 786–88; Hedegård, *Söderblom, påven*, 141–42. The remark was given by Nathan Söderblom in the concluding sermon of the Stockholm conference.

7. Söderblom, *Christian Fellowship*, 121; Söderblom, "Evangelisk katolicitet," 92–93; Werner, *Världsvid men främmande*, 331–37. Differences in the understanding of Christian unity were decisive to the choice of declining the invitation to the Stockholm conference. The Catholic Church still welcomed cooperation in ethical issues, however only if faith issues were not involved. See: Werner, *Världsvid men främmande*, 336–38.

It is thought provoking that events in ecumenical history, which are known as starting points for new development, pioneering, and growth, are not always characterized by unanimous friendship. The process of building up the Life and Work movement in connection to Stockholm 1925, shows that ecumenical history is a history of both advance and setback when it comes to the formation and sustenance of friendship. Ecumenical history recalls that dispute, theological disagreement, and national enmity may consolidate mistrust between Christians from different nations and traditions.

Our own time and international situation may not appear so distant from the situation of the pioneers of the early Life and Work movement. Their hopes and fears, their visions and struggles, somehow appear familiar when a new current of ecumenism grows and expands today, almost a hundred years later. Receptive Ecumenism is developing at a time when friendship, between churches and between nations, is not self-evident. This calls for further reflection on the initial question: What role can Receptive Ecumenism play when there is a lack of friendship? The history of the Life and Work movement provides some clues.

When studying the circumstances of the development of the Life and Work movement, the odds seem stacked against it. Preceded by dispute between church leaders and embedded in an historical situation of national rivalry, any progress of the movement may seem highly unlikely. Nevertheless, the Life and Work movement unfolded, took shape, and eventually formed a fundamental part of the World Council of Churches.[8] In this framework, Life and Work ecumenism is still a vital current of the international ecumenical movement today. It continues to provide energy and inspiration to ecumenists engaging in the development of social justice, post-colonial criticism, peace theology, and feminist theology. Life and Work ecumenism continually develops its heritage of social engagement, based in the time of its birth, when international peace was at stake and the peacemaking role of inter-church friendship was obvious. In the Life and Work movement, common social engagement became a seedbed for such friendship.[9]

---

8. Ehrenström, "Movements," 552–60, 568–79; Visser 't Hooft, "The Genesis," 697–719. The World Council of Churches was founded in 1948.

9. Kinnamon, *Can a Renewal Movement*, 22–23. Cf. Mudge, "Ecumenical Social Thought," 279–319. In this chapter, Mudge also calls attention to the role of the Faith and Order movement for the development of social thought in the history of the World Council of Churches.

Today, at a time when there is again a desperate need for greater trust between churches and between nations, Receptive Ecumenism creates new seedbeds for friendship, using however a different set of tools. Receptive Ecumenism does not in the first place turn the spotlight in an outward direction, towards society, but primarily in an inward direction, towards the need for interior renewal and learning from others.[10] Practicing Receptive Ecumenism implies reflecting profoundly on one's own attitudes, and thus also on the very basis of true ecumenical friendship.

However, as previously indicated, Receptive Ecumenism can be considered an advanced form of ecumenism which presupposes already existing bonds of ecumenical friendship. It presumes trustful relationships, since it involves displaying one's imperfections while acknowledging one's need for help, healing, and conversion.[11] Thus, it can be observed that other currents of ecumenism, such as Life and Work ecumenism, pave the way for Receptive Ecumenism. In common social engagement across Christian traditions, friendship comes into being. From this perspective, Receptive Ecumenism appears intertwined with and complementary to other currents of ecumenism in the worldwide ecumenical movement. Yet, receptive ecumenical vocabulary accommodates an idea of Receptive Ecumenism as a so-called "third phase ecumenism" in comparison to "first phase ecumenism," represented by the Life and Work movement, and "second phase ecumenism," represented by the Faith and Order movement.[12]

Reflecting on the ecumenical heritage from Stockholm 1925, the notion of ecumenical "phases" appears challenging. Phases usually follow upon each other, leave earlier phases behind, and may even outclass each other while testifying to an improved level of relevance. Therefore, I assume that the receptive ecumenical vocabulary of phases is a mismatch to the very principle and ethos of Receptive Ecumenism. On this basis, I suggest the alternative vocabulary of ecumenical "strands," in two senses of the word. First, strands are intertwined and craft a larger piece together. In ecumenical contexts, this may reflect the process of receiving inspiration from one another, and of supporting and being enriched by each other, while contributing in different ways to the movement towards the goal of Christian unity. This leads to the second sense

---

10. Pizzey, "On the Maturation," 112–19. Cf. Gehlin, "Asymmetry and Mutuality," 202–6.

11. Pizzey, *Receptive Ecumenism*, 20, 224.

12. Murray, "Introducing Receptive Ecumenism," 1–3.

of the word: strand in the sense of a shore at a sea, lake, or river. This is also the meaning of the word in Swedish, *strand*. In ecumenical contexts, it may signify the initiative of embarking on a common journey along the same river, however from different starting points and viewpoints. It may reflect the practice of bringing different insights and perspectives along when meeting fellow travelers on the same journey.

Rather than succeeding other phases of ecumenism, I argue that Receptive Ecumenism contributes to the international ecumenical movement *alongside* other strands of ecumenism. As such, it brings new insights and a well-needed infusion of energy to the ageing ecumenical movement. In response to the initial question, it first of all needs to be noted that Receptive Ecumenism serves the deepening and strengthening of existing ecumenical friendship. However, in the absence of such friendship, other ecumenical strands lay important foundations for the progress and accomplishment of Receptive Ecumenism. Accordingly, in *interaction* with other strands of ecumenism, Receptive Ecumenism creates, vitalizes, and infuses new life to ecumenical relations.

In the framework of such endeavors, receptive ecumenical methodology presents an array of tools for helping parties to lower their guard and continue the route of friendship. Receptive ecumenical methodology calls attention not to the flaws of others, but to one's own need for self-criticism and renewal. It turns the attention inwards, towards the spiritual dimensions of the ecumenical calling. This takes the present exploration to its second step, which focuses on the theme of spirituality, and approaches a new challenge.

SPIRITUALITY

Since its inception, Receptive Ecumenism has unfolded as a branch of spiritual ecumenism. Like other types of spiritual ecumenism, it is inward looking and calls for interior renewal and reform. This raises the question of whether Receptive Ecumenism bypasses issues that concern *social* renewal and reform.

Posed in a Swedish context, the question uncovers a challenge worth exploring. In Sweden, the Life and Work movement not only has a significant historical background but has also inspired an extensive ecumenical engagement in social issues. In the spirit of Life and Work, ecumenical theological reflection has given significant weight to social issues such as justice and peace.[13] Seen against this background, it becomes clear that Receptive Ecumenism, with its orientation towards interior renewal and reform within churches and traditions, addresses another set of needs and issues in the life of the ecumenical movement. From this viewpoint, it may even appear as if the struggle for a more just and peaceful society is left behind in Receptive Ecumenism. Thus, the following discussion calls attention to this seeming lack of social orientation in Receptive Ecumenism.

To begin with, it needs to be underscored that even though Receptive Ecumenism primarily focuses on the inward life of the believer and church community, it may not necessarily leave social concerns behind. I assume that social engagement and spiritual deepening are *interconnected* in Receptive Ecumenism just as in Life and Work ecumenism, although in two different ways.

Receptive Ecumenism testifies to this interconnection by means of accommodating the conviction that the path of prayer, conversion, and self-critical introspection can simultaneously be a path of service in a world torn by conflicts and crises. According to theologian Paul D. Murray, receptive ecumenical learning between separated Christian traditions witnesses to the possibility of living in reconciled difference for mutual flourishing in a world of blood-soaked conflict.[14] According to Murray, "This is the key issue of our living and dying together—the key question of our age—and it is clearly of relevance beyond the realm of ecumenically inclined theologians."[15] Hence, it can be observed that Receptive Ecumenism is oriented on the very *dispositions* for building peace with one another as Christians and in a wider societal context.

This can be compared to the interconnected and longstanding strivings of the Life and Work movement towards Christian unity and world peace.[16] These strivings were manifested already in the work of Nathan Söderblom. In tandem with his advocacy for peace, he pointed to the significance of striving towards a Christian unity which, in his view, had

13. This is well exemplified in the extensive work on justice and peace carried out in the Christian Council of Sweden. See e.g. Bäcklund (ed.), *Fred*.

14. Murray, "Establishing the Agenda," 19.

15. Murray, "Establishing the Agenda," 19.

16. Throughout the history of the Life and Work movement, strivings for Christian unity have been closely connected to endeavors for world peace. However, discussions on the unity of the churches and the unity of humankind have also been lively in the Faith and Order movement as well as in the Catholic Church in connection to the Second Vatican Council. See: Gehlin, *Pathways for Theology*, 14–19, 157–60.

to be grounded in inward reflection and the spiritual deepening of each believer.[17] This viewpoint is echoed today, in the contemporary work of the World Council of Churches for the overcoming of violence. In this context, peace is frequently discussed in terms of a spiritual path. Peace is understood as a spiritual journey which involves conversion, repentance, and asking for forgiveness. Churches are seen as trustworthy peacebuilders only if they commit to self-critical introspection.[18]

However, in the contemporary context of the World Council of Churches, the call to such a commitment is coupled with a call for *mutual accountability*. This means engaging with the question of whom one's church is accountable to. It entails developing mutually respectful relations in a spirit of sharing, and of acknowledging one's dependence on others. Mutual accountability implies fostering a sense of mutual belonging. It means being ready to take responsibility and being willing to make each other mutually accountable, even in a critical way.[19]

Considering the ecumenical debate on mutuality, it is possible to discern a crossroads that highlights the difference between Receptive Ecumenism and Life and Work ecumenism. Receptive Ecumenism does not call for consideration of the responsibility of anyone other than oneself and one's church. While Receptive Ecumenism does not bypass issues that concern social renewal and reform, it takes another route in terms of thinking and action when it comes to mutuality. Unlike Life and Work ecumenism, Receptive Ecumenism does not give primary weight to mutuality. It turns the spotlight towards one's own church and its role in the building of unity and peaceful relations. In consequence, neither mutuality nor dialogue are emphasized in Receptive Ecumenism.[20]

This feature of Receptive Ecumenism takes this exploration to its last step. This means approaching a third challenge, and the theme of imagination. The challenge becomes apparent when reflecting on the fact that Receptive Ecumenism is based neither on dialogue nor on mutuality. While dialogue and mutuality historically have been key to the development of ecumenical praxis and theology, the absence of these

---

17. See e.g. Söderblom, *Kyrkan och freden*, 48–57; Söderblom, "Evangelisk katolicitet," 67, 86. Aulén, *Hundra års*, 135–37.

18. Gehlin, *Pathways for Theology*, 127–43.

19. Tveit, *The Truth We Owe*, 314–21.

20. Balabanski & Hawkes, "Introduction," viii–ix; Gehlin, "Asymmetry and Mutuality," 197–212.

features evokes curiosity: In what ways does Receptive Ecumenism nurture ecumenical imagination?

IMAGINATION

The lack of any expectation of dialogue and mutuality in Receptive Ecumenism may appear challenging, when considering the way dialogue and mutual exchange have been core practices through the history of the modern ecumenical movement. As previously indicated, it also challenges the idea of mutual accountability, which has inspired the work of the World Council of Churches significantly in the last few decades. Receptive Ecumenism guides the imagination along *other* routes. It turns settled ecumenical perspectives upside down and provokes thought on ecumenical practices which may appear self-evident, such as dialogue and the search for mutual understanding.[21]

When discussing this challenge, another Swedish city will serve as a point of departure, namely the city of Sigtuna. In this city, the modern ecumenical movement finds yet another setting of importance to its historical development: the Sigtuna Foundation.[22] The sociologist and director Alf Linderman[23] highlights the vision which has guided life at the Foundation through its history as well as in contemporary times: to provide a place where people of different convictions, standpoints, and confessional backgrounds can meet, not however with the aim of convincing or changing the other, but with the aim of understanding oneself better in the light of the encounter with the other.[24]

It can be noted that this vision is kindred to Receptive Ecumenism's emphasis on learning and receiving, and with its dissociation from practices of teaching and giving. Receptive Ecumenism takes guard against tendencies towards convincing or changing the other. Concentrating on processes of learning, it aims at facilitating the development of a deeper self-understanding, in the light of the new knowledge that emerges from the encounter with other Christians and their traditions.[25]

---

21. I discuss the receptive ecumenical non-expectation of mutuality more in depth in Gehlin, "Assymmetry and Mutuality."

22. The Sigtuna Foundation was the location of the Fifth International Conference on Receptive Ecumenism in 2022.

23. Alf Linderman was the director of the Sigtuna Foundation 2001–2023.

24. Hagerman & Gabrielsson, *Det är det mänskliga mötet*.

25. Murray, "Families of Receptive Theological Learning," 86–88; Murray, "Establishing the Agenda," 12–17.

Receptive Ecumenism encourages attitudes of curiosity and willingness to learn.[26] However, it needs to be observed that Receptive Ecumenism takes the process of learning one step further. Focusing on learning, it seeks to inspire the imagination of new possibilities in the midst of brokenness.[27] As such, I assume, Receptive Ecumenism corresponds with essential aspects of a *moral imagination*, as it has been expounded by researchers of peace studies and cognitive science.

The peace researcher John Paul Lederach explains that moral imagination implies the capacity to think, see, and listen in new ways. The role of moral imagination is to give life to that which does not yet exist. It means trusting that new development is possible. It also means to set in motion such processes of development that are difficult to imagine under present conditions. According to Lederach, moral imagination is the capability to imagine and generate initiatives, which are rooted in our everyday challenges, but still reach beyond these challenges in order to break destructive patterns and cycles.[28] In the light of moral imagination, the imaginative dimensions of Receptive Ecumenism stand out clearly. Receptive Ecumenism stimulates the imagination of how to solve problems, bring new life to frozen relations, and break destructive patterns in the life of the churches. Insights gained from the traditions of others become imaginative springboards for new developments. They become sources for healing and renewal.

Moral imagination brings, moreover, a conceptual basis for understanding the close connection between imagination and self-critical introspection, which can be discerned in Receptive Ecumenism. Expounding the bases of moral imagination, cognitive scientist Mark Johnson stresses that the human capacity of imagining alternative standpoints, and finding new solutions to conflicts and problems, relies on the readiness to let one's thoughts grow beyond one's present viewpoints and standpoints. This, however, requires acknowledging the weaknesses and deficiencies of the metaphors and stories that presently frame one's thinking. Moral imagination, Johnson underscores, implies transforming the limits of one's convictions and engagement while discerning and

---

26. Hawkes, "Nurturing and Nourishing," 89–94.

27. This can be observed when studying the development of Receptive Ecumenism as an "ecumenism of the wounded hands." Cf. Murray, "Introducing Receptive Ecumenism," 4–5.

28. Lederach, *The Moral Imagination*, 27–29.

articulating alternative perspectives.[29] Moral imagination, I suggest, elucidates central dynamics in Receptive Ecumenism. It facilitates a deeper understanding of how the acknowledgement of weaknesses and deficiencies in churches and traditions can form springboards for the imagination and realization of new development. In Receptive Ecumenism, actions of self-scrutiny serve the discernment of alternative paths beyond rooted and sometimes destructive patterns.

However, in Receptive Ecumenism, dialogue and mutual exchange are not the primary means for discerning these paths. Receptive ecumenical methodology does not in the first place provide tools for mutual understanding. Instead, it aims at finding ways for living together in long term disagreement, in likeness with its forerunner in the field of interreligious dialogue: the method of scriptural reasoning. Rather than promoting agreement or consensus, it emphasizes the valuation of diversity. In encounters with the particular gifts of others, Receptive Ecumenism encourages attitudes of appreciation, wonder, passion, and love.[30] As such, it reflects the idea of a "holy envy," articulated by the Swedish bishop and biblical scholar Krister Stendahl. He called believers to listen to the adherents, not to the enemies, of other religions, and never compare one's own best to the other's worst. Stendahl stressed that true religious understanding involves leaving room for holy envy, which means being willing to recognize elements in other religious traditions that one admires and wishes would find greater scope in one's own religious tradition.[31] The idea of holy envy has inspired many pioneers of interreligious dialogue in the last decades. Now, it is certainly breaking through in the ecumenical field through attitudes inspired by Receptive Ecumenism.

Almost a hundred years after the historic conference in Stockholm 1925, the ecumenical movement is experiencing a new boost of energy. With Receptive Ecumenism, a new ecumenical current is born. This time the initiative comes from the Catholic Church.[32] In the last two decades, Receptive Ecumenism has developed and taken root in contexts influenced by different church traditions. In some of these contexts, the

---

29. Johnson, *Moral Imagination*, 200–3.

30. Murray, "Families of Receptive Theological Learning," 76–88. Cf. Adams, "Long-Term Disagreement," 154–71.

31. Boys "Turn It," 293.

32. As an ecumenical current with its origins in the context of the Catholic Church, Receptive Ecumenism finds a primary source for its development in the work of scholars at the Centre for Catholic Studies at Durham University, UK.

ecumenical engagement has long historical roots, like in the Swedish context. Here, new energy is received from the way Receptive Ecumenism guides the imagination on unexpected paths. It provokes thought on the established role of dialogue and mutuality, and it calls attention to one's need for learning and receiving from other Christian traditions.

Moreover, Receptive Ecumenism provides the ecumenical movement with new energy by means of drawing insight from yet another strand of engagement, connected to contemporary ecumenical commitment. This strand was existent, although embryonic, in Stockholm 1925, namely the strand of interreligious engagement.[33] Thus, by means of its methodology, Receptive Ecumenism confirms that the path of ecumenical learning and receiving can go beyond the well-trodden paths of the ecumenical landscape and reach into the terrain of interreligious engagement.

BIBLIOGRAPHY

Adams, Nicholas. "Long-Term Disagreement: Philosophical Models in Scriptural Reasoning and Receptive Ecumenism." *Modern Theology* 29/4 (2013) 154–71.
Aulén, Gustaf. *Hundra års svensk kyrkodebatt: Drama i tre akter*. Stockholm: SKD, 1953.
Balabanski, Vicky and Geraldine Hawkes. "Introduction." In *Receptive Ecumenism: Listening, Learning, and Loving in the Way of Christ*, edited by Vicky Balabanski and Geraldine Hawkes, vii–xiv. Adelaide: ATF, 2018.
Boys, Mary C. "Turn It and Turn It Again: The Vital Contribution of Krister Stendahl to Jewish Christian Relations." *Journal of Ecumenical Studies* 51 (2016) 281–94.
Bäcklund, Maria, ed. *Fred—detta vill kyrkorna i Sverige*. Sundbyberg: Sveriges kristna råd, 2014.
Ehrenström, Nils. "Movements for International Friendship and Life and Work 1925–1948." In *A History of the Ecumenical Movement*, Vol. 1, *1517–1948*, edited by Ruth Rouse and Stephen Charles Neill, 545–96. Geneva: WCC Publications, 2004.
Gehlin, Sara. "Asymmetry and Mutuality: Feminist Approaches to Receptive Ecumenism." *Studia Theologica: Nordic Journal of Theology* 74/2 (2020) 197–216.
———. *Pathways for Theology in Peacebuilding: Ecumenical Approaches to Just Peace*. Studies in Theology and Religion 27. Leiden: Brill, 2020.
Hagerman, Maja, and Claes Gabrielsson. *Det är det mänskliga mötet som räknas, a film about the history of the Sigtuna foundation* (2017). https://sigtunastiftelsen.se/om-oss/mansklig-motet/.
Hawkes, Geraldine. "Nurturing and Nourishing a Receptive Disposition through Process." In *Receptive Ecumenism: Listening, Learning, and Loving in the Way of Christ*, edited by G. Hawkes, V. Balabanski, 89–98. Adelaide: ATF, 2018.
Hedegård, David. *Söderblom, påven och det stora avfallet*. Örebro: Evangelii, 1953.

---

33. Even though interreligious engagement was not advocated during the Stockholm conference, its main organizer Nathan Söderblom had a profound interest in religion beyond Christianity. For further reading on this topic, see e.g. Jonson, *Jag är bara Nathan Söderblom*, 315–25.

Johnson, Mark. *Moral Imagination: Implications of Cognitive Science for Ethics*. Chicago: University of Chicago Press, 1993.

Jonson, Jonas. *Jag är bara Nathan Söderblom: Satt till tjänst*. Stockholm: Verbum, 2014.

Karlström, Nils. *Kristna samförståndssträvanden under världskriget 1914–1918 med särskild hänsyn till Nathan Söderbloms insats*. Stockholm: SKD, 1947.

———. "Movements for International Friendship and Life and Work 1910–1925." In *A History of the Ecumenical Movement*, Vol. 1, *1517–1948*, edited by Ruth Rouse and Stephen Charles Neill, 509–42. Geneva: WCC Publications, 2004.

Kinnamon, Michael. *Can a Renewal Movement Be Renewed? Questions for the Future of Ecumenism*. Grand Rapids: Eerdmans, 2014.

Lederach, John Paul. *The Moral Imagination: The Art and Soul of Building Peace*. Oxford: Oxford University Press, 2005.

Mudge, Lewis S. "Ecumenical Social Thought." In *A History of the Ecumenical Movement*, Vol. 3 *1968–2000*, edited by J. Briggs et al., 279–321. Geneva: WCC Publications, 2004.

Murray, Paul D. "Families of Receptive Theological Learning: Scriptural Reasoning, Comparative Theology, and Receptive Ecumenism." *Modern Theology* 29.4 (2013) 76–92.

———. "Introducing Receptive Ecumenism." *The Ecumenist* 51.2 (2014) 1–8.

———. "Receptive Ecumenism and Catholic Learning: Establishing the Agenda." In *Receptive Ecumenism and the Call to Catholic Learning: Exploring a Way for Contemporary Ecumenism*, edited by Paul D. Murray, 5–25. Oxford: Oxford University Press, 2008.

Pizzey, Antonia. "On the Maturation of Receptive Ecumenism: The Connection between Receptive Ecumenism and Spiritual Ecumenism." *Pacifica: Australasian Theological Studies* 28/2 (2015) 108–25.

———. *Receptive Ecumenism and the Renewal of the Ecumenical Movement*. Brill's Studies in Catholic Theology 7. Leiden: Brill, 2019.

Söderblom, Nathan. *Christian Fellowship and the United Life and Work of Christendom*. New York: Revell, 1923.

———. "Evangelisk katolicitet." In *Enig kristendom*, by N. Söderblom, E. Lehmann, K. B. Westman. Stockholm: SKD, 1919.

———. *Kristenhetens möte i Stockholm: Historik, aktstycken, grundtankar, personligheter, eftermäle*. Stockholm: SKD, 1926.

———. *Kyrkan och freden*. Stockholm: Bonniers, 1930.

Tveit, Olav Fykse. *The Truth We Owe Each Other: Mutual Accountability in the Ecumenical Movement*. Geneva: WCC Publications, 2016.

Visser 't Hooft, Willem Adolf. "The Genesis of the World Council of Churches." In *A History of the Ecumenical Movement*, Vol. 1, *1517–1948*, edited by Ruth Rouse and Stephen Charles Neill. Geneva: WCC Publications, 2004.

Werner, Yvonne-Maria. *Världsvid men främmande: Den katolska kyrkan i Sverige 1873–1929*. Uppsala: Katolska bokförlaget, 1996.

11

Receptive Ecumenism and Mission
Transformed Ecumenism for Transformed Societies

CALLAN SLIPPER

INTRODUCTION

I WANT TO MAKE what may seem to be at once an over-blown and yet an exciting claim for Receptive Ecumenism, namely, that it offers us a chance for a theologically and spiritually grounded form of mission, one that, for this very reason, should be more effective than many other forms. I am well aware that I am suggesting this in a moment when ecumenism itself is not prioritized by the churches. These same churches are nonetheless prioritizing mission, not least because, statistically at any rate, many of them are facing extinction. Ecumenism, on the other hand, is somewhere very close to the bottom of the "to-do list." Despite heartfelt affirmations by church leaders of the need to rebuild unity among Christians, as resources grow scarcer, they are regularly taken from ecumenism and deployed elsewhere. To speak anecdotally for a moment, during my time working ecumenically at national level for the Church of England, I saw this happen in several churches, including, rather drastically, in my own. The upshot of this is that many churches are seeking to improve missionally while sidelining ecumenism. This seems to me to be a colossal error, not least because it is contrary to the missional mandate of the Fourth Gospel where the Lord clearly links the communal health of the Christian community, and its mutual love and living experience of unity, with effective outreach to the world.[1] How can a divided church, battered by abuse scandals and institutional racism (to name just two of the ills that span multiple denominations) model the kingdom and speak with any credibility to a secularized society?

Before asking the core question of what Receptive Ecumenism adds to mission, I think we need briefly to look at the ecumenism implied by the Fourth Gospel's missional mandate, especially as seen in John 17. This sets the essential background to Receptive Ecumenism.

WHAT KIND OF ECUMENISM?

Let's begin by asking what kind of ecumenism is so important? There are many ways of building Christian unity—through prayer and worship, acts of kindness, symbolic gestures of solidarity, institutional cooperation, canonical and legal organization, common witness and, of course, with a certain pre-eminence, theological discussion and doctrinal understanding. While each of these is vital, they are all, however, secondary to the spiritual unity of living relationships. In fact, when Jesus prayed to the Father in John 17 it was this relational dimension, lived out in the intimacy of the inner life of God, that Jesus was speaking about: "May all be one. As you, Father, are in me and I am in you, *may they also be in us*, so that the world may believe that you have sent me" (John 17:21, my emphasis). The other things listed above that make up so much of the actual practice of ecumenical activity express and promote ecumenism's relational heart. What would be the use, to put it extremely to make the point, of having doctrinal agreement, a united structure, tokens of solidarity, or even of praying together if we all hate each other? It would

---

1. Apart from the *locus classicus* of John 17, especially 17:21–23, the Fourth Gospel is very clear about the need for a living community at the heart of Christian mission. Hence Jesus's new commandment that we love one another in John 13:34 is immediately glossed by the following verse: "By this everyone will know that you are my disciples, if you have love for one another." Moreover, the image of the vine and the branches, which indicates that all efficacy comes from Christ alone "because apart from me you can do nothing" (John 15:5), is about communal life not just because the idea of branches is plural but because the passage is put in the context of the second iteration of Jesus's commandment of mutual love (John 15:8–13). It is clear in this passage, just as in John 17, that the love in which Christians share is rooted in the eternal relationship of the Father and the Son (John 15:9).

be a sham unity. Only by sharing together in the love that God is in Godself, poured upon us by the Holy Spirit, can we achieve the goal of ecumenism however that is conceived.[2]

But let's be clear what is being suggested here. When Jesus prays for our unity, he is praying that we may be caught up into the relationship that he has with the Father and stating that in living out our unity we share in God's life and being: we in God and God in us. It is a remarkable claim. It says that God is truly present in the world through our unity. No wonder Jesus says that the world will know, that is, know by experience,[3] that God has sent him, even to the extent of recognizing the very same loving divine presence in his united disciples as was in Jesus himself: "I in them and you in me, that they may become completely one, so that the world may know that you have sent me and have loved them even as you have loved me" (John 17:23). It makes us, when we live this, the living and actualized mystical body of Christ, God's presence and action in the world.[4] This is mission, truly the *missio Dei* where God Godself, in the first person as you might say, reaches out beyond the outpouring of love within the mutuality and oneness of the Godhead to creation. Understood like this, ecumenism is the soul of mission. Simply by promoting ecumenism, therefore, Receptive Ecumenism promotes mission. But, as we shall see, there is more to it than that.

THE RECEPTIVE APPROACH

To dwell, however, in the soul of mission, living in God's overflowing love as he reaches out to creation, requires conversion; for us to share in the divine mission we need to be fit for it, able to be channels, however

---

2. Of course, there are many visions of the goal of the ecumenical journey. The lack of clarity here is a significant factor in the lack of ecumenical energy among the churches. See, for instance, Meyer, *That All May Be One*, 1–2 and 151–52.

3. The Greek word for "know" used in John 17:3 and 23 is *ginōskein*, which is more than simply intellectual knowledge but rather knowing by experience, the effort to learn and ability to recognize something for what it is. Such knowledge of "the only true, and Jesus Christ whom you have sent" is entering a relationship where it is encounter with the other, not merely knowledge about the other. This picks up on the Hebrew word for "know" used in the Old Testament which is "yada," a term used for personal relations and intimacy. See Slipper, *Enriched by the Other*, 6.

4. This notion is behind Paul's use of the image of the body of Christ, especially in its earlier instances as found in Romans and 1 Corinthians. It is rooted in the Semitic notion that sees "body" as coterminous with what we might call "person," that is, one who exists within the world and is an agent in it. The image is developed and given a different emphasis in Ephesians and Colossians.

rudimentary, of his love. Receptive Ecumenism is, first of all, an approach that aids this conversion. Of course, there is always more to conversion than any way of doing things, any process, however holy. We cannot participate in God without God's gift to us in Christ: the finite cannot attain the infinite from its own resources. So, at the base of the necessary conversion there is the grace of God received in the context of a real spiritual life. *Metanoia* is not merely the means of embarking upon spiritual practice but is also the constant effect of the daily grind of living out our spiritual discipline with God's help. What Receptive Ecumenism gives us is a methodology for *metanoia* in an ecclesial setting. How so?

It seems to me that three moments can be discerned in the process of Receptive Ecumenism. They can be characterized in various ways that can be outlined as: *repentance*, which is when as an ecclesial communion we connect with, recognize, and take responsibility for our own failings; *reception*, which is when we look with love at another ecclesial communion and see the wonders that are there and learn from them; and *restoration* when within the integrity of our own communion we take what we have learned and apply it, regaining what was implicitly already ours as members of the body of Christ. The process begins in conversion and ends in conversion as we are restored to health as the living body of Christ. Given that this is always done in the context of at least two ecclesial communions, it is always reciprocal: each is learning from the other. This means that although there is a fundamental act of honesty and humility in the moment of repentance, there is also an acceptance that there are positive things that each communion can offer. For at the same time as each communion opens itself up to the look of love from the other, it is also recognizing that it has gifts within itself. Yet at the moment of reception these gifts are discovered anew through the gaze of the other communion. Finally, a new relationship is forged in the moment of restoration as the communions involved are interpenetrated, as it were, by the gifts that come from each other. This restoration makes them all more distinct from each other, more themselves as they recover *in their own way* what they have found and, at the very same time, also all become closer, more united to the other as they can see how the other communion is now more like them, perhaps it would be better to say how, in a real sense, they are in the other and the other is within them: a perichoretic relationship.

The similarity here with the wording of the Fourth Gospel is not by chance. Receptive Ecumenism opens us up to a relationship of love, and the deepened unity it renders available to us mirrors the love heightened to an infinite extent in God whose very being is love. This, then, is a further way that Receptive Ecumenism profoundly benefits mission: it enables a particularly intense form of Christian unity, bringing about a Christifying conversion and a more Christ-shaped relationship among the communions involved.

RECEPTIVE MISSION

But Receptive Ecumenism offers another, related, possibility for mission. To understand this let's undertake an imaginative exercise. We will imagine two persons meeting. To do this effectively we have to notice that although Receptive Ecumenism is about communions coming together and understanding themselves in the light of the other, it is in fact persons who meet and conduct the conversation. It is persons who repent, receive, and restore. Receptive Ecumenism is thus a form of loving that can be undertaken by individual persons because it is always a process practiced by persons, in other words, it is about persons in relationship. So, in our exercise two persons meet, one a Christian and the other not. To make it easier to picture and to avoid using clumsy forms such as "he or she," let's imagine them both to be women. They get into conversation and strike up a friendship as they chat. The Christian, aware of her own fragility and limitations, begins to learn things from the other about how she sees things and finds her own worldview and her approach to life challenged. She accepts her discoveries and starts to adopt the things she has learned into her own Christian framework. Her friend, reassured by the deep listening she has received and perhaps surprised by finding things in herself that are more valuable than she had thought, feels free to recognize her own needs or even perhaps shortcomings, and she begins to notice things in her friend that respond to these, offering healing. Most surprisingly of all, she finds the spark of faith in her friend touches some of the deepest longings of her inner self. Within her the sense that Christ is beautiful and real begins to dawn. This is genuine evangelization, but without a whiff of coercion.

Of course, not all evangelistic encounters or even all dialogues will be like this. Sometimes there is a need to challenge or to witness to Christ in an assertive way, and mission is not only a matter of person-to-person conversation but includes many other forms of communication. Nonetheless dialogue, either one-to-one or between groups, is an effective way of sharing the joy of the Gospel,[5] most especially because it offers the real possibility of engaging with other persons out of love and building relationships of mutual care and concern.

For this to happen, of course, the dialogue partners must value each other and give each other space to express themselves. It sets up an interesting form of equality since in the approach proposed by Receptive Ecumenism, the dialogue partners are simultaneously lesser and greater than each other because they are simultaneously learners and teachers. It puts all on an equal footing without diminishing either the gifts or the frailties that any of the dialogue partners may have. Such truthful equality means that a pattern of behavior rooted in this approach opens up the possibility of a profound conversation in which both parties are valued, can admit their vulnerabilities, and grow together in an appreciation of the truth. For a Christian this cannot but be deeply liberating. No longer are we forced to try to seem always full of the answers, always wonderful, always somehow better than the recipient of our message. Such an approach, indeed, accords more with the reality of the church which, when all goes well, is full of wounded healers[6] and which, in any case, as the hospital for sinners,[7] contains not just those who fail in commonplace ways but also those whose behavior can go to the extremes of abuse and criminality. It is thus a relational process in touch with personal and ecclesiastical failing, free from the murmurs of triumphalism. Therefore, it can be truly authentic: a witness to Christ and not to ourselves.

Dialogue shaped by the process at work in Receptive Ecumenism, therefore, really can manifest the very soul of mission, that is, despite its eye-watering inadequacies the church can still be the lived expression of the divine in history. This accords with what is expressed in the Church of England's seminal document, *Mission-shaped Church*.[8] At one point

---

5. This phrase, obviously, is borrowed from the title of *Evangelii Gaudium* which, indeed has a section devoted to the need to build up relationships in the context of evangelization (87–92) and affirms that "the Gospel tells us constantly to run the risk of a face-to-face encounter with others, with their physical presence which challenges us, with their pain and their pleas, with their joy which infects us in our close and continuous interaction" (88).

6. This expression of Henri Nouwen (see Nouwen, *Wounded Healer*) is picked up by Paul Murray's pungent expression regarding Receptive Ecumenism: "Healing gifts for wounded hands."

7. See Matt 9:13; Mark 2:16; Luke 5:32. The first to use the description of the church as a "hospital for sinners" is attributed to various people; nonetheless, the idea is rooted in patristic writing.

8. The Archbishops' Council, *Mission-shaped Church*.

the document quotes a previous theological statement from the Church of England's House of Bishops which asserts that the Church is more than a voice speaking about divine things but is rather the living experience of them, making the powerful claim:

> The church does more than merely point to a reality beyond itself. By virtue of its participation in the life of God, it is not only a sign and instrument, but also a genuine foretaste of God's Kingdom, called to show forth visibly, in the midst of history, God's final purposes for humankind.[9]

But honesty, that is, an awareness of the facts, means that *Mission-shaped Church* immediately goes on to say:

> As such it [the Church] is always incomplete. The inevitable weakness and sinfulness of the Church at any particular time cannot simply be excused, but it is, through God's grace, the place where forgiveness and the power for a change of life can be seen and experienced.[10]

Receptive Ecumenism's approach copes very well with this double nature of Christian experience: both the amazing gifts of grace and the struggle of living up to the grace that has been given. For Receptive Ecumenism is grounded not just in gifts but in weakness, which is to say it is grounded in the reality of our condition.

WALKING WITH CHRIST

This groundedness then opens up the possibility for the ensuing dialogue to be extremely fruitful. In the ecumenical sphere mutual learning leads to discovering more of Christ by seeing his gifts to another ecclesial communion. In mission, a parallel process can take place. The dialogue partners enter on a journey together where each learns from the other, and since that learning is a coming closer to what is true, it is a coming closer to the Truth, to Christ. The wonderful thing is that in our learning from others, Christians need have no fear of losing Christ, indeed, aided by the sense of our own frailty, we are going out to meet him. Correspondingly a non-Christian dialogue partner is also on the journey towards Truth, and so to Christ. In a receptive process neither party is dominated or intimidated by the other, but within their own freedom and integrity,

---

9. *Mission-shaped Church*, 95 n. 62.
10. *Mission-shaped Church*, 96.

each learns from the other. Such a fundamentally truthful and respectful way of conducting dialogue is life-giving, especially at the point when the partners apply what has been discovered. It is a dialogue that walks with Christ, the way, the truth, and the life (see John 14:6).

We should notice, also, that the pattern it follows is that of Christ's saving love as enjoined upon the Christian community of Philippi by the Apostle Paul (see Phil 2:5–11). It is what *Mission-shaped Church* calls "a model for the practice of mission."[11] Each dialogue partner, in an act of humility and self-giving, pours itself out to the other and, at the same time, receives from the other. This is a rich process that mirrors both the incarnation and its salvific climax on the cross:

> The incarnation involves an exchange, the dignity and power of which it is humanly impossible to grasp, only faith can give us a tiny glimpse of its reality: God becomes one of us, even to the extent that he accepts suffering and death . . . This exchange is relived every time there is an act of inculturation. God in Christ enters more fully into our human condition; we share more fully in his life. We die in Christ to that which is sinful, and we rise to a creative newness in human relationships through the transforming power of Christ.[12]

In the receptive pattern of relationship, the "act of inculturation" is a real learning on both sides. For this very reason it can open the reality of Christ in a way that is non-invasive, respectful of the integrity of those who come to know him in this way, and honest in its expression since the sharing comes within a context of recognized weakness.

CONCLUSION

What we see here, therefore, is a form of mission that is ethically responsible since it is deeply respectful and, while not glossing over any side's weakness, it holds nothing back. It is for each dialogue partner a shared journey to Truth. Applying the approach of Receptive Ecumenism to mission would be, indeed, a significant step towards the new society that Christian evangelization seeks to achieve: a world formed by the kind of love that Christ modelled. And this, of course, is set in the context

---

11. The idea of a model is in this context being applied to church-planting. The core point of its being a relational pattern for mission more broadly, nonetheless, still holds good. *Mission-shaped Church*, 88.

12. Arbuckle, *Grieving for Change*, 118 quoted in *Mission-shaped Church*, 88.

of an ecumenism that is also travelling upon this same journey, and so relating receptively brings with it the realization (in all its inevitable flaws and struggles with human failings) of a church that is already beginning to live as a transformed society in the renewal it experiences. Moreover, since the church is called to be the sign and foretaste, as well as the instrument, of the society God wishes to bring about, both the church's renewed way of being, which it shares in mission with others, and the receptive approach it uses in the process of that missional sharing, mean it can be a transforming presence in society, giving to others what it practices itself. A church that lives out receptive learning will be a ferment of receptive relationships in the world round about it, building a transformed society. This kind of church offers those it serves a pattern of relating that helps them reflect the trinitarian love within and flowing from the Godhead. How very different from the pattern of mutual imposition that is so common, especially in politics, often making society in many places like a mini war, when not, sadly, at times becoming actual war!

BIBLIOGRAPHY

Arbuckle, Gerald. *Grieving for Change: Spirituality for Refounding Gospel Communities.* London: Chapman, 1991.

The Archbishops' Council, *Mission-shaped Church: Church Planting and Fresh Expressions of Church in a Changing Context,* London: Church House, 2004.

Ford, David F. *The Gospel of John: A Theological Commentary.* Grand Rapids: Baker Academic, 2021.

Francis, Pope. *Evangelii Gaudium.* Vatican City: Libreria Editrice Vaticana, 2013.

Meyer, Harding. *That All May Be One: Perceptions and Models of Ecumenicity.* Translated by William G. Rusch. Grand Rapids: Eerdmans 1999.

Millar, Virgina; Moxon, David, and Pickard, Stephen, eds. *Leaning into the Spirit: Ecumenical Perspectives on Discernment and Decision-making in the Church.* Cham, Switzerland: Palgrave Macmillan, 2019.

Moynagh, Michael with Philip Harold. *Church for Every Context: An Introduction to Theology and Practice.* London: SCM, 2012.

Murray, Paul D., Gregory A. Ryan, and Paul Lakeland, eds. *Receptive Ecumenism as Transformative Ecclesial Learning: Walking the Way to a Church Re-Formed.* Oxford: Oxford University Press, 2022.

Newbigin, Leslie. *The Gospel in a Pluralist Society.* London: SPCK, 1990.

Nouwen, Henri J. *Wounded Healer: Ministry in Contemporary Society.* Garden City, NY: Doubleday, 1972.

Slipper, Callan. *Enriched by the Other: A Spiritual Guide to Receptive Ecumenism.* Cambridge: Grove, 2016.

Thomson, John B. *Sharing Friendship: Exploring Anglican Character, Vocation, Witness and Mission.* London: Routledge, 2015.

12

"Mutual Flourishing" in the Church of England

An Opportunity for Internal Receptive Ecumenism?

DIANE RYAN

INTRODUCTION

THE CHURCH OF ENGLAND recently celebrated 30 years since the first ordinations of women to the priesthood, but the Act of Synod which legitimized this[1] permitted the continuation of two integrities; those who welcomed the ordination, and those who continued to oppose it. In this way, rather than seeking reconciliation between the opposing points of view, it allowed both viewpoints to continue as authentic expressions of the Church of England. The Five Guiding Principles,[2] to which all clergy are required to assent, were advanced to ensure the "mutual flourishing" of all, whatever their views on this subject. These principles attempted to ensure that all parts of the church continued to recognize each other as part of the same—one church with two identities. Parishes were permitted to pass resolutions requesting only male priests

---

1. Priests (Ordination of Women) Measure 1993.
2. House of Bishops' Declaration on the Ministry of Bishops and Priests.

serve their church and requesting extended episcopal oversight from a bishop who had not ordained women. Several Traditional Catholic[3] parishes requested this, and a small but increasing number of Conservative Evangelical parishes, with the creation of "Provincial Episcopal Visitors" or "flying bishops" taking on part of the role of the diocesan bishop for these churches, leading to further ecclesiological anomalies. The result has been a church with elements resembling an ecumenical relationship, and I have therefore looked to ecumenical methodology and resources to reflect on the situation.

Paul Lakeland has already suggested that churches could make use of an "internal receptive ecumenism."[4] For Monica Furlong this reflects the challenge involved in wrestling with division within the denomination: "It seems to me that the Church of England finds it easier and more rewarding to be ecumenical with Roman Catholics, Orthodox Christians and Methodists than to try to build bridges, however tenuous, within the differing branches of its own family."[5] So, taking up Furlong's challenge and Lakeland's suggestion, I will reflect on my own experiences in the Diocese of Sheffield to explore whether Receptive Ecumenism can offer a way to understand and improve relations between those with different views in the Church of England. In particular I will explore the Receptive Ecumenism themes of woundedness, hospitality, unilateralism and vulnerability in relation to the experience of women priests in the church.

DEVELOPING RECEPTIVE RELATIONSHIPS

The central question of Receptive Ecumenism, as posed by Murray, is "What can *we* learn, or *receive*, with integrity, from *our* various others in order to facilitate our own growth together into deepened communion in Christ and the Spirit?"[6] It thus puts emphasis on our own ecclesial needs and lack, and understands the church as a learning community, receptive to the gifts and insights of others. The goal of this endeavor is that all parties are changed; although the impetus comes from one quarter, and may not be reciprocated, recognizing that we cannot force the

---

3. The self-designation 'Traditional Catholic' is used to refer to those of High Church background who do not agree with the ordination of women and request alternative or extended episcopal oversight from a Traditional Catholic bishop in another diocese.
4. Lakeland, "Give and Take," 7–8.
5. Furlong, *The C of E: The State It's In*, 341.
6. Murray, *Receptive Ecumenism and the Call to Catholic Learning*, ix–x.

other to engage. Nonetheless, the aim is that all grow in unity with each other and with Christ, in contrast to approaches that aim for the ultimate discarding of one position in favor of the other. The starting point lies in recognition of one's own ecclesial woundedness, and desire for healing; it is a position of humility, of attending to the log in our own eye before commenting on the splinter in our neighbor's eye. Mary McLintock Fulkerson acknowledges the importance of recognizing the wound for healing: "Wounds generate new thinking,"[7] and Paul Avis notes the impetus towards wholeness: "There is a dynamic and a momentum in *koinonia* that seeks to overcome that impairment, just as the human body's natural healing properties will work to heal over a wound."[8]

This is an appropriate methodology to utilize in the present context, as the Church of England is experiencing its current situation as a wound, employing the phrase "impaired communion,"[9] which was previously used of relations with other denominations, to describe its internal relationships. Women priests continue to report instances of discrimination and bad behavior beyond those legalized by these Guiding Principles. Gabrielle Thomas's research on women's experiences in the churches shows remarkable similarities of experience across the denominations and highlights some shocking and unkind behaviors.[10] Meanwhile, the proposed appointment of an assistant bishop who would not ordain women, to be Diocesan Bishop of Sheffield, was withdrawn after opposition from within and beyond the church, leaving people from his Traditional Catholic background feeling that their "mutual flourishing" was being denied them.

Thomas recognizes that for dialogue to be effective, the participants need to show their wounds, not just put out the best china tea set,[11] metaphorically speaking. This requires trust that these wounds would be recognized by the other participants, and not made worse by rejection, and alongside confidentiality in the meetings she highlights the role of hospitality in making participants feel comfortable enough to share the wounds of their experiences.

I experienced an occasion when hospitality enabled relationships to develop, leading to an ecumenical thawing of attitudes. The Chrism

7. Fulkerson, *Places of Redemption*, 12.
8. Avis, *Seeking the Truth of Change in the Church*, 166.
9. Church of England, *Episcopal ministry*, 161.
10. Thomas, *Receiving the Gift*.
11. Following Murray, "Introducing Receptive Ecumenism," 5.

Mass, held in Holy Week, is an occasion for priests and deacons to renew their vows to the bishop, as well as collecting oils for use in the parish in the coming year. Traditional Catholic priests in this diocese celebrate an alternative Chrism Mass with their visiting bishop and some do not attend the diocesan one. Leaving on one side the implications for episcopal oversight, this sign of division at a significant time of the church's year is experienced as a wound in the church, so with another female colleague I decided to also attend the alternative Chrism Mass, wearing our clerical collars. Unsure how we would be received, we were in fact warmly welcomed and encouraged to stay for refreshments and chat. I followed this positive experience by attending the following year and handing to the Traditional Catholic Dean a card assuring my "brother priests" of my prayers for their ministry.

In the context of the Traditional Catholics' warm hospitality, where they were on "home ground" this seemed possible and a step towards healing. I don't know what effect my attendance had on this group of priests; perhaps none. This too, Receptive Ecumenism reminds us not to expect. We are each to take responsibility for our own learning and actions, not requiring the other to follow suit. Risto Saarinen's work on recognition is pertinent here, as obviously the aim is for mutual recognition of ministry: that these priests would offer prayers for their sister priests at the Chrism Mass. In Saarinen's terms this would be R1E, a recognition of equals.[12] But reading this through the lens of Receptive Ecumenism we see that reciprocity cannot be required. This lack of reciprocity may lead to sorrow and further wounding, but we can choose an attitude of appropriate realism, avoiding such expectations.

Receptive Ecumenism also recognizes the place of pain in the process of reconciliation. While the "pain of disunity" at the communion table has long been prescribed as an incentive to greater work for ecumenism, Receptive Ecumenism offers a place where that pain can be recognized and held. In the image of holding out wounded hands,[13] we see an acceptance of our own wounds, not trying to hide them from the other. An important first step may be the mutual acceptance that our divisions are a wound in the church and that we are all in need of healing. Thomas's project also showed the importance of a community in healing

---

12. Saarinen, *Recognition and Religion*, 35–37.
13. Murray, "Introducing Receptive Ecumenism," 5.

some of the wounds we present: the support of other women helped some to continue in difficult situations in their own church.

Saarinen states that "because the theory of recognition holds that we need both universalism and difference, it may become a friend of the ecumenical movement."[14] He, and Minna Hietamäki, build on social analysis to delineate different levels of recognition, and apply these to what can be observed of ecumenical relationships between churches. They describe recognition as a spectrum between toleration as a minimum relationship, and agreement and consensus as a fuller relationship (Saarinen), or identification—acknowledgement—recognition (Hietamäki). In both of these analyses, there are different levels of recognition available for different relationships, which involve different levels of agreement with the institution or individual represented.

Hietamäki, studying the development of relationships between the churches at the World Council of Churches, notes a directional movement with a subject and object of recognition. Thus, individual or institution A may recognize individual or institution B as a fellow Christian or church (X), perhaps because of an agreement on baptism as expression of belonging in the church. Such recognition would be a judgement based on their understanding of B, which implies a relationship of power from A to B, so to avoid misrecognition, a dialogical relationship of discovery is recommended. This has resonance with the practice of Receptive Ecumenism and leads to a deeper recognition than the "Christologically mediated recognition," where various subjects (A1, A2 etc) recognize Christ as God. In this setting, the subjects are in a sibling relationship united with each other through their common object, recognition of Christ as God. Hietamäki describes this as a "weak variant" of recognition, but it does avoid the power aspect of the A—B—X relationship. This relationship is strengthened by the institutions acknowledging that the Christ they proclaim allegiance to desire his followers to recognize each other, "that the world may believe." This recognition enables churches to "recognize each other 'as belonging fully to His body.'"[15]

Although Saarinen states that "even a one-sided recognition may be better than nothing,"[16] mutual flourishing in the Church of England is aiming for something deeper than this. Currently, recognition is incomplete, consisting of recognition of men's orders by women while

14. Saarinen, "The Changing World as Challenge for the Churches," 43.
15. Hietamäki, "Ecumenical Recognition," 208.
16. Saarinen, "The Changing World as Challenge for the Churches," 43.

not everyone recognizes women's orders. Thus, Hietamäki's category of Christologically-mediated recognition offers a creative way forward, as it avoids the possibility of misrepresentation, and offers the possibility of movement towards mutual recognition. In the visit to the Chrism Mass, we were welcomed to join in prayer as fellow members of the Body of Christ, a mediated recognition, and over the refreshments afterwards we shared stories of common struggles with diocesan offices and building problems, a partial recognition of the shared role of priest. The level of mutual recognition that already exists across the Church of England lends momentum towards further reconciliation.

DEVELOPING RECONCILED RELATIONSHIPS

Miroslav Volf's work exhibits a deep commitment to reconciliation between churches and between faiths, and his early work *Exclusion and Embrace*[17] emphasizes the importance of human reconciliation as part of God's work of reconciling all creation to himself. (2 Cor 5:18–19). He explores reconciliation with the metaphor of an embrace, containing four movements: "opening the arms, waiting, closing the arms and opening them again."[18] To make the move towards reconciliation, individuals must prepare themselves by "de-centering," making space for the other, and by being radically open to the other as they are. In these ways it echoes the movement of Receptive Ecumenism, which opens the hands and makes space to receive the gifts of the other. Further, the embrace does not leave its participants unchanged; each must be prepared to "undertake a re-adjustment of its identity in the light of the other's alterity."[19] These are not light undertakings and emphasize the challenge of the task of reconciliation.

The initial gesture of opening the arms serves to "de-center" the body, creating a void that longs to be filled, a desire for the other. As an uncompleted circle, the opened arms represent a wound requiring healing. There is space for the other to enter as he or she is, but the choice to enter into the embrace or not remains with the other. In the second moment of waiting, the initiator experiences openness with vulnerability, unable to protect him or herself. Expressing respect for the other, who "cannot

---

17. Volf, *Exclusion and Embrace*.
18. Volf, *Exclusion and Embrace*, 141.
19. Volf, *Exclusion and Embrace*, 110.

be coerced or manipulated into an embrace,"[20] the initiator waits for an indeterminate time, for the other to respond. The third movement is one of closing the arms. Even within the context of this successful embrace, the initiator must take care to respect the boundaries of self and other, and not over-exert their power. Volf implies here that an embrace is mutual and reciprocated, but it would seem to me that there may be instances where the level of enthusiasm for such action is different on each side, or where a power imbalance cannot be completely overcome. The risk for the other of accepting the embrace is that the initiator may exert their power to entrap the other, and not allow them to regain their freedom. Thus, the fourth and final action, which may not seem part of the embrace, but is nonetheless essential, is the opening again of the arms. In this way, the parties do not become an undifferentiated "we" but retain their individual identity, changed, but still who they were.

This understanding of reconciliation as embrace, challenging as it is, may offer a way forward in the situation of mutual flourishing. By naming the difficulties involved in movements towards reconciliation, it challenges participants to decide whether they truly desire reconciliation. Thomas suggests that what we have at the moment is less "mutual flourishing" than "independent flourishing" protected by buffer zones.[21] Following her understanding, those within the church should consider carefully whether they desire mutual flourishing sufficiently to undertake the costly movements towards reconciliation. This is a particular issue for women in the church who have experienced long years of exclusion from the structures of the church, and whose openness and vulnerability have not always been received with generosity or mutuality. Is it appropriate to ask of such women further openness and vulnerability in reaching out in reconciliation to their Traditional Catholic and Conservative Evangelical colleagues?

Issues of power and vulnerability are also made visible by this image of an embrace. Although Volf describes the "successful" embrace as a movement of mutuality, it is clear that one party takes the initiative. This action could flow from power or vulnerability, and it is interesting to see that in different contexts both ordained women and those who oppose them can be seen as having power or vulnerability. The initiator may feel able to act because of their relative power in the situation; Indian

---

20. Volf, *Exclusion and Embrace*, 143.
21. Thomas, "*Mutual Flourishing.*"

theologian Muthuraj Swamy contends that the stronger party should be the initiator of moves towards reconciliation.[22] Or their greater awareness of the wound caused by division may lead some to risk being vulnerable and initiate an embrace despite being the weaker party. Here again, the existence of "buffer zones" mitigates against work towards reconciliation because it insulates people from the pain of disunity. In this respect the recent judgement that "there is a duty not to cause pain where it can be avoided"[23] may be seen as mitigating against the work required to enable a truly mutual flourishing. This judgement was given in response to a query regarding the advanced publication of the identity of celebrants at the Eucharist at Wakefield Cathedral. The Independent Reviewer agreed with a congregation member that names of priestly celebrants at each service should be published in advance so that individuals could decide to avoid services led by women, as it was stated that attending such a service but being unable to receive communion, or walking out of the service, would cause the congregation member pain. The possibility of pain caused to the woman celebrant in such a situation was not mentioned. However, in ecumenical contexts, for example in interchurch couples, it is the regular experience of the pain of being unable to share communion that is a powerful motivation for action to resolve this wound.[24]

This analysis of reconciliation as embrace also highlights issues of identity which remain central to the concerns of Traditional Catholics within the Church of England. Anxious that their particular gifts and tradition might be lost within the Church of England, they are wary of anything that might diminish that identity. Volf distinguishes between differentiation, which is what God does in creation, separating darkness from light but valuing both, and exclusion, where division is made and only one side is valued. In embrace, it is clear that the identity of both participants is preserved. Respect for the other requires that sufficient space is made to accommodate the other, and that even within the embrace the two identities remain distinct. The end of the embrace requires the reassertion of individual identity, although it is recognized that "a genuine embrace cannot leave both or either completely unchanged."[25] This may offer the appropriate reassurance to those concerned about their identity, that reconciliation will not necessarily

---

22. Swamy, *Reconciliation*, 116.
23. Fittall, *Wakefield Cathedral*, 38.
24. See Ryan and Ryan, "From Experiment to Encounter," 10–12.
25. Volf, *Exclusion and Embrace*, 147.

require a dissolution of identity. With this confidence may come the freedom to change to the extent anticipated by the embrace.

VULNERABLE RELATIONSHIPS

A theological understanding of human vulnerability, seeing it as a vital part of Jesus's experience, has been developed by writers of disability theology, emphasizing that people with disabilities are not outside of Christian experience. However, they have also served to highlight the vulnerabilities that all people experience from time to time and normalize these as also part of Christian experience. "Vulnerability is the warp and woof of being human, and accepting our vulnerability opens us up to others."[26] Here we can see how accepting our own vulnerability feeds into the beneficial attitudes that we need to develop in order to practice reconciliation and Receptive Ecumenism, and conversely, "refusing to own up to our vulnerability cultivates an aversion to difference. This, in turn, yields ideologies of exclusion and violence."[27] Therefore, an understanding and acceptance of our own vulnerability, which might be an inner work of prayer, becomes a vital precursor to the pursuit of unity. Where undertaken in company, along the lines of Spiritual Ecumenism, a common understanding of our vulnerability before God and each other enables participants to offer their wounds for healing, confident that they will be treated with care.

Difficulties arise, however, in situations where there is not a mutuality of acceptance of vulnerability, or a reluctance to display that vulnerability. Where there is a lack of trust, people will be fearful of showing weakness. This includes some situations of mutual flourishing within the Church of England. Can we still proclaim the way of vulnerability where there is only one-sided recognition? In human interaction, as we saw in Volf's metaphor of embrace, a willingness to make oneself vulnerable involves an element of risk but can call forth an answering response in the other which acknowledges the risk taken and opens the way to mutuality. For example, attendance at the Chrism Mass of the Traditional Catholics, was a vulnerable position for me. However, this vulnerability enabled the Traditional Catholic priests to show welcome and hospitality in a space where they felt comfortable and unthreatened. There was a partial recognition, as priests engaged in conversation about

26. Reynolds, *Vulnerable Communion*, 107.
27. Reynolds, *Vulnerable Communion*, 110.

ministry. There was also opportunity for the development of the Life and Works aspect of ecumenism, with an animated discussion about parish building projects, which led to an invitation to a patronal festival, showing how easily one form of engagement can lead to another form. All these outcomes resulted from the decision to choose a position of vulnerability on this occasion.

An earlier occasion of vulnerability was less clear in its outcomes. Following the self-exclusion of a group of Traditional Catholic priests from a diocesan event at which the Dean of Women's ministry was presiding at communion, I engaged one Traditional Catholic priest in conversation. Clarifying that this was the first such occasion in the diocese, there was a frank exchange of viewpoints, during which the experience of wound was clear. He considered that the bishop was requiring clergy to do something against their consciences, which I countered, making a distinction between receiving communion and his attendance at the service, which is not prohibited by his conscience. Drawing on the thinking contained in this work and my own experience as an Anglican attending Catholic services where I am not invited to receive communion, I offered the challenge that because a thing is painful, does not mean that it is not appropriate to do. Here, my willingness to be vulnerable, while eliciting no immediate agreement, did enable an exchange of views to be made, in the context of previous "Faith and Order" type discussions with this individual, and a deeper understanding of the opposing positions was gained. This example shows that there is still considerable division over the recognition of ministries, and movement towards reconciliation will be a long process, in which all aspects of internal ecumenical engagement, Life and Work, Faith and Order, and Spiritual and Receptive Ecumenism will be required.

Vulnerability is a key attitude in the process of reconciliation, and, expressed as humility, is key to Receptive Ecumenism. Instead of pretending that everything is fine, we need to be ready to together acknowledge our wounds and weakness. Where we are not able to do this, "by projecting our own fear of vulnerability onto others, we become cut off from the wellspring of our own flourishing: mutual dependence."[28] Here the link between acceptance of vulnerability and flourishing within a context of mutual dependence is made clear. In the context of mutual flourishing, vulnerability can be a way to open up a relationship and is an important

---

28. Reynolds, *Vulnerable Communion*, 111.

component of reconciliation. Practicing vulnerability in other Receptive Ecumenism contexts could develop the confidence to offer this in intra-church, mutual flourishing relationships also.

BIBLIOGRAPHY

Avis, Paul D. L., ed. *Seeking the Truth of Change in the Church: Reception, Communion, and the Ordination of Women*. London: T. & T. Clark, 2004.
Church of England. *Episcopal Ministry: The Report of the Archbishops' Group on the Episcopate*. London: Church House Publishing, 1990.
Church of England, House of Bishops. House of Bishops' Declaration on the Ministry of Bishops and Priests (GS Misc 1076) 2014.
Fittall, William. *House of Bishops Declaration on the Ministry of Bishops and Priests. Wakefield Cathedral—Report of the Independent Reviewer*, 2019.
Fulkerson, Mary McClintock. *Places of Redemption: Theology for a Worldly Church*. Oxford: Oxford University Press, 2007.
Furlong, Monica. *The C of E: The State It's In*. SPCK, London, 2000.
Hietamäki, Minna. "'Ecumenical Recognition' in the Faith and Order Movement." *Open Theology* 1/1 (2015) 204–19.
Lakeland, Paul. "Give and Take." *The Tablet*, 14th July 2018, 7–8.
Murray, Paul D., ed. *Receptive Ecumenism and the Call to Catholic Learning: Exploring a Way for Contemporary Ecumenism*. Oxford: Oxford University Press, 2008.
Murray, Paul D. "Introducing Receptive Ecumenism." *The Ecumenist* 51/2 (2014) 1–8.
Reynolds, Thomas E. *Vulnerable Communion: A Theology of Disability and Hospitality*. Grand Rapids: Brazos, 2008.
Ryan, Diane, and Gregory A. Ryan. "From Experiment to Encounter: Receiving Interchurch Families in a Synodal Church." *Journal of Marriage, Families & Spirituality* 30/1 (2024) 6–20.
Saarinen, Risto. "The Changing World as Challenge for the Churches: New Frontiers of Ecumenical Recognition." In *Catholicity under Pressure: The Ambiguous Relationship Between Diversity and Unity*, edited by Dagmar Heller and Peter Szentpétery, 37–54. Leipzig: Evangelische Verlagsanstalt, 2016.
Saarinen, Risto. *Recognition and Religion: A Historical and Systematic Study*. Oxford: Oxford University Press, 2016.
Swamy, Muthuraj. *Reconciliation: The Archbishop of Canterbury's Lent Book 2019*. London: SPCK, 2018.
Thomas, Gabrielle. *"Mutual Flourishing": Learning Receptively from Thomas Aquinas* [Seminar paper]. Theology and Ministry. Abbey House, Durham University [2nd May], 2019.
———. *Receiving the Gift: Using Receptive Ecumenism to Explore Women's Experiences of Working within Diverse Churches in England*, 2019. In: https://www.durham.ac.uk/media/durham-university/research-/research-centres/catholic-studies-centre-for-ccs/Women-and-the-Churches-Shorter-Report-compressed.pdf.
Volf, Miroslav. *Exclusion and Embrace: A Theological Exploration of Identity, Otherness, and Reconciliation*. Nashville: Abingdon, 1996.

13

Transforming Ecumenism Through an Ecumenism of the People

Joan Patricia Back

INTRODUCTION

ONE OF THE MAJOR concerns in the ecumenical movement today is around reception and implementation of the progress that theological dialogues have achieved. The churches have celebrated significant milestones, but the question is how can these not only be received but also channeled into action? The challenge of transformation has been addressed in the ecumenical world over recent years. The search for ways of transformation can be aligned with two key words: "journey" and "pilgrimage" which have now acquired an ecumenical significance.[1] Ecumenical transformation takes place on the Emmaus road that we walk along together with Jesus.[2]

In this chapter I offer some insights into a transformation that comes from an ecumenical spirituality lived within the Focolare Movement,

---

1. For example, WCC General Assembly message 2013, "Join the Pilgrimage of Justice and Peace." https://www.oikoumene.org/news/message-of-the-wcc-assembly-we-intend-to-move-together.

2. See Pope Francis 25 January 2014: "Unity will not come about as a miracle at the very end. Rather, unity comes about in journeying; the Holy Spirit does this on the journey." https://www.vatican.va/content/francesco/en/homilies/2014/documents/papa-francesco_20140125_vespri-conversione-san-paolo.

which has given rise to a "dialogue of life"—a dialogue which lends itself as a vehicle for Receptive Ecumenism by facilitating the mutual exchange of gifts and the translation of our discovery into daily life.[3]

A NEW ECUMENICAL WAY: SPIRITUALITY

Since the beginning of the twenty-first century, ecumenists have been suggesting spirituality as a new ecumenical way and emphasizing the necessity of an ecumenism rooted in spirituality and not just based on theological dialogue. This new direction has been supported by prominent figures of the World Council of Churches and the Pontifical Council for Christian Unity. Samuel Kobia stated, "We need to rediscover spirituality as a primary way of engaging the ecumenical agenda."[4] Cardinal Kurt Koch highlighted the priority of a new ecumenical spirituality rather than ecumenical activity.[5]

This growing consensus on ecumenical spirituality to give a renewed impulse and a renewed soul to the ecumenical movement is orientated towards an "ecumenism of life." Here again within the two bodies we find a consensus on this perspective. Konrad Raiser spoke about the necessity of "an ecumenism of the heart. Not only of the spirit, of the intellect, but an ecumenism I would say of life"[6] while Walter Kasper suggested that something needs to fill, with "real life," what he calls this "transitional period" of incomplete *communio*. His proposal that to the "ecumenism of love" and "ecumenism of truth," which both naturally remain very important, must be added an "ecumenism of life."[7] Koch perceived the inextricable link between these three "ecumenisms" and a "renewed ecumenical spirituality."[8]

Often ecumenical spiritualities are born from charisms which the Holy Spirit enlarges in Christians of different churches, which generate new impulses towards deeper relations among Christians. As Yves Congar reminded us "ecumenism is first of all a fact of the Holy Spirit"[9] and we can look upon the charisms he bestows on the church of Christ as

3. Cf. Slipper, "A Discipline for Living."
4. Kobia to the 19th World Methodist Council July 2006.
5. Koch, "Ecumenical Spirituality."
6. "Ce qui'il faut, un oecuménisme de vie" in *La Croix* 23 gennaio 2001, 17.
7. Kasper, "*Prolusio 2001*," 19.
8. Koch, "Ecumenical Spirituality," 35.
9. Congar, *Spiritualità ecumenica*, 158.

agents of transformation. The transformative role of spirituality within the Catholic Church since Vatican II has had ecumenical consequences. In the ever-growing convergence among the churches regarding an ecclesiology of communion, the need for a spirituality of communion has emerged for an efficient functioning of that ecclesiology.[10] In this context Kasper's comment on *Novo Millennio Ineunte* is significant "It is particularly important for us also to develop a "spirituality of *communio*" (*NMI* 42f), in our own Church and between the Churches."[11] Chiara Lubich sees Focolare in this perspective :

> The Holy Spirit . . . has also given new charisms to the Church today which render a spirituality of communion possible . . . The charism of unity of the Focolare Movement is among these new movements and its "spirituality of unity" provides a full response to the need for such a new spirituality.[12]

Some charisms have given life to spiritualities that are lived by Christians of different churches, forming movements and communities characterized by an ecumenical lifestyle.[13]

Lived spirituality creates communion and "the commitment to a 'spirituality of communion' gives a renewed impetus to ecumenism."[14] This is precisely what Focolare's spirituality tries to do and as Pope John Paul II pointed out:

> Deepening in particular the spirituality of unity, you prepare yourselves to cooperate better with the Holy Spirit, the divine leaven of the unity of the People of God and of all humanity.[15]

Kasper underlines this:

> I believe that by starting with a purer and clearer understanding of ecumenical spirituality, we can move towards a renewed and more profound ecumenical practice, capable of providing a new

---

10. See, for example, ARCIC II, *The Church as Communion*.

11. Kasper, "*Prolusio* 2001," 20.

12. Lubich, "A Spirituality of Unity within Diversity," 192.

13. Some communities live out a prophetic dimension of an "already, but not yet" unity among them. For example: the Taizé Community, Chemin Neuf, Focolare Movement, and the Emmanuel Community.

14. John Paul II, "Talk to Bishops, Friends of the Focolare, 2003."

15. "To the XIX Meeting of Bishops Friends of the Focolare Movement." *L'Osservatore Romano*, 17 February 1995 (my trans.).

impetus to the ecumenical quest and of releasing it from its current difficulties, aporie and crises.[16]

Bearing all this in mind, I will now take a closer look at Focolare's spirituality of unity.

FOCOLARE'S SPIRITUALITY OF UNITY

Around Chiara Lubich's charism of unity emerged a gospel-based experience centered on the testament of Jesus, "that all may be one" (John:17:21). I would like to underline though, as Lubich did, that "the spirituality of unity, which flowered in a particular movement is now a universal patrimony."[17] This is, in keeping with the understanding of the nature of a charism, something destined for the good of the whole body of Christ. From the beginnings of Focolare, she saw that living the Word of God made those living the Word "One." In 1948 she wrote:

> May we be united, Father, in the Name of the Lord, living the Word of life that makes us one . . . I thought of grafting plants, where the two parts that have been peeled make contact with the living part of the branch and become one. Why? Because the two parts that make contact are both "alive." When are two souls able to be consumed in one? When they are "alive," that is, when the human has been peeled away . . . and, through the living Word of Life, incarnating it, they are living words. Two living words can consume themselves in one, if one of them is not alive, the other one cannot unite itself.[18]

From this insight, Focolare's spirituality based on two cornerstones, both fundamental for building unity, developed: "Jesus Crucified and Forsaken" (cf. Matt 27:46; Mark 15:34) and the "presence of Jesus in the midst" (cf. Matt 18:20). These emerged in the early 1960s as key concepts of Chiara Lubich's ecumenical thought.

Jesus in Our Midst Facilitates Receptive Ecumenism

Lubich's understanding of the presence of Jesus in the midst of those who are united in His name (Matt 18:20) became, just before Vatican

---

16. Kasper, "*Prolusio 2003*," 30.
17. Lubich, *The Holy Spirit: The Unknown God*, 128.
18. Lubich, *Early Letters: At the Origins of a New Spirituality*, 130.

II, "the strong point" of Focolare's ecumenical lifestyle.[19] Jesus, present among Christians from different churches, united in His love, opened up an ecumenical way: to be one in Christ (Gal 3:28). The experience of "being one" in this spirituality implies not only living a life in Christ, individually on one's own, but as a communitarian experience. Lubich likened this experience to that of being like "living cells" of the mystical body of Christ, because His presence among them "activated" that sacramental bond which exists through our common baptism and makes it "function," opening channels for a new "lymph" to enter into this body. These channels facilitate the exchange and sharing of gifts, a practice fundamental to Receptive Ecumenism.

As Focolare's ecumenical lifestyle developed with the "dialogue of life," living with Jesus in their midst laid the basis for a fundamental element of living Receptive Ecumenism to take place: the sharing of each other's gifts and learning from them.[20] For example, with the Orthodox, Focolare's spirituality was in tune with the writings of the early church fathers; their concept of living God's Word resonated with Lutherans and Reformed Christians; the emphasis on listening to the Holy Spirit found them in unity with Pentecostals.

Jesus Crucified and Forsaken as a Model for Living Receptive Ecumenism

To be so united as to have the presence of Christ among us in this spirituality requires a life modelled on that of Christ's *kenosis,* embodied in Jesus's cry on the cross "My God, my God, why have you forsaken me?" (Matt 27:46; Mark 15:34). His embrace of suffering, his humility is a spiritual key that facilitates dialogue. It enables us to face every painful situation of disunity and opens the door to entering into the Paschal mystery of the Resurrection: "the Risen Lord in us takes the place of the forsaken one."[21] It requires self-emptying, a postponing of our ideas in order to make room to listen to the other person. This is not something purely intellectual but involves concrete actions in receiving the other's proposals. A transformation takes place in the soul when this spiritual threshold is crossed. In the words of Paul "I have been crucified with Christ; and it is no longer I who live, but it is Christ who lives in me." (Gal 2:20).

19. Lubich, *Jesus in Our Midst,* 136.
20. Cf. Lubich, *My Ecumenical Journey,* 109.
21. Lubich, *Living Dialogue,* 61.

Therefore, in every division the countenance of Jesus crucified is seen as a suffering to be "embraced" and involves our adherence to God's plan in the sense of Col 1:24: "I am completing what is lacking in Christ's afflictions for the sake of his body, that is, the church." In this unitive "embrace," it is the Holy Spirit who gives strength and courage to face every difficulty involved in Receptive Ecumenism. In order to receive the gift from a church different from one's own it could involve an intellectual momentarily "putting aside" one's own ecclesiastical tradition, "emptying" oneself, to be open to listen to another church's understanding on the same subject. This does not conflict with the Receptive Ecumenism tenet of integrity, because discernment is through the Holy Spirit's presence; nor does it impede the process of becoming more Catholic, more Anglican etc. Indeed, it could result in a rediscovery of your own church, seen in a new light.

In these two cornerstones of the spirituality of unity, we find the key to a "living dialogue" which has much to offer to live other dimensions of ecumenism: God's presence among Christians of different churches in prayer together, in social activities and in theological dialogue. For instance, theologians can experience a new spiritual starting point in dialogue with Jesus among them. Over the years dialogues like ARCIC have experienced the presence of the Holy Spirit, who illuminates them as they seek to explore the truth together, to heal wounds, to enter a process of purification of historical memory but here there is an additional gift.

A DIALOGUE OF THE PEOPLE—DIALOGUE OF LIFE

Earlier I cited ecumenists speaking of the necessity of an ecumenism of life. It is in this context that I want to present the importance of a living dialogue, a "dialogue of the people" that is characteristic of Focolare's spirituality and life. "People" here denotes the whole people of God from the laity to Bishops, from children to the elderly. This dialogue is based on living out the Gospel and on the communicating of experiences.

Currently Christians of over 350 different churches worldwide are in contact with Focolare and this has given birth to a reality that Lubich defined as the "dialogue of life" or a "dialogue of the people." The experience of unity that comes from the presence of Jesus in the midst undergirds all dialogues, making them effective and receptive, and this is the foundation of the "dialogue of life"; Christ in our midst builds up the *koinonia* among Christians in daily life.

In 1996 Chiara Lubich became aware of this "living dialogue" at a meeting in London of over a thousand people belonging to Focolare from different churches. Reflecting on this "people," whose unity was tangible, she understood it was the fruit of the spirituality of unity lived out in daily life. She saw the ecumenical potential of Christians united in their common patrimony and the life of grace deriving from a common baptism. It is important to underline that this dialogue does not exclude other forms of dialogue nor is it in conflict with institutional ecumenism or an alternative to theological dialogues, quite the contrary. It is the basis of them all, undergirding the other aspects of ecumenism providing the *humus* on which the results of theological dialogues can be received and lived by the Christian "in the pew."[22]

Thus, this new form of dialogue—an "ecumenism of the people" can be a vehicle for Receptive Ecumenism—a people who are like an ecumenical yeast that leavens unity between the churches through the "dialogue of life."[23] I will share some fruits of this "living dialogue" that illustrate how the inculturated dialogue of life is the humus on which the various ecumenical dimensions are born and developed.

Latin America

In Mexico, in 2021, Focolare members after the Week of Prayer for Christian Unity began an ecumenical project of "virtual visits to churches to promote unity." The intention was to make ecumenical contacts ongoing and "launch the people" into a journey of communion and fraternity. Among their objectives was to know and esteem the riches that each tradition possesses and to live and express the Christian faith in their own environment.

In 2022 a central ecumenical commission was formed to generate an ecumenism of life. The first session involved over a hundred enthusiastic participants and was successively seen by more than 1,700 people who in turn invited others. During the year, nine virtual visits were held, involving an explanation of one church, followed by dialogue in

---

22. Metropolitan Emilianos Timiadis put it like this: "Ecumenical progress heavily depends upon the wide vision of a healthy and enlightened spirituality. In the absence of these conditions interest in ecumenical relationships becomes just an academic pursuit without fruitful repercussions in the future." Timiadis, *La spiritualità ortodossa*, 95. My translation.

23. Pope Francis speaks of recovering the knowledge that we are part of a people and of "regenerating bonds of trust and belonging": *Let Us Dream*, 107.

small groups to facilitate a reciprocal sharing and to build up friendship. Social media helped in generating this ecumenical community that welcomed more than 10,500 people from Ecuador, Peru, Argentine, Venezuela, Colombia, Costa Rica, Honduras and the USA, as well as different Mexican cities, in just the first two months.[24]

Asia

Since 2019 Focolare members Jane Roble and Robert Samson have been the executive secretaries of the Episcopal Commission on Ecumenical Affairs (ECEA) of the Catholic Bishops Conference of the Philippines. The commission developed out of meetings in the Focolare Centre with pastors of different churches and with ecumenical groups all over the Philippines. They attribute this to the "dialogue of life" saying that dialogue for them started with life and from the heart.

The year 2021 was proclaimed by the Catholic Church in the Philippines as the Year of Ecumenism, Interreligious Dialogue, and Indigenous Peoples. A meeting with thirty theologians of different churches took place at the Focolare Centre in Quezon City, a venue chosen because everyone felt at home there. There, the Ecumenical Initiatives Forum was established, a body of theologians from different Christian churches that would function as a think-tank group to organize the activities for the Quincentennial Celebration of Christianity.

In 2021 the annual Bishops' three-day dialogue/seminar was organized by this forum which drafted a common statement by the Christian churches, a joint statement of the Catholic Church in the Philippines with the Iglesia Filipina Independiente or IFI (the Philippine Independent Church), out of which emerged the mutual recognition of the sacrament of baptism. Archbishop Angelito Lampon also suggested that we could learn not just the things that we have in common, but the things that differentiate us from one another, in order to get to know each other better and be enriched by the process of learning. Roble and Samson write:

> Before discussing the subjects proposed it was agreed to a premise that we would all set aside our opinions and ideas, expertise and experiences to give God the first place and be an empty vessel to welcome the other who would be presenting something.

---

24. See https://t.me/EcumenismoVisitasVirtuales.

After several virtual meetings, a common statement by the Christian churches was drafted and approved and was launched on Pentecost Sunday 2021.[25]

Africa

From the Democratic Republic of the Congo, Marisa Sechi of Focolare is involved with a group of young people from different churches, united in a federation called the Church of Christ in Congo (which comprises ninety-five churches including Lutheran, Baptist, Presbyterian and Anglican) and with the Orthodox Church. During the opening service of the Week of Prayer for Christian Unity 2021 she was concerned that there were no Orthodox present. She discovered that the Orthodox Church had not been officially invited, which led to a misunderstanding that the Orthodox did not want to participate in ecumenical events. She suffered because she saw how hurt her Orthodox friends, who felt excluded, were. There had been some bureaucratic hiccup, and this was less than a week before the official service that concluded the Week of Prayer.

To overcome protocols and accelerate the process she phoned the Catholic bishop and the Protestant bishop and together they resolved the issue and invited all the Orthodox to be present. The conclusion she came to was that through the friendship and trust built up through a dialogue of life, she had helped to resolve what could have led to estrangement with the Orthodox.

Europe

For over fifty years Lutherans and Catholics have lived together in a small ecumenical town at Ottmaring near Augsburg (Germany). Members of two Lutheran communities heard Chiara Lubich speaking in Darmstadt in 1961. They were attracted by Focolare's evangelical lifestyle and emphasis on unity. The communities were very diverse, but all felt called to work *"that all may be one."* Chiara Lubich and pastor Klaus Hess, leader of the Brudershaft vom Geimeinsamen Leben, were convinced that it was the will of God to begin an ecumenical town. So

---

25. See https://cbcpnews.net/cbcpnews/one-ecumenical-family/ and https://cbcpnews.net/cbcpnews/celebrating-the-gift-of-faith-learning-from-the-past-and-journeying-together.

Okumenisches Lebenszentrum was born and became a permanent witness of "living dialogue."[26]

An experience from Pozzuoli, (Italy) exemplifies something Koch highlighted:

> spiritual ecumenism proves credible only if it is accompanied by what can be called practical ecumenism. In this sense, the Focolare Movement has implemented in an increasingly concrete way the consequences of the charism of unity, also dealing with social issues up to the sphere of the economy.[27]

A relationship developed between Focolare members and Pentecostal pastor Perna and his wife. They had heard about the ecumenical experience of the "pink boutique" inside the Pozzuoli women's prison, with its walls painted pink, with colored curtains and shelves, contrasting with the greyness of the cells. This was a place where inmates, often abandoned or far from their families, can receive weekly personal care products, etc. things that help to improve their "look" and increase their self-esteem. At the same time, they are able to share their problems with one another.

Friendship between Focolare and the pastor and his wife grew and together they participated in ecumenical prayer times in the prison, in the diocese and in their church and in various charitable activities towards the poor. The pastor told them of a dream: to open a welcome center in a deprived area. The "House of Welcome," love without borders, a house open to all, regardless of their faith, race or culture was born.

Middle East

Since May 10th, 2013, the day of friendship between the Orthodox Coptic Church and the Roman Catholic Church has been celebrated. In Alexandria (Egypt) Sami Creta a young Catholic man from Focolare and his friend Anis from the Coptic Orthodox Church had an idea to mark the day by creating a special event: a Coptic modern art exhibition in the Jesuit Cultural Center. The idea behind this was to get the heads

---

26. See Decker and Schmid, *Okumenisches Lebenszentrum Ottmaring*, 126.

27. Koch, "Cristiani Insieme in Tempo di Pandemia: Il contributo della spiritualità ecumenica di Chiara Lubich per accrescere l'unità tra i discepoli di cristo," Focolare Ecumenical Conference Castelgandolfo (Italy), 28 May 2021, http://www.christianunity.va/content/unitacristiani/en/cardinal-koch/2021/conferences/presentation-at-ecumenical-conference-of-focolare-movement.html.

of the two churches in Alessandria together in an informal way. They accepted and one hundred participants attended from both churches. The following year the initiative to meet was taken by the two church leaders themselves and the friendship day was held in a Coptic Orthodox monastery. Pope Tawadros then started a tradition to honor a figure for services to the church: Catholic one year and Orthodox the next. This all began from the dialogue of life.

CONCLUSION

Through the lens of "transforming ecumenism" I have looked at the "dialogue of life" as lived out in Focolare's spirituality of unity, as a vehicle for implementing Receptive Ecumenism. It enables Christians of different churches to build up a spiritual unity and create that space where informative and formative dialogue can take place, facilitating the sharing of gifts.

The experiences illustrate ecumenical transformation in different *milieux.* illustrating how the "dialogue of the people" contributes towards Receptive Ecumenism on different levels, from spiritual encounters to undergirding theological dialogue.

BIBLIOGRAPHY

Anglican–Roman Catholic International Commission (ARCIC II). *The Church as Communion* (1990), https://www.anglicancommunion.org/media/105242/ARCIC_II_The_Church_as_Communion.pdf.

Congar, Yves. *Spiritualità ecumenica in Saggi ecumenici: Il movimento gli uomini, i problemi.* Rome: Citta Nuova, 1986.

Decker, Michael, and Severin Schmid. *Okumenisches Lebenszentrum Ottmaring.* Munich: Neue Stadt, 2008.

Francis, Pope (with Austin Ivereigh). *Let Us Dream: The Path to a Better Future.* New York: Simon & Schuster, 2020.

John Paul II, Pope. *Talk to Bishops, Friends of the Focolare Movement 13 February 2003.* https://www.vatican.va/content/john-paul-ii/en/speeches/2003/february/documents/hf_jp-ii_spe_20030213_bishops-focolari.

Kasper, Walter. "*Prolusio* for the Plenary of the Pontifical Council for Promoting Christian Unity, November 2001." In Pontifical Council for Promoting Christian Unity, *Information Service* 109 (2002/1–II), 20.

———. "*Prolusio* for the Plenary of the Pontifical Council for Promoting Christian Unity, November 2003." Pontifical Council for Promoting Christian Unity, *Information Service* 115 (2004/1–II), 30.

Koch, Kurt. "Plenary Theme: Ecumenical Spirituality, Main Report Rediscovering the Soul of the Whole Ecumenical Movement (UR8). Necessity and Perspectives of

an Ecumenical Spirituality." Pontifical Council for Promoting Christian Unity, *Information Service* 115 (2004/1–II), 34–35.
Lubich, Chiara. *Early Letters: At the Origins of a New Spirituality*. New York: New City, 2012.
———. *The Holy Spirit: The Unknown God*. London: New City, 2018.
———. *Jesus in Our Midst: Source of Joy and Light*. London: New City, 2019.
———. *My Ecumenical Journey*. London: New City, 2020.
———. "A Spirituality of Unity within Diversity." In *Searching for Christian Unity*, edited by Cardinal Walter Kasper. New York: New City, 2007.
Pontifical Council for Promoting Christian Unity. *Information Service* 109 (2002/1–II), http://www.christianunity.va/content/unitacristiani/en/acta-oecumenica/information-service-/information-service-1091.html.
———. *Information Service* 115 (2004/1–II), http://www.christianunity.va/content/unitacristiani/en/acta-oecumenica/information-service-/information-service-1151.html.
Raiser, Konrad. *The Challenge of Transformation: Ecumenical Journey*. Geneva: WCC Publications, 2018.
Slipper, Callan. "A Discipline for Living According to the Spirit: Chiara Lubich and Receptive Ecumenism." In *Receptive Ecumenism as Transformative Ecclesial Learning: Walking the Way to a Church Re-formed*, edited by Paul D. Murray, Gregory A. Ryan, and Paul Lakeland. Oxford: Oxford University Press, 2022.
Timiadis, Emilianos. *La spiritualità ortodossa*. Brescia: Morcelliana, 1962.

14

Searching for a Deeper Unity
Towards Relational Receptive Ecumenism Through the Lens of Interchurch Families

Doral Hayes

INTRODUCTION

An interchurch family exists where each partner in the relationship comes from a different Christian tradition. In this chapter I argue that such families are a specific lived example of Christian unity and that they present an opportunity to the church to further develop receptive ecumenical practice. For many interchurch couples their homes are a lived ecumenical experience and place of hope, as well as being a place of witness to the pain caused by Christian disunity. The Association of Interchurch Families[1] (AIF), published a paper stating that interchurch families, "have a significant and unique contribution to make to our churches' growth in visible Christian unity."[2] Having been raised in an interchurch family, as well as working professionally with interchurch families in the English ecumenical scene for over a decade I too believe that greater unity is possible, and that interchurch families can help illuminate what is needed to

---

1. Information about Association of Interchurch Families is at www.interchurch-families.org.uk

2. Association of Interchurch Families, *Interchurch Families and Christian Unity*, 1.

strengthen and develop receptive ecumenical practice. Here I present the start of a theological response to these experiences that have led to a desire to celebrate, challenge, and further develop Receptive Ecumenism by offering a critical account through the lens of interchurch families, calling for something more dynamic, resilient and relational which seeks to support the churches in their ecumenical journey.

By starting with a brief account of Receptive Ecumenism through the lens of interchurch families, I acknowledge its contribution to ecumenical practice before considering its limitations and challenges. The level of giving and receiving that is seen in the experience of those in interchurch marriages presents a practice informed account of ecumenical relationality that is different from other aspects of church life. In this chapter I intentionally talk about interchurch couples, however, when I use the term interchurch families, I am referring to the whole family unit which may also include children who are also significant to interchurch families' specific experience of Christian unity. An interchurch couple's relationship presents an example of Receptive Ecumenism, a committed and authentic relationship, and a willingness to engage with the worship and traditions of another church. It is necessary to clarify, that in drawing attention to the specific experience of interchurch families I do not seek to idealize family life or interchurch families in particular. Each family is unique, interchurch family or not, and experiences the pain and complexities for life. What an interchurch couple demonstrates is a deep, honest and lasting form of commitment to each other alongside faith life in two different church communities. If real ecumenical progress is to be made, it can only happen when those engaged in ecumenical activity and dialogue are genuinely open to change, through real and honest ecumenical relationships and interchurch families offer an example of such a relationship. Finally, I will briefly engage with open and relational theologian, Thomas Jay Oord, considering how his thought resonates with the experience of interchurch couples and can support the development of Receptive Ecumenism, creating what I am calling Relational Receptive Ecumenism.

RECEPTIVE ECUMENISM THROUGH THE LENS OF INTERCHURCH FAMILIES

At the heart of Receptive Ecumenism is a humility that each tradition has something to learn from the other, it requires an acknowledgment that every tradition has places of imperfection and weakness, asking the question, "What do we need to learn and what can we learn—or receive—with integrity from our others."[3] This acknowledges that each Christian tradition has places of pain, that none are perfect and that learning something from the other requires a spiritual and theological humility and openness as well as a long-term commitment. Significantly, this is not an ecumenical model that encourages letting go of one's own tradition but one that emphasizes "embracing more" through deeper understanding.[4] As such Receptive Ecumenism is by nature dynamic and requires relationship; it cannot be carried out in isolation but requires engagement with the other and so is open, not clinging to a static position, but embracing growth and change. It is a method that requires a committed relationship, as only with commitment to the ecumenical process and journey, on all sides, can real ecumenical progress be made. What interchurch couples offer is a lived example of this commitment, integrating theological reflection and worship, alongside practical service to two churches as well as mutual healing through their loving partnership. As Rowan Williams writes, interchurch couples experience "the joys of a family life rooted in love and mutual commitment alongside the pain of our ecumenical divisions."[5]

Although much progress has been made in ecumenical relations, today, both at a local and national level, my experience leads me to believe that it is still easier for Christians to come together in service and mission than it is to discuss together the thorny and potentially divisive areas of doctrine. For example, in over six years working within English local ecumenism I have witnessed a significant focus on social justice activities and community witness and much less appetite for, and even an avoidance of, theological discussion. Within an interchurch marriage, theological issues cannot be avoided as they are present daily in the home, for example in the shared raising of children, as well as in prayer and at church as part of shared worship, and so interchurch partners' ecumenical and personal lives are intimately intertwined.

Paul Murray writes of the originality and creativity of God at work in the world as he examines the Trinity alongside the "interwoven character of these three moments of Christian discipleship,"[6] by which he is

---

3. Murray, "In Search of a Way," 621.
4. Hendricks, "Interchurch Families and Receptive Ecumenism," 11.
5. Williams, *A Letter of Greeting*, 1.
6. Murray, *Reason, Truth and Theology in Pragmatist Perspective* 136.

referring to the virtues of faith, hope and love. This interweaving dynamic between faith, hope and love resides within receptive ecumenical theology and practice. It begins with faith in God, found and exercised through the worship and teachings of a Christian tradition, and leads to hope for greater unity between the churches which can then, through receiving from one another, lead to a greater love of other Christians and the churches they serve. Reading this through the lens of interchurch families, I observe that for interchurch couples this process works slightly differently. Although it does start with faith in God, the ecumenical journey also has love of the other as a starting point, this love for the other leads to a deeper commitment to the ecumenical process. Martin Reardon writes: "We fell in love with one another and found, whether we liked it or not, that we were part of the ecumenical movement."[7]

The experience of interchurch couples has been written about over the last fifty years, with a significant contribution made by Ruth Reardon, co-founder and former life president of the Association of Interchurch Families.[8] The contribution to ecumenism by interchurch families was recognized by Pope John Paul II who stated in a speech to interchurch families in 1982, "You live in your marriage the hopes and difficulties of the path to Christian unity."[9] The distinct ecumenical space interchurch couples inhabit is described well by Pastor Konrad Raiser, former General Secretary of the World Council of Churches.

> Each marriage is built on a covenant in which the partners promise to stay together whatever may arrive; they engage together in a process of discovering unity in diversity. The particular identities of the partners, formed before their marriage, do not disappear even though they are being transformed by the experience of common life. The unity of the couple is never simply a given; it has to be built and shaped in a lifelong process. The two partners become one, but their very union remains alive and viable only as they grant each other the freedom to remain themselves and distinct.[10]

---

7. Reardon, M., "We Love Each Other" 4.

8. See, *inter alia*, Reardon, R., "No Blueprint," "Eucharistic Sharing," Interchurch Families as Ecumenical Instruments."

9. AIF, *About Our Work*.

10. Raiser, *Opening Ecumenical Space*, 1.

This specific experience leads to a broader faith held within two traditions, and a hope of greater unity both in the home and in the churches they serve.

This is an example of what Murray expresses as a "moment of faithful attendance to the reality of things held in being by God as source and sustainer."[11] Here Murray speaks of attending to the reality of things. Family is a real part of everyday life; it is at times messy involving both joy and pain, and all are interconnected on a daily basis. It is this everyday practice of ecumenism that forms a distinct and deeper form of dialogue. Gabrielle Thomas uses the language of "wounds" and "gifts" in her work on the practice of Receptive Ecumenism which also speaks into the complexity of a deeper relationship experienced in a domestic context.[12]

It is also worth noting that most receptive ecumenical practice has involved those working at a high level within the churches, which has resulted in certain voices dominating—in particular male clergy—leaving other voices much harder to hear. Therefore, the ecumenical growth and learning that has taken place in the domestic sphere has been rarely heard by church leaders and institutions. Where the experience of interchurch couples can be of value to the churches is in an open, honest, and loving discussion of faith and unity, and—although not without pain and disagreement—remaining in relationship. Interchurch couples offer to the churches a lived experience of the loving, attentive, and egalitarian relationship that Receptive Ecumenism requires but so far has not been able to fully live out in practice. Pam McElroy, who is in an interchurch marriage herself writes, "If a couple who perhaps started off suspicious and defensive about one another's church affiliation can come to experience a deep and growing unity in Christ, and feel at home in two different church traditions, surely there is a wider message there?"[13] I believe there is a wider message for the churches if they are willing to receive it and although there is not space within this chapter, a closer analysis of the contribution and potential of interchurch couples towards Christian unity is required.[14]

11. Murray, *Reason, Truth and Theology in Pragmatist Perspective*, 136
12. Thomas, *For the Good of the Church*.
13. McElroy, "My Other Parish," 7.
14. Editor's note: Shortly before going to press, The International Academy for Marital Spirituality (INTAMS) published a themed journal issue on this topic: *Marriage, Families & Spirituality*, 30/1 (2024). See also Diane Ryan, "Not Problems but Pioneers."

THE ACHIEVEMENTS AND LIMITATIONS OF RECEPTIVE ECUMENISM

Although relatively new in the ecumenical landscape, over the last two decades Receptive Ecumenism has been used within ecumenical practice across the globe. For example, within the Anglican Roman Catholic International Commission (ARCIC)[15] and as part of the work of the International Anglican Roman Catholic Commission for Unity and Mission. In 2016 Pope Francis and Archbishop Welby commissioned pairs of Bishops from the Roman Catholic Church and Anglican Communion to make an eight-day pilgrimage. The purpose was to provide "an opportunity for the bishops to discuss the ecumenical context in their own countries and to learn from the experience of each other."[16] This was Receptive Ecumenism in action, at the highest level in the Anglican and Roman Catholic Churches. It was symbolically significant and is to be commended, but it also raises questions such as what happened after the eight days of pilgrimage? What impact did this time together have on Christian unity in the longer term? From an interchurch couples' perspective, it should also be considered—if eight days together is thought to help further Christian unity—what impact can years, or even decades, of shared life such as those experienced by interchurch couples have?

In England, Receptive Ecumenism has been used by the national ecumenical instrument, Churches Together in England (CTE) which has a membership of over fifty national churches. CTE has been proactive in encouraging the use of Receptive Ecumenism both in their meetings and by offering material for a course to be utilized at a local level.[17] Additionally, following a very challenging situation regarding the nomination of the CTE Fourth Presidency in 2019,[18] there has been a renewed focus on Receptive Ecumenism as member churches considered what they can learn from the other as well as how to disagree well.[19] The experience of interchurch families of deep disagreement whilst remaining in relationship could have been a valuable resource at this time.

Although Receptive Ecumenism has been useful to ecumenical dialogue there are some critiques, I would like to make which point to

---

15. ARCIC, *Walking Together on the Way.*
16. IARCCUM, *IARCCUM Bishops Pairs,* 1.
17. CTE, *Course: Embracing the Other,* 1.
18. CTE, *Churches Together in England Statement on the Fourth Presidency,* 1.
19. CTE, *CTE Enabling Group Autumn 2021,* 1.

my own hopes for something increasingly impactful within ecumenical practice. Firstly, Receptive Ecumenism can appear to appeal to the church's agenda for self-improvement, each denomination engaging with the process to improve its own position. The original intention of Receptive Ecumenism is to further Christian unity; however, when engaged in without this as a genuine aim it could be seen as a method that feeds on the other rather than seeking mutual benefit and walking forward together in greater unity. Here Receptive Ecumenism can learn from the experience of interchurch couples who because of their love for each other are more likely to desire the growth and fulfilment of the other. Furthermore, through my professional experience with English ecumenism, I have come to understand that the vision of Christian unity and understanding of ecumenism by different churches is so varied that there is not a mutually understood definition nor clearly defined purpose to shared work. This is confirmed in a report commissioned by CTE that concluded that within the member churches of CTE there was more of desire for "an ecumenism of action,"[20] rather than a sense of calling for the churches to reach spiritual or ecclesial unity. When the goal of ecumenism is to simply work together it has an impact on the depth of unity that can be reached. Receptive Ecumenism also aims to be a spiritual practice but within the churches, and even within the ecumenical movement, ecumenism is rarely seen as a spiritual practice but largely focused on theological knowledge or missional objectives. What Jesus prays for in John 17:21 is an intimacy with each other that resembles the three persons of the Trinity. To truly follow Christ, the churches should desire this spiritual unity as well as a practical unity to better serve the world through mission and social justice. Although there can be discussion and even some practice of Receptive Ecumenism, if there is not a vision of a deeper unity and an openness to be changed by the other it can lead instead to more of an intent to take good ideas and appropriate them.

Secondly, even when using Receptive Ecumenism in formal church dialogues and ecumenical engagements the conversations can be polite and controlled. Subjects of division are discussed infrequently, there is rarely space for the consideration of the issues of the deepest grievance and pain, and if they are discussed, there is seldom an attitude that is open to even a small change of position. There is a need to learn to

---

20. Mladin, Fidler, and Ryan, *That They All May Be One*, 20.

disagree well and still remain on the path to unity, rather than threatening to walk away from the discussion and even from the relationship. Significantly, even when taking the approach of Receptive Ecumenism, there is rarely the time to develop close relationships as ecumenical dialogue meetings happen only a few times a year, often with a packed agenda. Time and space are needed to develop trust in relationships and so often people only make this time with those who are already like them. Learning from the example of an interchurch couple, the commitment of more time needs to be given to receptive ecumenical practice for change and transformation to be possible.

What the churches require in order to move towards greater unity is something less planned and polite than what is often found in current ecumenical dialogues, something that can be seen in the messiness of domestic relationships and specifically within interchurch families. For greater unity to develop, a closer bond is required that creates resilient relationships and that goes beyond professional courtesy and distance. Receptive Ecumenism offers a starting point for this especially with its inbuilt relationality but "we need to reemphasize the spiritual within the ecumenical"[21] creating a deeper connection. A deeper connection requires trust as the basis for a resilient relationship, only through deep friendships, and significantly within marriage, can both people be honest, even impolite and angry with each other and know the other will not leave the conversation or relationship. A confidence is required, knowing that the other will stay, even if there is disagreement, and that they can move forward together. It is here where the example of interchurch couples can model a closer and more resilient form of ecumenical relationship, a relationship based in love and commitment to the other as well as shared faith in God and a desire for greater spiritual unity.

TOWARDS RELATIONAL RECEPTIVE ECUMENISM

When looking at the development of receptive ecumenical practice through the lens of the lived experience of interchurch couples I have found the work of theologian Thomas Jay Oord compelling. In my ongoing work I am considering what his Open and Relational Theology might have to contribute to ecumenism as his approach and understanding of God resonates with aspects of the experience of interchurch couples.

---

21. Pizzey, *Receptive Ecumenism and the Renewal of the Ecumenical Movement*, 226.

Open and Relational theists place great emphasis on the view that any understanding of God is incomplete, including their own. Oord writes, "I believe an open and relational view of God makes most sense overall. But I am not certain, I do not know God fully and so I cannot be 100% sure. I look at reality through limited and sometimes distorted lenses, which means my vision is cloudy."[22] Such honesty and humility demonstrates the characteristics required for sincere receptive ecumenical practice. An openness to being wrong, to being challenged, and to an expanded perception of God resonates with my observation of the spirituality of interchurch couples who challenge each other towards a deeper faith and broader practice through their contribution to life in two churches. It also sits well alongside a Receptive Ecumenical approach acknowledging that something can be learnt from another tradition that will have an impact beyond themselves. Cardinal Kasper recognizes this in a letter to the 2nd International Gathering of Interchurch Families, "Praying together, reading and pondering the Scriptures together, encouraging others to do so, will have an effect within and beyond your families."[23]

The term Open and Relational Theology covers a diverse range of views but according to Oord what open and relational theists usually have in common are three ideas.

> 1. God and creatures relate to one another. God makes a real difference to creation and creation makes a real difference to God. God is relational. 2. The future is not set because it has not yet been determined. Neither God nor creatures know with certainty all that will actually occur. The future is open. 3. Love is God's chief attribute. Love is the primary lens through which we best understand God's relation with creatures and the relations creatures should have with God and others. Love matters most."[24]

Little has been written about Christian unity by Oord, who has written extensively about the "adventure" of God's love,[25] and that relationships with God and others have the potential for "transformation."[26] Interchurch couples are a specific example of the transformational quality of

---

22. Oord, *Open and Relational Theology*, 14.
23. Kasper, *Message from Cardinal Walter Kasper*, 1.
24. Oord, *Uncontrolling Love*, 107.
25. Oord, *Uncontrolling Love*, 220.
26. Oord, *Thomas Jay Oord*, 1.

God's love, as the deep affection held between the couple leads to their faith being transformed as they learn more of each other's faith and tradition. Pam McElroy writes "conscious of doctrinal disagreements and the need for sensitivity, and yet the week-by-week experience of "the other parish" can be deeply enriching."[27]

Oord also uses the language of journeying in his description of how understanding of God evolves,[28] with God as a constant partner, even if at times unrecognized. This also mirrors the journey that interchurch couples can take together with God, starting at different points but coming to a place of lived unity through daily shared faith and practice. In *Interchurch Families and Christian Unity*, the language of journeying is also used, for "in marriage they bind themselves in a life-long covenant to love and serve one another in what becomes their shared journey together to the kingdom of heaven."[29] What is significant here is that the original goal of the two Christian partners when deciding to get married was not greater Christian unity, but yet they are living Christian unity in their home on a daily basis, however imperfectly, and as part of two faith communities. As such their journey is different from that of other Christians on the ecumenical journey, who have not experienced Christian unity in their own intimate lives, and whose focus is on the churches who are still separated. This is reflected in the experience of Kay Flowers, a protestant partner in an interchurch marriage who writes of a conversation a Catholic priest: "turning to me, he said that, from what he had seen, I had a vibrant relationship with Jesus, and I participated in the life of the parish far more than many Catholic members."[30] I would argue that interchurch couples have a vision for both unity and to know more of God and that this is as deep and ongoing as is Oord's journey to know God. It is only as partners in an interchurch family that they are daily being opened to continually learn more of God through their shared life, spiritual practices and expression of faith.

Oord, influenced by the work of Sallie McFague, uses metaphors to describe the movement of God within the world. He describes the freedom that can be found in a relationship with God, who is like "wind rather than cement" and "an inspiring jazz leader," this is a picture of a loving dynamic God who responds to creation with its imperfections

27. McElroy, *My Other Parish*, 1.
28. Oord, *Uncontrolling Love*, 108.
29. AIF, *Interchurch Families and Christian Unity*, 2.
30. Flowers, "Learning to Forgive," 14.

and contradictions and who Oord perceives as an agent of "perfect change."[31] It is the dynamic nature of God within Oord's work that speaks to what interchurch families can bring to Receptive Ecumenism. Although Receptive Ecumenism seeks to bring about change in those who practice and within the churches, the reality of current practice is that it is usually restricted to professional relationships where there is little freedom for movement or mutual change. Oord's understanding of the relationality of God includes movement and mutual change through the God–creature relationship and this resonates with the experience of mutual changing over the lifetime of an interchurch marriage. As Ruth Reardon wrote after the death of her husband Martin, "Marriage is for this world, but the love and unity between us is a participation in God's own love and is therefore eternal. One day I too will be called to the fuller knowledge of that love in our Father's house."[32]

Relationality is at the heart of Oord's work, he writes that God and creation are in relationship together, that "God is a living and universally active but invisible being"; "unchanging in essence but an everlastingly changing experience."[33] This is how Oord makes sense of a loving God in a world that contains so much pain and suffering, it also resonates with the experience of families, including interchurch families, where there also exists the complex mixture of love and pain. Oord argues that instead of being detached, God is active and involved in the world and makes it clear that this is not a relationship of equals, after all God is God; but cites many biblical examples of where God responds to the actions of humanity with both emotion and thought which brings about a mutual change. This mutual change is key to the formation of a more relational Receptive Ecumenism and is required by both individual Christians, and the churches if they are to move towards greater unity. Through the course of their relationship, interchurch couples demonstrate mutual shaping of their faith, it is through their especially committed relationship, rooted in love for God and for each other, that they are able to become prophetic pragmatists,[34] living today the unity they seek for their churches.

---

31. Oord, *Open and Relational Theology*, 38.
32. Docherty, "Eulogy," 2.
33. Oord, *Open and Relational Theology*, 39.
34. West, *Cornell West Reader*.

CONCLUSION

The lived experience of interchurch couples provides not only an example of Receptive Ecumenism in action but a real hope that a deeper unity between the churches is possible. The unity expressed by interchurch couples in their lives as families of faith also shines a light on the deficiencies of Receptive Ecumenism as it is currently utilized. For the churches to move towards greater unity, recognition is needed of the requirement for committed, more intimate, and spiritual relationships rooted in a love of God and of each other. Moreover, it is impossible to avoid conflict and pain in family life and within ecumenical practice there is a need to engage with disunity, including areas of pain and disagreement. Through engaging with the work of Thomas Jay Oord it is possible to see mutual change within the relationship between God and creation. This underlines the importance of relationships, and specifically the potential of interchurch families as models of resilience and hope that can help further develop Receptive Ecumenism and start to form a more fruitful and relational model, one that is a relational Receptive Ecumenism.

BIBLIOGRAPHY

Anglican Roman Catholic International Commission (ARCIC III). *Walking Together on the Way*. London: SPCK, 2018.

Association of Interchurch Families. *About Our work*. https://www.interchurchfamilies.org.uk/about.

———. *Interchurch Families and Christian Unity*. London: Association of Interchurch Families, 2003.

Churches Together in England. *Churches Together in England Statement on the Fourth Presidency*. https://cte.org.uk/churches-together-in-england-statement-on-the-fourth-presidency/.

———. *Course: Embracing the Other*. https://cte.org.uk/about/ecumenism-explained/receptive-ecumenism/course-embracing-the-other/.

———. *Enabling Group Autumn 2021*. https://cte.org.uk/egautumn21/.

Docherty, Paul. "Eulogy for Ruth Reardon, 1930–2022." https://www.interchurchfamilies.org.uk/ruth-reardon.

Hendricks, Paul. "Interchurch Families and Receptive Ecumenism." *One in Christ* 46/1 (2012) 2–12.

International Anglican Roman Catholic Commission for Unity and Mission. *IARCCUM Bishops Pairs*. https://iarccum.org/bishop-pairs/.

Flowers, K. "Learning to Forgive." *Journal of the Association of Interchurch Families*, 12/1 (2002) 14.

Mladin, Natan, Rachel Fidler, and Ben Ryan. *That They All May Be One*. London: Theos, 2017.

Kasper, Walter. *Message from Cardinal Walter Kasper to the 2nd International Gathering of Interchurch Families*. www.interchurchfamilies.org/index.php/conferences/international/rome-2003/messages/message-of-cardinal-walter-kasper.html.

McElroy, Pam. "My Other Parish." *Journal of the Association of Interchurch Families*, 2/1 (1994) 7.

McFague, Sallie. *Models of God*. Minneapolis: Fortress, 1987.

Murray, Paul D. "In Search of a Way." In *The Oxford Handbook of Ecumenical Studies*, edited by Geoffrey Wainwright and Paul McPartlan, 613–29. Oxford: Oxford University Press, 2021.

———. *Reason, Truth and Theology in Pragmatist Perspective*. Leuven: Peeters, 2004.

Oord, Thomas J. (2010) *Open and Relational Theology: An Introduction to Life Changing Ideas*. USA: SacraSage, 2021.

———. *Postmodern and Wesleyan*. Available at: http://thomasjayoord.com/index.php/blog/archives/postmodern_and_wesleyan . (accessed 2 September 2024).

———. *The Uncontrolling Love of God: An Open and Relational Account of Providence*. Downers Grove, IL: InterVarsity, 2015.

Pizzey, Antonia. *Receptive Ecumenism and the Renewal of the Ecumenical Movement: A Path of Ecclesial Conversion*. Brill's Studies in Catholic Theology 7. Leiden: Brill, 2019.

Raiser, Konrad. *Opening up Ecumenical Space*: Address at the International Meeting of Interchurch Families at the Ecumenical Centre, Geneva, 25 July 1998. www.interchurchfamilies.org/index.php/conferences/international/geneva-1998/opening-up-ecumenical-space-geneva.html.

Reardon, Martin. "We Love Each Other." *Journal of the Association of Interchurch Families* 7.1 (1999) 4.

Reardon, Ruth. "Eucharistic Sharing: Informing our consciences." *Journal of the Association of Interchurch Families* 9/2 (2001) 12–15.

———. "Interchurch Families." In *The Oxford Handbook of Ecumenical Studies*, edited by Geoffrey Wainwright and Paul McPartlan, 459–67. Oxford: Oxford University Press, 2021.

"No Blueprint." *Journal of the Association of Interchurch Families* 1/2 (1993) 1, 16.

Ryan, Diane. "Not Problems but Pioneers: Interchurch Families and Receptive Ecumenism." In *Receptive Ecumenism as Transformative Ecclesial Learning: Walking the Way to a Church Re-formed*, edited by Paul D. Murray, Gregory A. Ryan, and Paul Lakeland, 181–92. Oxford: Oxford University Press, 2022.

Thomas, Gabrielle. *For the Good of the Church: Unity, Theology and Women*. London: SCM, 2021.

West, Cornell. *Cornell West Reader*. New York: Civitas, 1999.

Williams, Rowan. *A letter from the Archbishop of Canterbury 19 June 2003*. www.interchurchfamilies.org/index.php/conferences/international/rome-2003/messages/archbishop-rowan-williams-canterbury.html.

15

When the Legwork Fails
A Local Experience of Forgetting Receptive Ecumenism

Erik Ringheim

INTRODUCTION

THE ECUMENICAL MOVEMENT HAS had its ups and downs through the years, and different emphasis and different approaches have created different atmospheres. Some have helped the visible unity of the Church to thrive, whilst others have caused denominations to turn inwards and reflect. Furthermore, ecumenism exists in different layers: ecumenical organizations like the World Council of Churches; multilateral agreements like the Porvoo agreement; bilateral relations with church leaders, and so on. In addition to all of those, there is the local context.

This chapter is focused on what went wrong in the local ecumenical context in the municipality of Sollentuna, Sweden. It shows the devastating results that follow when you fail to do the legwork of ecumenism and hence demonstrates the importance of curiosity, humbleness, and integrity. It shows why Receptive Ecumenism is an important tool to heal wounds and how it is a methodology that can help the church in its local setting. It is, after all, through the relationships with, and kindness of, people from different denominations meeting each other in everyday life that trust, love and the visible unity of the church can take root.

The aim of my investigation was to discover why the flourishing ecumenical youth work in the municipality of Sollentuna ceased to be, and to do so through the lens of Receptive Ecumenism. In the event, it revealed how quickly mistrust and even jaundiced perspectives can take control when we fail to do the legwork. It is a narrative of local experience on the importance of (Receptive) Ecumenism, showing what can happen if time is not invested in maintaining as well as establishing ecumenical relationships, and in developing trust between the persons involved.

My reflection on this experience has been theology pursued *in via*,[1] and as such has changed and grown as my research progressed, affected by developing new perspectives on the material at hand, and as a result of prayer within our local ecumenical setting. It does not represent the full picture, nor every aspect of the events that took place, but should be seen as a contribution to the greater picture. If others can avoid our mistakes, I am truly happy. It is my contribution to *setting the ecumenical table with our broken crockery*.

SETTING THE SCENE

In February each year there is a school break in Sweden called *sportlovet*—originally intended as a break from school to get out in the woods for cross country skiing, ice skating or other sporting activity. The parish of Sollentuna, Church of Sweden, and the local Pentecostal church, Sollentuna pingstförsamling, decided to go on a joint ecumenical ski trip to the ski resort of Trysil in Norway for this school break in 2017. There were about 130 participants, aged fifteen to twenty, in addition to four pastors—two from each denomination. We had rented some big houses to live in and a large venue at the local hotel for the worship services and for recreation.

The aim of the ski trip was to get our youngsters to get to know each other, thus widening their horizon of Christianity, to have worship services together, thus widening the liturgical horizon and just to share life, meals and generally have a great time together, thus becoming closer friends, and to embark further on the road to unity and peace.

Before the trip the pastors from the two congregations had pre-meetings to discuss what we should bring from our respective tradition

---

1. Coakley, *God, Sexuality and the Self*, 33.

to the trip and what we should leave at home. Since we have quite different styles of worship and liturgy, different views on the baptism of children, understanding and practices regarding LGBT persons, and so on, it was important to us to bring everything to the table *before* the trip. We discussed theology and customs with mutual respect and in a spirit of curiosity toward the other tradition. Our aim was to bring to the ski trip an emphasis on our similarities rather than our differences.

The 2017 ski trip was a great success. The youth got to know each other, the ski slopes were great, and we had worship services that highlighted both Lutheran and Pentecostal styles of service. Bishop Krister Stendahl's famous phrase "holy envy"[2] really came in to play during our time together. As a Lutheran, I felt an appreciative envy with the Pentecostal worship band, their kind of loose organizational structure and their great ability to use technical equipment and their freely formulated prayers. And the pastors from the Pentecostal church appreciated some of the organizational skills and economic muscle of the Lutheran parish. In terms of worship, some of their youth said that they for the first time "understood" the Eucharist thanks to the liturgy, and the explanations made.

When we returned home after *sportlovet* and school started again the youth from different denominations began hanging out with each other at the schools and we, the pastors, started to prepare for next year's trip. It was everything we had hoped for and we said, "let's do this again next year." But this is where the legwork started to crumble. Planning for the following year, 2018, we only had one pre-meeting among the pastors because we were the same team as in 2017, and the success of the previous year was still with us. I think this is called hubris!

During the 2018 trip itself we had a few squabbles. We started to long for some important parts of worship from our own traditions rather than sharing freely in each other's. Different organizational styles became apparent, as did the fact that we had different linguistic interpretations and therefore different expectations, even when the same words were being used. For example, what is actually meant when we say someone is a "youth leader"?

Following this trip, a more protectionist attitude towards "our" youth at home became evident: "What if our youngsters hang out in the

---

2. "Holy envy" is from Stendahl's three rules for interfaith dialogue::"Let the other define herself ('Don't think you know the other without listening'); compare equal to equal (not my positive qualities to the negative ones of the other); and find beauty in the other so as to develop 'holy envy.'" Stendahl, "Interview."

Pentecostal church on Fridays instead of ours?" and vice versa. Nonetheless, we considered that the trip had, overall, been a positive experience—just not as good as the first one. And so, we decided to go to Trysil a third time, in 2019. We had such a great experience from the first trip, and, despite the issues mentioned above, a generally positive experience from the second trip. Perhaps the problematic elements of the second trip were nothing more than a bump in the road?

THE ERODING LACK OF LEGWORK

Here is where we really failed. For the 2019 trip, we didn't have a single pre-meeting involving the pastors. We didn't talk about theology or what we appreciated in the other denomination and people. We did not talk about what we should leave at home and what to bring. It was especially complacent of us on this occasion since the Lutheran parish had a new pastor from the Church of Sweden who didn't have the ecumenical experience and who would obviously have benefitted from a preparation with other members of the ecumenical team. In short, we didn't do the work.

That year of 2019 revealed a dramatic change in the attitude within and between the groups. Instead of showing interest in the other denomination we started comparing our own "good work" with their deficiencies. We quickly entered a downward spiral of mistrust and complacency. There were of course individual exceptions to this general ecumenical collapse, but the overall feeling was that the groups got more divided within our shared accommodation. We had two distinct groups within the camp and the things that we had left at the table back home in the first-and second- years' pre-meeting now returned with a vengeance. The Pentecostal pastors greatly missed the soteriological invitation at the worship service, while the Lutherans bemoaned the lack of organization and formal liturgy. Questions about faith and being "a true Christian believer" were asked of each other's traditions. And so, at the end of the 2019 trip we went our separate ways—as did the remainder of our joint ecumenical work with the youth. Even in the schools we could notice a tension. A serious rift had opened up between us.

ANALYSIS: WHAT WENT WRONG?

Over the course of three years, we had gone from an open ecumenical endeavor to questioning each other's faith and leadership. I got a question from one of the Pentecostal pastors: "You know, I have to ask—is it true that priests in the Church of Sweden don't believe in God? "I was as baffled as offended, but actually not all that surprised. The Lutheran and Pentecostal churches in Sweden have such different history, structures, governance, and understanding of mission that our different ways of serving Christ may (mis)lead someone to that conclusion. Let me explain.

The Pentecostal movement in Sweden grew through the nineteenth century, much as a dissenter movement in reaction to a very strict—and rather dull—Lutheran state church. In Sweden, up until 1868, you were not allowed to meet and pray together without the presence of a Lutheran priest. A skepticism regarding state church was formed in line with the awakening and pietist movements, who reacted against the idea that one could not rejoice in the Lord if you didn't do it in a state church manner,[3] Until 1996 a newborn child automatically became a member in the Church of Sweden, if at least one of the parents was a member. Of course, this kind of practice raises questions about the grounds of membership of the church, and the meaning of saying that someone is a Christian under these terms.

Not only does the ecclesiology of the Pentecostal church differ in many ways from the Church of Sweden but there are also significant differences in baptismal theology, styles of prayer, how worship services are celebrated, how the church buildings are constructed and used, and so on. Many of these are familiar and significant *loci* to consider in ecumenical relationships, as can be seen in the many formal dialogues on these issues between churches, but some of what went wrong on the ski trip was due to what are sometimes called "non-theological" factors (although some practical theologians would dispute this designation), such as how we organize things and how we govern and finance our work.

Let us have a look at governance and finance and how that affected our ski trip. How did the formal organizational culture provide different entry points to the experience of being church? The Church of Sweden in Sollentuna has some thirty-five thousand members, five churches, three chapels, three funeral grounds, almost ninety employees. We have a territorial view of what constitutes our parish boundaries (the whole geographical area of Sollentuna) and we have a massive church–state legacy to deal with. Like the state we have elections every fourth year to the parish, the diocese, and the general synod. In these elections, secular parties, the same as those that sit in parliament, can field candidates.

---

3. Bexell, *Sveriges kyrkohistoria*, 39.

We have a lot—*a lot!*—of regulations, policies, and funding formalities to administer.

For example,. if you, as a Church of Sweden parish member, want to borrow a room to host a reception after a baptism service, you must fill out forms, get keys, codes and cleaning instructions. We treat you almost like a customer whom we don't know and trust, because we don´t know all thirty-five thousand of our members (even if we know quite a lot of them), unlike the way our Pentecostal friends know their congregation.

Sollentuna Pingstförsamling, by contrast, is congregational and has some six hundred members,[4] many of them families who have worshiped there over several generations. They all know each other. They assemble both in the church building and outside of its walls—because "church is where the people are." They have five employees, not all of whom are full time. Attending our initial meeting before the first ski trip we met in their church building and I asked who all the different people and groups in the various rooms were, and what were they doing there, and the pastor replied: "I don't know—everybody has got their own key."

The Church of Sweden in Sollentuna has help from the state to collect the membership fees of 0.73 per cent of members' income while Sollentuna Pingst retains the traditional model of tithing a tenth of income for church members. These differences in governance and finance pose questions and have effects on activities such as the ecumenical *sportlovet* trip. How do we organize such a trip when we come from completely different organizational structures? What is required and expected of participants in terms of payment? Can we, or must we, have the same discount for the participants? Do we have the same resources to subsidize places? Should we each have the same number of participants since our churches are so different in size?

Different ecclesiological understandings of what the church *is* go hand in hand with the practicalities of how to organize things. Ecclesiology sets the framework not only on how to explore questions of faith, theology, worship and tradition but also on how churches live everyday life as congregations. When we failed to do the actual legwork, therefore, we not only failed in curiosity about theology but also in understanding what theology means for ecclesiology and thus, what it means for all the big and small questions involved in organizing an activity like the ski trip. To have understood the ecclesiological framework could

---

4. https://www.facebook.com/sollentunapingst/ 20220617.

have saved us a lot of friction. When we stopped preparing together, we effectively stopped asking ourselves the basic question of Receptive Ecumenism: *What is it that we in our tradition need to learn and receive, with integrity, from others?*[5]

A significant contribution of Receptive Ecumenism to the ecumenical scene is its emphasis on a non-proselytizing approach. It rejects the notions that "I" shall teach "you" in order for you to become more like me.[6] Nor is it interested in simply comparing doctrines (learning *about* the other). It is more than just setting out one's own tradition. Rather it is how, with integrity, the unity of the church actually can evolve (learning *from* the other). If we can be united only if your tradition is transformed to look like mine, we are a long way off from unity.

Even in such practical fields as government and finance we can and must learn from each other.[7] Is it a law of nature that the Church of Sweden needs to have all these documents just to have a member of the church have a reception after a baptismal service? Can we learn something from our Pentecostal friends about the trust-administration-axiom/balance? And for our Pentecostal Friends in Sollentuna, what might they learn from the Church of Sweden's "professionalism" about knowing "who is in the house." They are in fact moving in that direction. According to their website they want to organize access to be a little less "everybody's house" and a bit more or a managed process.[8] Without this, you might never know if you could throw something out—because you didn't know to whom it belonged!

When we had our ecumenical ski trip we didn't have the framework of Receptive Ecumenism, nor its theories or methodology. We just wanted to ski, worship, and get to know each other, to "live" together. And maybe that is what Receptive Ecumenism is—to *live* together. When you actually share lives with someone, you will sooner or later have to deal with vulnerability. I believe it to be the single most important thing in any relationship—to be vulnerable with each other. Everyone can have fun together, but you can only be vulnerable with the ones you trust. To have a true relationship is to have trust, earnest talk, and to share. In fact, to love.

---

5. Gehlin, "Receptive Ecumenism," 31, following Paul Murray.

6. Slipper, *Enriched by the Other*, 18.

7. This principle was also recognized in a 2009 UK project on the local church. See Marcus Pound, "Receptive Ecumenism and the Local Church."

8. https://sollentunapingst.se/vad-gor-vi/nya-kyrkan-fragor-svar/ 20220617.

In Swedish trust is called *tillit*. It is a palindrome and is spelled the same way front to back and vice versa. It can stand as a sign that trust must come from both ways. From you and me. Trust is a leap of faith. And that leap of faith is putting my weakness into your hands and hoping you will not take advantage of it, but to cherish it.

In our setting, as the trust eroded, so did the willingness to do things together. We became two groups side by side instead of two groups intertwined. We all became more exclusive within our own tradition not only in the big cabins in Norway but also when we came back home. We had less and less to do with each other. This phenomenon is not unique for a church setting—you can see it all over society, both in relationships and even between countries, when trust erodes, protectionism takes its place. When this happens, instead of cherishing different kinds of faith in Christ and recognizing that people have different needs and styles of worship, we "protect" our group. That is what happened with us. Instead of being happy that our youngsters talked about Christ *at all*, we were anxious about whether they did it in *our* particular way.

There is a declining rate of new members and baptisms in the Church of Sweden and with that comes a knee jerk reaction of "protecting" one's own tradition. Churches in the global north and west are in some sort of crisis: we do not have as many celebrations of baptism, we have fewer members, and we struggle to make our voices heard through the "white noise" of social media. But instead of responding by making more together, we tend to intensify the focus on our own group: how can we save *this* church/parish/group? In the spring of 2021, Rev Dr Kenneth Mtata had a seminary session at the gathering for all the priests and deacons in the diocese of Stockholm. He said that he, coming from an African context, noticed how we in the north were occupied in seeing our own crisis of declining memberships and failed to see the growing numbers in the south: aren't we *one* church under God?

* * * * *

The years passed after the last ski trip and we had some sporadic encounters where we politely talked with each other, but there was still a large gap between us—we had not split as friends. The lack of legwork had put us in this position. Ecumenism needs time and effort to build that *trust* that eventually enables the gift of Receptive Ecumenism: to challenge our own tradition; to be vulnerable; and to have that "holy envy" of the other's tradition. And now we had none of these: we didn't have a ski trip; we didn't have those glad encounters in the schools; we didn't have anything but awkward meetings in the local shopping center.

But there is a plot twist.

A FRESH START?

In 2021, Sollentuna Pingst were about to build a new church building and were in need of temporary housing between demolishing their current one and the new one being ready. So they reached out to us in the Church of Sweden, Sollentuna, in late spring of 2021. I saw this as a possibility of a fresh ecumenical start—and I also saw it as a perfect opportunity to confirm that my analysis of what had gone wrong was correct. So when the opportunity arose, I presented my theory of the lack of legwork when we had a meeting and asked them what they thought about it. This did not go at all well . . .

You know how it is when people look at each other as if they have a silent communication? I suddenly realized what I had done wrong. I started from myself and applied my views, my insight, to their experiences. I was more interested in having a confirmation *that I was right* instead of actually asking them why they thought the ski trip had failed. I did the opposite of Receptive Ecumenism. So I took a step back, listened to where the Spirit was leading and asked again, but now with the intention of actually seeking their point of view, and also affirming the mistakes that we in the Church of Sweden, Sollentuna, had made along the way. The atmosphere in the room shifted. It changed immediately; suddenly there was fresh air to breathe. An ecumenism of the wounded hands made that shift possible. The very act of analyzing and reflecting on the problem became in itself a testing ground of how to start to try to set things right again, with the help of Receptive Ecumenism. To bring your brokenness to the table is hard and requires trust—a trust that only comes with the sharing of brokenness.

POSTSCRIPT

In March of 2023, as I write, we are in the final process on how to help our Pentecostal friends out with space to live and a place of worship while their new church is being built. During the next eighteen months their congregation will share our church. Of course, this will not go without friction, and that is okay, we now know about the importance of doing the legwork. We are again establishing a trustful relationship between our congregations. Our hard-earned experiences have now become a point of reference on what not to do. Our wounds are in the process of healing into valuable and humbling scars.

BIBLIOGRAPHY

Bexell, Oloph. *Sveriges kyrkohistoria. Folkväckelsens och kyrkoförnyelsens tid.* Verbum förlag AB, Stockholm. 2003.

Coakley, Sarah. *God, Sexuality and the Self. An Essay "On the Trinity."* Cambridge: Cambridge University Press, 2013.

Gehlin, Sara. "Receptive Ecumenism. A Pedagogical Process." In *Sharing and Learning: Bible, Mission, and Receptive Ecumenism*, edited by Petter Jakobsson, Risto Jukko, and Olle Kristenson, 31–41. Geneva: WCC Publications, 2021.

Pound, Marcus. "Receptive Ecumenism and the Local Church." In *Receptive Ecumenism as Transformative Ecclesial Learning: Walking the Way to a Church Re-formed* edited by Paul Murray, Gregory A. Ryan, and Paul Lakeland, 211–24. Oxford: Oxford University Press, 2022.

Slipper, Callan. *Enriched by the Other: A Spiritual Guide to Receptive Ecumenism.* Cambridge: Grove, 2016.

Stendahl, Krister. "An Interview with Krister Stendahl: 'Accountability' is a better leadership quality and value than 'servanthood,'" interview by Yehezkel Landau, *Harvard Divinity Bulletin*, Winter 2007, https://bulletin.hds.harvard.edu/an-interview-with-krister-stendahl/.

16

Towards a Model of Transformative Ecumenical Asceticism in Sophrony Sakharov and Basil Pennington

EMIL M. MĂRGINEAN

INTRODUCTION

RECEPTIVE ECUMENISM, PARTICULARLY WHEN centered on the broad spectrum of spirituality and asceticism, holds significant potential for fostering transformative learning and making a substantial impact within Christian communities. This approach involves dialogue and mutual exchange, with a specific focus on spiritual practices and disciplines that shape one's faith journey.

Receptive Ecumenism has a great impact when it is centered on the broad spectrum of spirituality and asceticism and it supports transformative learning, as a form of deepening interior conversion.[1] Getting inspired by other spiritual traditions is a core element in this paradigm. Receptive Ecumenism allows individuals to immerse themselves in the spiritual practices and traditions of others. By doing so, they gain a deeper understanding of diverse spiritual pathways, contemplative practices, and ways of connecting with the Divine. Asceticism involves self-discipline and focusses on practices aimed at spiritual growth and transformation.

---

1. Pizzey, *Receptive Ecumenism*, 31.

Receptive Ecumenism allows believers to adopt ascetic disciplines from different traditions that resonate with their own spiritual journey. This assimilation of ascetic practices can lead to personal growth, self-awareness, and a stronger commitment to the Christian faith. Therefore, my aim is to create a comparative case study of two Christian traditions, based on spirituality and ascetic practices, which introduces a model of ecumenical asceticism. This model is a transformative asceticism, which I see as a form of Receptive Ecumenism, and in its incipient phase it works as an instrument for inner (personal) transformation. In a second phase, it could become an instrument for ecclesial transformation, as a form of expansive growth within traditions.

This chapter is centered on two important authors of Christian spiritual literature: Sophrony Sakharov and Basil Pennington. Both authors lived in the same time period, in the twentieth century. Fr. Sophrony Sakharov was a monastic and archimandrite of the Eastern Orthodox Church. He was born in Russia, but lived most of his life abroad, twenty-two years in Mount Athos, Greece, and fifty years in Western Europe, being the abbot of the Monastery of St. John the Baptist in Essex, England. He is an influential contemporary author in the Orthodox Church and in 2019 the Ecumenical Patriarchate decided to canonize him, and he is now referred to as Saint Sophrony the Athonite. He is known for the famous biography of Saint Silouan the Athonite, his master, but also for his masterpiece *We Shall See Him As He Is* and other treatises on prayer and spiritual direction. Dom Basil Pennington was a Roman Catholic minister, a Cistercian monk and an influential author who initiated the *Centering Prayer* movement at St. Joseph's Abbey in Spencer, Massachusetts, USA, during the 1970s. They met at the Orthodox monastery in Essex,[2] England, and they both shared in the spiritual and ecumenical tradition of Mount Athos. Pennington spent a few months in a monastery on Mount Athos and published a journal of his trip which records his stay, his experiences, theological conversations and ecumenical sharing.[3]

Both authors elaborated influential models of asceticism and spiritual life for the Christian West, while exploring and adapting the Eastern Byzantine liturgical and ascetical tradition. Their writings suggest a stable model of what I call transformative *ecumenical asceticism*. This concept was firstly introduced in a report of the Commission on Faith

---

2. See the details of the visit in Bolshakoff and Pennington, *In Search of True Wisdom*, 134–41.

3. See Pennington, *The Monks of Mount Athos*.

and Order of the World Council of Churches in Geneva, 1985,[4] although with a slightly different meaning, that of self-emptying in order to be more receptive to the voice of the Spirit. Saint Sophrony reiterated and expanded the same concept when he spoke about fruitful forms of ecumenism. In his view, asceticism, as an art of learning how to live without sin, should be the main driving force of any ecumenical encounter.[5] One could notice that in this case, asceticism and spiritual practices take a positive turn and depict a process of striving for perfection or deification. This is very much in line with the experience of Basil Pennington, in his reflection on the time spent on Mount Athos:

> Another significant element was the ecumenical sharing and insights. For Orthodoxy, as for most of the great religions, monasticism is at the heart of the Church, of the spiritual life of its peoples. Therefore, ecumenical dialogue in the monastic context and at the level of spiritual practice and experience has a primary importance."[6]

Starting from spiritual practices, one can build an ecumenical framework of deep transformative learning, a personal experientialist approach which has the potential of becoming properly ecclesial.

COMMON CONCEPTS

In this section, I would like to center my chapter on three concepts common to their theological thought which are relevant for a process of transformative ecumenism: *an extended vision of the world; inner transformation;* and *typologies of ascetic progress.*

An Extended Vision of the World

Saint Sophrony has a very rich discourse on the cosmic dimension of the Christian life. In his works, one could find over three hundred references to the cosmos, cosmic energies and cosmic life, elements which

---

4. "This requires from us great spiritual discipline, what might be called a peculiar 'ecumenical asceticism' which kills self-serving passions and destroys self-constructed expectations, and places all hope in the unsearchable judgments and inscrutable ways of the Lord who has gathered us together for this work and leads us on according to an agenda of his making, not ours. If any of us, therefore, have come with our own agendas, claiming to know where we are going and what we must produce, let us discard them right now." See Best, *Faith and Order Renewal.*

5. Saharov, *Taina vieții creștine,* 160.

6. Pennington, *Jubilee,* 1.

shape his ecclesiology.[7] Therefore, on a spiritual and ascetic level, this cosmic perspective provides unity among people, uniting races and cultures in a single heart and the ascetic practice takes a new form, evolving from an individual act to a communitarian act. Asceticism becomes a work of the Church in its mission of transforming the world and, therefore, every single voluntary ascetic gesture adds to the general work of the Church. Sophrony says, "We should prepare ourselves to understand this, for then we will become, in part, like Adam before the fall, and we will begin to carry in us all the mankind, the whole of Adam, as something unitary, created by God."[8] Once a person senses this divine dimension above the created cosmos, his vision evolves, and he or she sees the entire humankind as one single being. He realizes that his personal value is inestimably greater than that of the entire created cosmos because of his likeness to the divine image.

When it comes to Dom Basil, it is easy to see that he was influenced a great deal by the writings of Thomas Merton. He perceived the Divine Being as infinite love that transcends the boundaries of expression of any religious system.[9] This extended vision played an important role in his ecumenical activity and inter-religious dialogue, especially in his missionary work in China and India. Also, he understood from Thomas Merton that a mature theology involves going through a broad process of transformation, overcoming the limited consciousness of the old self, and going beyond this border, accepting change and novelty. Therefore, when he discussed the outcome of Vatican II, he concluded:

> It reached out and said: 'potentially, everybody in the world is part of the people of God and that all are called to join into . . . the transcendence of the human family into the communion with the Divine.[10]

It is easy to notice his strong appeal for an extended vision of the world, focusing on the inherent unity of humankind.

One can see that the discourses of Sophrony and Basil have a very clear ecumenical flavor. The cosmic dimension of the world is the

---

7. This is my approximation computed by using dedicated software tools.
8. My translation from Romanian. See Saharov, *Cuvântări Duhovnicești I*, 101.
9. See a video-interview of Basil Pennington, "The Infinite Capacity for Love."
10. Pennington, "Vatican II." This video is excerpted from an interview by Ann Overton for the Mastery Foundation, recorded on April 30th, 1995.

key-element in a deeper understanding of the unity of the human race with the Divine.

Inner Transformation

The second point is related to a process of transformation, on how this extended vision of the world can be implemented in today's world. Being part of two distinct Christian traditions, they proposed slightly different daily practices, which ultimately have a very strong common basis. Both are rooted in the pre-existing praying tradition of the Christian Church.

A contemporary example of bringing the hesychastic practice of Jesus Prayer from Mount Athos to the city is Saint Sophrony the Athonite. He is the one who brought the *Jesus Prayer*, the prayer of the heart, or the prayer of a single thought, to his monastery in contemporary England. It is not only that he instructed his fellow monks and nuns to use this prayer in a private manner, but, due to practical reasons they successfully used this prayer during the daily services or prayer times in the church. In a multi-national community, like the monastery of St. Sophrony, where individuals have various native languages, the Jesus Prayer serves as a universal prayer that transcends linguistic barriers. Also, the use of the Jesus Prayer is deeply rooted in the Orthodox monastic tradition, and it is often integrated into liturgical worship as a way to emphasize the importance of personal prayer and spiritual growth within the context of community worship. In its expanded form, the prayer is: "Lord Jesus Christ, Son of God, have mercy on me, a sinner," but the most common form in the early sources is a shorter one: "Lord Jesus Christ, have mercy on me." Repeated during the day, this short prayer has a strong transformative power.

Some of the disciples of Thomas Merton from Saint Joseph's Abbey, Basil Pennington, Thomas Keating and William Meninger, built an ascetic program of prayer and contemplation, based on the monastic rule, but adapted to the contemporary lay context, called Centering Prayer. This practice was inspired by *The Cloud of Unknowing*, a 14th century Christian spiritual writing and is the result of mixing the natural theology of Thomas Aquinas and the mysticism of Teresa of Avila and John of the Cross, with some aspects of Jung's theory (and of other contemporary psychologists) of the subconscious mechanism. The basics of Centering Prayer are as follows:

Sit relaxed and quiet.

1. Be in faith and love to God who dwells in the center of your being.
2. Take up a love word and let it be gently present, supporting your being to God in faith-filled love.
3. Whenever you become aware of anything, simply, gently, return to the Lord with the use of your prayer word.

After twenty minutes let the Our Father (or some other prayer) pray itself.[11]

Both methods are contemplative and transformative. They are also strongly ecumenic and inclusive. They are not just technical methods for professional clergy or specialized lay people but are an invitation open for all. This perspective is what the group from Saint Joseph's Abbey coined as "contemplation for all."

It is true that one could identify some differences of implementation, particularly with respect to how these methods deal with different challenges that might arise during the act of prayer. Let us take distracting thoughts for instance. In Centering Prayer, the emphasis is not much on fighting with the thoughts, on the negative struggle. The authors were inspired by John of the Cross, who sees no absolute need for the strict elimination of any thought, but rather encourages trying to keep the mind unattached to such thoughts or trying to convert the negative thoughts to positive thoughts. In Jesus Prayer, the Eastern Orthodox tradition is stricter in terms of dealing with distracting thoughts in that while the ascetic is still in the process of purification from passions and his or her prayer is marked by a strong feeling of repentance. The regular path is that distracting thoughts should be stopped right from the beginning.[12] There is no need to have any dialogue with the thoughts and to discern which of them might be beneficial or not. Still, St. Gregory of Sinai seems to partly support the approach of the authors of Centering Prayer when it comes to dealing with the evil thoughts: "So when thoughts invade you, in place of weapons call on the Lord Jesus frequently and persistently and then they will retreat."[13]

---

11. Pennington, *Challenges in Prayer*, 108.

12. Thoughts and images should be excluded from the practice of the Jesus Prayer, as St. Gregory of Sinai teaches. See Ware, "The Jesus Prayer."

13. See Gregory, "On Prayer."

When trying to identify some non-Orthodox aspects which shaped the current form of Centering Prayer, my feeling is that Centering Prayer is essentially aligned with the Orthodox understanding and theology. It is more a question of external appearance, which is obviously related to the context in which this practice has developed. The current form, which has similarities with Transcendental Meditation, was meant to be an answer to the growing number of Roman Catholics embracing Zen Buddhism or Hindu philosophies and lifestyles; it was contextual. There is also the inner void that it creates—it promotes a certain state of stillness which is not so visibly filled by the personal presence of God, as in the Orthodox practices and prayers. Fundamentally, however, it is a Christian practice of contemplation and prayer to a personal God but adapted to the needs of a specific audience.

In this second stage of inner transformation through transformative learning, there is the possibility of a change of perspective from inner conversion to ecclesial conversion. Transformative learning will bring about changed circumstances and open up new possibilities,[14] therefore the prophetic witness of ascetics could determine a certain flow and spiritual movements in the Church. These could be spiritual practices which enrich the daily life of different denominations. My sense is that in the context of theological discourse, the progression towards intentional ecclesial practices constitutes the second phase in an ecumenical journey. The initial stage, however, could commence with a spirituality inherent in the people of God. This approach leans towards a form of ecumenism rooted in the laity, emphasizing a lay-driven ecumenism as the preliminary step, distinct from a solely ecclesial ecumenism. Community involvement, seeking spiritual guidance, promoting unity and love, engaging in dialogue and collaborative initiatives, praying for Church transformation, are all tools which could create a deep ecumenical connection among Christians and a sense of belonging to the same spiritual fountain which is the Early Church.

Typologies of Ascetic Progress

When it comes to evaluating spiritual progress, the two authors have slightly different views, although these do not exclude the other's perspective. I have identified two typologies of ascetic progress in their writings

---

14. Pizzey, *Receptive Ecumenism*, 197.

and my sense is that they have a common root, and the external differences are in fact aligned with the mainstream of their tradition.

In general, spiritual life is an invitation to an increasing reception and absorption of the divine life, reaching a state of full harmony between God's life and human life. Humans become able to acquire perfection, deification, and union with God by grace. In order to reach this harmonious state, Orthodox theology—based on the experience of previous generations—has identified a certain ascending path, in the form of a ladder, which begins with the basics and the virtues and is completed with living a full life in God. This is what Saint Sophrony proposes when it comes to understanding one's spiritual progress, a progressive and methodical approach to spiritual development. The model of *vertical ladder* presupposes that one must complete some basic steps in order to reach and fully enjoy the next steps. This image is similar to climbing a ladder where every rung represents a level of spiritual growth.

Dom Basil, as an exponent of the Western tradition, redesigned this model and understood that man can receive the complete gift of the Spirit at any time, as something which is not conditioned by a certain spiritual level. This is the model of a *horizontal ladder*, a metaphor often used to describe the idea that individuals can experience spiritual growth and receive the fullness of the Spirit at any point in their journey, without being restricted by a linear progression or a predetermined spiritual level. This metaphor suggests that one can ascend or descend on the ladder of spiritual growth, accessing different levels of spiritual experience at any time. Of course, the lives of the saints show that God offers His grace to whomever He wants and when He wants, but what the Eastern Orthodox theology wants to point out, especially through the voice of Saint Sophrony and his master, Saint Silouan, is that there must be a continuous and steady process to acquire God's life. This does not exclude any unexpected gifts of grace, but it is a warning that any gift, if not supported by a solid spiritual foundation, could be lost far too quickly. Orthodox Christianity places a pronounced emphasis on personal transformation and inner renewal as integral components of the spiritual journey. In this tradition, the weight of significance is notably directed towards the cultivation of an individual's inner life and the ongoing process of spiritual transformation. Henceforth, in this perspective, the initiation of any ecumenical process must commence with an emphasis on inner transformation, which could create a favorable environment for ecclesial transformation.

CONCLUSION

The main thesis of this chapter is that asceticism is a key-element in any transformative ecumenical encounter, which starts with inner transformation. The two authors, Sophrony Sakharov and Basil Pennington, although they belong to two different Christian traditions, have a largely similar discourse related to the ecumenical value of the spiritual practices and experiences. The model they propose is an expanded asceticism, which is not an exclusive privilege of athletes of contemplation, but it is an inclusive form of preparation for the works of grace, accessible to every single person. Thus, it is characterized by a deep consciousness of universality and centered on the inherent and ontological unity of humankind.

This comparative approach puts asceticism (as a process of positive inner transformation) at the foundation of the inter-confessional and ecumenical dialogue. Ascetic practices often involve intentional self-discipline, reflection, and spiritual cultivation, fostering qualities such as openness, humility, and a deepened understanding of one's faith. Asceticism, irrespective of specific traditions, often shares common principles related to self-discipline and spiritual growth. I believe that focusing on these shared elements can provide a foundation for dialogue among individuals from different confessional backgrounds. Also, as humility is an important element in any ascetic practice, people involved in ascetic discipline may be more receptive to the perspectives and beliefs of others, creating a conducive environment for ecumenical dialogue. Asceticism's emphasis on the inner journey allows individuals to appreciate the diversity of spiritual paths while recognizing a shared commitment to inner transformation. This shared commitment can serve as a unifying factor in ecumenical dialogue; this is unity in diversity.

This type of ecumenism is thus both *receptive* and *positive* as it actively listens to the spiritual experiences of others, collecting the spiritually profitable elements from these encounters.

BIBLIOGRAPHY

Best, Thomas F. *Faith and Order Renewal. Reports and Documents of the Commission on Faith and Order*. Stavanger: WCC Publications, 1985. https://archive.org/stream/wccfops2.138/wccfops2.138_djvu.txt.

Bolshakoff, Serge, and Basil Pennington, eds. *In Search of True Wisdom: Visits to Eastern Spiritual Fathers*. New York: Society of St. Paul, 1991.

Gregory of Sinai. "On Prayer: Seven Texts." https://orthodoxchurchfathers.com/fathers/philokalia/gregory-of-sinai-on-prayer-seven-texts.html.

Pizzey, Antonia. *Receptive Ecumenism and the Renewal of the Ecumenical Movement: The Path of Ecclesial Conversion*. Brill's Studies in Catholic Theology 7. Leiden: Brill, 2019.

Pennington, Basil. *Challenges in Prayer: A Classic With a New Introduction*. Liguori: Liguori, 2005.

———. *Jubilee: A Monk's Journal*. Ramsey, NJ: Paulist, 1981.

———. "The Infinite Capacity for Love." https://youtu.be/uf11FmlNa2g.

———. *The Monks of Mount Athos: A Western Monk's Extraordinary Spiritual Journey on Eastern Holy Ground*. Woodstock: SkyLight Paths, 2003.

———. "Vatican II." https://www.youtube.com/watch?v=c_gXiUybBls.

Sakharov, Sophrony. *Cuvântări Duhovnicești I*. Alba-Iulia: Reîntregirea, 2004.

———. *Saint Silouan, the Athonite*. Yonkers: St Vladimirs Seminary Press, 2021.

———.. *Taina vieții creștine*. Suceava: Accent Print, 2014.

———. *We Shall See Him As He Is: The Spiritual Autobiography of Elder Sophrony*. Platina: St. Herman of Alaska Brotherhood, 2006.

Ware, Kallistos. "The Jesus Prayer in St Gregory of Sinai." https://bogoslov.ru/article/2588738.

17

Receptive Ecumenism and Ecumenical Mission

Two Sides of the Same Coin

RISTO JUKKO

INTRODUCTION

MANY SKEPTICAL VOICES HAVE been heard in recent years related to the ecumenical movement with its goal of visible unity. Although many important ecumenical documents have been published,[1] there seems to be a widespread problem regarding their reception, and at the same time ecumenism is considered to be a highly abstract matter only for experts. At the very least it can be said that consensus ecumenism is stagnating. Some, though not all, theologians have even spoken about an "ecumenical winter" that can be traced back at least to the 1990s, if not earlier.[2] However, in spite of the fact that ecumenism, for various

---

1. E.g., the *Joint Declaration on the Doctrine of Justification*, signed by the Lutheran World Federation and the Roman Catholic Church in 1999. Working on another level can be mentioned the unity statement adopted by the WCC 10th Assembly in Busan, South Korea, in 2013, (https://www.oikoumene.org/sites/default/files/Document/PRC_01_1_ADOPTED_Unity_Statement.pdf) and the WCC convergence document of 2012, *The Church: Towards a Common Vision* (https://www.oikoumene.org/sites/default/files/Document/The_Church_Towards_a_common_vision.pdf).

2. Pizzey, *Receptive*, 4; Mayer, "Language Serving Unity?," 205.

reasons, seems to have lost some of its urgency, winter is not the only season of the year. Walter Kasper is of the opinion that "there is no reason to be discouraged or frustrated, or to speak of an 'ecumenical winter.'"[3] One sign of an "ecumenical spring" is Receptive Ecumenism, a recent Catholic-inspired ecumenical approach.

A key idea of Receptive Ecumenism is to work on ecumenism from a receptive or receiving perspective. In stating this, it says nothing profoundly new, as it has been said, and rightly so, that "reception is constitutive for the life of faith and for the Church itself."[4] The act of receiving can be said to be characteristic of the church and of a Christian life. Reception, in the sense that Receptive Ecumenism understands it, indicates movement towards oneself and also includes a dimension of welcoming what is being received.[5] This meaning also avoids a risk of understanding "reception" from only a purely linguistic, technical, or instrumental perspective.[6] The immediate focus of Receptive Ecumenism is not so much on potential converging points or on visible unity. The direction is no longer from one individual to the other in the sense of seeking to teach doctrine or express his or her own convictions to the other without listening, but instead the approach is intended to be receptive in the sense that each is open and ready to learn from the other in encounters and dialogues and, if necessary, to be open to change and conversion.[7] This process, when each tradition brings its own distinct gifts to the common ecumenical table, is mutually enriching.

The approach of Receptive Ecumenism seems to be a postmodern expression and application of John 17:21, but seemingly only of the first half of the verse. Hence, the intention of this article is to see what the implications of the second half of John 17:21 are for the relationship of Receptive Ecumenism to ecumenical mission. As has been rightly stated, ecumenism needs to integrate mission and unity.[8]

---

3. Kasper, *Harvesting the Fruits*, 8.

4. Rausch, "Reception Past and Present," 498.

5. See, e.g., *Online Etymology Dictionary*, https://www.etymonline.com/word/reception (accessed 11 Aug. 2023).

6. Cardinal Johannes Willebrands points out that "obvious danger." Willebrands, "The Ecumenical Dialogue and its Reception," 5.

7. See, e.g., *Unitatis Redintegratio* (1964), §7.

8. Paul Avis states that "mission must be integrated with unity in our thinking and in the agendas of our churches. Mission and unity should not be seen as two separate or even as two complementary activities. *We cannot afford that disjunction*." Avis, *Reshaping Ecumenical Theology*, ix (my emphasis).

This article will follow two parallel tracks: the first deals with Receptive Ecumenism, and the second focuses on ecumenical mission, particularly as it has been expressed by the World Council of Churches (WCC) Commission on World Mission and Evangelism (CWME). The article will then bring these two tracks together to show how the two, in general terms, unity and mission, are in fact two sides of the same coin.

RECEPTIVE ECUMENISM

Receptive Ecumenism has been connected to, among other things, both fundamental theology and comparative ecclesiology.[9] The influence of a variety of theological currents within it can be regarded as one of its advantages, but they may also signal that more work still needs to be done on it to give it greater theological precision. The philosophical roots of Receptive Ecumenism rest in Nicholas Rescher's pragmatic idealism. When the various elements of his thinking—"subtle realism, expansive coherentism, and recursive fallibilism"—are combined, the result leads to a human understanding "shaped by inherited stances, assumptions, values, and received knowledge, all with varying levels of associated significance and embeddedness."[10] Rescher's ideas have influenced Receptive Ecumenism by giving it the need for self-critical engagement with others, while, in the process, revealing its weaknesses.

The ground-breaking idea of Receptive Ecumenism is to use ecumenical encounters as a privileged context for fostering "personal and ecclesial growth into more intensely configured communion in Christ and the Spirit."[11] This necessarily leads to ecumenical learning, not only across traditions but also within traditions. Basically, Receptive Ecumenism argues that ecclesial growth, conversion, and maturing do not result in Christian traditions being reduced but precisely to their "becoming more appropriately Anglican, more appropriately Lutheran, more appropriately Methodist, more appropriately Orthodox, etc."[12] And more appropriately and fully Catholic. When the focus is on conversion, ecclesial or individual, this is an *ad intra* perspective in relation to ecumenism. In this, Receptive Ecumenism situates itself against the ecumenical versions

---

9. Kasper, "'Credo Unam Sanctam Ecclesiam'"—The Relationship between the Catholic and the Protestant Principles in Fundamental Ecclesiology"; Mannion, "Receptive Ecumenism and the Hermeneutics of Catholic Learning."

10. Murray, "Receptive Ecumenism and Catholic Learning," 8.

11. Murray, "Receptive Ecumenism and Catholic Learning," 7.

12. Murray, "Receptive Ecumenism and Catholic Learning," 16.

of "the lowest common denominator" which is the idea that if we can find such denominators in our respective traditions, this would be the springboard to more unity. Receptive Ecumenism is a unilateral, *ad intra* process that focuses on learning and receiving from the other.[13]

Receptive Ecumenism hopes to add the following self-critical question to the ecumenical agenda: "What, in any given situation, can one's own tradition appropriately learn with integrity from other traditions?"[14] There is an implicit hope, though not an explicit demand, that other Christian traditions would be open and ready to ask themselves the very same question. This is an *ad extra* perspective given to Receptive Ecumenism by Catholic learning, seeking the truth about what can be learned from the other. This can happen when one church puts itself in a vulnerable position in relation to others, displaying openly its weaknesses rather than its strengths, and concentrating inwardly on itself, and in particular, on its wounds.[15]

One important characteristic of Receptive Ecumenism is that it is a form of Spiritual Ecumenism. The difference between these two is that Receptive Ecumenism "should expand the range of Spiritual Ecumenism to include institutional and ecclesial conversion, not just personal conversion."[16] The difference is thus one of scope, and the importance of Spiritual Ecumenism both for the initial development of Receptive Ecumenism and its further development cannot be overestimated.

The primary aim of Receptive Ecumenism is "transformative conversion via a process of ecclesial learning."[17] With this aim in mind, Receptive Ecumenism does not abandon full structural unity as the aim of ecumenism, as it claims that reconciled diversity without structural unity will never be a sufficient substitute for the unity and catholicity of the church.[18]

In modern Catholicism the roots of Receptive Ecumenism can be discovered in the Vatican II (1962–1965) documents and in particular in the Decree on Ecumenism *Unitatis Redintegratio*. The ecumenical movement is mentioned in positive terms in paragraph 3:

13. Murray, "Families of Receptive Theological Learning," 87.
14. Murray, "Receptive Ecumenism and Catholic Learning," 12. See also Pizzey, *Receptive Ecumenism*, 19.
15. Pizzey, *Receptive Ecumenism*, 20, 21.
16. Pizzey, *Receptive Ecumenism*, 28.
17. Pizzey, *Receptive Ecumenism*, 32.
18. Murray, "Receptive Ecumenism and Catholic Learning," 12.

> For men [separated from full communion with the Catholic Church] who believe in Christ and have been truly baptized are in communion with the Catholic Church even though this communion is imperfect. The differences that exist in varying degrees between them and the Catholic Church—whether in doctrine and sometimes in discipline or concerning the structure of the Church—do indeed create many obstacles, sometimes serious ones, to full ecclesiastical communion. The ecumenical movement is striving to overcome these obstacles.[19]

Another base document for ecumenism in the Roman Catholic Church is Pope John Paul II's open and courageous approach to his own papal ministry in his encyclical letter *Ut unum sint,* On Commitment to Ecumenism (1995). In the encyclical letter the pope invites theologians and leaders of other Christian traditions to think of his ministry as a sign of unity rather than division when he says:

> For a whole millennium Christians were united in "a brotherly fraternal communion of faith and sacramental life . . . If disagreements in belief and discipline arose among them, the Roman See acted by common consent as moderator" . . . This is an immense task, which we cannot refuse and which I cannot carry out by myself. Could not the real but imperfect communion existing between us persuade Church leaders and their theologians to engage with me in a patient and fraternal dialogue on this subject, a dialogue in which, leaving useless controversies behind, we could listen to one another, keeping before us only the will of Christ for his Church and allowing ourselves to be deeply moved by his plea "that they may all be one . . . so that the world may believe that you have sent me" (John 17:21)?[20]

ECUMENICAL MISSION

Receptive Ecumenism is not a "rarefied academic discipline," as it involves both theology and practice.[21] This is precisely what ecumenical mission is also about: it involves both theology and practice. Its theological foundation is in the Triune God and the self-communication of the divine Trinitarian life. The false impression of mission being only "practical" rather than theological, has possibly been transmitted by

---

19. *Unitatis Redintegratio,* §3.
20. John Paul II, *Ut Unum Sint,* §§95, 96.
21. Pizzey, *Receptive Ecumenism,* 21.

the decision of the Edinburgh World Missionary Conference in 1910 to leave out discussions related to doctrinal matters.[22] The Continuation Committee of the Edinburgh Conference and, later, its successor, the International Missionary Council, which was founded at Lake Mohonk, USA, in 1921, did not place on their agenda those doctrinal matters related to relations between churches. It is noteworthy, however, that the impetus for the matters of faith and order came from the World Missionary Conference in Edinburgh in 1910.

However, recent documents published by missiologists demonstrate that mission involves *both* theology *and* practice. For instance, two important ecumenical mission documents have been published in the 2010s, and both of them show the direction that mission has been moving in. The first is an official WCC mission statement titled *Together towards Life: Mission and Evangelism in Changing Landscapes* (*TTL*). This was adopted by the Central Committee of the WCC in 2012 and presented to the member churches of the WCC in 2013 at the World Council of Churches' 10th Assembly in Busan, South Korea.

One of the most significant new emphases in the document is on the mission of the Holy Spirit (*missio Spiritus*) within the Trinitarian concept of mission, i.e., the mission of God (*missio Dei*).[23] Another novelty in the mission document is the concept "mission from the margins." Even if it has been criticized for being theologically somewhat vague, it basically means a change of perspective in mission, highlighting the role of the marginalized in society as agents in mission, which means those who have not had a voice or the possibility to act or make themselves visible, fully participate in God's mission along with other actors. They are examples of how mission also affirms life in all its fullness.[24]

The mission document is a call to evangelism in confidence, in humility, and with respect for others. *TTL* §83 says: "Evangelism is sharing one's faith and conviction with other people and inviting them to discipleship, whether or not they adhere to other religious traditions. Such sharing is to take place with both confidence and humility and as an expression of

---

22. Ross, "The World Missionary Conference," 7–12.

23. *TTL* §11.

24. *TTL* §102 says: "*We affirm that the purpose of God's mission is fullness of life (John 10:10) and that this is the criterion for discernment in mission.*" (original emphasis). Cf. ". . . it is important to recall that the gospel is about promise before it is about obligation and that its challenge lies (. . .) precisely in a call to greater life and nourishing." Murray, "Receptive Ecumenism and Catholic Learning—Establishing the Agenda," 15.

our professed love for our world." The good news of Jesus is a message to be transmitted to every generation and to the whole world, and it leads to repentance, conversion, faith, and baptism (*TTL* §84).

TTL is firmly based on and acknowledges the new landscapes of World Christianity. The world had seen many changes since 1982, when the first WCC mission statement, *Mission and Evangelism: An Ecumenical Affirmation*,[25] was officially adopted. The demographic shift of Christians from the Northern hemisphere to the South, and in particular to Africa, has become a fact that Western Christianity hardly noticed to begin with.

With World Christianity, world mission has become polycentric. *Missio Dei*, God's mission, refers to the fact that God's mission is on the move in this world. As God's mission is movement, it necessitates both deep theological reflection and also practical action that is holistic. Mission is practical because the triune God has become flesh in Jesus Christ, in the form of a servant—for the sake of our salvation (Phil 2:6–8). The very first sentence of the WCC mission document *TTL* (§1) is a creedal confession: "We believe in the Triune God, who is the creator, redeemer, and sustainer of all life" and it goes even deeper in the next paragraph: "Mission begins in the heart of the Triune God and the love which binds together the Holy Trinity overflows to all humanity and creation." (*TTL* §2). This divine origin of mission makes it impossible for humans to define "mission" precisely.

TRANSFORMING MISSIONARY DISCIPLES

The second important ecumenical mission document produced in the 2010s is entitled *The Arusha Call to Discipleship*.[26] It is an outcome document of the WCC Conference on World Mission and Evangelism in Arusha, Tanzania, in 2018. It is a short but theologically dense call to transforming discipleship, and it affirms that "we are called to follow the way of the cross, which challenges elitism, privilege, and personal and structural power (Luke 9:23)."[27]

The unanimous adoption of the document at the World Mission Conference in Arusha in 2018 was not a surprise, as one of the most

---

25. https://archive.org/details/wccmissionconfo50/mode/2up (accessed 11 Aug. 2023).

26. E.g., in Jukko, ed. *Call to Discipleship*, 12–14. The references to *The Arusha Call to Discipleship* in this article are to this edition.

27. *The Arusha Call to Discipleship*, 13.

prominent emphases in recent ecumenical mission theology has been discipleship. It is strongly linked with the life and ministry of Jesus and starts with the gospels. Discipleship refers to the fundamental equality of Christians. For any follower of Jesus, there can be no other road than the way Jesus Christ showed them—after all, he called himself "the way" (John 14:6). In relation to mission, the disciples are not only called to follow Jesus, but they are also sent out in mission. The relationship between discipleship and mission is reaffirmed in *The Arusha Call to Discipleship*, in which disciples are called to proclaim the good news of Jesus Christ in word and deed, moving in the Spirit.[28]

Discipleship is transforming because disciples transform the context or the society in which they live. But there is another dimension of transforming discipleship, too. It is transforming also in the sense that being with Jesus transforms his followers. Missionary discipleship does not mean a nominal membership of a church, which expresses itself through a Christian going to church only on Sunday and after the worship service immediately returning home in order to do the same again the following Sunday. Transforming missionary discipleship includes and necessitates a change—sometimes a radical change—in the disciple's values, attitudes, and behavior, and for this to happen individually, collectively, and ecclesially. Being a disciple of Jesus means being where Jesus is and with those people with whom Jesus is.

Discipleship has also been highlighted in the Catholic Church. In the Vatican II documentation, the ecclesiological document, the Dogmatic Constitution on the Church, *Lumen Gentium*, affirms the responsibility of being a witness to Christ: "The obligation of spreading the faith is imposed on every disciple of Christ, according to his state (ability)."[29] Not surprisingly, the Vatican II missiological document Decree *Ad Gentes*, On the Mission Activity of the Church, expresses the same missionary character of the disciple: "... every disciple of Christ, as far in him lies, has the duty of spreading the Faith."[30] Pope John Paul II in his encyclical letter *Redemptor Hominis* (1979) affirmed the importance of Christ's call to follow him.[31] In his apostolic exhortation

---

28. E.g. *The Arusha Call to Discipleship*, 12.

29. *Lumen Gentium*, §17.

30. *Ad Gentes* §23.

31. "Therefore, if we wish to keep in mind this community of the People of God, ... we must see first and foremost Christ saying in a way to each member of the community: 'Follow me'. It is the community of the disciples, each of whom in a different

Evangelii Gaudium (2013) Pope Francis has underscored the relationship between mission and discipleship, stating that through baptism Christians are always "missionary disciples."[32]

At its General Assembly in Indonesia in November 2019, the World Evangelical Alliance pledged itself to intentional, holistic disciple-making in the 2020s.[33] The evangelical Lausanne Movement, in its document *The Cape Town Commitment* (2010), refers to discipleship,[34] and so does the Anglican Communion. Archbishop Justin Welby has said: "The best decision anyone can ever make, at any point in life, in any circumstances, whoever they are, wherever they are, is to become a disciple of Jesus Christ."[35]

RECEPTIVE ECUMENISM AND ECUMENICAL MISSION

Looking more closely at the two parallel tracks, Receptive Ecumenism and ecumenical mission, it becomes clear that they are in fact one and the same track. First, the theological foundations of both are deeply embedded within a Trinitarian framework, in God's trinitarian nature: Three in One, One in Three. That God is one, and yet triune, sending the Son and the Spirit, is a mystery. In the same manner, God's work in the world cannot be divided between the three Persons of the Trinity.[36] Humans cannot understand the Trinity, but the ecumenical striving after unity and mission in the following of Jesus can be perceived as human beings' imperfect attempts to understand a little better something of the mystery of the Trinity.

The emphasis on God's triune nature makes it possible, always firmly within the Trinitarian framework, to see why both Receptive Ecumenism and ecumenical mission relate strongly to both pneumatology and ecclesiology and thus to Christology. Christology is "incomplete" without pneumatology, and being based on Christology and pneumatology, within the Trinitarian frame, Receptive Ecumenism and ecumenical mission are ecclesiological and also ecclesial. We are dealing with the one mission of

way . . . is following Christ." Pope John Paul II, *Redemptor Hominis*, §21.

32. Pope Francis, *Evangelii Gaudium*, §120.

33. World Evangelical Alliance, "Welcome to the Decade of Disciple-Making."

34. Lausanne Movement, *The Cape Town Commitment*, 2010, Part II, 3B–3C.

35. The Anglican Consultative Council, *Intentional Discipleship and Disciple-Making*, xi.

36. An old theological maxim (dating probably before Augustine, 354–430) affirms that *opera trinitatis ad extra indivisa sunt*.

the one church of the one God. "We need to show that God's mission in the world is at the heart of our work for unity."[37]

Secondly, Receptive Ecumenism is a form of Spiritual Ecumenism, which is the soul and heart of the ecumenical movement.[38] It is described to be "a Spirit-driven movement of the heart, mind, and will"[39] and it is "properly a matter of the heart before it is a matter of the head."[40] This emphasis on the work of the Spirit and spirituality links Receptive Ecumenism strongly with mission. It can be affirmed that spirituality is directly related to "a reconciled church capable of proclaiming the good news to all," and spirituality in mission was affirmed at the Edinburgh World Missionary Conference in 1910.[41] Spirituality is vital for mission as it is the spirituality of the church that sustains mission. Mission spirituality "gives the deepest meaning to our lives and motivates our actions."[42] All ecumenism is spiritual, and so is mission. Worship, prayer, and meditation enable the church to engage and fulfill its mission. It would be a step in the wrong direction if spirituality were left aside or relegated to the last place in ecumenical mission. "Since God is the primary agent of mission and God works through the power of the Holy Spirit, it is through openness to the Spirit that mission takes effect in human life."[43] *Together towards Life* expresses in many paragraphs how mission is a "Spirit-driven" movement, "the mission of the Holy Spirit within the mission of the Triune God."[44]

Thirdly, both Receptive Ecumenism and ecumenical mission emphasize conversion. In the New Testament the Greek words *epistrephō* (ἐπιστρέφω) and *metanoia* (μετάνοια) are two of the most frequently used words in the sense of "turn around from a wrong way" (e.g. Luke 22:32; 2 Cor 3:16; Acts 15:3; 1 Thess 1:9; Acts 3:19; 26:18, 20) and

---

37. Avis, *Reshaping Ecumenical Theology*, 186.

38. "This change of heart and holiness of life, along with public and private prayer for the unity of Christians, should be regarded as the soul of the whole ecumenical movement, and merits the name, 'spiritual ecumenism.'" *Unitatis Redintegratio*, §8.

39. Murray, "Receptive Ecumenism and Catholic Learning," 16.

40. Murray, "Receptive Ecumenism and Catholic Learning," 15.

41. Ladous, "Spiritual Ecumenism," in Lossky et al., eds. *Dictionary of the Ecumenical Movement*, 1069.

42. TTL §3.

43. Ma and Ross, "Introduction: The Spiritual Dimension of Mission," in Ma and Ross, eds. *Mission Spirituality and Authentic Discipleship*, 9.

44. *TTL* §11. See also e.g. §16, and §18: "What is clear is that by the Spirit we participate in the mission of love that is at the heart of the life of the Trinity."

"repentance, radically thinking anew" (e.g. Mark 1:4, 15; Acts 2:38; 3:19; 11:18; 20:21; 26:20). However, it seems that "conversion" is not a precisely defined concept in the New Testament even if a call to conversion is always linked with the Kingdom of God, indicating an attitudinal reorientation to God and to our fellow human beings. Only God can bring about conversion, as conversion is a work and gift of God.[45]

The Vatican II Decree on Ecumenism, *Unitatis Redintegratio*, combines ecumenism and conversion in a strong fashion: "There can be no ecumenism worthy of the name without a change of heart. For it is from renewal of the inner life of our minds, from self-denial and an unstinted love that desires of unity take their rise and develop in a mature way."[46] The Vatican emphasis is picked up by Receptive Ecumenism as it emphasizes continuing ecclesial conversion, leading to a deepening and expanding growth within traditions by means of receptive learning from and across traditions. In that sense, conversion is a movement away from the presupposition of mutuality in ecumenism, because there is a unilateral willingness to conversion. Its aim is a greater flourishing of one's own ecclesial tradition (*ad intra*). The process of growth and change is a "way of hope-filled conversion."[47]

Conversion has become a major concept in Protestant mission with the phrase "conversion of heathens," defined by William Carey in 1792 as the aim of mission. Two levels have been distinguished: one is at a personal level, which means adopting the Christian religion and a personal acceptance of faith. The WCC mission documents freely admit the necessity of conversion and not only of those who are not Christians but of Christians themselves. The first official WCC statement on mission, *Mission and Evangelism: An Ecumenical Affirmation* (1982), says: "The calling is to specific changes, to renounce evidences of the domination of sin in our lives and to accept responsibilities in terms of God's love for our neighbor . . . Thus, the call to conversion should begin with the repentance of those who do the calling, who issue the invitation."[48] The conversion should begin with Christians who call others to the

---

45. Love, "Conversion," in Moreau, ed. *Evangelical Dictionary of World Missions*, 231; Löffler, "Conversion," in Lossky et al., *Dictionary of the Ecumenical Movement*, 253.

46. *Unitatis Redintegratio*, §7.

47. Murray, "Receptive Ecumenism and Catholic Learning," 12; slightly different expression, "grace-filled conversion," in Murray, "Families of Receptive Theological Learning," 86.

48. *Mission and Evangelism*, §§11, 13.

Kingdom of God. This self-scrutinizing exercise should lead to humility, as expressed in the second official WCC mission document, *Together towards Life: Mission and Evangelism in Changing Landscapes*, issued thirty years later (*TTL* §22): "We need a new conversion (*metanoia*) in our mission which invites a new humility in regard to the mission of God's Spirit." *TTL* (§81) includes "'the invitation to personal conversion to a new life in Christ and to discipleship.'" And *The Arusha Call to Discipleship* (2018) recognizes that "the Holy Spirit continues to move at this time, and urgently calls us as Christian communities to respond with personal and communal conversion, and a transforming discipleship."[49] Here "communal" addresses Christians, but can be understood to go beyond the borders of Christian communities.

Even if both Receptive Ecumenism and ecumenical mission emphasize the necessity and high importance of conversion, there seems to be a difference here in terms of the scope of conversion. Receptive Ecumenism seeks both personal and ecclesial conversion to Christ through the Spirit, whereas mission seeks both personal and communal (including ecclesial but going beyond and further) conversion to Christ through the Spirit. The difference of scope is due, in my understanding, to the difference of directions—*ad intra* and *ad extra*—between them.

Fourthly, as already noted, Receptive Ecumenism presents to the ecumenical agenda the following self-critical question: "What, in any given situation, can one's own tradition appropriately learn with integrity from other traditions?"[50] In other words, what can I and my church, my community, or my fellowship learn or receive from others? Receptive Ecumenism focuses intentionally on receiving and on intra-Christian learning. The direction is *ad intra*. Here again, there is common ground shared by ecumenical mission and its emphasis on missionary discipleship. A disciple is a learner, a receiver, as is the case in Receptive Ecumenism. However, there is an additional element in mission that seems to complete the basic set-up and direction *ad intra* of Receptive Ecumenism.

Mission, due to its intra-trinitarian origin, is a movement of loving and giving (*TTL* §2). Its question would be: "How, in any given situation, can one appropriately love the other person and, if possible, share one's faith with integrity with the other?" The direction of mission is *ad extra*. Mission always looks first outward, not inward. It means sending,

---

49. *The Arusha Call to Discipleship*, 12.
50. Murray, "Receptive Ecumenism and Catholic Learning," 12. See also Pizzey, *Receptive Ecumenism*, 19.

loving, sharing, giving. Only after its sharing, giving and submitting itself in a vulnerable position in relation to the other comes *ad intra*: What, in this position in relation to the other, can one appropriately learn with integrity from other (Christians and non-Christians)? This attitude and position are strongly emphasized in missionary discipleship. Mission is looking at not only the non-Christians but also the Christians (Luke 10:29ff; Matt 5:43–48).

And yet, unsurprisingly, there are similarities even in this emphasis. As Receptive Ecumenism emphasizes conversion into Christ and learning, discipleship is precisely that: it necessitates repentance, conversion (Mark 1:15) and learning: "Take my yoke upon you, and learn from me; for I am gentle and humble in heart, and you will find rest for your souls" (Matt 11:29). A disciple of Jesus not only learns about him but learns from him when following Jesus. A disciple learns from the Master. It is also learning from one another, in the community of disciples. It necessitates humility and endurance, as the learning process may be slower than expected. "Then he said to them [to the disciples], 'Do you not yet understand?'" (Mark 8:21; cf. Matt 16:9; Luke 18:1).

Missionary discipleship is always ecumenical. Discipleship is a call to mission, as *The Arusha Call to Discipleship* so strongly articulates, and mission belongs to every Christian through baptism. In the same way, Receptive Ecumenism can be undertaken by any follower of Christ, at least on some level.[51] Receptive Ecumenism acknowledges baptism as the basis for the ecumenical endeavor of learning, and thus, in consequence, for discipleship. This similarity is based on Christ's exhortation to follow him, given to every Christian:

> As disciples of Jesus Christ, both individually and collectively:
> We are called by our baptism to transforming discipleship: a Christ-connected way of life in a world where many face despair, rejection, loneliness and worthlessness."[52]

Baptism is a sacrament of unity. The term 'Christ-connectedness' appeared at the WCC Conference on World Mission and Evangelism in Arusha, Tanzania, in 2018: "Discipleship is more than learning about

---

51. E.g. Pizzey, *Receptive Ecumenism*, 78, 131. See also Murray, "Families of Receptive Theological Learning," 90.

52. *The Arusha Call to Discipleship*, 13.

Jesus. To become a disciple is to follow Jesus. At the heart of discipleship, then, is Christ-connectedness—a disciple is bound to Christ."[53]

CONCLUSION

Receptive Ecumenism and paradigms of ecumenical mission are responses to post-modernity, post-colonialism, and the rise of World Christianity in a post-Christian era. They emphasize the importance of conversion and learning, both collectively and personally. And they both emphasize interaction and relationality, but in slightly different ways. Receptive Ecumenism places more emphasis on *ad intra*, for the sake of unity, whereas mission places greater emphasis on *ad extra*, for the sake of common witness, and as a consequence, it emphasizes unity *ad intra*, as missionary disciples of Christ. Both need each other, as growing visible unity is a witness in itself, and credible witness (mission) is not possible without unity (theology) and consequent cooperation (praxis). "There is a unity dimension of mission and a mission dimension of unity."[54]

These two parallel tracks cannot be kept separated from one another, because both have their starting point and finishing point in the triune God and the mission of God. That is why Receptive Ecumenism and the ecumenical mission movement can work together in order to find a theological and biblical basis for the practical and integrated solutions that they may propose together to global problems. The ecumenists and missiologists are challenged to do so together, converting together, learning from each, and bringing the results as witnesses forward for the benefit of all. However, the motivation and desire are based on the unity in mission. "If our unity does not eventuate in missionary outreach to the world, and specifically in evangelization through giving public testimony to the truth of God's revelation and saving action in Jesus Christ, it is not the unity for which Christ prayed."[55]

Receptive Ecumenism and ecumenical mission are "inextricably related." Paul Murray affirms that "intra-ecclesial matters of structural, spiritual, and practical renewal and extra-ecclesial matters of witness, sacramentality, and mission are inextricably related."[56] The WCC Central

---

53. Hyde, "Following Jesus," 9.
54. Avis, *Reshaping Ecumenical Theology*, ix.
55. Avis, *Reshaping Ecumenical Theology*, 194.
56. Murray, "Receptive Ecumenism and Catholic Learning—Establishing the Agenda," 18.

Committee affirmed in its meeting in Rolle, Switzerland, in 1951: "Thus the obligation to take the Gospel to the whole world, and the obligation to draw all Christ's people together both rest upon Christ's whole work, and are indissolubly connected. Every attempt to separate these two tasks violates the wholeness of Christ's ministry to the world."[57] The same was stated in 1982 by the WCC mission statement *Mission and Evangelism: An Ecumenical Affirmation*: "There is a growing awareness among the churches today of the inextricable relationship between Christian unity and missionary calling, between ecumenism and evangelization. 'Evangelisation is the test of our ecumenical vocation.'"[58]

On the one hand, mission history shows clearly that missionaries have not always been good listeners to others. Mission work has not always brought unity. The ecumenical mission movement needs to repent, convert, and learn to learn. The emphasis on learning in Receptive Ecumenism is something which ecumenical mission needs to learn from Receptive Ecumenism. In this, of course, missionary discipleship is most helpful, bringing ecumenical mission to a position of weakness and woundedness, to readiness to learn from others. The mission movement needs to learn that God "has made known to us the mystery of his will, according to his good pleasure that he set forth in Christ, as a plan for the fullness of time, to gather up all things in him, things in heaven and things on earth." (Eph 1:9–10). Learning from Receptive Ecumenism about an eschatological understanding of truth and a more self-critical and humble engagement with others is something that the ecumenical mission movement can gain from Receptive Ecumenism and become "Receptive Ecumenical Mission."

On the other hand, Receptive Ecumenism needs to learn from ecumenical mission. To put it more generally, unity needs mission, for the sake of the Christian witness: "The goal of ecumenism is to reach unity so that Christians can properly bear witness to Christ."[59] Learning from others as a path to deeper unity with them is a necessity in the search for Christian unity, but Christians cannot stop at simply learning for themselves (*ad intra*). Christian faith is also directed *ad extra*, as a witness to Christ in service of word and deed to the world. Without this

---

57. https://archive.org/details/fourthmeetingofcounsel/page/66/mode/2up?view=theater (page 66 in the "Minutes and Reports of the Fourth Meeting of the Central Committee"; accessed 11 Aug. 2023).

58. *Mission and Evangelism*, §1.

59. Pizzey, *Receptive Ecumenism*, 179.

outward-looking and love-motivated outward dimension, the search for unity to serve only oneself or one's own ecclesial structures becomes functional, an aim in itself. In the worst case, if we concentrate only on our own learning and our own transformation, it may lead to ignoring our neighbors and their needs. Transforming missionary discipleship underlines the triune God's overflowing love as its motive and the basis of the theology and practice of mission. The dual nature of transforming missionary discipleship—both personal and community-oriented—can help Receptive Ecumenism to remember the "world outside" and to change it from being an ecumenical method to a process of becoming "Receptive Ecumenism in Mission," "to properly bear witness to Christ."[60] The result is the acknowledgement of the two sides of the same coin: unity and mission.

BIBLIOGRAPHY

Ad Gentes. Decree On the Mission Activity of the Church 1965. https://www.vatican.va/archive/hist_councils/ii_vatican_council/documents/vat-ii_decree_19651207_ad-gentes_en.html.

"The Arusha Call to Discipleship." In *Call to Discipleship: Mission in the Pilgrimage of Justice and Peace. World Council of Churches Commission on World Mission and Evangelism Documents 2018–2021*, edited by Risto Jukko, 12–14. Geneva: WCC Publications, 2021.

Avis, Paul. 2010. *Reshaping Ecumenical Theology: The Church Made Whole?* London: T. & T. Clark.

The Cape Town Commitment. Lausanne Movement 2010. The Cape Town Commitment - Lausanne Movement.

Francis, Pope. *Evangelii Gaudium*. 2013 http://w2.vatican.va/content/francesco/en/apost_exhortations/documents/papa-francesco_esortazione-ap_20131124_evangelii-gaudium.html.

Hyde Riley, Merlyn. "Following Jesus: Becoming Disciples, Mark 6:1–13." In *Called to Transforming Discipleship. Devotions from the World Council of Churches Conference on World Mission and Evangelism*, edited by Risto Jukko, Jooseop Keum, (Kay) Kyeong-Ah Woo, 7–14. Geneva: WCC Publications, 2019.

Intentional Discipleship and Disciple-Making: An Anglican Guide for Christian Life and Formation. London: The Anglican Consultative Council, 2016.

John Paul II, Pope. *Redemptor Hominis*, The Redeemer of Man, 1979. https://www.vatican.va/content/john-paul-ii/en/encyclicals/documents/hf_jp-ii_enc_04031979_redemptor-hominis.html.

———. *Ut Unum Sint*, On Commitment to Ecumenism, 1995. https://www.vatican.va/content/john-paul-ii/en/encyclicals/documents/hf_jp-ii_enc_25051995_ut-unum-sint.html.

---

60. Pizzey, *Receptive Ecumenism*, 230.

Jukko, Risto, ed. *Call to Discipleship: Mission in the Pilgrimage of Justice and Peace. World Council of Churches Commission on World Mission and Evangelism Documents 2018-2021*. Geneva: WCC Publications, 2021.

Kasper, Walter, Cardinal. "'Credo Unam Sanctam Ecclesiam'"—The Relationship between the Catholic and the Protestant Principles in Fundamental Ecclesiology." In *Receptive Ecumenism and the Call to Catholic Learning. Exploring a Way for Contemporary Ecumenism*, edited by Paul D. Murray, 78-88. Oxford: Oxford University Press, 2008.

———. *Harvesting the Fruits: Basic Aspects of Christian Faith in Ecumenical Dialogue*. London: Continuum, 2009.

Ladous, Régis. "Spiritual Ecumenism." In *Dictionary of the Ecumenical Movement*. 2nd edition, edited by Nicholas Lossky et al., 1069-70. Geneva: WCC Publications, 2002.

Löffler, Paul. "Conversion." In *Dictionary of the Ecumenical Movement*. 2nd edition, edited by Nicholas Lossky et al., 253-54. Geneva: WCC Publications, 2002.

Love, Richard D. "Conversion." In *Evangelical Dictionary of World Missions*, edited by A. Scott Moreau, 231-22. Grand Rapids: Baker, 2000.

Lumen Gentium, Dogmatic Constitution on the Church, 1964. https://www.vatican.va/archive/hist_councils/ii_vatican_council/documents/vat-ii_const_19641121_lumen-gentium_en.html.

Ma, Wonsuk, and Kenneth R. Ross. "Introduction: The Spiritual Dimension of Mission." In *Mission Spirituality and Authentic Discipleship*, edited by Wonsuk Ma and Kenneth R. Ross, 1-9. Oxford: Regnum, 2013.

Mannion, Gerard. "Receptive Ecumenism and the Hermeneutics of Catholic Learning—The Promise of Comparative Ecclesiology." In *Receptive Ecumenism and the Call to Catholic Learning. Exploring a Way for Contemporary Ecumenism*, edited by Paul D. Murray, 413-27. Oxford: Oxford University Press, 2008.

Mayer, Annemarie C. "Language Serving Unity? Linguistic-Hermeneutical Considerations of a Basic Ecumenical Problem." *Pro Ecclesia* 15/2 (2006) 205-222.

Mission and Evangelism: An Ecumenical Affirmation—A Study Guide for Congregations 1983. https://archive.org/details/wccmissionconfo50/mode/2up .

Murray, Paul D. "Families of Receptive Theological Learning: Scriptural Reasoning, Comparative Theology, and Receptive Ecumenism." *Modern Theology* 29/4 (2013) 76-92.

———. "Receptive Ecumenism and Catholic Learning—Establishing the Agenda." In Paul D. Murray, ed. *Receptive Ecumenism and the Call to Catholic Learning. Exploring a Way for Contemporary Ecumenism*, 5-25. Oxford: Oxford University Press, 2008.

Pizzey, Antonia. *Receptive Ecumenism and the Renewal of the Ecumenical Movement*. Brill's Studies in Catholic Theology 7. Leiden: Brill, 2019.

Rausch, Thomas P., SJ. "Reception Past and Present." *Theological Studies* 47 (1986) 497-508.

Ross, Kenneth R. "The World Missionary Conference, Edinburgh 1910—A Fountain-Head." In *Ecumenical Missiology: Changing Landscapes and New Conceptions of Mission*, edited by Kenneth R. Ross, Jooseop Keum, Kyriaki Avtzi, and Roderick R. Hewitt, 7-12. Oxford: Regnum, and Geneva: WCC Publications, 2016.

Together towards Life: Mission and Evangelism in Changing Landscapes 2012, https://www.oikoumene.org/sites/default/files/Document/Together_towards_Life.pdf.

Unitatis Redintegratio, Decree on Ecumenism 1964, https://www.vatican.va/archive/hist_councils/ii_vatican_council/documents/vat-ii_decree_19641121_unitatis-redintegratio_en.html.

Willebrands, Johannes, Cardinal. "The Ecumenical Dialogue and its Reception." *Bulletin/Centro Pro Unione* 27 (1985) 3–8.

World Evangelical Alliance. "Welcome to the Decade of Disciple-Making." https://disciplemaking.worldea.org. (accessed 2 September 2024).

18

Listening, Discipleship, and Church in Mission

An Evangelical Perspective

BERTIL EKSTRÖM

I HAVE BEEN PART of the group in Sweden that over a couple of years worked with the concept of Receptive Ecumenism and mission and it has been an important learning process for me. I appreciate Dr Risto Jukko's contribution to this volume. There are many aspects where his analysis and reflection find echo and agreement in the missiological discussions around the world today. And we have been in some of them together.

My involvement in ecumenical dialogue has primarily been as a representative of the World Evangelical Alliance (WEA) as director of the Mission Commission. That has given me the opportunity to meet peer leaders from the other Christian families, participate in the Global Christian Forum and engage in different processes in the production of important documents such as *The Common Word*, *Christian Witness in a Multi-Religious World*, and the Edinburgh 2010 *Common Call*. I was also part of the group from World Evangelical Alliance (WEA) invited to attend the Commission on World Mission and Evangelism (CWME) consultation in Manilla 2012, working on the *Together towards Life* document, so well presented by Risto Jukko.

In this chapter I would like to make some brief comments on three areas by way of response to Risto Jukko's chapter: listening; discipleship; and church in mission.

LISTENING

Speaking from a "Southern" perspective, there has been a tendency to replicate what we have seen and absorbed from the mission initiatives that have reached our countries and cultures. The difficulty in listening to each other in our home countries has often been reflected on the "so called" mission fields where we work. Sometimes national leaders have overcome barriers, sometimes they have even deepened the barriers between the different Christian traditions. Furthermore, there has often been more of an apologetical approach to others than an openness to listen and learn. There is no doubt that apologetics has been important in the history of the church, for good and for bad, but it presupposes telling others what we believe in, rather than promoting dialogue and listening. The proposed dialogue that we have seen in more recent decades, between Christian traditions, but also with other religions, as well as with other institutions globally and in local cultures and societies, is a much needed one and we recognize that we, from our Evangelical perspective, have not always been open to that.

I think, though, it is worthwhile listening to the other "documents" and "challenges" produced by the Lausanne Movement and other Christian networks, mainly as a result of the 2010 conferences. I believe that true Receptive Ecumenism cannot limit itself to one part of the enormous spectrum of Christian traditions—the so-called "traditional" or "mainstream" churches—but must also include those new communities such as those that have emerged in the Global South.[1] The dialogue contributes to deconstructing prejudices and removing barriers. It provides the opportunity to build bridges and give us all new perspectives on theology, church, and our part in God's mission, but also how we see our world and our society. In addition, as we are experiencing it at the present time, it offers great opportunities to listen and learn. I think I speak for many church and mission leaders in the Global South when I say that "please,

---

1. Four main Christian conferences were held in 2010, celebrating the centenary of the 1910 Edinburgh Conference. Two of them were of special importance: the Edinburgh 2010 Conference and the Lausanne 2010 Cape Town Conference. The respective documents can be found in https://www.oikoumene.org/resources/documents/edinburgh-2010 and https://lausanne.org/content/ctc/ctcommitment.

don't keep this dialogue narrow, but broaden it." Of course, it is a challenge to get some people to join the roundtable!

DISCIPLESHIP

Our Latin American emphasis on mission has been on the Kingdom of God as a present reality in society today.[2] That affects the way we live as individual Christians and maybe even more so, how we live and act collectively as the Church of Christ. The concept of the Kingdom is holistic and refers to all the different dimensions of human life and of God's creation. It is a present reality that promotes and defends the values and the principles of the Kingdom. At the same time, it anticipates the full coming of the Kingdom in the future.

There is no doubt that this concept of the Kingdom has to start within the church itself. There is a need for conversion and a humble attitude, I would say, in all our churches, regardless of tradition and origin. The lack of true discipleship and of committed leadership has created a church that in many ways is expanding but is not influencing society as it should. Thank God, there are many exceptions in all Christian traditions.

CHURCH IN MISSION

I affirm the need for a missional ecclesiology and an ecclesial missiology![3] This would speak about a church sent into its local society and sent into the whole world. It is impossible to separate church and mission, as Risto Jukko points out in his chapter. A church that is not missional in the sense that it is not an integral part of the *Missio Dei*—*God's* mission—is not a biblical church. A missional church collaborates with God in His mission to reconcile all creation with himself. And it does this by being a therapeutic community that embraces the poor, the weak, the marginalized, the wounded and the sinner. At the same time, the church is sent out to proclaim the Good News of salvation to the ends of the earth.

On the other hand, any missiology that does not include the church is also crippled, halting. The Great Commission, in its various versions in the gospels, speaks about making disciples and baptizing them, in other words, integrating people into the Body of Christ, the Church. Mission

---

2. See, for example, Escobar, *The New Global Mission*, 107, 168; Padilla, *Mission Between the Times*, 169.

3. See Ekström, *The Church in Mission*, 95–102.

should aim to include people in the worshipping church of Christ. And that does not exclude, of course, all the other important things that mission work may do out of a holistic understanding of the Gospel. There is a need to not only reflect about how mission has been understood and practiced in history but also how it is being lived out today.

CONCLUSION

In many ways the document from Cape Town—*The Cape Town Commitment*—and the World Council of Churches/Commission on World Mission and Evangelism document have a lot in common. I find commonality not only in the theological foundations—Trinitarian, Christological, Pneumatological, Church based and Holistic—but, also in many of the ideological and practical affirmations and challenges dealing with peace, righteousness, reconciliation, environment, poverty, justice, and the proclamation of the Good News of salvation. My conclusion is that we have been listening to each other and, certainly, also to God! International conferences in Receptive Ecumenism may not be as representative as we would like but they shows that there is a possibility of learning from each other. Although we will not all be able to join the same church, at least not on earth, there is plenty of room and possibility to find ways of walking together towards life.

I finish with an analogy that comes from the Amazon region. The Amazonas River in Brazil is formed by two rivers, the Solimões River, which flows downstream from Peru (where it is called Amazonas) and the Rio Negro, which has its birth in Colombia (where it is called Guaiana). When the Solimões River and the Rio Negro meet in the city of Manaus the waters do not initially mix. For six kilometres it is possible to see the dark blue water from Rio Negro and the brown water from Solimões running in parallel. It is like they have to get used to each other and slowly blend until they become "one" united river. By definition, the river is one, but the reality is that two rivers are running side by side. The phenomena occurs because there is a difference in temperature, density and speed between the two rivers. Eventually one mighty river reaches the Atlantic Ocean some seventeen hundred kilometres downstream in a powerful encounter with the salty waters.

Receptive Ecumenism is for me something similar to the Amazon River. We may come from different backgrounds, traditions, theological understandings and experiences and need some time to listen, understand, dialogue and find the common foundations for our Christian faith. As we do that, unity in the Body of Christ is recognized and perceived, since we are by definition "one in Christ" (John 17), and a solid basis for cooperation is built. The impact on society will be powerful and the Kingdom of God will be manifested on earth as an anticipation of the final establishment of the eternal Reign of God.

BIBLIOGRAPHY

Ekström, Bertil, ed. *The Church in Mission—Foundations and Global Case Studies*. Pasadena, CA: William Carey Library, 2016.

Escobar, Samuel. *The New Global Mission—The Gospel from Everywhere to Everyone*. Downers Grove, IL: IVP, 2003.

Padilla, René. *Mission Between the Times—Essays on the Kingdom*. Grand Rapids: Eerdmans, 1985.

Part III

Expanding the Horizons

Prologue to Part Three
River Ecumenism

Sven-Erik Fjellström

THE WORD RETREAT PROBABLY makes us think of silence and, where possible, solitude in faraway places. You might be surprised then if I share my experience of making a week-long retreat in London in February 2002. Equipped with a London Underground map, a travelcard and a copy of St John's Gospel I had decided to make my own retreat in a busy city for a week. It was up to me to keep my silence. My plan was to read a chapter from the Gospel of John every day—and then step out into the streets so see where and how the Gospel was happening today.

I easily found repentance preachers, like John the Baptist, in many street corners. And I found people like Nathanael, with political visions for another world, sitting "under fig trees" outside the parliament. I also imagined Nicodemus and Jesus sitting and talking in a language foreign to me—but I felt that they were sharing issues important for life. I closed my eyes and prayed for them. And there were many wells of Sychar, both inside and outside churches where fair and open faith dialogue took place. As I came to the end of the week it struck me that chapters 1—7 of the gospel all contain *water* (the amniotic fluid in chapter 3, is called "foster water" in Swedish). And so I allowed myself some reflections:

The stories in John 1—7 reminded me of how people can "come to faith" in very different ways. Some (John 1) want and need a physical breaking up, like the disciples of John the Baptist. Others (John 3) need time and space for intellectual reasoning, like Nicodemus. Still others have a lot of experience but are longing for places where they can be met with respect and listened to, like the Samaritan woman (John 4). There are also those who have given up their waiting for a miracle to happen at the pool (John 5). My reflection made me realize how my own description of how to believe and follow Christ over the years has been rather static, perhaps even rigid. I also had to ask myself whether my own view on other churches was rigid in the same way? And when had I dared to start having positive expectations when I met people of other faith traditions? How might we imagine the living water of the Spirit in an ecumenical world?

I knew from school that the Nile River is one of the longest rivers in the world. From maps, of course, but also having had the privilege to fly over it a number of times, I came to realize how important it is for daily life, not only as a water provider for many nations, but everything from producing mud bricks for building to dams important for agriculture. I had imagined the source of the Nile River (the place where Stanley and Livingstone met) as a small brook somewhere at the beginning of it all. But in fact, eleven countries contribute to the river. And the place we call the source is huge! Millions of liters of water meeting, but also coming fresh from underground at Jinja in Uganda.

But there is also a lot of tension around the river. Building a dam can be interpreted as stealing from the other—a recent example are the tensions between Ethiopia and Egypt over the major hydroelectric dam being built in Ethiopia. Some years ago, I heard about the Nile Eleven Project from a fellow traveler to Uganda. The project was started in order for those who shared and benefited from the Nile to work with one another in mutual respect and with humility. How can we see the grandeur of the source and respect each other? The project has also contributed to and supported many cultural initiatives.[1]

I am brave enough to confess to all of you that I have developed an allergic attitude towards some of the ecumenical images we create—specifically trees! Such images risk, in my view, showing which branch is bigger or precedes the other. And they also remind us of the splits. Even the river metaphors tend to place some of us as more important. Could imagining a River Nile Ecumenism help us?

Having had the privilege some years ago to go out by boat to see the incredible meeting place of sources at Jinja, I was deeply moved. The massive Nile River comes flowing from Lake Victoria in Tanzania,

---

1. https://www.utne.com/arts/arts-and-culture-the-nile-project-bringing-the-river-basin-together-and-to-the-world/.

which in its turn gets water from Rwanda and Burundi. But my greatest surprise was that millions of liters of water came up *from underground* every second. What can we learn from this? The abundant and living streams from the wellspring of God are present among us. Living along the river gives us a wider perspective of both receiving and contributing. Has the time come for us in the Northern hemisphere to adopt a humbler attitude, where we no longer look at ourselves as the mainstream? Could Receptive Ecumenism—"River Nile Ecumenism"—help us along the way to this humility and respect for each other?

The Nile also brings us back to the riverbanks in Egypt in the book of Exodus. When everything was hopeless, some brave women became tools to change it all and make an exodus possible. A Nile Exodus perspective can encourage us to pray for brave and "God fearing midwives" (Exod 1:17) who have courage enough to see new and wider perspectives when the rest of us say that change is probably not possible in the ecumenical landscape? Or we can pray for Spirit filled workers like Bezalel and Oholiab (Exod 35:30–35) who were not only filled "with divine spirit, with skill, intelligence and knowledge in every kind of craft" (v. 31) but were also equipped "to *teach*" (v.34). Perhaps the story in Exodus 35 shows a participatory pattern for our ecumenical work?

Let us pray, then, for the transforming and challenging streams from the wellspring that can make us brave in this world. As a closing prayer in this spirit, I here share a free translation of stanza five of the Swedish hymn *Guds källa har vatten till fyllest*:

> So here in the world, give us courage
>
> to live as the Master once taught
>
> The wellspring of God is the power
>
> that helps us to serve Him with love.[2]

---

2. Original Swedish text by Bo Setterlind, 1978.

19

A Living Conversation
Mutual Learning within the Lutheran Community

CHEDIEL SENDORO *and*
KARIN JOHANNESSON

INTRODUCTION BY SVEN-ERIK FJELLSTRÖM

MEETING AND MUTUAL LEARNING within a Church denomination is not typically called "ecumenism" However, the Church of Sweden decided, together with the Christian Council of Sweden, to contribute to the Fifth Receptive Ecumenism International Conference at Sigtuna in 2022 by drawing on a learning process between two Lutheran Churches— specifically from week-long seminars where the bishops from the Church of Sweden (CoS) and the Evangelical Lutheran Church in Tanzania (ELCT) were together in 2015 and 2019. Sweden and Tanzania have a long political history together: several examples can be mentioned from independence onwards. Looking at Church history, missionaries from the Church of Sweden came long before independence and Tanzania is the country where hundreds of Swedish missionaries have worked over the years. The era of many missionaries is over, and the relationship today has of course, many new faces.

Jumping forward to 2009 brings us to the year when the Church of Sweden made its decision permitting same-sex marriages, a decision which put strain on the relations with two big Lutheran churches on the African continent, namely The Evangelical Mekane Yesus Church in Ethiopia, and the ELCT in Tanzania. During a meeting in Dodoma the ELCT issued what has been known as the Dodoma statement, setting out their position on this issue, and strongly opposing such a development.[1]

Nonetheless, in 2011, the former Church of Sweden Archbishop Anders Wejryd was invited by the former Presiding Bishop of the ELCT, Alex Malasusa to make a three week visit to the ELCT. It was presented as a visit where the two bishops wanted to show that even if the churches had different theological views, they could still sit at the same table. And in 2013, at the 50th anniversary of the ELCT, Archbishop Wejryd made a formal invitation to the ELCT bishops to come to Sweden for a Common Bishops' Meeting in August 2015. They met for a week of sharing of the Bible and contextual reflections on *three* churches—the ELCT, the Church of Sweden, and the church that we meet in the book of Acts. The intention was that the bishops also should have time on their own for frank sharing—so nothing was communicated from the group sessions where they were completely on their own, as bishops. Before going for visits in dioceses of the Church of Sweden, a joint statement was issued.[2]

In May 2019 the Swedish bishops were invited to Tanzania for a second week together. The method for sharing was similar, and the bishops made a new joint statement.[3] The 2019 meeting in Tanzania was followed by visits in several dioceses. During a visit to the Mwanga diocese, Bishop Karin Johannesson and Bishop Chediel Sendoro started planning how they could share their experience using a receptive ecumenical perspective. This chapter presents each of their reflections on these inter-Lutheran conversations in the light of Receptive Ecumenism.

---

1. http://www.elct.org/news/2010.04.004.html.

2. https://www.lutheranworld.org/sites/default/files/message_august_28_2015_3.pdf.

3. https://www.svenskakyrkan.se/filer/190508%20-%20Joint%20Statement%20-%20bishops%20from%20ELCT%20and%20Church%20of%20Sweden.pdf.

BISHOP CHEDIEL SENDORO, MWANGA DIOCESE, EVANGELICAL LUTHERAN CHURCH IN TANZANIA

In considering mutual learning within the Lutheran family, I want to talk about Receptive Ecumenism at two different levels:

1. Mutual learning within the Lutheran family at a local level, i.e. within the Evangelical Lutheran Church in Tanzania (ELCT); and
2. Mutual learning within the Lutheran family at a global level with reference to two conferences of the Church of Sweden and the ELCT bishops.

Mutual Learning within the Lutheran Family at a Local Level; An Example of the Evangelical Lutheran Church in Tanzania

What many people do not know about the Evangelical Lutheran Church in Tanzania (ELCT), is the fact that it comprises several Lutheran churches with different traditions and from different Lutheran backgrounds. In my opinion, the ELCT remains a *federation* of Lutheran churches in Tanzania. It is not a single Lutheran Church.

The first Lutheran missionaries from Europe came to Tanzania (then Tanganyika) towards the end of the nineteenth century. These missionaries came at different times, from different mission societies, with different Lutheran traditions, and even from different countries. The end result was the formation of seven different Lutheran churches within the country. These were:

1. The Lutheran Church of Uzaramo-Uluguru;
2. The Lutheran Church of Usambara-Digo;
3. The Lutheran Church of Southern Tanganyika;
4. The Lutheran Church of Northern Tanganyika;
5. The Evangelical Church of North Western Tanganyika;
6. The Lutheran Church of Central Tanganyika; and
7. The Lutheran Church of Iraqw.

These seven Lutheran churches had different traditions according to the missionaries that started or those who further developed the work. In time, these different mission societies felt that they needed to cooperate somehow. In 1952 the mission societies came to an agreement to form the Mission Coordination Committee with an aim of having a forum where these missionaries could discuss matters of common interest.[4] As the political movements for independence grew in the country, so too changes took place in the running of churches, and African members, particularly the clergy, demanded greater participation in the daily running of the churches.

A journey which began with formulating the Mission Coordination Committee, and later (1956) developing a constitution that required the seven local Lutheran churches to have a common practice in choosing leaders,[5] culminated in the formation of the Evangelical Lutheran Church in Tanganyika (ELCT) on June 19th, 1963. As I mentioned earlier, this was not a single Lutheran church, but a federation of seven local Lutheran churches which were in the beginning referred to as synods.[6] For these seven Lutheran churches, with seven different traditions, from more than seven different backgrounds, to come together under one umbrella as the Evangelical Lutheran Church in Tanganyika they surely needed a spirit akin to Receptive Ecumenism—of being open to learn from one another and remaining tolerant of each other.

You can imagine that even after the seven churches came together in 1963, each of them continued to grow and give birth to new dioceses that inherited the traditions of the mother-dioceses. As at June 2022, we have twenty-six dioceses and we expect one new "baby" in October 2022. We surely live and need to continue living with the spirit of Receptive Ecumenism within the Evangelical Lutheran Church in Tanzania.

Among the many differences existing in the Lutheran family within the ELCT, two are more vivid. Firstly, there exists two systems of episcopacy: apostolic succession and non-apostolic succession. Until now, thirteen dioceses follow the apostolic succession system while the remaining thirteen follow the non-apostolic succession system. Secondly, we do not have the same position on the issue of women's ordination. At the time of writing (2022), one diocese does not accept women ordination while two others say they do accept it, although their practice suggests otherwise. The first ordination of a female pastor took place in 1991 in Iringa Diocese. Among the dioceses that accepted women's ordination, and the most recent to celebrate its first ordination of a woman was the diocese in Mara Region in 2021. The period in-between

4. Bavu 1987, 34–36. See also Kimambo 1999, 78.
5. Bavu 1987, 35–38. See also Kimambo 1999, 78.
6. Hildebrandt 1987, 236–38.

has been of individual dioceses learning from others, discussing in their decision-making bodies and deliberating.

Despite such differences and the fact that we have not reached full unity as one single church, the ELCT dioceses enjoy being together and feel proud to identify themselves as the Evangelical Lutheran Church in Tanzania. In this way, the dioceses in the ELCT have been growing together as one church with different traditions inherited from the first seven Lutheran churches that came together in 1963. Maybe staying together with our existing differences is far more enriching than if we could have been united under a single style of church. And so the process of mutual learning goes on.

Looking further afield, the relationship between the Evangelical Lutheran Church in Tanzania and the Church of Sweden also has a rich and growing history. In the next section, I will focus only on how this relationship has facilitated mutual learning between the two churches, both being Lutheran. Two bishops' meetings will be cited as portraying the image of this mutual learning among and through the bishops of these two churches.

Mutual Learning within the Lutheran Family at a Global Level: An Example of the Evangelical Lutheran Church in Tanzania and the Church of Sweden

The relationship between the Church of Sweden and the Evangelical Lutheran Church in Tanzania has a rich history which is still developing. On this occasion, I want to focus only on how this relationship has facilitated *mutual learning* between the two churches, each Lutheran. Two bishops' meetings will be cited as portraying the image of this *mutual learning* among and through the bishops of these two churches.

> The Church of Sweden has a long-standing relationship with the ELCT and we would now like to devote time to getting to know each other better as leaders in the worldwide church. We will highlight how our different conditions affect our way of being a church.[7]

These were the key words of Archbishop Antje Jackelén of the Church of Sweden announcing the Joint Bishops' Conference with the ELCT in Rättvik, Sweden. In this meeting, fourteen bishops from the

---

7. Press Release, 12 August 2015.

ELCT visited the fourteen bishops of the Church of Sweden. During their time together, they had discussions, bible studies, the eucharist and prayers. These four elements were always introduced and led by two bishops (one from each church). As stated in the words of Archbishop Antje, the main purpose of the conference of the bishops of these two largest member churches of the Lutheran World Federation was to meet as church leaders, to strengthen confidence in each other and understand each other's contexts and challenges.

In this first conference, the bishops chose to base their discussions on the Acts of Apostles. Explaining this selection, Archbishop Antje said in her press release, "We are doing this because there we find a story about people who tried to interpret their contemporary context and be a church in it. These Bible stories describe how completely new relationships were formed between different languages and cultures, and we want to be inspired by this."[8]

Considering different contexts and different theologies shaped by contexts of the two churches, one would expect—and surely find—a good number of differences. However, it was possible to stay together because each church was open to learn from the other. Instead of separating, the differences became a rich ground for learning and therefore enriching one another. Through sharing, meditating and reflecting, the bishops agreed that they had common interests and goals. With this, they found it important for the two churches to continue coming closer so that they might further strengthen one another. This was a result of listening to one another with a mind that is open to learn from the other. At the end of the first conference, the twenty-eight bishops came up with a joint statement and a commitment to act. Finally, the ELCT bishops were invited by the bishops of the Church of Sweden to visit their different dioceses.

To reciprocate the generosity of the Church of Sweden, the ELCT invited the bishops of the Church of Sweden to Tanzania in May 2019. The conference was held in Moshi, Kilimanjaro and was attended by thirty-two bishops (thirteen from Church of Sweden and nineteen from ELCT). This second meeting was a continuation of the first one. This time the guiding theme of the conference was "Proclaim the Gospel: The Church in the Public Space." Under this theme, the bishops chose to focus on three major areas: a) Proclaiming the gospel in our

---

8. Press Release, 12 August 2015.

contexts; b) Being baptized into the weakness and the power of Christ; c) Challenging injustice—what is our mission?

Once again, the bishops spent their time together focusing on these three areas under the main theme through sharing, discussions, bible studies, the eucharist and prayers. It was a time for them of fellowship with and learning from one another. The bishops from the Church of Sweden also had an opportunity to see how the ELCT is present in the public space through provision of social services. This was experienced by visiting a church-owned referral hospital, the Kilimanjaro Christian Medical Centre, and a church-owned deaf school, the Mwanga School for the Deaf. To conclude this mutual learning exercise, the thirteen bishops from the Church of Sweden were invited as individuals or small groups to visit a few ELCT dioceses.

At the close of this second conference all 32 bishops came up with a joint statement bearing a call to the two churches and their own commitment to do the following:

- to scale up our commitment to address the causes of and the impact of climate change and loss of biodiversity on people's livelihoods;
- to encourage young people to engage in the relationship between our churches;
- to promote interfaith dialogue and friendly co-existence, especially between Christians and Muslims;
- to support each other in claiming and prophetically utilizing public space;
- to pray regularly for each other, especially on Reformation Day, October 31st, and to share concrete needs in prayer;
- to promote diversity, equality and respect in church leadership—especially women in leadership roles;
- to continue developing and deepening Christian education and teaching;
- to engage in *diakonia*, advocacy, social justice and gender justice so that we "leave no one behind."

This joint statement further verified that the meeting was fruitful in terms of *mutual learning* and understanding one another better. More areas of common interest were further identified, while emphasis on common goals and strategies was deepened.

Reflecting on the experience of these meetings of bishops, and the history of the ELCT, it is clear to us that mutual learning is not limited to a context with different churches. It is possible to mutually learn even in what we consider to be one and the same church. It is important to value the differences as adding flavor to the fundamental requirement of staying together so that we can learn and enrich one another. Indeed, without such differences, staying together would be such a boring experience!

BISHOP KARIN JOHANNESSON, UPPSALA DIOCESE, CHURCH OF SWEDEN

The first time I heard about Receptive Ecumenism was in Helsinki some ten years ago. I was then working on a research project on Lutheran theology and ethics in a post-Christian society. My assignment within this project was to discuss how Martin Luther understood sanctification, i.e., the believer's growth in holiness. More precisely, I wanted to bring three Lutheran theologians with different interpretations of Luther's understanding of sanctification in dialogue with each other. Professor Risto Saarinen and I had booked a meeting since I needed theoretical perspectives and research methods that would help me to set the stage for such a dialogue in the book that I was working on. When we met, Professor Saarinen suggested that I might find some useful perspectives in Receptive Ecumenism that I could benefit from. So, my first acquaintance with Receptive Ecumenism came to me when I tried to get dissenting Lutherans to talk to each other about an issue that I believe is of vital importance for the endurance of Christian faith and, in a broader perspective, for the survival of life on earth.

What I appreciated about Receptive Ecumenism when I first met it was that I finally got tools that helped me bring up really important issues on the agenda in ecumenical conversations. There is a liberating problem orientation in Receptive Ecumenism that evokes my enthusiasm. I am sure that many of you have had similar experiences. We know what is at the top of the agenda in our own Christian tradition. We know what is discussed when our bishops meet, when the diocesan board meets, on the debate pages of our newspapers, or during intense discussions in the parishes. And we know that these issues are rarely the issues we talk about when we meet representatives of another Christian tradition. Then we address other issues. Often the issues we then address are neither controversial nor particularly engaging. Sometimes I have had my head full of questions that I really struggle with while I have participated in a quite boring ecumenical dialogue that have revolved around some minor detail that I can hardly perceive as significant today. Receptive Ecumenism can bring new life to our encounters with Christians belonging to other traditions since it revolves around real problems that are important to those who take part in the dialogue. *Receptive Ecumenism can also bring new life to conversations within our own Christian tradition.* The bishops of the ELCT and the Church of Sweden can testify to this.

A Deeper Understanding of Receptive Ecumenism

My understanding of Receptive Ecumenism has developed further through the joint meetings that the bishops of the ELCT and the Church of Sweden have had. I was not present at the first meeting in Rättvik in Sweden, but when the bishops met in Tanzania, I got the opportunity to make my first visit to that country. I had then been a bishop for a couple of months.

The bishops' joint meeting in Moshi opened my eyes to an important aspect of Receptive Ecumenism which I had previously not noticed. Earlier, I thought that Receptive Ecumenism helps us deal with challenges, issues, or problems in our own Christian tradition that we ourselves have already identified. The dialogue with the bishops in the ELCT made me realize that Receptive Ecumenism can also help us to discover important issues, major challenges, or difficulties that we ourselves have not yet discovered. Through the dialogue with another tradition, we can discover issues that we must address and talk more about within our own Church. *Receptive Ecumenism can help us to discover blind spots in our own tradition.*

Our joint bishops' meeting in Moshi and the dialogue that I and Bishop Sendoro have had when we have prepared for this conference have helped me to discover a challenge that I think that we need to talk more about within the Church of Sweden. It is probable that I was able to discover this challenge more easily because the dialogue between the bishops of the ELCT and the bishops in the Church of Sweden is about mutual learning within one and the same Christian tradition. When the bishops met in Rättvik and Moshi, everyone knew that we were all Lutherans. Therefore, our conversations were in several ways like the dialogue I wanted to promote when Professor Saarinen introduced me to Receptive Ecumenism. It was a dialogue within one and the same tradition that not everyone interpreted in the same way. Not all bishops that took part in our joint bishops' meetings interpret our common Lutheran tradition in the same way. As Bishop Sendoro has explained, sometimes the differences are due to historical circumstances. Sometimes we interpret our common tradition differently since our social or economic circumstances are different. I think we in the Church of Sweden need to talk more about the diversity that exists within our own Lutheran tradition.

Diversity and Anxiety in the Church of Sweden

The dialogue with the bishops in Tanzania made me realize that we in the Church of Sweden sometimes have an ambivalent approach to diversity. During our joint bishops' meeting in Moshi, I discovered that the bishops of the ELCT in several respects are more different from each other than the bishops in the Church of Sweden are. You notice this already at first glance. In the Church of Sweden, all bishops have the same pectoral cross. Our purple shirts may differ slightly in shade and model, but the variation is not very great. This means that the bishops in the Church of Sweden often look alike. Consequently, people mix us up from time to time. When we were in Tanzania, I discovered that the bishops in the ELCT had different pectoral crosses and they did not have the same color or design of their shirts. This diversity was a huge advantage when I forgot the name of one of the Tanzanian bishops. I could still easily refer to him by describing him as "the bishop with the glittering cross."

In the years that have passed since our visit to Moshi, I have had reason to think on a slightly deeper level about how we handle diversity within the Church of Sweden. The dialogue with the bishops in the ELCT made me aware of a particular anxiety within the Church of Sweden which I had not discovered before. This anxiety is closely connected with how we in the Church of Sweden use the term "Lutheran." We sometimes use it as a fence that shuts out certain things, for example the use of a ciborium. That is to say; we sometimes use the term "Lutheran" to create a unity by excluding some parts of the diversity that exists within the Christian tradition. At times, we exclude things that could very well be included in a Lutheran tradition without jeopardizing our basic beliefs.

At other times, we use the term "Lutheran" in a way that implies that everything that is good and valuable within the Christian tradition is highlighted as Lutheran. When I have pointed out that something that the Church of Sweden says in an official document is not only Lutheran but Christian, I have got the answer that it is important for ecumenism that we only comment on our own tradition. The problem with that approach is that it easily leads us to stress, for example, the love of the Bible or the joy of God's grace as something particularly Lutheran. This seems to be to be a kind of religious imperialism.

The mutual learning in which the bishops in the ELCT and the Church of Sweden have been involved has made me think about how we can use the term "Lutheran" in a way that is in accordance with Martin Luther's intentions. Luther did not want us to describe ourselves as Lutherans. Instead, he wanted us to describe ourselves as Christians. That makes me think that everything that we as Lutherans can understand as Christian ought to be part of our tradition. If that is the case, the term "Lutheran" will be redundant but Christian friendship and mutual learning will still be significant. The joint bishops' meeting in Tanzania testifies to this.

Mutual Learning in a Wider Context

When we gathered in Moshi, our mutual learning especially focused on issues concerning the Church in the public sphere. Our conversations highlighted some important differences between Tanzania and Sweden. When we bishops in the Church of Sweden speak out publicly on a political issue, we are often criticized from within the church. In Tanzania, criticism instead comes from outside, from the politicians. The bishops in Tanzania and the bishops in Sweden do not expose themselves to the same risks when they speak out on controversial issues. In Sweden, we risk being ridiculed. Sometimes people also leave the Church of Sweden because they do not appreciate what we say. In Tanzania, the consequences of the statements that the bishops make in public may be more far-reaching.

It is important that Christians in Africa and Europe, for example, support each other when the church needs to speak out on controversial issues that are discussed in public. When the bishops of Tanzania dare to take a stand to protect people's lives and dignity, the bishops of the Church of Sweden need to show that we stand behind our colleagues. It must be clear to the public in Tanzania that the bishops have Swedish friends who support them. In the same way, sometimes it must be obvious to the public in Sweden that the bishops in the Church of Sweden have friends in Tanzania who support us.

The visit to Tanzania deepened my learning about the importance of Christians from different countries standing together when we defend human dignity in the public sphere. During a visit to Italy, I was reminded that this also applies when we belong to different Christian traditions. In Italy, I went to Lampedusa, together with a Roman Catholic priest and an Anglican priest. Our mutual learning was focused on the human dignity of the refugees traveling across the Mediterranean. We walked around outside the detention camp where they are guarded by the military while waiting to be moved somewhere else. The camp is in a pit, and it was terribly hot there. A few kilometers away, the tourists were sunbathing on the beaches. In the evening, the local priests and we who were visiting went out to dinner together. When it was time to pay, it turned out that the restaurant owner did not want us to pay for the dinner. She was so happy that a Lutheran bishop, an Anglican priest, and three Roman Catholic priests were there together. She wanted to contribute to our friendship by serving us for free. And she also wanted us to address the situation on Lampedusa in public.

As churches, we need to listen to and learn from each other. We also need to be involved in mutual learning with society at large. The restaurant owner taught us that we need to say something about the refugee situation on Lampedusa. We hopefully taught her that a Lutheran, Anglican, and Catholic clergy can enjoy a good dinner together, without quarreling. That is also a way of bearing witness in the public space. In a similar way, the joint bishops' meetings in Rättvik and Moshi bore a witness in the public sphere. Lutheran churches, with different theological views, can also sit at the same table. The former Archbishop in the Church of Sweden, Anders Wejryd, and the former Presiding Bishop of the ELCT, Alex Malasusa, gave us an example of this in 2011. It now falls to us to continue setting such examples in the future.

BIBLIOGRAPHY

Bavu, Immanuel K. *Karne Moja ya Injili ya Kilutheri; Dayosisi ya Kilutheri ya Mashariki na Pwani 1887–1987*. Evangelical Lutheran Church in Tanzania (booklet), 1987.

Hildebrandt, Jonathan, *History of the Church in Africa: A Survey*. Achimota, Ghana: Africa Christian Press, 1987.

Kimambo, Isaria N. "The Impact of Christianity among the Zaramo: A Case Study of Maneromango Lutheran Parish." In *East African Expressions of Christianity*, edited by Thomas Spear and Isaria N. Kimambo, 63–82. Oxford: James Currey, 1999.

Murray, Paul D., ed. *Receptive Ecumenism and the Call to Catholic Learning. Exploring a Way for Contemporary Ecumenism*, Oxford: Oxford University Press, 2008.

Press Release, 12 August 2015, https://www.mynewsdesk.com/uk/svenska_kyrkan/pressreleases/bishops-from-sweden-and-tanzania-meet-in-raettvik-1206497.

20

Touchstone and Transformation
Christian Relationships with Judaism as Challenge and Tool for Receptive Ecumenism

CLARE AMOS

INTRODUCTION

THIS CHAPTER TAKES ITS starting point from, and is framed within, two thought-provoking comments about the relationship between Christianity and Judaism made by two great German speaking theologians, one Protestant and the other Roman Catholic, one who died more than fifty years ago, the other full of years and enjoying a well-deserved retirement.

The first comment was made by the Swiss Protestant theologian Karl Barth: "In the final analysis there is really only one main ecumenical question: that of our relations with the Jewish people"

The other was offered by Cardinal Walter Kasper, in 2002 while he was President of the Pontifical Council for Promoting Christian Unity, a role which included responsibility for the Vatican's Pontifical Commission on Religious Relations with the Jews. During a speech to mark the 37th anniversary of the promulgation of the document *Nostra Aetate*, Kasper said, "[W]e Catholics became aware with greater clarity that the faith of Israel is that of our elder brothers, and, most importantly, that

Judaism is as a sacrament of every otherness that as such the Church must learn to discern, recognize and celebrate."[1]

I take Barth's remark as my starting point and conclude by reflecting on the significance of Kasper's comment. I bear in mind the conference at which this chapter was originally presented as a short paper, and I have drawn on the document shared then as a background resource, "The Key Principles and Core Values of Receptive Ecumenism."[2]

ONLY ONE QUESTION

To begin with Barth. It is challenging to track down where and when he said those exact words, or presumably their German original. Certainly the sentence reflects Barth's thinking. Even in 1933 we find Barth writing a letter which included the remark, "Theologically speaking, the question of how to relate to the Jews is surely the pivotal question of the whole history of our time," though not including the word "ecumenical." Also relevant is the throw-away line which appears in *Church Dogmatics*, that the "modern ecumenical movement suffers more seriously from the absence of Israel than of Rome or Moscow" (*CD* IV, 3.2).[3]

However the precise comment itself appears to be quoted (with a marginal difference that may be due to translation from German into English) in Paul M. Van Buren, *A Theology of the Jewish–Christian Reality, Part 2, "A Christian Theology of the People Israel,"* Harper & Row, 1983 (paperback edition 1987), 351–52. Van Buren references it as being found in *Freiburger Rundbriefe*, 27, 1976, cited in *Handreichung* 39, 102, published by the Evangelische Kirche im Rheinland. He states that the words were addressed by Barth in 1966 to the members of the Vatican Secretariat for Christian Unity. Presumably this was a speech given during Barth's visit to Rome in that year which led to the publication of *Ad Limina Apostolorum* which included key questions that Barth raised about *Nostra Aetate* and other Vatican 2 documents. The actual speech does not appear in *Ad Limina Apostolorum*. The full quotation of Barth's words (as given by Van Buren) is,

---

1. Kasper, "Address on the 37th Anniversary of *Nostra Aetate*," Oct. 28, 2002

2. Centre for Catholic Studies, Durham University https://www.durham.ac.uk/research/institutes-and-centres/catholic-studies/research/constructive-catholic-theology-/receptive-ecumenism-/ (accessed 18/9/2023).

3. Barth, *Church Dogmatics* IV, 878.

> There exist today many good relations between the Roman Catholic Church and many Protestant Churches, between the Secretariat for Christian Unity and the World Council of Churches; the number of ecumenical study groups and working groups is growing rapidly. The ecumenical movement is clearly driven by the Spirit of the Lord. But we should not forget that there is finally only one genuinely great ecumenical question: our relations with the Jewish people.[4]

It is fascinating to discover more about the context of Barth's 1966 visit to Rome. It is well-known that Barth had been invited, as probably the pre-eminent Protestant theologian of the twentieth century, to attend two sessions of the Second Vatican Council, but illness had prevented him, and his 1966 visit was a compensation for this—also making clear his overall support for the work of the Council.

However there is an extensive Barthian "backstory" that has only recently been publicized in an article by Daniel M Herskowitz.[5] Herskowitz details not only the earlier process and drafts of the document that eventually emerged in October 1965 as *Nostra Aetate,* but also Barth's involvement with this process, partly at the request of leaders in the world Jewish community, especially Abraham Joshua Heschel. The original aim of Cardinal Augustin Bea, President of the Council for Promoting Christian Unity, had been that a statement about Jews, Judaism and the Roman Catholic Church's relationship to the Jewish people, would form part of the Decree on Ecumenism. But this was eventually not adopted, due to pressure both from conservative Roman Catholics, on religious grounds, and leaders of the Uniate Churches in the Middle East, on political grounds. Instead, the text on Judaism formed a major part of the *Declaration on Non-Christian Religions (Nostra Aetate)* which appeared as one of the last major documents of the Council in October 1965. Herskowitz's article makes clear that Barth was not only party to the discussion as to whether the Council's comments on Judaism should be incorporated in a document on "Ecumenism" or in a document on "Non-Christian Religions," but was also involved in the discussion about some sensitive parts of the eventual text, in particular whether the traditional charge of "deicide" which had been levelled against Jews during much of Christian history should be rebutted.

---

4. Van Buren, *A Theology of the Jewish–Christian Reality*, 351–52.
5. Herskowitz, "Karl Barth and Nostra Aetate."

In the context of Barth's earlier involvement with this conflicted process, the question he addresses in *Ad Limina Apostolorum* in relation to the Decree on Ecumenism is telling: "Why is the most grievous, the fundamental schism—the opposition of Church and synagogue (Rom 9–11; Eph 2)—not dealt here, but only spoken of as the relation of the Church to "Abraham's stock" in the Declaration on the Relationship of the Church to Non-Christian Religions?"[6]

There is much to unpack in an assertion that Christian relations with Judaism constitutes the one main ecumenical question for the churches in our—or at least Barth's—day. In what sense is this the case? Indeed, in what sense is Barth using the word "ecumenical"? Is he using this word "ecumenical" to speak of Jewish relationships with Christianity being on a par with, say, Anglican relationships with the Roman Catholic Church? Or is he viewing Christian relationships with Judaism as a sort of external test case, which can constitute a marker to judge how seriously the individual churches are really committed to learning ecumenically from each other about an issue, namely their relationships with Judaism, that none of them can afford to ignore and which all need to work at together?

HOW WIDE CAN ECUMENISM BE?

Before exploring this further I offer clarification of how I am using the word "ecumenical." In some contexts the word "ecumenical" is now being used more widely, and, in my view unhelpfully, in relation to interreligious dialogue. While I was in post at the World Council of Churches, I worked with others to try and clarify its usage, which led to the production of a short booklet, *Called to Dialogue*. The following comments about "ecumenism/ecumenical" are largely drawn from that booklet.

Although the 1951 Central Committee of the World Council of Churches noted that the word *ecumenical*, "comes from the Greek word for the whole inhabited earth" the reality is that both for the Roman Catholic Church and for the World Council of Churches the center and goal of "ecumenism" remains "the visible unity of the churches in one faith and in one Eucharistic fellowship." Normatively therefore, the term *ecumenism/ecumenical* refers to intra-Christian or inter-church dialogue and engagement. In common speech the word *ecumenical* is used as a synonym for *inter-church/intra-Christian*. However, since the 1990s a variety of epithets have been applied to the term "ecumenism" intended

---

6. Barth, *Ad Limina Apostolorum*, 30.

to suggest its application not only to intra-Christian but also to interreligious dialogue. These include "a new ecumenism," "a wider ecumenism," "macro-ecumenism," and "whole world ecumenism." Sometimes the expression "Abrahamic ecumenism" is used, specifically to speak of relationships between Jews, Christians, and Muslims. The WCC document *Common Understanding and Vision of the WCC* (*CUV*), commended by Central Committee in 1997, comments as follows: "More recently, a growing number of voices from the churches . . . have spoken of the need for "a wider ecumenism" or "macro-ecumenism"—an understanding which would open the ecumenical movement to other religious and cultural traditions beyond the Christian community" (*CUV* §2.6).

However, this same document then goes on to suggest, "These ambiguities surrounding the understanding of 'ecumenical' create the real danger of introducing competitive divisions into the ecumenical movement. What is the meaning and purpose of this movement? Who are its subjects? What are its goals and methods or forms of action?" (*CUV* §2.7).

There seems to be almost inherent unclarity about the term *ecumenical* which has become more apparent precisely because of such use in relation to interreligious concerns. Perhaps we can put it like this. If indeed the term *ecumenical* means something broader than ecclesiastical intra-Christian or inter-church-focused dialogue, namely "an element of common responsibility for the household of life," it could then be argued that to add adjectives such as *new* or *wider* in front of it when referring to interreligious engagement is actually misleading, because it then implicitly narrows the scope of the stand-alone word *ecumenism*, resulting among other things in the sense of competition which CUV §2.7 notes. What we need to do is to recover a generous ambiguity for the word *ecumenism* by itself, and an acknowledgement that it speaks of vision as well as actuality.

In view of this I prefer not to use the word "ecumenical" to describe "interreligious dialogue." On the other hand, I consider that the goal of "ecumenism" should not simply be institutional church-focused unity, but include the vision of how that unity can enable reconciliation in the whole inhabited world (*oikoumene*).

Given such an understanding of ecumenism, in what sense might it be appropriate for Barth to speak of Christian relations with Judaism as an "ecumenical question"? And does such a definition elucidate the developments in the Roman Catholic Church during Vatican II with which Barth seems to have been in dialogue?

As we have already noted, whether Christian relations with Judaism should be seen primarily as an "ecumenical" or "interreligious" concern formed part of the story, and the politics, of Vatican II. A statement on Christian relations with Jews which was originally intended to form part of a Decree on Ecumenism, was separated from it, and then the scope of the document *Nostra Aetate* was widened to refer also to relationships with Muslims, and eventually also briefly to relationships with Hinduism, Buddhism and other faiths. The section on Judaism is considerably longer than any of the others. But what has often been noticed is that whereas *Nostra Aetate* refers to these other religions using terms and ideas with which adherents of these religions would have been comfortable and familiar, its reflection on Judaism is offered almost entirely from a Christian perspective drawing from New Testament texts which refer to Jews and Judaism, and would not have been how most Jewish people chose to refer to themselves. So, for example,

> The Church . . . cannot forget that she received the revelation of the Old Testament through the people with whom God in His inexpressible mercy concluded the Ancient Covenant. Nor can she forget that she draws sustenance from the root of that well-cultivated olive tree onto which have been grafted the wild shoots, the Gentiles. Indeed, the Church believes that by His cross Christ, Our Peace, reconciled Jews and Gentiles. making both one in Himself."[7]

Based on the evidence of *Church Dogmatics*, such a description of Judaism would probably have been quite congenial to Barth himself.

But is this ecumenism? Or indeed "Receptive Ecumenism"?

Given a description of Receptive Ecumenism which speaks of an "openness to growth, change, examination of conscience and continual grace-filled conversion" it is worth noting that reference to the long history of Christian mistreatment of Jews only gets a mealy-mouthed apology in *Nostra Aetate*. Internal Catholic pressures had led to the removal of the explicit rebuttal of the charge of deicide in an earlier draft of the document and though it was noted that the Church "decries hatred, persecutions, displays of anti-Semitism, directed against Jews at any time and by anyone," there was no overt admission that the church

---

7. *Nostra Aetate* §4.

and its adherents had been guilty of such actions many times over many centuries. Ultimately *Nostra Aetate* is important not so much for what it said positively for Jewish–Christian relationships, regarding which it was comparatively conservative, but because its official status opened up the floodgates for future discussion, both in the Roman Catholic Church and in other parts of Christendom.

On that visit to Rome referred to in *Ad Limina Apostolorum*, Barth was to pose two challenging questions to *Nostra Aetate*:

- On what grounds does *Nostra Aetate* speak of the past and present history of Israel in the same breath with Hinduism, Buddhism and Islam as a "non-Christian religion"?
- Would it not be more appropriate, in view of the anti-Semitism of the ancient, medieval and to a large degree the modern church, to set forth an explicit confession of guilt?

When in 1974, almost a decade after the original promulgation of *Nostra Aetate*, a further official text *"Guidelines and Suggestions for Implementing Nostra Aetate"* was published, it was much less reticent in its language about Judaism than the original document. After a preamble it opens with a note that reads almost like a confession, and with language that resonates with Receptive Ecumenism:

> To tell the truth, such relations as there have been between Jew and Christian have scarcely ever risen above the level of monologue. From now on, real dialogue must be established. Dialogue presupposes that each side wishes to know the other, and wishes to increase and deepen its knowledge of the other. It constitutes a particularly suitable means of favoring a better mutual knowledge and, especially in the case of dialogue between Jews and Christians, of probing the riches of one's own tradition. Dialogue demands respect for the other as he is; above all, respect for his faith and his religious convictions."[8]

The condemnation of antisemitism in this 1974 document is also more explicit than in *Nostra Aetate* and is linked to a demand that Christians should strive to acquire a better knowledge of the basic components of Judaism and how Jews define themselves. The expression "the mystery of Israel" is introduced in this document as a part of pondering the mystery of the Church.

8. *Guidelines*, I, Dialogue.

Significantly, by the time that the 1974 document was published, Roman Catholic relations with Judaism had been organized to distinguish relations with Judaism from relations with other religions, designating the Commission for Religious Relations with the Jews as a body linked to the Pontifical Council for Promoting Christian Unity[9] rather than the Pontifical Council for Interreligious Dialogue. In the most recent official statement offered by the Roman Catholic Church on Judaism, the 2015 *Gifts and Calling of God are Irrevocable,* this location is justified as follows:

> From a theological perspective it also makes good sense to link this Commission (for Relations with Judaism) with the Council for Promoting Christian Unity, since the separation between Synagogue and Church may be viewed as the first and most far-reaching breach among the chosen people.[10]

About ten years earlier, Cardinal Jorge Mejia, a previous Secretary to the Commission, in a speech during celebrations to mark the thirtieth anniversary of the Commission's establishment, acknowledged the ambiguity of locating the Commission under the umbrella of the PCPCU:

> Maybe this solution is not the best since it might create the misunderstanding that the goal of these relations is the establishment of a unity, as with other Christians; and this, as is now clear, is absolutely not the case with Judaism. From another point of view, however, there is a true relationship between ecumenical commitment in the strict sense and the relations with Judaism, at least in the sense that this relation is a vocation shared by all Christians and thus can truly help their mutual reconciliation.[11]

It is however important, given the stated aim of Receptive Ecumenism of learning from one's dialogue partner, that the decision whether to describe Jewish–Christian dialogue as "interreligious" or "ecumenical" should be one in which Jewish partners also have the right to a view. There is an unusual and intriguing reference made in 1968 by Immanuel Jacobovits, Chief Rabbi of Great Britain that a priority for relations between Jews and Christians should be to establish, "if not a religious ecumenism,

---

9. Now the Dicastery for Promoting Christian Unity.
10. *Gifts,* I, 3.
11. Jewish–Christian Relations—Documents (notredamedesion.org) The Creation of the Commission for Religious Relations with the Jews and Its Work, November 2004.

at least a moral ecumenism."[12] Although Jacobovits, like many more traditional Orthodox leaders, was nervous about theological dialogue with Christians, he believed strongly that Jews and Christians should work closely together to address issues of personal and social morality that had arisen in the modern age. However, this self-owning of the term "ecumenism" by a Jewish leader to describe Jewish–Christian relations in this way is unusual, if not unique, although Jewish leaders have generally been affirmative when Christians have considered dialogue with Judaism as qualitatively different from Christian dialogue with other non-Christian religions. From the Jewish perspective, such a "special relationship" is seen as at least a partial assurance against Christian missionary activity directed towards the conversion of Jews to Christianity.

THE CHALLENGE OF JUDAISM FOR THE WORLD COUNCIL OF CHURCHES

To return to Karl Barth. Barth had an influential and ambiguous relationship with the World Council of Churches, particularly in the first decade of its existence, so it is interesting to compare briefly the WCC positions on Christian relationships with Judaism with those of the Vatican. The WCC has, by and large, seen the issue of Christian relations with Judaism initially as a missional question, then as an interreligious one, rather than an ecumenical one. Certainly, since the establishment of the WCC interreligious office in 1971 responsibility for relationships with Judaism has been located there along with relationships towards other religions. The fraught story of the second WCC Assembly at Evanston in 1954, during which a text on the "Hope of Israel" was excluded from the Assembly statement on "Christ our Hope," cast a long shadow over later developments, and for both political and religious reasons, the admission of Orthodox Churches to WCC membership in 1961 influenced the direction of travel.

There is one substantial theological WCC report on the theology of Jewish–Christian relationships produced by a Faith and Order Commission meeting in Bristol in 1967, and thus before the setting up of the WCC interreligious office. The report resulted from a collaboration between Faith and Order and a particular group, the Committee on the Church and the Jewish People, originally established in 1931 by the International Missionary Council and which "joined" the WCC in 1961 along with the

---

12. Schaffer, "The Merits of 'Moral Ecumenism.'"

rest of the IMC. Presumably the report was to some degree prompted by concurrent Roman Catholic initiatives. That it is a Faith and Order report is significant, though it does not necessarily carry the implication that Christian relations with Judaism are an "ecumenical" concern.

There are two short reflections in this report which are relevant. The first is a discussion linked to the self-understanding of the Church. Is the Church to be seen primarily as the Body of Christ or as the People of God? The report suggests that if the Church views itself as the former, then:

> The Jewish people are seen as being outside. The Christian attitude to them is considered to be in principle the same as to men of other faiths and the mission of the Church is to bring them, either individually or corporately, to the acceptance of Christ, so that they become members of his body.

If however,

> the Church is primarily seen as the people of God, it is possible to regard the Church and the Jewish people together as forming the one people of God, separated from one another for the time being, yet with the promise that they will ultimately become one . . . the Church should consider her attitude towards the Jews theologically and in principle as being different from the attitude she has to all other men who do not believe in Christ. It should be thought of more in terms of ecumenical engagement in order to heal the breach than of missionary witness in which she hopes for conversion.[13]

The second issue raised by the Bristol report does not depend on one's answer to that earlier question. It is the explicit assertion that:

> The Church's rethinking of her theology with regard to the question of Israel and her conversation with the Jewish people can be of real importance to the ecumenical movement. In this way questions are posed which touch the foundation and the heart of Christian faith. Though these questions are also being asked for other reasons, it is our experience that here they are being put in a particularly penetrating form.[14]

---

13. WCC Commission on Faih and Order, *The Church and the Jewish People*, IV, "The Church and her Witness."

14. WCC Commission on Faih and Order, *The Church and the Jewish People*, V, "Ecumenical Relevance."

Later WCC statements in 1982 and 1988 did not add much to what was said in 1967. The Bristol report marks the last time when the WCC "wrestled" with the question of the theological nature of the relationship—and in what sense it might be called "ecumenical"—between Christianity and Judaism.

CONCLUSION

So are Jewish–Christian relationships an "ecumenical" question or not? And what are the learnings from and for the ideology of Receptive Ecumenism? There are two stated tenets of Receptive Ecumenism into which the Jewish–Christian relationship may make a special contribution:

The first tenet is, "Our traditions are limited as well as life-giving, wounded as well as grace-bearing: we need to show rather than to hide our wounds and to ask our others to minister to us."

The second tenet is "The openness to growth, change, examination of conscience and continual grace-filled conversion that lies at the heart of Christian life pertains as much to the ecclesial as to the personal."[15]

In my response to these principles I would want to suggest the following features of the Jewish–Christian relationship justify—but also interrogate—its description as "ecumenical":

At the most fundamental level, the task for the Christian churches to relate to Judaism encourages or even requires them to work together "ecumenically," and because it is "a vocation shared by all Christians" it can also help their mutual intra-Christian learning and reconciliation. As noted in the WCC report from the Bristol conference in 1967, serious theological Christian engagement with Judaism requires discussion of issues which appear in a particularly penetrating way to touch the "heart of Christian faith." The theological re-thinking that these issues require can (and perhaps should) have important implications for serious "ecumenical" engagement between churches.

Above I quoted as one of the "key principles" of Receptive Ecumenism the need for "examination of conscience and continual grace-filled conversion." The difficult history of the Christian–Jewish relationship over many centuries, culminating in the genocide of the twentieth century is certainly an area where Christians and institutional Christianity need to "examine their conscience." This has been deeply challenging for the churches, though in western Christianity at least, the engagement

---

15. *The Key Principles and Core Values of Receptive Ecumenism.*

between Jews and Christians has now contributed to a "conversion" and a repudiation of long-held views such as the charge of deicide. In this sense Christian engagement with Judaism can act as a "transformative touchstone" whose effects can spill over into other relationships, both in intra-Christian contexts, and in terms of the churches' relationship to the wider world.

It would however be a mistake to suggest that there is no further need for Christians to "examine their conscience" in relation to their attitudes to Judaism. In many Christian churches an "unthinking" supersessionism vis-a-vis Judaism is still common currency. In practical terms it frequently shows itself in the use of the Bible, especially in worship. It is notable, for example, how in the Revised Common Lectionary (Common Worship Lectionary), the Old Testament readings that are thematically "connected" with the Gospel for the day often seem to suggest rather simplistically that Christians have replaced Jews as "the people of God." To move beyond such a "supersessionist" attitude requires serious reflection by Christians on the nature of the Bible. However this challenge can and should encourage Christians to reflect more generally on our use and abuse of scripture, and thus offers another example of the Christian–Jewish relationship as a potential "touchstone" for mutual intra-Christian learning.

There are other areas where Judaism and Christianity can (and should) learn from each other in a way that is central to the vision of "Receptive Ecumenism." In a foreword he wrote for a collection of essays published in 2011[16] Cardinal Walter Kasper commented "Israel and the churches need each other and are dependent upon each other. A true ecumenism without Israel is not possible." Kasper refers at this point to the way that, in his view, Judaism and Christianity need each other, to guard against tendencies in Judaism to become over particularistic and reclusive, and in Christianity to become ahistorical and succumb to a form of gnosticism.

Yet it is an earlier comment of Kasper—offered in 2002 and quoted in my introduction—with which I want to conclude. It speaks to me evocatively of the possibility of Judaism becoming for Christianity an agent of "Receptive Ecumenism." Kasper suggests that "Judaism is as a sacrament of every otherness that as such the Church must learn to discern, recognize and celebrate." This description of sacrament is

---

16. Cunningham et al, "Foreword," *xvi*.

powerful and resonates deeply with many Christian traditions. What does it mean to be a "sacrament of every otherness"? Perhaps it is something like this: if Christians are willing to accept and honor the sheer difference of Judaism in its own terms and not seek (as even *Nostra Aetate* initially sought to do) to present Judaism through Christian eyes, that very humility of learning can be sacramental, enabling our transformation, which will then have implications for our engagement with other Christians, and for the ecumenical movement itself. At its most profound—and if it is truly dialogue—Christian engagement with Judaism can help us to discover that difference, "otherness," as much as similarity, can be the starting point for our growth.

BIBLIOGRAPHY

Barth, Karl. *Ad Limina Apostolorum: An Appraisal of Vatican II*. Translated by Keith R. Crim. Richmond, VA: John Knox, 1968.

Barth, Karl. *Church Dogmatics IV/3.2*. Edinburgh: T. & T. Clark, 1962.

Philip A. Cunningham et al. *Christ Jesus and the Jewish People Today*. Grand Rapids: Eerdmans, 2011.

Dicastery for Promoting Christian Unity. "Guidelines and Suggestions for Implementing the Conciliar Declaration *Nostra Aetate*, 1974." http://www.christianunity.va/content/unitacristiani/en/commissione-per-i-rapporti-religiosi-con-l-ebraismo/commissione-per-i-rapporti-religiosi-con-l-ebraismo-crre/documenti-della-commissione/en3.html.

———. "The Gifts and the Calling of God are irrevocable (Rom 11:29): A Reflection on Theological Questions Pertaining to Catholic–Jewish Relations on the Occasion of the 50th Anniversary of "*Nostra ætate*" (No. 4) http://www.christianunity.va/content/unitacristiani/en/commissione-per-i-rapporti-religiosi-con-l-ebraismo/commissione-per-i-rapporti-religiosi-con-l-ebraismo-crre/documenti-della-commissione/en.html.

Herskowitz, Daniel M. "Karl Barth and Nostra Aetate: New Evidence from the Second Vatican Council." *Journal of Theological Studies* (2021). 343–74.

Kasper, Walter Cardinal. Address on the 37th anniversary of *Nostra Aetate*, Oct. 28, 2002, accessed via website of Council of Centers on Jewish–Christian Relations, https://ccjr.us/dialogika-resources/documents-and-statements/roman-catholic/kasper/wko2oct28.

———. "Foreword" in Philip A. Cunningham et al, *Christ Jesus and the Jewish People Today*. Grand Rapids: Eerdmans, 2011, x–xviii.

Mejia, Jorge Cardinal. "The Creation of the Commission for Religious Relations with the Jews and Its Work" 23/11/2004 http://www.notredamedesion.org/en/dialogue_docs31ab.html?a=4a&id=15.

Schaffer, Gavin. "The Merits of 'Moral Ecumenism': Secularism, Suspicion and Jewish–Christian Relations in Twentieth-Century Britain." *Journal of Ecclesiastical History* 74/3 (2023) 618–43.

Van Buren, Paul M. *A Theology of the Jewish–Christian Reality, Part 2, "A Christian Theology of the People Israel."* New York: Harper & Row, 1983 (paperback ed. 1987).

Vatican II. Declaration on Non-Christian Religions (*Nostra Aetate*), October 1965, https://www.vatican.va/archive/hist_councils/ii_vatican_council/documents/vat-ii_decl_19651028_nostra-aetate_en.html.

World Council of Churches. *Called to Dialogue: Inter-religious and Intra-Christian Dialogue in Ecumenical Conversation—A Practical Guide*. Geneva: WCC Publications, 2016.

———. *Common Understanding and Vision of the WCC*. Geneva: WCC Publications, 1997.

World Council of Churches Commission on Faith and Order. *The Church and the Jewish People ("The Bristol Report")*. Geneva: WCC Publications, 1967. https://www.jcrelations.net/statements/statement/the-church-and-the-jewish-people.html.

21

Wider Ecumenism
A Pilgrimage towards Cosmic Christ Consciousness

MATHEW CHANDRANKUNNEL, CMI

INTRODUCTION

WIDER ECUMENISM IS A movement that incorporates deep theological interactions among Christian denominations. It is a way of life that lives in dialogue with an openness towards all humanity as the children of an all-embracing God who may belong to the numerous religious traditions spread across the globe, and it is care for nature—with all its living organisms, plants and the material world within which we humans exist and of which we are endowed to be stewards or shepherds. As a title and concept, Wider Ecumenism was first presented by Fr. Eugene Hillmann, CSSp, a Catholic missionary who worked among the Masai tribe in Northern Tanzania.[1] His book, *The Wider Ecumenism* (1968) grappled with the question of mission and the implanting of Christianity in places where it was unheard of.[2] Fr Hillmann argues that "it is impossible and even unnecessary to preach Christianity to all people." According to him, the majority of people who are not Christians will

---

1. Hillmann, *Wider Ecumenism*, 160.
2. Starkloff, *Aboriginal Religion*, 287–319.

be saved through their response to the events affecting their lives in which grace is working anonymously, based on Karl Rahner's concept of "Anonymous Christians." Oswin Magrath had also written an article entitled "Wider Ecumenism" and I am yet to trace who originally proposed the term.[3] However, the unsung hero of Wider Ecumenism in India is Rev Dr M. A. Thomas, who propagated and practiced this method of ecumenism in India by establishing the Ecumenical Christian Centre (ECC) at Bangalore in 1963. His relentless visionary thinking and creative dynamism nurtured the ecumenical movement in India and influenced both the WCC and the Catholic Church in India through a close collaboration with the institutions he built up along with leaders from other Churches and from the secular world.[4] Though there have been many prominent theologians of ecumenism in India, in this chapter I briefly present the wider ecumenical vision of M. A. Thomas, and how it could be further extended and flourish, incorporating values embedded in the spiritual, religious and cultural matrix from the East and the West and thus become a tool for the integration of all the trajectories and trends in the ecumenical movement.[5]

---

3. Magrath, *Ecumenism*, 624–8.

4. For a detailed account of the life, vision, and influence of M.A. Thomas, see Chandrankunnel, *Epiphany*.

5. As the Director of ECC from 2016 to 2021, I had the ample opportunity to go through the articles M. A. Thomas has written, the manuscripts he had kept without publishing, the notes he collected, the reports he wrote for the annual general body meetings, and the trimonthly meetings held at ECC for administrative purposes. I saw in the reports that after fifteen years of service of M. A. Thomas as the founding Director of ECC, many were approached and a few were selected to write a book on M. A. Thomas. However, none came to fruition and hence I took it up as my challenge to write a book on the evolution of the thought for the establishment of ECC, its execution and smooth functioning of ECC and its overall impact in India and especially among the World Council of Churches. I wrote the manuscript after consulting all possible sources at ECC and elsewhere and come up with the manuscript, *The Semantic Epiphany: the Methodological Oeuvre and the Ecumenical Vision of M. A. Thomas* which could not be published due to the impact of Covid-19 and the lack of funds for publications. So this chapter is a summation of the manuscript and the details are elaborated here on the life of M. A. Thomas, his vision, execution and functioning of ECC, his theological contributions, and his concerns for the people and the birth pangs he suffered in this endeavor. His concern for the people and angst for the people's sufferings, lamentation towards Jesus Christ when things were not going in the way he expected were all described in his poems, which were published. The chapter carries some of the quotations from the poems published as M. A. Thomas, *Traffic Lights*.

WIDER ECUMENISM AT THE ECUMENICAL CHRISTIAN CENTRE

The foundational concept of Wider Ecumenism which is practiced and promoted at the Ecumenical Christian Centre (ECC) is formed from the integration of Ecumenism and Interfaith Dialogue. Integrating all the diverse experiences he had from different religious traditions, Rev Dr M. A. Thomas, the founder of the ECC, evolved and practiced the wider ecumenism which was also promoted by the missionary movements and later crystallized into the theology and practice of the World Council of Churches. Through his in-depth interactions with interfaith fellowship, Thomas fused interfaith dialogue into the concept of wider ecumenism. The practice and promotion of this wider dimension of ecumenism at ECC and its transmission to other global forums such as the WCC in was through Thomas's direct involvement.

The ECC breathes wider ecumenism. When a program is organized at the ECC, its starts with a prayer service incorporating all religious traditions rather than a specific Christian tradition. Moreover, every day in ECC campus, at 8 AM all staff members assemble either in the chapel or in the open Green Quadrangle and recite a few prayers from different religious traditions. From the Christian tradition "Our Father" is recited. Then St Francis of Assisi's most secular prayer "Make me an instrument of peace..." is recited by all initiated by the prayer leader. The prayer session is concluded by the chanting of the great prayer from the Upanishads, *"Asato Ma Sat Gamaya."* After a few minutes of silence, everyone goes to their own respective duties and works previously assigned to the staff members. All ECC staff, therefore, from the director to the sweeper, all take leadership in the prayer session in rotation without an exception. So the day of work begins with the multireligious prayer of kindly praying to the One Almighty God to lead us from the unreal to the real, from ignorance to truth, from death to eternity and to be an instrument of peace and respecting each and every one as the child of God and praying to the *"Abba"* to deliver each days food and to forgive us as we are forgiven in order to give a sense of belonging to the cosmic brotherhood. This is an openness towards the wider humanity, united in search for the eternal values and to be always an instrument of forgiveness, peace and happiness in order to create an egalitarian community where everybody is accepted, appreciated and respected. Everyday morning this multireligious legacy of wider ecumenism is continuously renewed at ECC, to connect with the whole of humanity and with the totality of creation.

DIALOGUE WITH RELIGIONS

Traditionally, the Catholic Church held that "outside the Church there is no salvation." However this exclusivist mentality is challenged by an understanding of salvation in and through the role of Jesus Christ which allows an inclusive openness towards the larger humanity of the earth. The Catholic Church's acceptance and appreciation for "what is good in all the religions" is evident at Vatican II and produced *Nostra Aetate*, the "Declaration on the Relation of the Church to Non-Christian Religions." This new perspective generated an openness that allowed unprecedented theological investigations including Karl Rahner's "Anonymous Christians"[6] and Raimundo Panikkar's "Unknown Christ of Hinduism."[7] Hans Küng was also a pioneer, emphasizing the need of dialogue among the religions and bringing to the popular imagination the idea that "peace among the religions is necessary for world peace."[8] From such theologians, mainstream Churches accepted and appreciated the importance and the necessity of being in dialogue with the other religions. Thus, the perception of other religions as evil changed to an attitude of openness, appreciation, acceptability, respectability and fellowship. Adopting the basic arguments of Rahner, Panikkar and Küng, many churches accepted that the value system of Jesus Christ is visible and entrenched in other religious traditions, and if a person followed his or her conscience and their religion, they may receive the eternal redemption revealed in and through Jesus Christ.

Though a synonymous concept to salvation in Christianity could not be found in the Buddhist tradition, a similar concept of *kenosis* is available in the important Buddhist concept of Bodhisattva developed in the Mahayana-Vajrayana tradition also was appreciated by the Vatican II.[9] A Bodhisattva withholds their enlightenment until the elimination of the suffering of all other beings and thus supports them to transcend their own suffering. Perhaps influenced by such deeper levels of understanding these concepts of salvation and *kenosis* from both the

---

6. Conway, *Anonymous Christian*.
7. Panikkar, *Unknown Christ*.
8. Küng, *World Religions*.
9. Holm, *Nestorian Monument*.

traditions, both His Holiness Dalai Lama and the Abbot of the Cistercian Monastery in France, were able to greet each other with a surprise invitation to meditate together.[10] The evolved consciousness of these great leaders of modernity enabled them to contemplate on the Divine as the best way of encounter rather than a conversation. Through this practical example they brought to us the dimension of the divine in their mutual presence and fused their own individual consciousnesses into the One and single cosmic consciousness. Here physical identities merge and only the divine remains, as water droplets merging into the ocean lose individual identities.

All religious traditions search for meaning and purpose in life. In Christianity it is believed that this movement is guided by the Holy Spirit and thus entrenched into the love and empathy of Jesus Christ. Thus, a genuine dialogue, a rational process of receptibility, reciprocity, and hospitality will definitely lead us towards fellowship, peace and harmony in order to evolve us into higher dimensions of consciousness.

REDEMPTIVE DISCIPLESHIP: FOUNDATION FOR AN ECUMENICAL ENCOUNTER

All Christian denominations are based on the theology of the incarnation, life, death and resurrection of Jesus Christ. Whatever the doctrinal differences, most churches hold the divinity and humanity of Jesus Christ and His resurrection which gave redemption to humanity. Jesus in his life always proclaimed that God the Father had sent him to the humanity to raise them up as children of God and always followed the desire—commands of His Father. A radical obedience of Jesus Christ is visible in his life from the birth in the manger towards the exaltation on the cross of suffering, pain and death. It is indeed a *kenosis*, a self-emptying as St Paul described in his letter to the Philippians. It is in and through self-emptying that Jesus enriched others. Redemptive discipleship invites everyone to follow this radical obedience and self-emptying.

Dietrich Bonhoeffer's writings speak of the radical obedience and self- emptying of Jesus Christ, and M. A. Thomas was highly influenced by this great revolutionary activist theologian, often quoting him in his writings, sermons and lectures. Redeemed by the resurrection of Jesus Christ, every Christian is invited to be a disciple in this manner and

---

10. Shared by His Holiness Dalai Lama in my numerous encounters with him in India.

expected to witness Jesus Christ. The disciples of Jesus underwent this transformation after the advent of the Holy Spirit. Even today in our contemporary times all Christians are invited to follow this redemptive discipleship to evolve towards an ecumenical consciousness, by discovering the value system of Jesus Christ underpinning the doctrinal positions of the denominational Churches. According to M. A. Thomas, the redemptive discipleship could only be expressed in and through *diakonia* (service) and *marturia* (witness), the core value of Jesus Christ which invite all of us to totally dedicate in the transformation of the wider humanity. By serving the poor, eradicating ignorance, healing the sick, caring for the orphans and thus to become the salt of the earth and light of the world. Hence, Thomas gave priority to these dimensions of service and witnessing, evolved from his radical discipleship towards the core value system of Jesus, for the integral transformation of the people, rather than in dialogue with the numerous denominations of Churches to be either in an organic or collegial relationship.

Both in India and abroad, Thomas encountered obstinate divisive doctrinal positions which led him towards disillusionment with the whole process of ecumenical dialogue. It is clear from his life that he was looking for alternative means and ways of being meaningful for and in humanity. He felt frustrated with ecumenical dialogue's focus on theological arguments and the hard dogmatic positions held by churches and leaders. Thus, instead of pursuing ecumenical dialogue with the goal of organic unity or a communion ecclesiology, he plunged into the service of humanity and the witnessing of Christ which he thought could be built upon the radical discipleship, enabling him, even reformulating the concept of mission itself. For M. A. Thomas, then, mission is an invitation to serve the mystical body of Christ as is emphatically elucidated by Paul through his epistles. It is the ultimate breaking of the bread and wine as the body and the blood of Christ participating in the last supper, crucifixion, death and resurrection, were by capitulating everything in Jesus Christ, a conceptual foundation initiated in the very beginning of Christianity. It is not a retreat to the past but a reformulation of everything as Paul and Irenaeus advocated in order to produce day by day, a stronger synthesis founded on the mystery of the mystical body of Christ and love of neighbor. This new Adam, Jesus Christ, empowered through the resurrection, is not a dominant master of creation but a steward, caring, nurturing and protecting the entire creation, leading towards a permanent eschatological transformation which is yet to be realized. Here Jesus

Christ is embodied as Cosmic Christ, who enwraps the whole creation as alpha and omega with cosmic scope and hope. This transformation of the entire creation and wider humanity will be the summing up of today's sciences and the faith-revelation that imparted to humans as a gratuitous gift given in and through Jesus Christ directed lovingly for the progress of all humanity in the glorified Christ Consciousness.

M. A. Thomas was a person of integration and holistic outlook and so he evolved a strategy to balance both these dimensions of service and witnessing as a fundamental mission, with the horizontal and the vertical perspectives on life and beyond life, extending oneself towards the other and deeply immersed towards witnessing Christ, towards a Christo- centrism. In Thomas's outlook, the mission of the Church is to serve not only humanity but also, as envisaged by St Paul in Romans 8, participating in the groaning of the entire creation. Hence, Thomas was a forward looking visionary, emphasizing the need to prioritize climate change, environmental protection etc., in our role as the carers of nature. He thus created a theological vision of a total and integral summation of the ecological consciousness and the human consciousness merging into the Cosmic Consciousness of Jesus Christ. Thomas pioneered a visionary model of wider ecumenism, going beyond the restricted conceptual boundaries of ecumenism among the Christian denominations to incorporate interfaith dialogue and even ecological awareness, all culminating towards a Cosmic Christ Consciousness.

SANATANA SAT GURU AS COSMIC CHRIST

Joseph Sittler, the keynote speaker of the third WCC Assembly held at New Delhi in 1961, presented a Christology connecting the Cosmos and humanity interpreting Col 1:15–20, integrating the whole cosmos including nature into the redemptive mystery of Christ. M. A. Thomas participated in the 1961 WCC Assembly in New Delhi. This lecture can be interpreted as the first Christology of Ecology, or Christology of Nature, where Sittler exhorted that nature need to be protected since Christ redeemed everything in this cosmos.[11] Thomas was influenced by these new theology of nature and we could see that when he established ECC, caring for the nature was an important aspect that was emphasized at ECC from its very inception and continued with an international conference in January 2020, "Climate Change, Ecology and Religion" where

---

11. Sittler, "Called to Unity."

participants from all over the world including Russia, Australia, New Zeeland and from all over India.[12]

Creation and redemption are the two sides of the same coin as envisaged by Paul in his letters, especially in Rom 8:19-22, Eph 4:4-7 and Col 1:15-20. In the letter to the Colossians, Paul established the centrality of Christ in the Christian faith and thus, he proposed a Christology for the entire creation. Paul emphasized that Christ is the true image of God and hence the revelation of God, the whole existence and essence of everything is brought in and through him. This Christ is imperishable and susceptible to corruption. Thus, as the perfect image of God, Paul argued that Christ is the true and only mediator between God, man and the entire creation, leading to the cosmic significance. The whole universe came into being in and through Christ and once again brought into a proper relationship with God. Christ is thus, active both in the new creation as the redeemer and as God's own paramount agent. Paul, thus, in a stunning way, integrated here the temporal and the eternal or the terrestrial and the transcendental into a unique whole. The primacy and supremacy of Christ over everything and fullness and meaning of everything are acknowledged and fulfilled in Christ. Paul through these theologically deep conceptual analysis and interconnectivity of God, cosmos and humanity knitted us into an inextricable continuum. God's plan of redemption is already at work in the creation itself in and through the logos as Jesus Christ. Christ is the sustainer and it is in Christ, cosmos and humanity are coherent as both are dependent on Christ. Thus, Paul asserts that the coherence of the cosmos and the humanity are due to the primacy and pervading of Christ over everything, stretching towards a cosmic significance of Christ. The unity, solidarity and coherence of the God–Cosmos–Humanity continuum is due to the Cosmic Christ which holds together without susceptibility to chaos. Thus, Paul maximizes the significance of the person of Christ into a cosmological order.

M. A. Thomas expressed and asserted this cosmic role of Jesus Christ by placing titles like mediator, unifier, sacrament, bridge builder and many other meaningful references through his lectures, articles and poems. In one article he made a shift of emphasis from Christ–Church–World towards Christ–World–Church almost following the Pauline cosmic

---

12. This international conference was organized by the author where many participants from most of the religious traditions from India and abroad participated. Many Buddhist masters and monks participated in this conference where they elucidated on the concept of Green Tara, a feminine Bodhisattva.

paradigm.[13] According to Thomas, the unity of humankind is achieved in and through Christ as well as the unity of the Churches. As Paul envisaged, Christ is the aim, goal and purpose of human progress and evolution and in this process, M. A. Thomas avoided both cultic/ritualistic dimensions and proselytizing tendencies. In the Cosmic Christology, the *Kerygma* is obviously *Diakonia* leading towards *Koinonia*. M. A. Thomas was practicing and popularizing this Cosmic Christology and his characteristic trademark of propagating it was through *Diakonia*, namely service to his fellow humans and the inhabitants of this cosmos.

The Cosmic Christ of M. A. Thomas's vision also evolved from the deep Indian Christian theology based on the deeply philosophical heritage and ethos evolved from the timeless spiritual and philosophical speculations of India. In many of his writings and lectures one could find the traces of this interest, and awareness of the contributions made by Vengal Chakkrai, Pandipetti Chenchiah, A. J Appasamy and other pioneering Indian Christian theologians. Jesus the incarnated "Word," the Divine Son dwelt among this world and lived, died and resurrected in a Jewish culture, experienced as Jesus the Messiah, translated into the pervading Greek culture as Jesus the Christ. In the process of incarnating Jesus Christ into various cultural matrixes, the Gospels and the epistles represented different theological motifs expressed through a variety of cultural modes. For example, John's gospel took up the Greek philosophical concept of the "Logos" in illustrating the incarnation of the Divine "Son" into the human flesh in space and time and the earthly cultural conditioning in the Jewish tradition. The Word–Logos who became a human being Jesus, lived amidst the Jewish cultural, spiritual milieu incorporating the Samaritan, Roman, Canaanite and other cultural traditions. Scores of other Christian thinkers took up the Greek, Roman and other cultural traditions in incarnating the Divine into their own cultural heritage and ethos. In continuation of this tradition of inculturation, St Thomas the Apostle came to India and integrated the cultural heritage with Christian values which the Thomas Christians in Kerala very rigorously and reverentially continue to live up to becoming Christian in Faith, Hindu in Culture and Asian in its roots.[14] Faith in Jesus was and is always in search of understanding the revelation in and through the

---

13. This is elucidated further in Chandrankunnel, *Semantic Epiphany*.

14. This expression was introduced by Fr Placid Podipara CMI, a historian and theologian of the Ancient Thomas Christians in defining their identity as Christian in the cultural matrix of India.

cultural ethos of India which is deeply incarnated in the daily lived experience of its people from the apostolic times. Though there have been attempts throughout the centuries to incarnate the Divine Son in to the Asian cultural context, for example to present Jesus Christ as *Sanatana Sat Guru*,[15] the reality of Asia such as poverty, caste-tribal inequality, multi-religious-spirituality context, especially, the Hindu and the Buddhist traditions, are the manifold expressions of Asia which is earnestly crying to incarnate and inculturate Christ into this rich cultural ethos of Asia. In short Christ is to be born into the Asian milieu necessitating the contextualization or inculturation of Christianity in Asia.

UNIVERSALIZING CHRISTIANITY

However, Asian theologians and other Asian thinkers have critically argued that Christianity has been built upon a Western philosophical and cultural bulwark. Therefore, the Indian theologians observe that the word inculturation has to be patterned on the model of incarnation of the Word. Inculturation does not tell anything about the process or its implications in the concrete but must be examined in a particular context.[16] The Sri Lankan Theologian Aloysius Pieris, as an Asian, reflects on and echoes the same spirit that the Jordan and the Ganges of Asian Religions need to be flowing together incorporating the nomadic and the pastoral traditions of the Asiatic cultural context.[17] Poverty, hunger, illiteracy, malnutrition, dictatorships, lack of freedom, oppression etc., are pervading the half of the humanity that is more than three billion people and the question now is, how far the face of Christ is capable of entering into the sufferings of these people and how they could be drawn towards the salvific hope of resurrection in the horizon of their daily lives. For this purpose, the Church need to turn towards Christ who had concern for the multitude (Mark 8:2) and the Church needs to translate the Epiphany of Jesus Christ into the cultural milieu of Asia with its social, political, economic, spiritual, and religious dimensions. A search for the dignity of human person always affirms freedom, justice, and rights which must invariably involve rejecting the dehumanizing tendencies of capitalism, materialism, communism, imperialism,

---

15. For an argument of how Jesus the Messiah (a Jewish description) could be interpreted as *Sanatana Sat Guru* as the Greeks interpreted Jesus as Christ, see Chandrankunnel, "Logos as *Dharma*" in Thomas Kutty, *Biblical Spirituality*.

16. Valle, *Becoming Indian*.

17. Pieris, *Vatican II*.

colonialism, secularism, fundamentalism and casteism. This affirmation encourages a striving for the power of the people to change the course of their destiny based on the revelation of God's power in its intervention in history in order to create an inclusive community that shares the experience in the bondedness of the compassion and love of Christ. Throughout his life M. A. Thomas tried to incorporate and theologize these different Asian experiential estrangements into the theological parlance which one could find in his articles, lectures, poems and the courses he had evolved at the Ecumenical Christian Centre through decades of applied theology.

Many of the concepts and cultural categories that are enshrined in the spiritual wealth of Asia such as Satchidananda, Narahari, Guru, Boddhisatva have been used to portray the infinitely compassionate person of Jesus Christ who is both Divine and Human at the same time. Contemporary renderings of the wellness, happiness and wholeness concepts also need to be incorporated into our theological discourse to make an eventful impact on the youth of today who build their lives on these categories. We need a theology that vibrates according to the heartbeats of the Asian masses and their life world. Only then might we claim that the Churches really carry the torch entrusted to them by the activist and visionary, M. A. Thomas.

AUGMENTING ECUMENISM TOWARDS A UNIVERSAL CONSCIOUSNESS

It has been observed by many ecumenists that there is an ecumenical winter—a lack of ideas or vision, a crisis even. There is in fact a bankruptcy of vision not in a single field but many dimensions of humanity.[18] The unprecedented medical situation of Covid-19 and the raging wars fought in our neighborhoods show the collapse of international institutions, and the pervasive hopelessness among younger generations are the signs and symbols of these crises. The hegemony imposed by the unprovoked attacks on countries can be diagnosed as the sickness of humanity endowed with selfish unwarranted determinations that call us towards a redefining, reinterpreting and renewing our own priorities and transforming our way of life with a new mode of thinking, living and action. Edmund Husserl in 1936 detected a crisis in European civilization rooted in the advancement of technology and science which

---

18. Kasper, *Call to Unity*.

catapulted people towards more calculative rather than contemplative modes of action. This diagnosis and analysis were radically expanded by his disciple Heidegger.[19] In the same year, Franklin Roosevelt quoted Josiah Royce's 1914 book, *A Word for the Times*:

> the human race now passes through one of its great crises! New ideas, new issues,—a new call for men to carry on the work of righteousness, of charity, of courage, of patience and of loyalty.[20]

Royce developed the concept of the beloved community on the foundation of rationality as an antidote for the crises and problems of his time. This concept of beloved community was expanded by Martin Luther King (Jr), Nelson Mandela through their actions and incorporating the idea of *Ubuntu* which is inextricably intertwined with the existential foundations of the African Culture.[21] Archbishop Desmond Tutu through the Truth and Reconciliation Commission expanded it into the South African culture, integrating the suffering and pain encountered by the natives and trying to build peace with the colonial power that oppressed them. "I am because of we are" is a new way of looking up to the community and living the concept of *Ubuntu*, a concept inextricably interwoven with the values of the African tribal communities. In Asia, Mahatma Gandhi proposed the concept of "*Ram Rajya*"— a way of life, with interdependence and inclusiveness. A communitarian participation and interaction with other people to have trust, having an evolving community endowed with compassion, caring, humility, kindness, forgiveness, reconciliation and justice towards a life giving and life enabling through inter-dependence, are said to be the characteristics of the beloved community, whether it is termed as Ubuntu, Ram Rajya or Kingdom of God, which expresses the same basic characteristics and underpinning foundation. Hegel in his *Philosophy of History* enumerated how a person can become ethical through the social process of involving in the activities of the society. Thus, the global beloved community can be defined as an all embracing and interdependent relationality that discriminates none. This communitarian life derives a universal ethics in and through the involvement within the community. Justice is also absolutely interconnected with the beloved community. Pope Francis's encyclicals *Laudato Si* and *Fratelli Tutti* are a worldwide wakeup call for establishing such a beloved community.

19. Husserl, *European Sciences*.
20. Kalb, *Presidential Rhetoric*, 270.
21. Jensen, "Beloved Community."

Laudato Si is a clarion call for the whole inhabitants of the earth to be in dialogue with all the people to be concerned about our common home, the earth, our universe. Pope Francis reiterates the various crises like climate change, global warming, and the drastic environmental catastrophe that is impending to fall upon us. The root causes of the ecological crisis, according to Pope Francis are because of the materialistic and exploitative tendencies like reductionism, capitalism, communism and socialism that are prevailing upon us without giving the due respect we owe towards humans and nature. Therefore, he calls for a paradigm shift, a "new humanism capable of bringing together, the different fields of knowledge, including economics, in the service of a more integral and integrating vision. The tangible ways and the great ideals to build a just and fraternal society as a web of relationship in and through social life, participation in political processes and being active in the institutions that govern the society.

Fratelli Tutti explored these numerous avenues. Building up a universal fraternity through social relationship is envisaged as creating a fraternity in the style of the beloved community. Pope Francis exhorts Christians to see the face of Christ on every suffering person, the fundamental principle of Christian life. These analyses and explanations point towards the Good Samaritan par excellence, Jesus Christ. The foundation for creating such a new society or an open world based on love, care, trust, freedom, is therefore for a life in Christ. Therefore, in building up a just society, a beloved community, a welfare state, individuals and society need spiritual foundations, as Arnold Toynbee's ten volume study of civilizations concluded.[22] The Pope exhorts us to take up the "Good Samaritan" as a role model and there by indicates the role of Jesus Christ—a concept already established by St. Augustine in and through his *City of God*.

Missionaries, theologians, and philosophers all argue for the transformation of human society founded on a value system, a universal ethics which most religious traditions contain whether it is from the East or the West, with sacred books or with founders or without founders. Integrating the values and inculcating them into the hearts and minds of the people with a dynamic leadership style could transform any society into a beloved community, a community of love, care, concern and affinity. Such community or style of living are pervading over all cultural

---

22. Toynbee, *Study of History*.

traditions such as *Ubuntu* from Africa, *Lokasamgraha*—"Hold together the Whole World," *Vasudaiva Kudumbakam*—"The Whole Creation as a Family," *Loka Samastha Sukhino Bhavanthu*—"May the Whole Creation be in Happiness," from the Indian culture. They all express the same spirit of fellowship, a web of relationship which are proposed by the theologians, the ecumenical leaders and thinkers from all over the world. The transformation of the society became the main conceptual framework for the theologians and the thinkers as they have pinpointed on the wider humanity rather than exclusively on the Christian denominations called Churches. Though some theologians proposed and overwhelmed Christian communities with a conservative interpretations and narrow definitions of ecumenism, the present conception of the churches point to an all-embracing vision, stretching towards wider humanity.

ECUMENICAL CONSCIOUSNESS: PILGRIMAGE TOWARDS COSMIC CHRIST CONSCIOUSNESS

Wider Ecumenism, Transformative Ecumenism,[23] and Receptive Ecumenism are the main trajectories that could be found influential in the twenty first century. These movements all work among the humanity without looking for whether they are Christians or belonging to major or minor Christian denominations or atheists but considering all only as humans and involved in a compassionate, affectionate and healing works in and through Christ Jesus. As M. A. Thomas envisaged, whether we start from Christ, Church and World or World, Church to Christ or Church, Christ to World is irrelevant because all these three are inextricably intertwined to form as a continuum of love, care and nurturing, promoting service, sacrifice, justice and an interdependent communitarian co-existence as wider humanity. Almost the same idea has been placed by many of the theologians without the religious, social, cultural, gender and geographical barriers. As the famous evolutionist scientist, philosopher and theologian Teilhard de Chardin proposed, the origins of creation are from the Alpha, through a process of socialization,

---

23. Transformative Ecumenism is piloted by the Council for World Mission, which is a worldwide partnership of Christian churches. The 32 members are committed to sharing their resources of money, people, skills and insights globally to carry out God's mission locally. CWM was created in 1977 and incorporates the London Missionary Society (1795), the Commonwealth Missionary Society (1836) and the (English) Presbyterian Board of Missions (1847).https://www.cwmission.org/cwm-convenes-planning-meeting-on-together-in-transformative-ecumenism/ (accessed 26 November 2023).

planetization and *omegalization*, integrating the whole humanity and the entire creation including the whole of the living beings, especially from the simple amoeba to the complex humans and move towards the Omega, the Supreme Consciousness or in terms of the scientist philosopher David Bohm, the implicate and explicate orders.[24] Thus, the whole creation, the entire beings in the universe, evolve according to the law of the complexity consciousness, transforming the inner and the outer through the tangential energy, spearheading towards the ultimate being, the Super Consciousness which seems to be the trajectory, the future evolution of our universe as envisioned by some of the scientists who are spiritually driven. I think this is the trajectory humanity may need to foster and grow, one which could definitely guide the beings in this cosmos as its custodian, homo *custos*.[25] This is actually the vocation of a human being as well as the collective human society, the vocation of humanity and the collective future course of action: "the idea of logos helped to explain the unity of God and creation."[26]

In Greek, *Oikumene* means the inhabited world and *Oikos* means home. Thus, from these Greek words derive the two concepts, namely, Ecumenism and Ecology. Ecumenism, though the original term referred to as covering the entire inhabitable world, through the centuries it exclusively referred to the unified Christianity, or the entire Christian world. In the early days of Christianity, when conflicts arose, there were universal gatherings of Christian leaders in order to solve problems and settle theological conflicts and thus came up the connotation, the unified Church arriving at conflict resolutions through the collective decisions of the ecumenical councils. However, the real meaning is an all embracing one, exclusively for humanity and now incorporates the creation too in order to become an inclusive inextricable continuum. From *Oikos* evolves the meaning of managing our home, referring to the environmental caring and solving the ecological problems. So, integrating these two dimensions together, we could place the term, Ecumenical Consciousness as caring for the entire cosmos as a very inclusive term, referring to the totality of beings, from the simplest to complex apex life forms like *homo sapiens*. It is only the humans who are self-aware and thus, can be considered as being aware for the care of the entire cosmos. As already seen in *Laudato Si* and *Fratelli Tutti*, encyclicals dealing with the entire creation and the

24. De Chardin, *Phenomenon of Man*, *Divine Milieu*; Chandrankunnel, *Holism*.
25. Chandrankunnel, *Homo Custos*.
26. Zizioulas, *Being as Communion*.

totality of humanity, it is only humans who could care for the other and bring them into a unified whole through the role of being a steward, or a shepherd in the biblical terminology.

NECESSITY OF INTEGRATIVE ACTS OF THE WCC AND THE CATHOLIC CHURCH

The World Council of Churches (WCC) is the global body integrating Orthodox, reformed, Anglican, Congregationalists, Baptists, Presbyterians, Pentecostals, namely, all the Christian denominations other than the Catholic Church with the responsibility of encouraging and enabling the ecumenical movement and of articulating and disseminating an ecumenical vision. Every WCC assembly is a great exercise of interaction among all these Christian denominations where discussions, debates and organizational clarifications are enacted. In the 1968 Uppsala Assembly the theme was "Behold, I make all things new," while in the Vancouver Assembly in 1983, the theme "Jesus Christ—the Life of the Word," defined ecumenism by "emphasizing God's reconciling purpose as not being only for the church but the whole of humanity and the whole of creation. The Message of the assembly described the unity of God's people as "a sign by which the world may be brought to faith, renewal and unity."[27] In 2006, Porto Alegre, "God, in your grace, transform the world," reinforced the perspectives of transformation and unity. The next assembly, Canberra 1991, "Come, Holy Spirit—Renew the Whole Creation," was even more concerned that ecumenism should hold together an absolute commitment to the unity and renewal of the church and an absolute commitment to the reconciliation of God's world, namely, bringing together the entire creation. They commented, "We need to affirm the vision of an inhabited world (*oikumene*) based on values which promote a life for all."[28] The WCC's ecumenical vision therefore emphasizes and encompasses the renewal of Church and the world in the light of the gospel of God's kingdom. In the face of all threats to life, the WCC affirms the Christian hope of life for all those who are grounded on the incarnation, life, death and resurrection of Jesus Christ, the foundational experience of every Christian.

The 1998 Harare Assembly once again integrated the term ecumenical consciousness into the WCC constitution. There is an emphasis on

27. Gill, *Gathered for Life*, 2.
28. WCC Report, 268.

the growth of an ecumenical consciousness among the member Churches and among the humanity, namely, nurturing ecumenical consciousness as a vision of life and a community rooted in the cultural milieu.[29] Ecumenical Consciousness relates to the *Oikumene*, the whole inhabited world, of all religions and of all beings. Thus, ecumenism is not merely an exclusive process for the Christians alone but for the entire creation. Hans Küng has pushed this further, echoing the discussion above on a wider ecumenism: "For the first time in the history of the world we seem to be witnessing the slow awakening of global ecumenical consciousness and the beginning of a serious religious dialogue . . . Ecumenism should not be limited to the community of Christian churches; it must include the community of the great religions."[30]

Although Küng endorsed this wider perspective, not many in the WCC accepted this extended concept of ecumenism. Now however, such a broader perspective needs to be endorsed by the Churches together, following the lead of Pope Francis's encyclicals, and the WCC concept of Ecumenical Consciousness. This resource pooling, thinking and acting together by the Catholic Church and the WCC towards an Ecumenical Consciousness is definitely an openness towards Jesus Christ, to the world inculcating a collective and individual transformation of policies, attitudes and relationships. Definitely, it is indeed the need of the hour. I would like to quote from the WCC workshops where the longing of the entire creation is vividly narrated towards an ecumenical consciousness, a pilgrimage towards the Cosmic Christ Consciousness, through an inextricable intertwining:

> We long for the visible oneness of the body of Christ, . . . the wholeness of God's entire creation . . . to encounter with those of other faiths.[31]

CONCLUDING PROPOSAL

So, what might be the future course of action for realizing an ecumenical consciousness? As we have already seen the trajectories for an evolving ecumenical consciousness, different strands could be interpreted as methodological dimensions of the ecumenical movement. Receptive Ecumenism provides a modus operandi, a receptive encounter with the other,

---

29. Kessler, *Together on the Way*, 364.
30. Küng, *World Religions*, xiv.
31. "Our Ecumenical Vison," 267.

while Transformative Ecumenism provides the purpose of the movement and Wider Ecumenism provides the scope—the subject matter of ecumenism. In order to break free from the stagnation, crisis and bankruptcy of the ecumenical movement, the need of the hour is the thinking and acting together of the Catholic Church and the WCC along with other contemporary movements such as Focolare, Taizé, San Egido and the Iona Community. This has to be integrated with meaningful movements from other religious traditions and thus, all other leading movements from within and outside of the Churches to act together.

One site of action would be to organize a series of international conferences so that a wider ecumenical forum for thinking together could be established. The different strands of the ecumenical movement, the vibrant variant trajectories already available could be fused into an integral ecumenical consciousness incorporating all humanity and the totality of creation. The Catholic Church and the WCC, along with the other universal ecumenical and secular partners could enrich these processes of evolving such an integral ecumenical consciousness in order to build up a better future in partnership for the creation and humanity.

As we approach two millennia since the death and resurrection of Jesus Christ, and the establishment of Christianity as a movement for the redemptive transformation of the world, there is an opportunity for the churches. In order to be meaningful and relevant in the twenty first century, Christianity needs to become once again a movement, along with its ecumenical and interfaith partners. This process will be a challenge and opportunity for the integration of the totality of humanity and the entire creation. A decade of activity incorporating the entire world can bring together the humanity and creation to celebrate the redemptive salvific effect of Jesus the Messiah, The Christ, the Sat Guru in order to make a paradigm shift in our thinking, acting and living for the future, transcending the narrow boundaries of our own constructed fragmentation for a pilgrimage towards a holistic universality of the Cosmic Christ Consciousness.

BIBLIOGRAPHY

Augustine, Saint. *The City of God*. London: Penguin, 2003.
Conway, Eamonn. *Anonymous Christian—A Relativised Christianity?: An Evaluation of Hans Urs Von Balthasar's Criticism of Karl Rahner's Theory of the Anonymous Christian*. New York: Lang, 1993.

Chandrankunnel, Mathew. "Logos as Dharma, how Jesus the Messiah could be interpreted as Sanatana Sat Guru as the Greeks interpreted Jesus as Christ." In *Wider Contextualized Biblical Spirituality*, edited by Johnson Thomas Kutty and Mathew Chandrankunnal. New Dehli: Christian World Imprints. 2021.

———. *The Science and Philosophy of Holism*. Paper presented at the International Philosophical conference of Belarus, Minsk, 12 July 2019.

———. *Semantic Epiphany: The Theology of M. A. Thomas*, unpublished manuscript.

———. "The Vocation of Humans: From a Paradigm Shift from Homo Faber towards Homo Custos for the harmony of Creation." Paper Presented at the Asian Theologians Conference in Medan, Indonesia, 2019.

de Chardin, Pierre Teilhard. *The Divine Milieu: An Essay on the Interior Life*. New York: HarperCollins, 2001.

———. *The Phenomenon of Man*. Translated by Bernard Wall. New York: Harper Collins, 2008.

Congdon, David, W. *Rudolf Bultmann: A Companion to His Theology*. Eugene, OR: Cascade Books, 2015.

Francis, Pope. *Fratelli Tutti*. Vatican City: Libreria Editrice Vaticana, 2020.

———. *Laudato Si'*. Vatican City: Libreria Editrice Vaticana, 2015.

Gill, D (ed), *Gathered for Life: Official report of the VI Assembly of the World Council of Churches*. Geneva: WCC Publications, 1983.

Hillmann, Eugene, CSSp. *The Wider Ecumenism, Anonymous Christianity and the Church*. New York: Herder & Herder, 1968.

Holm, Frits, V. *The Nestorian Monument: An Ancient record of Christianity in China*. Whitefish. MT: Kessinger, 2018.

Husserl, Edmund. *The Crisis of European Sciences and Transcendental Phenomenology: An Introduction to Phenomenological Philosophy*. Studies in Phenomenology and Existential Philosophy. Evanston, IL: Northwestern University Press, 1970.

Jensen, Kipton and Preston King. "Beloved Community: Martin Luther King, Howard Thurman, and Josiah Royce." *AMITY: The Journal of Friendship Studies* 4/1 (2017) 15–31.

Kalb, Deborah, Gerard Peters, and John T. Woolley, eds. *State of the Union: Presidential Rhetoric from Woodrow Wilson to George W Bush*. Washington, DC: CQ, 2007.

Kasper, Walter. *That They All Be One: The Call to Unity Today*. London: Burns & Oates, 2004.

Kessler, D., ed. *Together on the Way: Official Report of the Eighth Assembly of the World Council of Churches*. Geneva: WCC Publications, 1999.

Küng, Hans. *Christianity and the World Religions: Paths of Dialogue with Islam, Hinduism, and Buddhism*. Translated by Peter Heinegg. London: Fount, 1987.

———. *Tracing the Way: Spiritual Dimensions of the World Religions*. London: Continuum, 2006.

Magrath, Oswin. "The Wider Ecumenism." *New Blackfriars* 49/580 (1968).

"Our Ecumenical Vision." *Ecumenical Review* 50/3 (1998) 266–67.

Panikkar, Raimundo. *The Unknown Christ of Hinduism: Toward an Ecumenical Christophany*. Maryknoll, NY: Orbis, 1981.

Pieris, Aloysius. *Give Vatican II A Chance: Yes to Incessant Renewal, No to the Reform of Reforms*. Bangalore: Claretian, 2012.

Sittler, Joseph. "Called to Unity." *Ecumenical Review* 14 (1962) 177–87.

Starkloff, Carl F, SJ. "Theology and Aboriginal Religion: Continuing 'The Wider Ecumenism.'" *Theological Studies* 68 (2007).

"Report of the Report Committee, WCC 7th Assembly." *Ecumenical Review* 43/2 (1991).

Thomas Kutty, Johnson and. Chandrankunnel, Mathew, eds. *Wider Contextualized Biblical Spirituality*. New Dehli: Christian World Imprints. 2021.

Thomas, M. A., *Traffic Lights*. Bangalore: ATC, 1991.

Toynbee, Arnold J.A. *Study of History*. 10 vols. Oxford: Oxford University Press, 1987.

Valle, Vijaya Joji Babu. *Becoming Indian: Towards a Contextual Ecclesiology*. Doctoral Thesis. KU Leuven, Belgium, 2010.

Zizioulas, John D. *Being as Communion*. New York: St Vladimir's Seminary, 1997.

22

Receiving and Beyond
Receptive Ecumenism and Wider Ecumenism

PENIEL RAJKUMAR

INTRODUCTION

RECEPTIVE ECUMENISM IS, IN some ways, about drinking deeply from the wells of the wisdom of the "other," so that these waters may quench our thirst, cool our feet as we "walk the talk" of ecumenism, and water the seeds of imagination that have been planted in our hearts and minds across the ages. My chapter will focus on how the transformative possibilities of both "wider ecumenism" and "Receptive Ecumenism" can be freed to further the causes of both the ecumenical and interreligious movements.

In some ways the DNA of my paper lies with two questions: First, what is the breadth of our ecumenicity? This relates to the issue of the inclusion of religious and cultural others in the idea of ecumenism, especially through ideas such as wider or macro ecumenism. Second, what is the depth of our receptivity? This probes questions about those spaces where reception is needed in current ecumenical witness? However, a caveat at this point may be necessary—true to the nature of DNA, it is possible that these two points will never be explicitly visible in this article. They will, rather, be interspersed with the big question—what can Receptive

Ecumenism receive from wider ecumenism to make ecumenism more transformative in the context of World Christianity?

WHAT IS THE BREADTH OF OUR ECUMENICITY?

The idea a wider ecumenism or a macro-ecumenism, by which is meant the opening of the ecumenical movement "to other religions and cultural traditions beyond the Christian community,"[1] has not been without its problems and has been the source of much discussion within the ecumenical movement. I will not use this paper to debate the appropriateness of the term "wider ecumenism" but will use the term to mean the macro-ecumenism of interreligious dialogue.

It should be noted that the concept of "wider ecumenism" emerged in response to the accusations that the ecumenical movement was parochial in its focus and did not pay sufficient attention to other global questions relating to the wholeness and healing of humanity or the whole creation. Ecumenists like Wesley Ariarajah argue for it from a theological basis. Especially given that the ecumenical movement was at a point where it had radically reassessed its theology of religions, the question of how ecumenical the concept of "ecumenism" should be, was no longer seen as a question of semantics or inclusion.[2] Rather it was seen as a theological question, (which) "has to do with a reassessment of our understanding of God, of the scope of God's saving work, and of the agents of God's mission."[3] It was a call for discernment, the tone of which resonates quite closely with the biblical text that undergirds the fifth international Receptive Ecumenism conference: "Listen to what the spirit is saying to the churches." According to Ariarajah:

> The call for a "wider ecumenism," therefore, is a call to discernment. It is an attempt to make more sense than before of the conviction we hold that the Spirit of God is active in the world. It is an attempt to give more meaning than before to our belief that "the earth is the Lord's and the fullness thereof, the world and those who dwell in it."[4]

Theology was not the only reason for the focus on wider ecumenism. Another important reason was a recognition of the shift in world

---

1. World Council of Churches, "Common Understanding," para 2.6
2. Ariarajah, "Wider Ecumenism," 327.
3. Ariarajah, "Wider Ecumenism," 327.
4. Ariarajah, "Wider Ecumenism," 327–28.

Christianity towards the non-western world. The new ecumenical reality was one that consisted of churches which were "tiny minorities in an ocean of humankind, who lived by other faiths."[5] Therefore, Christians in different parts of the world, such as for example in Asia, saw God at work among their neighbors of other faiths and refused to "believe that God's reconciling and redeeming work in these societies is put on hold until the churches are able to overcome divisions that are part of another age and culture."[6] For these churches their day-to-day life had to be lived alongside communities of other faiths, and not through ecumenical histories and memories that were foisted on them from outside which they were now forced to believe was the core of their ecclesial identity. These were histories of which they were perpetual outsiders and latecomers. Hence, in some ways the call for wider ecumenism was also an attempt to put a spoke in the wheels of such foisted identities and memories.

Broadly speaking, wider ecumenism was seen as one way for the ecumenical movement to rise above its captivity to the problems of twentieth century Europe and to a global vision that is still rooted in North Atlantic understanding of the church and its mission."[7] It takes seriously the changed landscape of World Christianity as well as the challenge to "unthink the West" from our ecumenical imagination, to use a phrase by the South African missiologist Vuyani Vellem.[8]

In such a context, one question that wider ecumenism could pose for Receptive Ecumenism today as it tries to engage with the question of difference, is whether the differences that are addressed and the methods that are employed to address these difference are those that could inadvertently replicate and reinforce the broad Eurocentricity of ecumenism or can they help overcome the Eurocentric taint of ecumenism? If so in the context of the changing face of World Christianity, where does the ecumenical future lie?

WHAT IS THE DEPTH OF OUR RECEIVING?

Miguel De La Torre, a Cuban–American theologian, makes an important point that for ecumenism to be more transformative and global it needs to move beyond its current Eurocentric trajectory. According to Torre,

---

5. Ariarajah, "Wider Ecumenism," 327.
6. Ariarajah, "Wider Ecumenism," 327.
7. Ariarajah, "Wider Ecumenism," 328.
8. Vellem, "Un-thinking the West," 2.

"failure to ask questions concerning power relationships leads to a traditional engagement in ecumenism, along with its normative dissimulation, which becomes complicit with global structures of oppression that maintain a partially masked attempt to incorrectly understand the world than correctly initiate transformation."[9] Torre goes on to argue that "those who have drunk from the Eurocentric ecumenical Kool-Aid all too often lack the ability to differentiate between the proverbial blink and wink of disenfranchised communities, and thus, their attempt for religious unity lacks gravitas within communities on the underside of the Eurocentric thirst for critical analytical tools capable of raising consciousness."[10] This for him should provide the impetus for the "goal of ecumenism . . . to move beyond its current Eurocentric-led trajectory."[11]

This demands a willingness to be transformed by the voices and vision of those who have been "othered" by traditional ecumenism, or those relegated to the margins of the current ecumenical imagination which has let the Eurocentricity of ecumenism to march on, unchallenged and not criticized. How do we challenge this?

Very often Christians at interreligious dialogue tables talk about the interreligious dialogue in terms that resemble a Pentecostal celebration of diversity—of speaking in many tongues. However, one of the lessons that Christians have often learnt on the tables of interreligious dialogue is the need for a linguistic shift—the need for a new Pentecost experience within the Church. The Pentecost experience that I am alluding to is a different one. This Pentecost experience will be marked not by the gift of *speaking in many tongues*, but by the gift of *listening with many ears*. It is the Pentecost experience of the ears.

Matthew Chandrankunnel's chapter, among others, alludes to the transformative power of ecumenism. The Pentecost experience of listening can be part of the redemptive politics of transformation. Both Receptive Ecumenism and interreligious dialogue help us recognize the need to cultivate listening as an ethical form of political presence and participation. Public theologian Luke Bretherton interprets listening as "a way for churches to practice humility in their negotiation of political

---

9. De La Torre, "World Christianity?" 67.
10. De La Torre, "World Christianity?"67.
11. De La Torre, "World Christianity?" 67.

life."[12] Listening, according to Bretherton, serves as an "antidote to self-glorification, idolatry, and regimes of control."[13]

We live in a context where both religious and secular institutions have become exemplars of an "anthropology of domination"—marked by narcissistic self-love and unscrupulous self-assertion, based on the idolatrous worship of power. In such a context Bretherton says that, "listening is a therapy for the self-love or pride that attempts to "pursue illusions of self-sufficiency both in relation to God and neighbor."[14] Like a vaccination it "inoculates the church against developing false securities because in listening one has to deal with the world as it is rather than acting on the basis of our projected fantasies or idolatrous means of escape."[15]

Bretherton's thoughts are complemented by the late Rabbi Jonathan Sacks, who in his book *The Dignity of Difference* emphasizes the need to listen and be prepared to be surprised by others. Sacks writes:

> We must make ourselves open to their stories, which may profoundly conflict with ours. We must even, at times, be ready to hear of their pain, humiliation and resentment and discover that their image of us is anything but our image of ourselves. We must learn the art of conversation, from which truth emerges, not, as in Socratic dialogues, by the refutation of falsehood but from the quite different process of letting our world be enlarged by the presence of others who think, act, and interpret reality in ways radically different from our own.[16]

Listening is a constitutive element of hospitality as it "trusts and gives space and time to those who are excluded from the determination of space and time by the existing hegemony."[17] If the church has to address the issue of division and discrimination we may need to embrace the challenge of becoming a listening space which is not over-dominated and over-determined by the voices of the dominant and powerful, that drown out all other voices, or predetermine how one can speak or what one may say. The church needs to become this community of the new Pentecost—and learn the gift of many ears—and let itself be re-signified by the voices and visions of the Others. The gift of listening—through

---

12. Bretherton, *Church and Contemporary Politics* 214.
13. Bretherton, *Church and Contemporary Politics*, 214.
14. Bretherton, *Church and Contemporary Politics*, 214.
15. Bretherton, *Church and Contemporary Politics*, 214.
16. Sacks, *Dignity of Difference*, 23.
17. Bretherton, *Church and Contemporary Politics*, 215.

attentive silence—can also be an active way of breaking the "conspiracy of complicit silence" in the face of injustice and inequality. It is an antidote to the politics of complicity based on convenience.

RECONFIGURING OUR ECUMENICAL SUBJECTIVITIES: OVERCOMING "*HOST*-ILITY"

So, how can Receptive Ecumenism be practiced in the context of wider ecumenism? One of the biggest learnings for me in my own interreligious journey came from a Confucian Christian Scholar Heup Young Kim, who in one of our dialogues challenged Christians to give up what he called the original sin of imperial Christianity—namely the sin of *Host*-ility—the perpetual will to play the host always.

Both wider ecumenism and interreligious dialogue invite us to cultivate an alternative imagination of our ecumenical subjectivity. They help us rethink our identity as Christian ecumenists in a radical way which embodies *kenosis* or self-emptying. We are subjects *as we receive*, we are ecumenists *alongside others* with whom we share the *oikos*— the whole inhabited earth. This demands that we nurture within us the moral resolve to cultivate an integrated sense of identity that embraces the wonder of realizing that "the path towards us often runs through the highways and byways of our neighbors"—a metaphor I borrow from Wesley Ariarajah, one of my distinguished predecessors in the WCC.

What might such imagination of ecumenical subjectivity be in the current context of World Christianity? My imagination of such subjectivity is what I would term as being "ecumenical innkeepers" and is drawn from a biblical example. Of many biblical characters who have challenged me in my engagement in ecumenical and interreligious dialogues the most challenging one has been a silent character in the bible who appears alongside a more famous character. This character is the innkeeper in what is popularly known as Jesus's parable of the Good Samaritan (Luke 10). There is something subversive about the innkeeper that I found to be of use in the context of interreligious as well as ecumenical dialogue.

If we pause for a moment and reflect on this parable, we will recognize that the force of the parable of the Good Samaritan rests on the shock and repulsion of Jesus's Jewish audience recognizing a despicable Samaritan as an unlikely or even undesired "do-gooder." As Crossan says, "the internal structure of the story and the historical setting of Jesus' time agree that the literal point of the story challenges the hearer to put together two impossible and contradictory words for the same person: 'Samaritan' (10:33) and 'neighbor' (10:36). The thrust of the whole story demands that one say what is a contradiction in terms: Good + Samaritan."[18]

However, this contradiction was shocking to Jesus's hearers only in their imagination, but to the innkeeper this was a challenge in flesh and blood. It is at this point that the innkeeper emerges as someone who doesn't let the power of prejudice stifle the possibility of transformation and holistic restoration even if it had been initiated by a repulsive and suspicious "outsider." There were several reasons why the innkeeper should have been suspicious of and hostile to the Samaritan. Was it not more likely that the Samaritan could have been the one who had assaulted the wounded man? Further if the innkeeper was aware through local gossip that the Priest and the Levite had actually seen a wounded man and continued on their journey, should he not have doubted what it was that made the Samaritan think of himself as being better and more righteous than the Priest or the Levite. Should not the Samaritan have shown the same, if not more humility than the Priest and the Levite, who acted in the best professional model, respected the privacy of the wounded man till the end, and did not take upon themselves the task of legislating new rules of intervention in social issues?[19] Further, one of the suspicions that the Jews had against the Samaritans which becomes clear in Josephus's writings was that the Samaritans took sides with the Jews during good times and disowned them when they were in trouble.[20] On what basis then could the innkeeper trust the Samaritan? Was it not possible that the Samaritan would never return to repay the balance, but would leave the victim with impossible debts to pay?

It is in such a context that the innkeeper silently replaces suspicion and hostility with trust and support. He opens the doors of his inn wide for him and makes him an "inn-sider." As a result, the Samaritan entrusts the wounded man entirely to the innkeeper and promises to come back. It is in this reciprocity of trust and mutual help that healing and restoration of wholeness is made possible. The challenge which the innkeeper poses to us today involves the risk of offering trust and goodwill in ecumenical and interreligious relationships where suspicion and hostility are easier, more likely and more justifiable.

18. Crossan, *In Parables*, 64.
19. See Wells, "The Jericho Affair," 17.
20. For more on this see Ford, *My Enemy is My Guest*.

In a divided world, ecumenism can be a source of healing and wholeness if it becomes more receptive and wider. In such a world one Good Samaritan may be good enough for the first aid which is lifesaving indeed, but to make the healing more complete we need innkeepers, their resources, their open doors, and their hospitality. Can both wider and Receptive Ecumenism challenge us to take on the role of innkeepers in contexts where agency for transformation lies beyond us?

Both Receptive Ecumenism and wider ecumenism challenge us to recognize our co-dependency on the "other." They teach us that we cannot close ourselves to the gifts the "other" brings. As a community called to be a sign of the Kingdom of God—the Church cannot shield itself from the "other." As a community of the people of God, the Church must have the confidence that God is present even in the outsider—which in the words of Stanley Hauerwas, is "a confidence made possible only because the community itself was formed by the presence of the ultimate stranger, Jesus Christ"[21]—the one who came to his own but whose own received him not, as we read in the gospel of John. Therefore the innkeeper as the in(n)sider challenges us to receive with gratitude the gift of the outsider. This is because it is only in the face of the "other" that we rediscover ourselves and recognize God.

Both Receptive Ecumenism and wider ecumenism challenge the Church to become what the feminist theologian Letty Russel calls "the church in the round," that is, around a table without any sides, edges or corners.[22] And if I were to borrow the words of a popular hymn, it is about becoming that table for a feast "to celebrate the healing of all excluded-feeling."[23] If we can achieve this, our ecumenical fellowship can truly be transformed into a table which both feeds us in our faith-imagination and also teaches us the right way to stay hungry—hungry for justice, peace and reconciliation which, in their concrete forms, embody God's hope for the world.

BIBLIOGRAPHY

Ariarajah, Wesley. "Wider Ecumenism: A Threat or a Promise?" *Ecumenical Review* 50 (1998) 321–29.

Bretherton, Luke. *Church and Contemporary Politics: The Conditions and Possibilities of Faithful Witness*. Oxford: Wiley-Blackwell, 2010.

21. Hauerwas, *The Peaceable Kingdom*, 85.
22. Russel, *Church in the Round*.
23. Kaan, *The Church is like a Table*.

Crossan, John Dominic. *In Parables: The Challenge of the Historical Jesus*. New York: Harper & Row, 1973.

De La Torre, Miguel A. "Is Ecumenism Even Possible in the Context of World Christianity?" *Ecumenical Review* 74/1 (2022) 58–68.

Ford, J. Massyngbaerde. *My Enemy Is My Guest: Jesus and Violence in Luke*. Maryknoll, NY: Orbis, 1984.

Hauerwas, Stanley. *The Peaceable Kingdom: A Primer in Christian Ethics*. London: SCM, 1983.

Kaan, Fred. "The Church Is Like a Table (Round-Table Church)." Carol Stream, IL: Hope, 1985.

Russel, Letty M. *Church in the Round: Feminist Interpretation of the Church*. Louisville: Westminster John Knox, 1993.

Sacks, Jonathan. *The Dignity of Difference: How to Avoid the Clash of Civilizations*. London: Continuum, 2002.

Vellem, V. "Un-thinking the West: The Spirit of doing Black Theology of Liberation in Decolonial Times." *HTS Teologiese Studies* 73/3 (2017) 2.

Wells, Samuel. "The Jericho Affair." *Christian Century*, June 29, 2004.

World Council of Churches. "Common Understanding and Vision of the WCC." https://www.oikoumene.org/resources/documents/common-understanding-and-vision-of-the-wcc-cuv#:~:text=The%20WCC%20provides%20a%20space,fuller%20manifestation%20of%20that%20unity.

23

Recognition of Others and Receptive Ecumenism

Risto Saarinen

INTRODUCTION

THE ECUMENICAL MOVEMENT HAS never embraced totalitarianism. Historically and theologically, it has sided with democracy and dialogical openness. In our day, when the heinous Russian attack on Ukraine has shaken the foundations of European politics, it is necessary to remind all Christians that ecumenism embraces human rights and democratic politics.

Democracy and human rights also mean a clear affirmation of plurality and toleration. Christians are called to live together with Muslims, members of other religions and secular people, including convinced atheists. Within the ecumenical movement, we also need to affirm the status quo of a plurality of churches with their somewhat different emphases. While we strive for unity, this striving cannot be one of a totalitarian nature. It is a search in which we are considerate and listen to our neighbors. The human rights of our neighbors are as important as the freedom to express our own convictions.

What does this late-modern democratic ethos mean in practice to our ecumenical spirit? For ten years, a multi-disciplinary team at Helsinki University has been involved with an academic research project on ecumenical recognition. We understand recognition as a democratic affirmation of each other within the sphere of a certain plurality.[1] While recognition means that some doctrinal differences are laid aside, it does not mean a complete unity or uniformity. Nordic Lutherans recognize the ordained ministry of German Protestants as well as that of the Church of England, but these three theologies of ordained ministry are not identical with one another.

What do we actually mean by such recognition? In political contexts, recognition means more than toleration but less than full uniformity. Leading theorists of societal recognition, such as Charles Taylor and Axel Honneth point out that liberal democracies need to complement traditional ideas of toleration with an active practice of recognition mechanisms.[2] It is not enough to tolerate sexual, religious or ethnic minorities but they need to be given an active voice in society. In some cases, such minorities need to have privileges in order to provide equal opportunities for the society at large.

For instance, the Sami people in Northern Finland have some privileges with regard to their means of living, and the people in the Åland islands are recognized as having some unique rights pertaining to their specific position between Sweden and Finland. Such recognized privileges are not in conflict with the overall equality of all citizens, as they are considered to contribute to the overall picture of equal opportunities. Religious groups in Finland also enjoy some privileges which can be grounded in terms of such politics of recognition.

In our ten-year research project in Helsinki we have come to the conclusion that churches and other religious communities practice recognition which in some sense resembles the acts of political recognition. At the same time, theological recognition is different from political, diplomatic and legal forms of recognition. In making visible the positive differences in a complex whole, churches can practice recognition which resembles societal recognition as a whole. For instance, the recent recognition of gays and lesbians in the Scandinavian established churches is an instance of their broader societal and political recognition.

However, when Christians recognize other Christians and churches recognize other churches, or when the churches recognize each other's practices, such as baptism or ordained ministries, something new and

---

1. Saarinen, *Recognition*; Faucher and Mäkinen, *Encountering*; Hirvonen & Koskinen, *Theory and Practice*.

2. Siep and Ikäheimo, *Handbuch*; Ikäheimo, *Recognition*.

distinctive is happening. This is theological recognition, a spiritual event which moves beyond diplomatic and legal measures.

THEOLOGICAL RECOGNITION

Theological and spiritual recognition has far-reaching conceptual roots in the Greek terms *epiginosko* and *anagnorisis* and the Latin term *agnitio*. When the New Testament speaks of *epignosis aletheias*, recognition of the truth, a spiritual encounter with God is at stake. The Latin expression *agnitio Dei* or *Christi* likewise focuses on a conversion event which changes the perspective of the one who recognizes. These theological events resemble the poetic and aesthetic events of transforming recognition.[3] For instance, when, in Acts 7:13, Luke relates how Joseph made himself known to his brothers in Egypt, he uses the word of Greek drama, *anagnorizesthai*, to recognize, which means a dramatic turn and a new relationship between the parties. This terminology is employed in some seminal documents of Vatican II. In the 1970s, when recognition started to be discussed as ecumenical method, leading theologians like Walter Kasper pointed out that recognition needs to be seen as a theological and spiritual event.[4] Our Helsinki work basically affirms this insight.

While it is possible to recognize events and states of affairs, such as priesthood or baptism, recognition is fundamentally an interpersonal event. Persons are recognizing other persons, and the matter at hand is like a platform of this interpersonal encounter. This may be the reason why churches can more easily recognize individual Christians from other communities than recognize the doctrines of others or their community as a whole. The event of churches recognizing other churches and their teaching is nevertheless also an interpersonal event. It is important to discuss doctrines and practices, but fundamentally we are always recognizing other Christians in the event of theological recognition. Ecumenism is thus primarily personal interaction and only secondarily something like "doctrinal mathematics."

Horizontal recognition among Christians is further based on the vertical recognition between God and human beings. We recognize God as person, and God recognizes us as persons. Doctrinal elaboration of this personal faith follows from this personal encounter. Horizontal recognition of other Christians is likewise a consequence of this primary

---

3. See Saarinen, *Recognition*, 42–54 and Boitani, *Riconoscere*.
4. See Saarinen, *Recognition*, 168–83 and Frank, *Confessio Augustana*.

vertical recognition which the Christian tradition names using Latin expressions like *agnitio veritatis* or *agnitio Dei*.

People with legal or canonical training may think of recognition as an act which changes the status of the object. When I am allowed to join some society, my status is changed into the membership status. When the state of Finland recognizes the state of Kosovo, Kosovo's diplomatic status changes. A canon lawyer may think that when my church recognizes a practice of another church, the status of that practice is changed. The one who performs the recognition remains an unmoved mover who does not need to change.

Such thinking is, on the one hand, quite appropriate . However, it represents the modern paradigm of legal and secular recognition. This is not the classical way of understanding theological recognition. The biblical and patristic way of speaking about recognizing the truth means conversion, an event in which I change myself in order to create a connection and to build a communion with God or other humans. With my own act of recognizing others I practice *metanoia*, I open my mind and heart to embrace others. This opening does not compromise my identity. On the contrary, it can be understood as a move from non-identity towards making visible my true identity. The one who recognizes others steps from shadows into light and becomes transparent, like Joseph who revealed himself to his brothers as high official in Egypt, thus changing both parties of the encounter.

In philosophical traditions, both sides of the act of recognition are normally affirmed. My act of recognition changes myself, but also the status of the other is in some sense transformed. When we create a mutual relationship, we are both open and more transparent than before. We have bonds of communion, but at the same time we see that the light of the truth also reveals the differences between us. Recognition is not about projecting myself to the other, but rather deals with the affirmation of the alterity of the other. This alterity may also enrich me, and in any case its recognition transforms my own way of thinking.

Let me illustrate this philosophical idea with an ecumenical example that will continue to be discussed in the next years in the Lutheran churches of Sweden and Finland. In the 1970s, the then-professor of theology Joseph Ratzinger called Catholics to consider how the Lutheran Augsburg Confession could be recognized as a Catholic document. Different proposals were drafted, and the main response of Catholic theologians focused on showing how the Augsburg Confession could be interpreted as a Catholic text. In many cases this is possible, since the short propositions are open to interpretation.[5]

Today we would say, however, that such Catholic reading of the Augsburg Confession aimed at something like cultural appropriation. In the Nordic countries, we have a history of cultural appropriation with the Sami people in Lapland. In former times we thought that if the Sami spoke Finnish and behaved like other Finns, then they would have achieved democratic equality. Today we understand that such a policy manifests colonialism and cultural appropriation.

This kind of recognition is a manifestation of the modern legal idea of recognition bringing about a change of status of the object in question. If Catholics interpreted the Lutheran Confession to look like a Catholic document, then Lutheran faces would lose their distinctiveness and resemble the normative Catholic countenance. When the minority is culturally appropriated to the majority, then a unity is apparently accomplished. This matter is philosophically complex, as universalism and cosmopolitanism, virtues that we call Catholic in theological language, are also important. We cannot become merely tribal societies without cosmopolitan features. I will, however, leave this side now undiscussed.

The old project of Catholic recognition of the Augsburg Confession is currently being reopened, especially in Germany. The volume *Die Confessio Augustana im ökumenischen Gespräch* provides extensive documentation of the discussion.[6] Generally speaking, Lutherans and other Protestants are today very clear that the Augsburg Confession should not be discussed in terms of Catholic cultural appropriation. Protestants cannot just be treated as little Catholics after five hundred years of separation. The distinctive identity of Lutherans, Anglicans, and the Reformed cannot be concealed with ecumenical cosmetics. For many, this identity is a resource and a richness. For many, it is also a historical truth.

The German volume contains articles that discuss recent philosophical and political theories of recognition and compare them with theological recognition. For many writers it is clear that the event of recognition changes both parties and is characterized by mutual openness and a person-centered approach to dialogue. In his concluding article to the volume, Cardinal Kurt Koch, the Vatican's leading ecumenist, considers the possibility of a Catholic recognition of the Augsburg Confession

---

5. Saarinen, *Recognition*, 178–80.
6. Frank, *Confessio Augustana*.

in its 500th anniversary in 2017. He admits that the earlier discussion did not properly understand the meaning of recognition.[7]

To an extent, Cardinal Koch assumes a legal and modernist understanding of recognition as the status change of the other. This is visible in his considerations of reading the Augsburg Confession as a Catholic text. However, Koch also employs the richer understanding of Walter Kasper, according to whom such recognition must be oriented to the ecclesial communion of today rather than to a historical text.

Most importantly, Cardinal Koch concludes that the "recognition of an ecclesial communion" must be a "reciprocal activity" and a "spiritual process." The foundation of such activity and process is the Holy Scripture and the confessions of faith. The Augsburg Confession can provide important help for such a process.[8] While these words are carefully balanced, they nevertheless avoid the dangers of cultural appropriation and merely legal understanding of recognition as status change of the object. Especially, the expressions "reciprocal activity" and "spiritual process" are significant here.

The contribution of Cardinal Koch would be even more promising if he discussed openness or even *metanoia* in this reciprocal and spiritual process. There is in his approach some underlying bondage to a legal or canonical interpretation of recognition. However, legal and canonical readings belong to the modernist paradigm, whereas recognition as a spiritual process manifests the classical theological understanding of this concept.

I have used the example of the Augsburg Confession to show that Catholic ecumenism has in many ways moved from a cultural appropriation of the other to the consideration of reciprocity and a spiritual, rather than canonical, understanding of recognition. What is still lacking to some extent is the affirmation of one's own openness and readiness for transformation. The work of Helsinki scholars on theological recognition argues that theological recognition needs such openness to realize that the alterity of the other cannot simply be handled by issuing a stamp of approval. We need a spirit of conversion.

---

7. Frank, *Confessio Augustana*, 388.
8. Frank, *Confessio Augustana*, 397–98.

RECEPTIVE ECUMENISM

I now move to the second part of my presentation. How does this ecumenism of mutual recognition relate to the paradigm of Receptive Ecumenism? Some time ago, I traveled to Durham with Sara Gehlin and Minna Hietamäki to discuss this issue with Paul Murray and other colleagues at the Centre for Catholic Studies there. We were received with warm hospitality and we had some wonderful discussions on this topic.

The first and maybe most obvious common point between Receptive Ecumenism and the recognition of otherness is the requirement of personal openness. In order to practice reception and recognition, you need to be open to accommodate new insights and achieve new learning. If your mind is only ready to evaluate others, not your own standing, *this is not for you*. The spirit of *metanoia* or conversion is exemplary for Receptive Ecumenism and recognition of otherness. Obviously, such *metanoia* does not mean that you change your mind constantly. The openness for new insights often means that you learn to be a better member of your own community through involving yourself with other traditions.

The second common point between recognition and Receptive Ecumenism is an attitude that takes the plurality of religious and other convictions seriously. If you think that a monocultural unity is the optimal state of mind and an optimal environment for the church, *this is not for you*. You need not be a modernist or a multiculturalist, but you need to take seriously the richness of our cultural universe and the alterity of others. Instead of cultural appropriation or colonization, you need to listen to others and practice some positive affirmation of them as they are. This attitude may be easier between persons than between doctrines. The affirmation of religious persons and their narratives is extremely important.

The third common point between the two, concerns a vision in which many different convictions can be affirmed as plausible. I may have a preference for my own tradition, but I also consider neighboring traditions and maybe also some more distant traditions as plausible. If you think that truth always requires consensus and full unity, *this is not for you*. This common point is academically linked with pragmatist philosophy as it appears, for instance, in Nicholas Rescher's so-called preferentialist plausibilism.[9]

---

9. Rescher, *Pluralism*.

According to this model, I may prefer one explanation, but consider some other explanations as plausible and some others as implausible. This is not relativism, but it is not absolutism or monocultural unity either. As truth-seeking groups, religious communities may resemble competing scientific explanations in this manner. Obviously, the analogy to science is limited, but I see no theological difficulties in allowing for this kind of truthful plurality. While my favorite gospel is Luke, I can also affirm the plausibility of Matthew, Mark and John. We adhere to preferred religious convictions by personal faith, and this means that we cannot rule out other similar options simply because we happen to prefer one particular conviction.

Let me clarify this point. Recognition procedures assume that I can appreciate options that differ from my own. This does not imply that I would recognize all possible options. Toleration and recognition have their external boundaries which can be defined in various ways. I use the English word "plausible" to define such options which I can recognize even if they differ from my own view. This means that there are also implausible options which I cannot recognize, because they seem to me as obviously false or morally problematic.

The openness and *metanoia* dimension of recognition means that when I consider other convictions as plausible, I continue to be open to the idea that my own preferred conviction may benefit from the insights of other plausible traditions. Lutherans, for instance, can certainly learn from the spiritual life of ancient churches. Lutherans also need help in understanding the charismatic and intercultural theology of new Christian movements. This openness does not mean that we compromise our own conviction. On the contrary, we may understand our own tradition better when we learn from others.

In sum, I have found three common points between Receptive Ecumenism and recognition of otherness, namely, personal openness, the awareness of plurality and the idea of agreement in terms of plausibility. This being said, I also want to outline some differences between these two approaches. The theology of recognition is academic by its nature and it has close ties with philosophical analysis and legal thinking. I have argued above that theological recognition also involves conversion and spirituality. However, the procedures as such are fairly intellectual and in some sense political. For these reasons, a theology of recognition may not provide a strong spirituality. Receptive Ecumenism is a much more "down-to-earth" movement. While its basic points can be and have been developed in an academic fashion, its great strength lies in group work at the grassroots level. It is a method of concrete learning and a practice of openness. It does not need legal or philosophical explanation, as its insights are very clear and continue the tradition of Roman Catholic spiritual ecumenism.

Receptive Ecumenism is also tactful and considerate in ways that recognition procedures may not be. In the academic discussion, the power relations between the one who performs recognition and the one receiving it are discussed at great length. Recognition measures involve power dynamics in which problematic hierarchies are sometimes manifested. The learning processes and grassroots work of Receptive Ecumenism may successfully avoid these issues of power.

This first difference, between the academic and spiritual, is for me personally a reason to involve myself more strongly with Receptive Ecumenism. Our two approaches are complementary in the sense that Receptive Ecumenism is strong and clear in grassroots communities in which the recognition approach may remain intellectual and political. Receptive Ecumenism can help others to become aware of the need for spirituality.

The second difference is concerned with the distinction between generic and specific. Receptive Ecumenism is a movement within theology, and it is tailored according to the needs of the churches in the specific cultural context of today. In particular, it outlines the way in which a bigger tradition, such as the Roman Catholic church, or the established Lutheran churches in the Scandinavian countries, can exercise ecumenical work in a manner that is considerate and avoids paternalism. Even more importantly, Receptive Ecumenism gives a signal that bigger and older traditions can learn and receive new things and that the smaller traditions can also contribute to the entire picture.[10]

This practice is inspiring, as it counteracts the view that large traditions remain "unmoved movers" who merely tell smaller communities how they ought to behave. The spirit of learning, openness, and *metanoia* concerns us all, and maybe even particularly the bigger churches. This specific contextual message is very appropriate in today's situation, in which many processes stagnate and the older traditions need to consider their life-form in the secular environment. It also manages to avoid the

---

10. See Murray, Ryan, and Lakeland, *Receptive Ecumenism as Transformative Ecclesial Learning*.

problem of cultural appropriation, a problem to which the younger generation is today especially sensitive.

At the same time, Receptive Ecumenism may be something that can only be understood within this particular setting of the churches. Due to its specific and spiritual character, it does not develop a general theory of religious interaction. It is an excellent virtue to be tactful and willing to learn new things, but this virtue only defines the human platform for more ambitious subsequent reflection. What actually happens when we begin to talk in this manner?

I am now thinking about Protestant theology in countries like Germany, Sweden and Norway. We have a long tradition of elaborate philosophical and theological hermeneutics. Sometimes it is a relief to discuss without the weight of hermeneutics. However, the tradition of our countries is to develop theology that can interact with politics and with diverse academic developments. The church needs to talk spiritually, but it also needs to be universal in order to connect its message with the society at large.

For instance, during the Covid-19 pandemic, the Swedish archbishop Antje Jackelén published several texts and a whole book about the effect of the pandemic on Christianity and Swedish society.[11] These texts are theological and spiritual, but they also connect with many different academic disciplines and with political rhetoric. With her elaborate hermeneutical skill, the archbishop builds bridges to Swedish society and creates theological positions beyond mere openness and tactful empathy.

My own conviction is that the theology of recognition can also be ecumenically constructive in this manner. Recognition is a topic which is discussed politically and academically, often as a cornerstone of multiculturalism and liberal democracy. At the same time, this concept has long Christian roots and a considerable theological potential. Recognition may be a generic concept in ways that Receptive Ecumenism is not. Let me add that some ecclesial processes, for instance, the recognition of the Augsburg Confession, require this kind of extensive hermeneutical elaboration.

This means for me that there may be another complementary way of doing work together with receptive ecumenists. The theology of recognition may be able to create bridges to politics, sociology and hermeneutics, enabling theologians also to display an understanding

---

11. Jackelén, *Otålig i hoppet*.

of plurality as the many competing plausible explanations of complex truth. We theologians should explain our traditions of encountering otherness and recognizing alterity. In doing this, we should keep our minds open so that we are able to learn something. In this manner, the theology of recognition can be a sister to Receptive Ecumenism. Maybe not a twin sister, but rather something like Martha for Mary, a sister who may be spiritually less advanced but nevertheless useful in her busy work with everyday bridge-building.

BIBLIOGRAPHY

Boitani, Piero. *Riconoscere è un dio*. Torino: Einaudi, 2014.
Faucher, Nicholas & Virpi Mäkinen, eds. *Encountering Others, Understanding Ourselves in Medieval and Early Modern Thought*. Oldenburg: de Gruyter, 2022.
Frank, Günter et al., eds. *Die Confessio Augustana im ökumenischen Gespräch*. Berlin: de Gruyter, 2021.
Hirvonen, Onni, and Heikki Koskinen, eds. *The Theory and Practice of Recognition*. London: Routledge, 2023.
Ikäheimo, Heikki. *Recognition and the Human Life-Form*. London: Routledge, 2022.
Jackelén, Antje. *Otålig i hoppet: Teologiska frågor i pandemins skugga*. Stockholm: Verbum, 2020.
Murray, Paul D., Gregory A. Ryan, and Paul Lakeland, eds. *Receptive Ecumenism as Transformative Ecclesial Learning: Walking the Way to a Church Re-formed*. Oxford: Oxford University Press, 2022.
Rescher, Nicholas. *Pluralism: Against the Demand for Consensus*. Oxford: Clarendon, 1993.
Saarinen, Risto. *Recognition and Religion: A Historical and Systematic Study*. Oxford: Oxford University Press, 2016.
Siep, Ludwig, and Heikki Ikäheimo, eds. *Handbuch Anerkennung*. Dordrecht: Springer, 2019.

24

Recognizing Our Gifts
Re-reading Receptive Ecumenism with Risto Saarinen

GREGORY A. RYAN

INTRODUCTION

RISTO SAARINEN'S STIMULATING CHAPTER brings alive some of the explorations we shared in Durham and Helsinki on the resonance between recent work on a theology of recognition and Receptive Ecumenism. By way of continuing that conversation in this chapter I would like to do two things. First, to respond to some of the similarities and differences which Saarinen has identified, and to suggest some further cases where research on religious recognition can help in the understanding and practice of Receptive Ecumenism. Second, to develop the conversation by considering a further situation in my own tradition where these principles and practices might be applied, namely the Catholic Church's journey towards greater synodality.

RECEPTIVE ECUMENISM

In recovering the classical senses of recognition as both transformative (conversion) and differentiating (self-preservation), and thereby going beyond the useful but limited modern legal and political senses,

Saarinen presents an intriguing ecumenical horizon, with the category of recognition presented as a practical Martha to Receptive Ecumenism's more spiritual Mary.[1] Nonetheless I would like to reinforce Saarinen's acknowledgement that although Receptive Ecumenism works well in the practical domain, and requires a spiritual conversion and discipline, it is by no means solely concerned with the interior dispositions of individuals. Rather it is intended quite explicitly to effect change in structures, habits, procedures, language and formulations, and theological discourse at various institutional levels. Thus,

> Receptive Ecumenism seeks to embody the full radical intent of Paul Couturier's spiritual ecumenism, by refusing any false reduction of it to simply the praying together and receiving of each other's spiritual and liturgical riches, and by embracing its full potential for structural, institutional, ecclesial and theological renewal.[2]

The dominant spirit is akin to Pope Francis's dream in *Evangelii Gaudium* for "a missionary impulse capable of transforming everything, so that the Church's customs, ways of doing things, times and schedules, language and structures can be suitably channeled for the evangelization of today's world rather than for her self-preservation." (§27)

Religious recognition and Receptive Ecumenism undoubtedly share some fundamental methodological orientations, including personal openness, rejecting appropriation of the other, and affirming a preferentialism or "committed pluralism," as Saarinen incisively observes. Drilling down into the dynamics of Receptive Ecumenism, recognition is indeed exercised in various ways. In the everyday, reflective sense used by Jean-Marie Tillard, Receptive Ecumenism requires traditions (or, rather, actors in traditions) to recognize a deficiency in their own conceptualization or practice of the gospel, or to recognize an aspect of another tradition which resonates more strongly with a sense of that gospel. Saarinen's presentation of religious recognition provides a framework for understanding this twofold dynamic of Receptive Ecumenism in a new and helpful way. Building on this, the first part of this chapter will explore how Receptive Ecumenism relates to two classical paradigms of recognition,

---

1. In addition to Saarinen's contribution to this volume, see his monographs *Recognition and Religion* and *God and the Gift*.

2. Murray, "Growing into the Fullness of Christ."

before proposing a way in which religious recognition helps clarify some problematic terminology often used in Receptive Ecumenism.

Paradigmatically, classical recognition involves the *transformation* of the subject—as recognizer or recognizee. The subject here is no cool, autonomous agent, but a living participant in the complex act of recognition, capable of change and growth in knowing and acting. The resonance with Receptive Ecumenism could hardly be more obvious, as the title of the collection of essays, *Receptive Ecumenism as Transformative Ecclesial Learning: Walking the Way to a Church Re-formed* indicates.[3] One of the recurring concerns in that volume is the desire expressed by Paul Murray from the beginning to avoid "instrumental learning"—the kind of pick and mix approach that simply transplants from one setting to another without becoming an occasion of potential transformation. Here, Receptive Ecumenism follows a model similar to transformative learning theory (TLT) insofar as the focus is on transformation of perspectives and the development of dispositions and habits, rather than surface level learning.[4]

One of the paradigms Saarinen identifies in his work on recognition is "the promise of self-preservation" in which a differentiation of horizons between the one recognizing and the one being recognized is foremost. This terminology illuminates the notion of "dynamic integrity" within Receptive Ecumenism in a new way. Within Receptive Ecumenism, integrity tends to be elaborated in terms of preserving the coherence of the receiving tradition, even as its web of traditions, practices, grammar, etc. is reconfigured or transformed in reception (hence *dynamic* integrity).[5] Contrary to any understanding of ecumenism as a move towards uniformity, Receptive Ecumenism exhibits a dynamic of self-preservation through the differentiation of horizons—which are constantly developing, not static. To recognize one's own potential for receiving a gift thus requires the receiver to abandon, or at least amend, any previous *mis*recognition of the other as not offering worthwhile gifts. Alongside this, there is a dynamic of correction to the corresponding misrecognition of one's own tradition as complete or fully adequate. Both sets of adjustments can proceed dramatically—in

---

3. Murray, Ryan, and Lakeland, *Receptive Ecumenism as Transformative Ecclesial Learning*.

4. On the parallels with TLT, see Ryan, "Preface," xii–xv.

5. See Murray, "Discerning the Dynamics," and "Discerning the Call"; Ryan. *Hermeneutics of Doctrine*, 82–121.

a sudden moment of insight—or incrementally, through intuition, experimentation, and iterative growth.

Nonetheless, the differentiation of the two traditions is maintained (albeit within a greater eschatological and Christological unity). Authentic ecclesial identity need not be sacrificed, but is, it is hoped, deepened within the whole body of Christ. In Murray's oft-cited words, the point is "not a matter of becoming *less* Catholic but of becoming *more* Catholic precisely by becoming more appropriately Anglican, more appropriately Lutheran," and so on.[6] This is more than simply uncovering the occluded other from a viewpoint of complete self-autonomy, towards which the modern paradigm of legal recognition of status tends. Although not stated in exactly the same terms, Receptive Ecumenism entertains an ethos of reconciled diversity akin to Saarinen's understanding of the body of Christ in which a genuine differentiation is valued and sustained between the different parts of the body.[7] Ecumenism is not an endless exchange of gifts asymptotically approaching homogeneity across the traditions. Rather, tensions and differences remain but can become sites of poietic diversity and "overflow," to borrow a term from Pope Francis's description of creative tension.[8]

Although it has received less attention in Receptive Ecumenism, a complementary integrity of the otherness of the (nominal) *giver* is equally vital. Saarinen's allusions to the danger of "cultural appropriation" in this regard are relevant here for ecumenical practitioners. Understanding that the value of a gift may sometimes be precisely in its substantive otherness—not to be appropriated, even with integrity, into another tradition, to be held in relationship rather than taken into possession—is a theme which has perhaps not received sufficient attention in the literature. In an ecclesial context, this might apply to an understanding of dynamic integrity in mutual reception of some Eastern and Western traditions, for example. This is not to say that otherness inhibits the possibility of reception—indeed it may be essential for transformative learning—but that such otherness must neither be minimized nor absorbed.

---

6. Murray, "Establishing the Agenda," 16. See also, against certain forms of kenotic ecumenism, Murray, "Growing into the Fullness of Christ."

7. Saarinen, *God and the Gift*, 145–46.

8. See, *inter alia*, Pope Francis (with Austin Ivereigh), *Let us Dream*.

"GIVER-LESS" RECEPTION?

What about the "odd" fact that in Receptive Ecumenism the giver generally seems passive, even unaware of their role as giver? Although the notion of reception implies the corresponding action of a giver, seen more explicitly when ecumenism is considered as an "exchange of gifts," in Receptive Ecumenism it is principally the *receiver* who is the active partner. If the metaphor of gift/reception is given full rein, this appears to leave Receptive Ecumenism open to the charge of appropriation or even exploitation ("extractivism"),[9] enriching oneself at another's expense, without consent.

Stated thus baldly, the weakness of such a critique can be seen plainly: "reception" in these ecumenical terms is not a zero-sum game. To learn from another does not necessarily equate to "taking" from them in any pejorative sense. Speaking of "learning" rather than giving/receiving is one way of correcting this misconception. Another is to attend to the actual characteristics required for this mode of receiving, which involve humility, openness, love and so on.[10] A third approach would be to refer to the hope that learning would be mutual, but not to presuppose it.[11] A fourth would be to recognize that when we talks of "gifts" in ecumenical settings, these goods are not so designated because they are in a gift-exchanges between churches but because they are already gifts (charisms) from God to the church, and as such not to be hoarded but shared. This involves more than a basic notion of tradition as handing on of the deposit of faith, and includes giving to others, enabled by the gifts one has oneself received and put into practice—something Saarinen very appropriately calls "poietic love."[12]

Notwithstanding these responses, Saarinen's work on the theology of gift offers another, strikingly original, way of making sense of this apparent anomaly. Here I must go beyond the material presented in the Saarinen's chapter to his underlying research, and in particular his treatment of "giving" as a ditransitive verb.[13] Very briefly, a ditransitive verb has two subjects (e.g., A gives X to B). In different cases of giving and receiving, either

---

9. I am indebted to Michael Nausner for suggesting this term.
10. See Pizzey, "Receptive Ecumenism and the Virtues."
11. Murray, "Establishing the Agenda," 17.
12. Saarinen, *God and the Gift*, 144. On *poiesis* in Receptive Ecumenism, see also Ryan, *Hermeneutics of Doctrine*, 141–46.
13. Saarinen, *Recognition and Religion*, 223–33.

the giver-gift or the gift-receiver complexes may be dominant. Saarinen analyses all six possible combinations of pairings, but for the purpose of Receptive Ecumenism two cases are particularly relevant, where the thing being received "presents itself." That is to say, the role of the giver as an active partner is minimal or non-existent, and this is starting to look a lot like the apparent oddness in Receptive Ecumenism.

The two cases which conform to this "thing-presents-itself" pattern are: a) one where the *giver* and thing are identified, with the thing (i.e. the "gift") being antecedent, and b) one where the *recipient* and thing are identified, with the thing again being antecedent.[14] Case (a) comes very close to one of two possible starting points for Receptive Ecumenism, namely where a particular aspect of another tradition shines out as attractive, even if the tradition in question is not actively offering it as a gift (something which distinguishes Receptive Ecumenism from mutual gift-exchange). Murray refers to this as an "ecumenism of desire," or an "ecumenism of love."[15] Conversely, case (b) mirrors the alternative starting point, when a dysfunction or wound presents itself as a warrant for looking outside the tradition in order to receive and learn—thus an "ecumenism of need." Understanding the odd "giver-less reception" of Receptive Ecumenism as a case of the thing presenting itself or of a gift being received from a "limited giver" provides a degree of refinement not hitherto available in the conceptual vocabulary of Receptive Ecumenism to describe its characteristic unilateral receptivity. It is a welcome outcome from these conversations.

SYNODALITY

Receptive Ecumenism's openness to plurality both as a mode of authentic spirit-infused Christian existence and as a locus for transformative learning is rightly described by Saarinen as a matter of virtue. But then he asks a very interesting question: "What actually happens when we begin to talk in this virtuous manner?" In the Catholic Church, this question is being posed in an unprecedented way in its dialogical and practical exploration of synodality, focused on a four-year "walking together" entitled "For a Synodal Church: Communion–Participation–Mission."

---

14. These are set out in Saarinen, *Recognition and Religion*, Table 4.1, 227. "Case (a)" in the present chapter relates to Case 2 in Saarinen's table, while my "case (b)" pertains to Saarinen's Case 5.

15. Murray, "Growing into the Fulness of Christ," 474.

The global synodal process taking place from 2021–24 is a site of interest not only in respect of ecumenism, but also recognition, involving paradigms of both self-preservation and transformation in its exploration of communion, mission, and participation. Key words of the current synodal process in the Catholic Church have been *spiritual listening* and *journeying together*. Although the terminology of recognition in the process is rarely explicit, an intent to seek transformative learning from the other is clear:

> A synodal Church is a Church which listens, which realizes that listening "is more than simply hearing." It is a mutual listening in which everyone has something to learn . . . all listening to each other, and all listening to the Holy Spirit. What the Lord is asking of us is already in some sense present in the very word "synod"—"Journeying together."[16]

So, what does happen when we begin to talk in this virtuous manner? The synodal process has perhaps started to answer this for the Catholic Church. The process is intended to include voices which have been insufficiently recognized—including those of laity, women, and LGBTQ+ people, voices from the Global South, and from societal and economic peripheries. Pope Francis's vision of a church which is listening and journeying together does not involve simply making legal judgements but is orientated towards a *metanoia* transforming spiritual and practical dimensions of individuals and communities. This can be seen in his nuanced but dogged resistance to using legal categories to deal with questions of sacramental readmission for divorced and remarried Catholics in the 2014–15 synods on the family, or married priests and female deacons in the 2019 Amazon Synod. It is made explicit in his repeated insistence that the current synod is not a parliament, the church is not a democracy, and that what is essential is discernment, not just debate.

For the Catholic Church, whatever the outcome of the current synodal process may be, it has already resulted in a remarkable recognition of previously under-acknowledged groups within the church. LGBTQ+ Catholics for example, have been recognized as a reality, not simply a pastoral problem of "homosexual tendencies"; and "LGBT Catholics" has become a familiar term in diocesan newsletters and activities within the last five years in England and Wales. Recognition in the current synodal process has not only gone beyond simple identification to interpersonal

---

16. Francis, *50th Anniversary*.

recognition through listening to diverse voices, and in keeping the voices alive at the different stages of synthesis from local to regional. It has also moved beyond a legal or canonical understanding of recognition and towards a realization that ecclesial conversion is needed.

Similar moves can be observed regarding women, laity, and other groups lacking a deeper sense of recognition within the Catholic Church. Recognition, which has not been widely used in analysis of synodality thus far, offers an important framework for interpreting this complex multi-layered ecclesial phenomenon in contemporary Catholicism. Each of the three key words for the 2021–24 synod: "Communion—Participation—Mission" depends on the exercise of certain kinds of recognition. Although communion and mission have been familiar tropes in Catholic ecclesiology since Vatican II, "participation," which risks—indeed demands—transformative recognition of all the members of the People of God, is the characteristic addition of the current synodal moment. Theologically, this participation is fundamentally Trinitarian, but the working document for the October 2023 synod also treats the term in a manner close to Saarinen's distinction between toleration and genuine recognition:

> Participation adds anthropological density to the concrete character of the procedural dimension. It expresses concern for the flourishing of human beings, that is, the humanising of relationships at the heart of the project of communion and the commitment to mission. It safeguards the uniqueness of each person's face, urging that the transition to the "we" does not absorb the "I" into the anonymity of an indistinct collectivity. It guards against falling into the abstractness of rights or reducing persons to subservient instruments for the organization's performance.[17]

Synodality also contains specifically ecumenical dimensions. Time and time again, synodality is described in terms of the walking together of *all the baptized*, not just those in full communion with the Catholic Church. There is no new ecumenical doctrine here—*Lumen Gentium* and *Unitatis Redintegratio* laid out this understanding at Vatican II, but synodality creates an opportunity for new practices to be explored. A renewed understanding and practice of listening to and learning from all the baptized opens a space for both Receptive Ecumenism and

---

17. Synod of Bishops, *Instrumentum Laboris* §56.

recognition to be practiced in contemporary Catholicism. Might the framework of recognition facilitate receptive ecumenical learning in new structural and procedural ways in a synodal Catholic church? How might baptized non-Catholics participate not only in occasional synods but in the life of the church at every level? More than observers and honored guests, certainly. What existing ecumenical initiatives might be given new energy, encouragement, and even fresh mandates by this new perspective in the Catholic Church?

The working document (*Instrumentum Laboris*) for the 2023 Synod lists areas where ecumenism and synodality might bear upon one another. They are significant for the future of Receptive Ecumenism in the Catholic Church, and worth quoting in full:

a. Through one Baptism all Christians participate in the *sensus fidei* (supernatural sense of the faith; cf. *LG*12), which is why in a synodal Church all the Baptized must be listened to attentively;

b. The ecumenical journey is an "exchange of gifts" and one of the gifts that Catholics can receive from other Christians is precisely their synodal experience (cf. *EG* 246). The rediscovery of synodality as a constitutive dimension of the Church is one fruit of ecumenical dialogue, especially with the Orthodox;

c. The ecumenical movement as a laboratory of synodality. In particular the methodology of dialogue and consensus-building experienced at various levels in the ecumenical movement could be a source of inspiration;

d. Synodality is part of the "continuous reform" of the Church, as it is principally through its internal reform, in which synodality plays an essential role, that the Catholic Church draws closer to other Christians (*UR* 4.6);

e. There is a reciprocal relationship between the synodal ordering of the Catholic Church and the credibility of its ecumenical commitment;

f. A certain synodality between the Churches is experienced whenever Christians from different communities come together in the name of Jesus Christ for common prayer, action and common witness, as well as regular consultations and participation in each other's synodal processes.[18]

---

18. Synod of Bishops. *Instrumentum Laboris*, B1.4.

While (a)–(d) demonstrate a close correlation with the principles and practice of Receptive Ecumenism,[19] item (e) relating to the Catholic church becoming a "more credible" ecumenical partner is particularly interesting in the light of Saarinen's proposal regarding bridge-building with society. In the same way that Christian churches showing they have an understanding and practice of plurality might build bridges in a world desperately in need of such hermeneutics, so too the plausibility of Catholic ecumenical engagement might be said to rest on the quality of recognition the Catholic Church can develop and demonstrate *ad intra* in its synodal processes in order to avoid a performative contradiction (and therefore a lack of coherence).

Saarinen's example of Archbishop Jackelén during the Covid-19 pandemic models how ecclesial plausibility is possible in the world because of a general hermeneutics of recognition which applies to society as well as to the special hermeneutics of theological and ecumenical recognition. For synodality and its intrinsic ecumenism, a somewhat similar role is played regarding society at large by Pope Francis's presentation of four dialectical principles for the renewal of society—or in Francis terms, for "building a people." These are at various times presented as tools for renewal of society, individual communities, and the church, and are characterized by the generic nature that has been identified in recognition. These principles, found in *Evangelii Gaudium* (2013) but presented by Francis as far back as 1974, take the form of four dialectical but unequal pairings:

- *Time is greater than space* (it is more important to initiate processes than to control spaces: transformation is possible)

- *The whole is more important than the part* (reconciled diversity: unity is a polyhedron, not a uniform sphere).

- *Unity prevails over conflict* (no need to fear dissensus, discussion and change)

- *Reality is more important than ideas* (persons are more important than ideology).

Building on Saarinen's argument in the previous chapter, we might say that synodality involves both the general hermeneutics of being *a* people as well as the special (theological) hermeneutics of being *the* People of

---

19. See Ryan, "Receptive Ecumenism in a Synodal Catholic Church."

God. While there is not space to explore this further, the indications are that recognition has potential to be a useful framework for understanding synodality *ad intra* and *ad extra,* and that what we might call the special hermeneutics of Receptive Ecumenism, "oriented towards a distinctive Christian destiny"[20] offers a particularly appropriate mode of spiritual and ecumenical performance within this general framework.

As Saarinen notes, in *theological* recognition "something new and distinctive is happening." Within synodality, this is especially apparent in the role afforded to the Holy Spirit as the key protagonist of the Synod. Applying a framework of recognition is provocative here: just as mature recognition requires more than identification, and limited or segregated rights, so synodality requires the church to recognize the Spirit, as it were, *inter-personally.* Thus, the synodal consultations have noted the need to better understand the relationship between freely distributed charisms (among the whole baptized faithful) and the institutional framework of the church, especially regarding ordained ministries:

> A great challenge of synodality that emerged during the first year is the harmonization of these gifts, without pitting them against each other, under the guidance of the pastors, and thus without opposing the Church's charismatic and institutional dimensions.[21]

The issue is helpfully sharpened when seen in terms of the church needing to move from a limited, modern paradigm of recognition which regards the Spirit in quasi-legal institutional categories employed by the church as an autonomous actor, to a recovery of classical modes, recognizing the Spirit and adopting a mode of openness to transformative conversion. Pope Francis's weaving of synodality and conversion is apposite here:

> Our current reflection on the Church's synodality is the fruit of our conviction that the process of understanding Christ's message never ends, but constantly challenges us. The contrary of conversion is "immobility," the secret belief that we have nothing else to learn from the Gospel. This is the error of trying to crystallize the message of Jesus in a single, perennially valid

---

20. Clooney, "Asymmetries," 288.

21. General Secretariat of the Synod, *Working Document for the Continental Stage,* §70.

form. Instead, its form must be capable of constantly changing, so that its substance can remain constantly the same.²²

Can the church therefore *recognize*, and not only tolerate, the voices of laity, women, LGBTQ+ people, and those from the peripheries in a synodal church? Can the church recognize, not just tolerate, the cry of the earth and the cry of the poor? Can the church recognize, and not merely tolerate, the Holy Spirit as synodal protagonist? Then, we might hear what the Spirit is saying to the churches.

BIBLIOGRAPHY

Clooney, Francis X. "Comparative Theology's Interesting Asymmetries with Receptive Ecumenism." In *Receptive Ecumenism as Transformative Ecclesial Learning: Walking the Way to a Church Re-formed*, edited by Paul D. Murray, Gregory A. Ryan, and Paul Lakeland, 287–99. Oxford: Oxford University Press, 2022.

Francis, Pope. *Address Commemorating the 50th Anniversary of the Institution of the Synod of Bishops.* 17 October 2015. https://www.vatican.va/content/francesco/en/speeches/2015/october/documents/papa-francesco_20151017_50-anniversario-sinodo.html.

———. *Christmas Address to the Roman Curia.* 22 December 2022. https://www.vatican.va/content/francesco/en/speeches/2022/december/documents/20221222-curia-romana.html.

———. *Evangelii Gaudium.* 24 November 2013. https://www.vatican.va/content/francesco/en/apost_exhortations/documents/papa-francesco_esortazione-ap_20131124_evangelii-gaudium.html.

Francis, Pope, with Austin Ivereigh. *Let Us Dream: The Path to a Better Future.* New York: Simon & Schuster, 2020.

General Secretariat of the Synod. *Working Document for the Continental Stage.* Available at https://www.synod.va/en/synodal-process/the-continental-stage/resources-and-tools/documents.html.

John Paul II, Pope. *Ut Unum Sint*, "On Commitment to Ecumenism." 25 May 1995. https://www.vatican.va/content/john-paul-ii/en/encyclicals/documents/hf_jp-ii_enc_25051995_ut-unum-sint.html.

Murray, Paul D. "Discerning the Call of the Spirit to Theological-Ecclesial Renewal." In *Leaning Into the Spirit: Ecumenical Perspectives on Discernment and Decision Making in the Church*, edited by Virginia Miller, David Moxon, and Stephen Pickard. Cham, Switzerland: Palgrave MacMillan, 2019).

———. "Discerning the Dynamics of Doctrinal Development: A Post-Foundationalist Perspective." In *Faithful Reading: New Essays in Theology in Honour of Fergus Kerr, OP*, edited by Simon Oliver, Karen Kilby, and Thomas O'Loughlin, 193–220. London: T. & T. Clark, 2012.

———. "Growing into the Fullness of Christ: Receptive Ecumenism as a Way of Ecclesial Conversion." In *Receptive Ecumenism as Transformative Ecclesial Learning: Walking*

---

22. Francis, *Christmas Address*.

the *Way to a Church Re-formed*, edited by Paul D. Murray, Gregory A. Ryan, and Paul Lakeland, 463–79. Oxford: Oxford University Press, 2022.

———. "Receptive Ecumenism and Catholic Learning—Establishing the Agenda." In *Receptive Ecumenism and the Call to Catholic Learning: Exploring a Way for Contemporary Ecumenism*, edited by Paul D. Murray, 5–25. Oxford: Oxford University Press, 2008.

Murray, Paul D., Gregory A. Ryan. and Paul Lakeland, eds. *Receptive Ecumenism as Transformative Ecclesial Learning: Walking the Way to a Church Re-formed*. Oxford: Oxford University Press, 2022.

Pizzey, Antonia. "Receptive Ecumenism and the Virtues." In *Receptive Ecumenism as Transformative Ecclesial Learning: Walking the Way to a Church Re-formed*, edited by Paul Murray, Gregory A. Ryan, and Paul Lakeland, 448–62. Oxford: Oxford University Press, 2022.

Ryan, Gregory A. *Hermeneutics of Doctrine in a Learning Church: The Dynamics of Receptive Integrity*. Studies in Systematic Theology 23. Leiden: Brill, 2020.

———. "Preface." In *Receptive Ecumenism as Transformative Ecclesial Learning: Walking the Way to a Church Re-formed*, edited by Paul D. Murray, Gregory A. Ryan, and Paul Lakeland, xii–xv. Oxford: Oxford University Press, 2022.

———. "Receptive Ecumenism in a Synodal Catholic Church." In *Living Tradition: Continuity and Change as Challenges to Churches and Theologies*, edited by Viorel Coman and John Anthony Berry, 276–90. Leipzig: Evangelische Verlagsanstalt, 2024.

Saarinen, Risto. *God and the Gift: An Ecumenical Theology of Giving*. Collegeville, MN; Liturgical, 2005.

———. *Recognition and Religion: A Historical and Systematic Study*. Oxford: Oxford University Press, 2016.

Synod of Bishops. *Instrumentum Laboris* for the First Session of the 16th Ordinary General Assembly, 4–29 October 2023. Available at https://press.vatican.va/content/salastampa/it/bollettino/pubblico/2023/06/20/0456/01015.html#en.

25

Becoming Through Participation
Flourishing Together at Multiple Boundaries

Michael Nausner

VULNERABILITY TOWARDS THE OTHER

What I love about Receptive Ecumenism is its insistence on the need of the other's perspective, and even on the necessity of vulnerability towards the other. In my encounter with the other—at the boundary—I start with asking what I can learn from the other, and I thereby implicitly acknowledge that I am poorer, even less myself without the perspective of the other. My identity is shaped in the encounter with the other, something Paul D. Murray, an initiator of Receptive Ecumenism, early on has compared with Emmanuel Lévinas's theory of the other: the other has a claim on me, an ethical demand.[1] This is radical and challenging at the same time: I fundamentally receive my vocation and my identity from the other, which means that—in a Lévinasian spirit—I need to surrender all totalitarian aspirations and be receptive instead, from the first moment of encounter. One senses that the flourishing of any identity or community is dependent on a certain vulnerability, i.e., a willingness to admit one's need for the other and an openness for receiving what one cannot give oneself. From this perspective, the boundaries

---

1. Murray, "Receptive Ecumenism," 290.

of identity are necessarily permeable and malleable, and in a certain sense we are shaped *at* the boundary of our respective communities rather than *by* it.[2] Identity is not a stable quality, but something that emerges in processes of listening encounters.

POWER INEQUALITIES IN ENCOUNTERS

A temptation of the approach of Receptive Ecumenism, however, seems to be a certain negligence of power relations. Who is doing the listening? What about the question of equality and mutuality? What does an approach of vulnerable listening mean in a situation of power-asymmetry? Are the demands of listening the same regardless of socio-cultural conditions? If the listener, say, is part of an institution of historical power represented by cathedrals, is it fair to have as a goal of the listening process in Receptive Ecumenism to become "*what we already are*" as Murray repeatedly emphasizes?[3] Does Receptive Ecumenism here risk becoming an exercise in self-affirmation? What are the risks of directing the focus exclusively "toward unilateral learning and receiving in a spirit of self-criticism?" This is how Sara Gehlin puts it, and she critically analyzes "the absence of mutual exchange in receptive ecumenism."[4] She thereby draws our attention to the fact that denominational, cultural, and creaturely boundaries never simply are innocent zones of encounter, but always also fields of contestation and power struggle. Questions of justice and equality need to be asked as well as questions of asymmetry and mutuality at the boundaries of encounter.[5] Boundaries are never only what one partner in the encounter perceives them to be. They are always also zones in which power inequalities come to the fore, and they continuously need to be negotiated. Therefore, a certain kind of *border thinking* needs to be practiced that has just relations and mutual accountability as a goal.[6]

FROM WIDER ECUMENISM TO ECO-ECUMENISM

For such a thinking it is important to keep the wider embeddedness of boundary dynamics in mind. No denominational boundary is ever

2. Tanner, *Theories of Culture*, 115.
3. Murray, "Receptive Ecumenism," 282, 291. (My emphasis)
4. Gehlin, "Asymmetry and Mutuality," 198.
5. Gehlin, "Asymmetry and Mutuality," 210.
6. Gehlin, "Asymmetry and Mutuality," 204f.

free from entanglement with more fundamental cultural and ecological boundaries. I think that responsible ecumenism is in continuous need of remembering the global, or rather the planetary implications of its approach. The term *oikoumene* in the Hellenistic and Roman world was used as a signifier for the reach of imperial power (cf. Luke 2:1). To unilaterally exercise power has a history in the use of the term, and to use it that way has been a common temptation in Christian tradition. But the term, of course, does not necessarily signify imperial aspirations; it also just means the *entire inhabited world*. This is what Wesley Ariarajah alludes to when he emphasizes the significance of a *wider ecumenism*, an ecumenism that seeks to bring together the plurality of religious traditions of the world.[7] I agree that this needs to be the background music of all our ecumenical endeavors, especially in times of global intermingling, geopolitical turmoil, and planetary crisis. Unity of the churches needs to be seen in connection with the unity of humanity as a whole.[8]

Against the backdrop of our current climate crisis, I think we need to understand this to mean not only the world inhabited by humans, but also the more-than-human world, the entire created world. To think ecumenically, then, means to think *ecologically* in the widest sense as well.[9] Human community cannot be abstracted from its material entanglement within creation.[10] True flourishing requires a mutually healing coexistence between humans and the more-than-human world. Ecumenism will benefit from being practiced against the background of the renewal of all of creation. To act ecumenically, then, means that every small step toward the human or more-than-human other is understood as an expression of *participation* in the renewal of *all* creation. The Benedictine theologian Simón Pedro Arnold has coined the term *eco-ecumenism* for such an approach, and he sees possibilities for a sensitive treatment of cultural as well as ecological boundaries in an attentive exchange with indigenous spirituality. "Original cultures," Arnold maintains, "have grown a wisdom and spirituality that integrates the cosmos in its original solidarity with mankind [sic.]. This is what we

---

7. Ariarajah, "Wider Ecumenism," 321.

8. Gehlin, "Asymmetry and Mutuality," 206.

9. See Matthew Chandrankunnel's chapter in the present volume where he argues for a *wider ecumenism/ecumenical consciousness* that combines ecumenical and ecological concerns embracing the totality of beings.

10. Keller, *Political Theology of the Earth*, 37.

call Indian eco-ecumenism."[11] Here we are encouraged to keep in mind the cosmic dimension of our ecumenical thinking and the need to never limit it to a denominational or ecclesial affair. Ecumenism is a matter of participation in God's creative activity in the entire creation!

Murray expresses this participatory dimension of ecumenism in a trinitarian way when he writes: "(E)ach of us individually, and each of the Christian traditions collectively, is called to a unique *participation* in God's love, God's Spirit, made visible for us in Christ."[12] To me participation is a key term for theology in general and ecumenical theology in particular. Faith is rooted in an experience of participation that always exceeds the participation in a specific community or denomination. As an expression of the participation in the renewal of all creation it necessarily has ecumenical, i.e., planetary significance, and it is essentially non-exclusive.[13] Participation, of course, has been an important term in ecumenical theology at least since the mission conference in Willingen 1952 when the concept of *missio Dei* was emphasized, which meant that mission never should be misunderstood as a unilateral activity of missionizing churches, but rather as a matter of participation in God's transformative activity in the world. In Willingen, the Cuban theologian Alfonso Rodriguez framed *mission Dei* as "the Christians' participation in co-creating the world with God."[14] Mission is not a product of the church but a participation in God's loving and creative presence in creation as a whole, "in God's ongoing work of liberation and reconciliation by the Holy Spirit."[15] In practice, however, such participation in God's reconciling work needs to be negotiated very concretely at various boundaries.

Given the poor track record of Western Christianity, not only in its relation to indigenous people in the global south but also in relation to the more-than-human world, attention to neglected and suppressed aspects of indigenous spirituality is of importance for a culturally and ecologically sensitive ecumenism. Such attention would also be in tune with a concern voiced in *Together Towards Life*, a document endorsed by the World Council of Churches in 2013. The document hints at the connection between colonial and ecological exploitation that is exemplified in the oppression and marginalization of indigenous people. "We regret,"

11. Arnold, "Decolonization and Interculturalism," 21.
12. Murray, "Afterword," 157. (My emphasis)
13. Nausner, *Eine Theologie der Teilhabe*.
14. Nagy, "Behind *Missio Dei*," 166.
15. *Together Towards Life* §§43, 17.

the document reads, "that mission activity linked with colonization has often denigrated cultures and failed to recognize the wisdom of local people. Local wisdom and culture which are life-affirming are gifts from God's Spirit. We lift up testimonies of peoples whose traditions have been scorned and mocked by theologians and scientists, yet whose wisdom offers us the vital and sometimes new orientation that can connect us again with the life of the Spirit in creation, which helps us to consider the ways in which God is revealed in creation."[16] Wholesome ecumenism in the spirit of the *Missio Dei* is an expression of Christianity's participation in the renewal of *all* creation, and I think we need a renewed recognition of the vital contribution of indigenous voices towards such an understanding of a wider ecumenism, an eco-ecumenism. For this to happen, the implications of the *Missio Dei* for "the right of self-determination for Indigenous people"[17] need to be recognized. I will return to such a recognition at the end of this chapter.

THREE INTERRELATED BOUNDARIES

In what follows I want to highlight the interrelation of the above-mentioned boundaries, the denominational, the cultural, and the ecological/creaturely boundaries. Thus, I proceed in three steps: First I provide a glimpse into my personal struggle with denominational, cultural, and ecological boundaries, second, I reflect on the relevance of cultural boundaries for the ecumenical encounter, and finally on ecological boundary negotiations as a necessary component of a wider ecumenism. My main incentive is to highlight the *embeddedness of the struggle around denominational boundaries in the cultural and ecological context*. In other words: our participation in a denominational community has always also cultural and ecological implications. And in turn the denominational, cultural, and ecological dimensions are aspects of our larger participation in God's renewal of creation.

MY OWN JOURNEY (OF MULTIPLE BELONGING)

In keeping with my conviction that all theology is contextual and therefore requires some basic reflection of a theologian's subject position, I want to give a brief glimpse into my personal identity formation and identity struggle at the three mentioned boundaries: denominational, cultural,

---

16. *Together Towards Life* §§27, 12.
17. *Together Towards Life* §§43, 17.

and ecological. I have spent more than fifty years of my life in a Methodist church community, more explicitly in the United Methodist Church, in Austria, Switzerland, Germany, the United States, and Sweden. I have worshipped, studied, ministered, and taught in these differing contexts, and I have been in intense conversation and communion with people from other denominations, cultures, and religions—always with a keen interest for boundary dynamics. After many years abroad I moved back to Sweden in 2017 and became a member of the Church of Sweden in 2019, but without abandoning my Methodist affiliation.

Now I am working as researcher at the Church of Sweden Unit for Research and Analysis in Uppsala. In my research during the last few years, I have developed a specific interest in the boundary between humanity and more-than-human creation, not least because of the obvious fact that this relation has been a relation of ruthless exploitation on the part of humanity in the West—often legitimized by Christian theology. There is a need to fundamentally rethink the role of humanity in creation, which is a key task for ecumenical theology in the wider sense.[18] This is the context out of which I am writing: Denominationally, culturally, and ecologically I feel that I am living *at*, and I am being shaped *by* these various boundaries and the specific power dynamics at play at them. Denominationally, culturally, and ecologically I am hybrid. I am neither totally this nor that. I am a hyphen-identity, Methodist and Lutheran, Austrian and Swedish, human and yet so intimately a part of the more-than-human world that a stable boundary between me and the more-than-human world is hard to draw. I describe these three aspects of my own hybrid identity not just for personal reasons, but because I think that a similar hybridity is common in times of global migration and that it needs to be reflected in Receptive Ecumenism or any other kind of ecumenism.[19] Otherwise, the contribution of the growing number of hybrid voices who do not entirely identify with one community or the other, will be neglected.[20] *Denominational, cultural, and ecological hybridity and their intersection need to be considered in an ecumenical world of*

---

18. Nausner, "Människan i skapelsen."

19. On the level of interreligious relations, such "multiple belonging" or "hybrid identity" has been reflected on in depth since the turn of the century by Catherine Cornille whose book *Many Mansions?* is a prime example for a constructive argument to include a critical reflection on such lived identity that goes against the grain of the policies of most institutionalized denominations or religions. – See: Cornille, *Many Mansions*, 1–6.

20. Simojoki, "Ökumenisches Lernen," 270.

intermingling. The dynamics of difference cuts through all our preconceived and constructed boundaries. Such intermingling needs to be kept in mind when reflecting cultural and ecological boundary dynamics.

CULTURAL BOUNDARIES

When it comes to cultural boundaries, during the last decades theology has learned from postcolonial theory that cultures cannot be understood as homogenous wholes interacting with each other across clearly identifiable boundaries.[21] Instead, processes of intermingling and of hybridization are a characteristic for cultural emergence. In times of global migration, most people have direct or indirect experiences of such intermingling and cultural hybridity. The German missiologist Claudia Jahnel has applied this insight to ecumenical exchange.[22] Inasmuch as religions and denominations function in analogous ways as cultures,[23] postcolonial theory can be applied also to denominational encounters. It is not only that "there can be considerable diversity of *opinion*" within traditions, as Murray points out,[24] but "theological issues mix with cultural and national identity."[25] Jahnel mentions three examples of such cultural-theological complexity: the theological message needs to be translated by 'vernacular speakers' and thereby be transformed, groups of resistance emerge *within* denominations to create an *internal* cultural-theological plurality, and finally believers exhibit double or multiple denominational or religious affiliations.[26]

In my home church in Örebro in Sweden, for example, people from over a dozen cultural and denominational backgrounds worship together under the umbrella of a Church of Sweden liturgy, and I know for a fact that many among them feel in-between, i.e., they have varying denominational and cultural affiliations and loyalties. Is this maybe already a version of the "unity as the full flourishing of difference in communion" which Murray sees as indicative for Receptive Ecumenism?[27] I do not think that we are there yet, since the norm still is the Church of Sweden

---

21. Gruber, *Intercultural Theology*.
22. Jahnel 2021, "Das universale Wort."
23. Tanner, *Theories of Culture*.
24. Murray, "Introducing Receptive Ecumenism," 3. (My emphasis)
25. Jahnel, "Das universale Wort," 19.
26. Jahnel, "Vernakulare Ökumene," 24–25.
27. Murray, "Introducing Receptive Ecumenism," 2.

language and liturgy regardless of the presence of a global ecumene. The issue of (cultural and denominational, let alone religious) multiple belonging is rarely spoken about. But I think there is the potential to develop what Claudia Jahnel has called a "vernacular ecumenism"[28] by which she means that Christ's universal significance always is incarnated in a specific cultural mix. We have no other access to the universal Christian message than via its concrete cultural expressions. These expressions need to change in accordance with the cultural processes of transformation and hybridization in every local context.

So, what does that mean for the listening process advocated by Receptive Ecumenism? Quoting the Spanish-Brazilian bishop Pedro Casaldáglia, Jahnel writes: "The universal Word only speaks dialect."[29] This means that listening to the denominational other in a general sense is not enough and maybe not even possible. Listening instead needs to start at the everyday encounter with the concrete cultural other, oftentimes already in one's own community of worship where various hybrid voices "from below" need to be taken into consideration.[30] In a sense, then, Receptive Ecumenism as a listening exercise will need to take place already within one and the same church. I commend therefore Murray's sensitivity of "taking into account the *socio-cultural* [. . .] *realities* of [. . .] traditions, rather than simply treating them as theorized doctrinal realities."[31] Indeed, (the proclamation of) doctrine alone does not create unity! Instead, lest it deteriorate into uniformity, unity as gift necessarily emerges as a lived reality in maintained socio-cultural diversity. My contention is that as soon as we tune in to our own and others' "socio-cultural realities" we will not only realize that the Word of God speaks dialect, but we will also realize how mixed these dialects are and how they witness to a vast variety of social and cultural conditions within any given denomination. A sustainable understanding of unity, therefore, is characterized by a keen attunement to the concrete conditions at the cultural boundaries of encounter.[32] It is a unity that feeds on the church's universality which only can be glimpsed through the concreteness of the other, so that it becomes a "concrete universality."[33]

28. Jahnel, "Vernakulare Ökumene," 32.
29. Jahnel, "Das universale Wort," 56.
30. Simojoki, "Ökumenisches Lernen," 269.
31. Murray, "Introducing Receptive Ecumenism," 5. (My emphasis)
32. Jahnel, "Vernakulare Ökumene," 33.
33. Olle Kristenson borrows this term from Edward Schillebeeckx. See Kristenson,

I ask myself: Can we see such "concrete universality" in our midst already? How do we deal with the inner variety of socio-cultural realities and the reality of multiple belonging within and beyond our own communities? Do we see the concomitant blurring of denominational boundaries as a possibility or a threat? Maybe the visualization of ecumenism by Sven Erik Fjellström at the Receptive Ecumenism conference in Sigtuna in June 2022 can be of help for taking the countless hybrid formations of Christian practice seriously as part of the one ecumenical family.[34] Fjellström challenged the customary image of the tree with branches as an appropriate depiction of the ecumenical movement since it evokes the impression of a clear and distinct identity of every individual branch. It allows for no internal hybridity, and it seemingly emphasizes the split instead of the connections. What, Fjellström asked, if we imagine the ecumenical movement as a river, a river he chose to call *Nile-Ecumenism*? (The Nile, Fjellström reminded his listeners, provides water for eleven nations!) Since churches are nourished by the same well, can the ecumenical movement not be imagined as a river? In terms of denominational and cultural boundaries, the image has the decisive advantage that it signals the various currents and intermingling of currents as interdependent, and the necessity of ecumenism as an intercultural phenomenon where cultural boundaries never are fixed comes to the fore.

ECOLOGICAL BOUNDARIES

I finally turn to the ecological boundaries and the need to reconsider them together in the ecumenical community, especially in times of climate crisis. I do so by referring to the traditions of the Swedish indigenous population. One of the key challenges the Church of Sweden is tackling these days is its—not least also *internal*—relation to the Sámi people, the indigenous people who are a vital part of Swedish culture and of the Church of Sweden. Traditionally the Church of Sweden has treated them as the religious and cultural other, creating thereby internal boundaries along which power imbalances were played out. Not only do the power dynamics of cultural/colonial boundaries come to the fore in this relation, but the questions of cultural and ecological boundaries converge. Sámi perspectives show with sobering clarity that cultural and ecological

---

"Universality and Particularity," 95.

34. See Fjellström, "Prologue to Part Three" in the present volume.

exploitation and appropriation have been the two sides of one coin from the first encounter with the colonizers. The need for material, but not least ideological, decolonization of the relations seems obvious.[35]

On November 24th, 2021, a solemn service of apology was celebrated in Uppsala cathedral, and a second one on October 23rd, 2022, in Luleå, i.e., in traditional Sámi territory—*Sápmi*. Representatives from the Church of Sweden were encountering representatives from the Sámi people around a bond fire situated at the high altar of each cathedral. An apology was formulated alongside an eight-step commitment to engage in reparations for the colonial injustices committed by the Church of Sweden through the centuries. Now the church is in the middle of a sensitive process of reconciliation. It is a process that demands an honest assessment of cultural and ecological boundary violations throughout the history of encounters between traditional Sámi populations and representatives for church and state.[36] The reconciliation process cuts to the core of who we are called to be—a community of reconciled and just diversity. Among the reconciliatory commitments the Church of Sweden has signed are the commitments to respect traditional Sámi spirituality and to make it visible *within* the Church of Sweden.[37] This to me equals an implicit acknowledgement of *inner* hybridity and of the necessity of a continuous negotiation of internal boundaries under the umbrella of the Church of Sweden.

My final reflection focuses on the question of what such recognition of traditional Sámi spirituality might mean for a renewed understanding of *ecological* boundaries. I believe that the gift of indigenous spirituality in general and of Sámi spirituality in particular can help the church to see the width and the depth of reconciled community that necessarily also needs to encompass the more-than-human world (see my reference to *eco-ecumenism* above). Indigenous spirituality can give fresh insights into our created world as animated. As humans we are not living on the surface of the planet, but we are an organic outgrowth of the ecosphere of which we are a part. Therefore, the customary view of humans living beyond, or above nature needs to be challenged since it fosters the

---

35. Johnsen, "Menneske først," 318–19.

36. The Church of Sweden has been a state church from its inception and until 2000.

37. "Church of Sweden to make public apology, commitments to Indigenous people of Sweden," The Lutheran World Federation (accessed September 20 2023.)

illusion that the difference between humans and the rest of creation can be understood as a clear-cut division line.

This is what becomes clear in the Sámi theologian Lovisa Mienna Sjöberg's study of the tradition of blessing in Sámi spirituality.[38] The land, or ground, is seen as a community populated by creatures of all kinds, not least also subterranean *ulddat* or *hálddit*. Traditionally, any Sámi narrative about the land as a living community has been brushed aside as superstition by the colonizing church. This, to me, is an example of the failed recognition of "the wisdom of local people" mentioned in *Together Towards Life* and, further, the categoric negligence of local wisdom also communicates a refusal to take the chance to be connected "again with the life of the Spirit in creation."[39] In times when a purely instrumental view of the more-than-human world has led to overwhelming ecological exploitation, Mienna Sjöberg describes the subterranean creatures or spirits as guardians of a balanced relation between humans and the land.[40] She sees them as an expression of a Christian contextual theology and in tune with a biblical vision of an enchanted creation.[41] By signaling human boundary violations, they communicate to humans how to relate to the more-than-human world in a respectful way. They remind humans that they are not the only agents in creation, and that a "continuous negotiation" with more-than-human agents is of paramount importance.[42] Mienna Sjöberg here joins the choir of many indigenous voices problematizing a hierarchical and distanced relation between humanity and more-than-human creation, a chorus that has gained momentum during the last decades. The worldwide ecumenical community needs these voices as a reminder that "reconciliation that does not include the whole of God's creation is incomplete and superficial."[43] There is a lot to learn from an indigenous understanding of the holiness of the land which prohibits an establishment of exploitative boundaries between humans and the rest of creation. Indigenous languages upholding a sacred relationship with the land are "storehouses of ecological well-being," much needed in times of climate crisis.[44]

38. Mienna Sjöberg, "Att leva i ständig välsignelse."
39. *Together Towards Life* §27, 12.
40. Mienna Sjöberg, "Att leva i ständig välsignelse," 196–203.
41. Mienna Sjöberg, "Adams barn," 23.
42. Mienna Sjöberg, "Adams barn," 31.
43. World Council of Churches, *Statement on Reconciliation with Indigenous People*.
44. World Council of Churches, *Statement on Reconciliation with Indigenous People*.

FLOURISHING TOGETHER AT MULTIPLE BOUNDARIES

With these reflections I hope to have contributed with some new perspectives to the wide and sprawling discourse around Receptive Ecumenism. If indeed Receptive Ecumenism, as Murray maintains, has as its goal mutual flourishing and the recognition of "the self in the other, the other in itself," such mutuality and "healing together"[45] needs to grow out of a recognition of power asymmetries in the encounters. But it also needs to take account of *internal* boundaries, i.e., denominational hybridity and multiple belonging. Maybe the *internal* listening to power and culture differentials needs to happen simultaneously with the *outward* ecumenical engagement for a tradition to truly be able to recognize "the other in itself." In addition, ecumenical endeavors, to my mind, need to recognize cultural and ecological contexts not as peripheral, but as ecumenism's necessary embeddedness. It is at the intercultural and inter-creational boundaries that reconciled ecumenical identities are emerging, which I exemplified by referring to the reconciliation process with the Sámi people. An ecumenical exploration of flourishing at intercultural and inter-creational boundaries may not only be the way forward for the Church of Sweden but for the entire worldwide ecumene.

BIBLIOGRAPHY

Ariarajah, S. Wesley. "Wider Ecumenism. A Threat or a Promise?" *Ecumenical Review* 74 (1998) 321–29.

Arnold, Simón Pedro. "Decolonization and Interculturalism: A Theological Point of View." *Voices from the Third World* 37 (2014) 15–28. Available online: http://eatwot.net/VOICES/VOICES-2014-1.pdf.

Cornille, Catherine (ed.). *Many Mansions? Multiple Religious Belonging and Christian Identity*. Eugene, OR: Wipf & Stock, 2010.

Gehlin, Sara. "Asymmetry and Mutuality. Feminist Approaches to Receptive Ecumenism." *Studia Theologica: Nordic Journal of Theology* 74 (2020) 197–216.

Gruber, Judith. *Intercultural Theology. Exploring World Christianity after the Cultural Turn*. Göttingen: Vandenhoeck & Ruprecht, 2018.

Jahnel, Claudia. "'Das universale Wort spricht nur Dialekt.' Postkoloniale Impulse für eine Ökumene der sinnlichen Einheit und eine ästhetische ökumenische Theologie." *Ökumenische Rundschau* 70 (2008) 42–56.

———. "Vernakulare Ökumene in transkultureller Einheit. Ökumenische Theologie nach dem Cultural Turn." *Interkulturelle Theologie/Zeitschrift für Missionswissenschaft* 1 (2008) 10–33.

Johnsen, Tore. "Menneske først, kristen så: Om teologi, rasisme mot samer og behovet for avkolonisering." *Kirke og Kultur* 126/4 (2021) 299–325.

---

45. Murray, "Introducing Receptive Ecumenism," 7.

Keller, Catherine. *Political Theology of the Earth: Our Planetary Emergence and the Struggle for a New Public*. New York: Columbia University Press, 2018.

Kristenson, Olle. "Universality and Particularity: A Contribution to the Interpretation of Gustavo Gutiérrez' Theological Reflection with a Focus on the Preferential Option for the Poor." *Swedish Missiological Themes* 99 (2011) 79–99.

Mienna Sjöberg, Lovisa. "Att leva i ständig välsignelse: En studie av sivdnidit som religiös praxis." PhD diss., Faculty of Theology, University of Oslo, 2018.

———. "Adams barn tillsammans i klimatkrisens tidevarv: Några reflektioner kring de osynligas plats i skapelsen." *St. Sunniva: Tidsskrift for feministisk teologi* 2 (2022) 22–33.

Murray, Paul D. "Afterword. Receiving of Christ in the Spirit: The Pneumatic-Christic Depths of Receptive Ecumenism." In *Receptive Ecumenism. Listening, Learning and Loving in the Way of Christ*, edited by Vicky Balabanski and Geraldine Hawkes, 157–70. Adelaide: ATF, 2018.

———. "Introducing Receptive Ecumenism." *The Ecumenist* 51/2 (2014) 1–8.

———. "Receptive Ecumenism and Catholic Learning. Establishing the Agenda." *International Journal for the Study of the Christian Church* 7 (2007) 279–301.

Nagy, Dorottya. "Behind *Missio Dei*. Reflections on the International Missionary Council's 1952, Willingen, Germany, Conference—One Possible Way of Commemorating after Seventy Years." *Verbum SVD*, 63/2–3 (2022), 161–88.

Nausner, Michael. "Culture-Specific and Cosmopolitan Aspects of Christian Coexistence. A Postcolonial Perspective on Ecumenical Relations." *Religions* 13/10, 896 (2022) 1–9. Online: https://doi.org/10.3390/rel13100896.

———. "Människan i skapelsen: Teologiska utgångspunkter för reflektion kring klimatfrågor och naturens rättigheter." Uppsala: Church of Sweden, 2021. Online: Människan i skapelsen—Teologiska utgångspunkter för reflektion kring klimatfrågor och naturens rättigheter. www.svenskakyrkan.se/naturens-rattigheter.

———. *Eine Theologie der Teilhabe*. Reutlinger Beiträge zur Theologie 2. Leipzig: Evangelische Verlagsanstalt, 2020.

Simojoki, Henrik. "Ökumenisches Lernen, Hybridisierung und Postkolonialismus. Versuch einer kritischen Verschränkung." In *Postkoloniale Theologien II*, edited by Andreas Nehring and Simon Wiesgickl, 256–70. Stuttgart: Kohlhammer, 2018,

Tanner, Kathryn. *Theories of Culture: A New Agenda for Theology*. Guides to Theological Inquiry. Minneapolis: Fortress, 1997.

Together Towards Life: Mission and Evangelism in Changing Landscapes. Geneva: WCC Publications, 2013.

World Council of Churches. *Statement on Reconciliation with Indigenous People*. Geneva: WCC Publications. 2022. https://www.oikoumene.org/resources/documents/statement-on-reconciliation-with-indigenous-peoples.

Index of Names

Appold, Kenneth, 91–92
Arbuckle, Gerald, 145
Ariarajah, S. Wesley, 280–81, 284, 314
Arnold, Simón Pedro, 314
Augustine, Daniela, 81
Avis, Paul D. L., 149, 204, 212, 216

Banks, Adele, 75
Barth, Karl, xxiii, 245–51, 253
Bea, Augustin, 247
Berdyaev, Nikolai, 41–42
Beskow, Nathanael, 123–24
Best, Thomas F., 195
Bevans, Stephen, 99
Bretherton, Luke, 282–83
Bridges Johns, Cheryl, xxi-xxii, 69–87, 88–92, 99

Carey, William, 213
Carter, David, xxi, 47–54, 63
Clarke, Sathianatan, 95, 98–99
Clooney, Francis X., 309
Congar, Yves, 112-4
Cox, Harvey, 81, 85
Crossan, John Dominic, 284
Cunningham, Philip A., 256

Derrida, Jacques, 29

Ehrenström, Nils, 126

Fjellström, Sven Erik, 121–24, 229–31, 232–33, 320
Ford, David F., 19
Francis, Pope, 18–29, 48, 50–51, 59, 109, 111, 115, 158, 164, 175, 211, 270–71, 275, 300, 302, 305, 308–10
Fulkerson, Mary McClintock, 149
Furlong, Monica, 148

Gehlin, Sara, xx, xxii, 7, 18, 125–37, 189, 294, 313–14
Girard, René, 40
Groupe des Dombes, 14–15

Han, David Sang-Ehil, 71
Hauerwas, Stanely, 286
Hawkes, Geraldine, 17–18, 132, 134
Herskowitz, Daniel, M. 247,
Hietamäki, Minna, 151, 294
Hollenweger, Walter, 78
Hoekendijk, Johannes, 15

Ignatius of Loyola, 14, 117

Jacobovits, Immanuel, 252–53
Jackelén, Antje, 236, 297, 308

INDEX OF NAMES

Jahnel, Claudia, 318–19
James, William, 13
Johannesson, Karin, xx, xxii, 3–6, 232–43
John XXIII, Pope, 18, 113
John Paul II, Pope, 12, 49–50, 160, 173, 207, 210–11
Johnsen, Tore, 320
Junge, Martin, 95

Kalu, Ogbu, 89
Kärkkäinen, Veli-Matti, 98
Karlström, Nils, 126–27
Kasper, Walter, xxiii, 57–58, 63, 65, 159–61, 178, 204–5, 245–46, 256, 269, 290, 293
Keating, Thomas, 197
Kimambo, Isaria N., 235
Kinnamon, Michael, 127–28
Kobia, Samuel, 159
Koch, Kurt, 159, 167, 292–93
Kristenson, Olle, xxii, 7, 18, 319
Küng, Hans, 262, 275

Lakeland, Paul, xxii, 11, 111–18, 148, 296, 301
Lederach, John Paul, 134
Levinas, Emmanuel, 38–40
Lubich, Chiara, xxii, 160–64, 166–67
Luther, Martin, 58, 239, 242

Ma, Wonsuk, 75, 212
Mejia, Jorge, 252
Meninger, William, 197
Merton, Thomas, 196–97
Meyer, Harding, 52, 140
Mienna Sjöberg, Lovisa, 321–22
Murray, Paul D., xix–xxi, 7–21, 23–24, 27, 35–38, 45, 57–58, 74–76, 78–79, 83, 101–2, 129, 131, 133–35, 148–50, 172, 174, 205–6, 208, 212–15, 217, 294, 300–304, 312–13, 315, 318–19, 323

Nausner, Michael, xxiii, 303, 312–24
Noble, Ivana, xxi, 33–46
Nouwen, Henri J., 143

Oord, Thomas J., xxii, 171, 177–81
Outler, Albert C., 49

Padilla, René, 223
Pennington, Basil, 193–201
Pieris, Aloysius, 268
Pizzey, Antonia, 126, 129, 177, 193, 199, 203, 206–7, 214–15, 218, 303
Pound, Marcus, 17, 189

Radner, Ephraim, 102
Rahner, Karl, 111, 117–18, 260, 262
Raiser, Konrad, 69–70, 74, 159, 173
Reardon, Martin, 173
Reardon, Ruth, 173, 180
Rescher, Nicholas, 205, 294
Reynolds, Thomas E., 155–56
Robeck, Cecil M., 90–91
Rowan, Williams, 30, 172
Rusch, William, 57, 59–60, 64–65
Ryan, Gregory A., xxiii, 11, 36–37, 45, 155, 176, 296, 299–311

Saarinen, Risto, xxiii, 150–51, 239, 241, 288–98, 299–304, 306, 308–9
Sacks, Jonathan, 283
Sakharov, Sophrony, 193–201
Schaffer, Gavin, 253
Sendoro, Chediel, xxii, 232–43
Simojoki, Henrik, 317, 319
Slipper, Callan, xxii, 138–46, 159, 189
Smith, James K.A., 78, 80–81
Söderblom, Nathan, xii–xv, 123, 127, 131–32, 136
Stăniloae, Dumitru, 42–45
Stendahl, Krister, 135, 185
Samy, Muthuraj, 154

Tanner, Kathryn, 313
Taylor, Charles, 80, 86, 289
Thomas, Gabrielle, 18, 149–50, 153
Thomas, M.A., 260–61, 263–67, 269, 272
Timiadis, Emilianos, 164
Torre, Miguel De La, 281–82
Turcescu, Lucian, 43
Tveit, Olav Fykse, 4, 132

Underwood, Kieren, 59

Van Buren, Paul M., 246–47
Vatican II, 12, 18–19, 47, 49–50, 114, 160, 196, 206, 210, 213, 250, 261–62, 290, 306
Vissert 't Hooft, Willem Adolf, 128
Volf, Miroslav, 62, 152–55

Wainwright, Geoffrey, 50, 60, 66
Walls, Andrew, 70
Weber, Max, 80
Welby, Justin, xx, 175, 211

Welch, Elizabeth, 78
World Council of Churches/WCC, xi, xvi, xxv, 22–23, 25–28, 35, 70–72, 74, 76, 90, 98–99, 123, 128, 132–3, 151, 158–59, 173, 183, 195, 205, 208–9, 213–17, 224, 247–49, 253–55, 260–61, 265, 274–76, 280, 284, 315, 322
Wesley, John, 64
Willebrands, Johannes Cardinal, 204

Yanoshevsky, Galia, 33–34
Yong, Amos, 81

www.ingramcontent.com/pod-product-compliance
Lightning Source LLC
Chambersburg PA
CBHW071151300426
44113CB00009B/1169